Video

Leeds City College
Technology
Campus

**This book is to be returned or renewed
by the last date stamped below.**

**It can be renewed by calling in person
or by telephone at: Library+
Floor 0, Cookridge St., Leeds LS2 8BL
Tel: 0113 386 1705**

FINES WILL BE CHARGED ON OVERDUE BOOKS		

by Kevin Daum, Matt Scott, Bettina Hein & Andreas Goeldi

WILEY

John Wiley & Sons, Inc.

Video Marketing For Dummies®

Published by
John Wiley & Sons, Inc.
111 River Street
Hoboken, NJ 07030-5774

www.wiley.com

WILEY

About the Authors

Kevin Daum is a marketer, speaker, and videomaker. He is the author of five books including two Amazon #1 best sellers, *ROAR! Get Heard in the Sales and Marketing Jungle* (John Wiley & Sons, Inc.) and *Green $ense for the Home* (Taunton Press) which won the 2011 Outstanding Book from the American Society of Journalists and Authors (ASJA). He is a columnist for Inc.com and *Smart Business* magazine.

Kevin is an Inc. 500 entrepreneur whose sales and marketing techniques resulted in more than $1 billion in sales. Drawing on his background in theater and business, Kevin shares his expertise to help individuals communicate effectively to reach their goals. His most recent venture is ROARing Video which helps companies communicate through humorous and compelling video.

Kevin is a graduate of the MIT Entrepreneurial Executive Leadership program and a longtime member of the Entrepreneur's Organization, where he has held several board positions. Kevin has designed, produced, and led award-winning executive training programs and events for C-level executives and entrepreneurs on four continents. The Entrepreneur's Organization has bestowed the Global Learning Award on Kevin's events three times, most recently in 2011. Previously Kevin was named one of the 40 people under 40 in San Francisco by the *Business Times* and in 2006 was named Distinguished Alum of the Year by his alma mater, Humboldt State University.

Matt Scott is a New York-based screenwriter, director, actor, video production manager, and film teacher, who has created original videos for FunnyOrDie.com and NBC's Dotcomedy site. His freelance work includes numerous documentaries and video projects for educational and theatrical clients. He also serves as a production manager for B Productions, the house video company for New York Fashion Week. Matt created ROARing Video with Kevin.

Bettina Hein is Founder and CEO of Pixability, a video marketing company headquartered in Cambridge, MA. Pixability's technology and services help companies worldwide—from Fortune 500 giants to small businesses—create and use video successfully for online marketing. Pixability's software optimizes and delivers videos to YouTube, Facebook, and other platforms.

Bettina is a serial technology entrepreneur who has built successful technology companies both in the United States and in Europe. Prior to Pixability, she co-founded the Swiss-based speech software specialist SVOX AG. SVOX was sold to Nuance Communications (NUAN) for $125 million.

Bettina was the initiator of START, an organization that advances entrepreneurship among college students. In 2000, START received the Ernst & Young Entrepreneur of the Year Award. Bettina is also the founder of the SheEOs, a network for female CEOs and founders of growth companies.

Bettina holds a Masters of Science degree from the Massachusetts Institute of Technology where she was a Sloan Fellow, a law degree from the University of Constance, and a degree in business administration from the University of St. Gallen. Bettina is a frequent speaker on the topics of video, marketing, and entrepreneurship, and she has presented at MIT, Harvard Business School, and conferences worldwide.

Andreas Goeldi is Chief Technology Office of Pixability, a video marketing company headquartered in Cambridge, MA. Pixability's technology and services help companies worldwide—from Fortune 500 giants to small businesses—create and use video successfully for online marketing. Pixability's software optimizes and delivers videos to YouTube, Facebook, and other platforms.

Andreas is an experienced Internet technologist and online marketing expert with a passion for film and video. He has worked in online marketing since the web's earliest days. He co-founded Namics, one of Europe's largest interactive marketing agencies, which was acquired by PubliGroupe. Andreas has worked on digital and online marketing strategies with companies such as Microsoft, Compaq, Nestlé, and Siemens. He also co-founded both Blogwerk. com, one of Europe's largest blog networks, and Buzzient, a U.S.-based social media analytics company. Andreas' passion for film and video started when he bought his first Super 8 camera at the age of nine years, and he started programming at the age of 12. Andreas holds an S.M. in Management of Technology from MIT and an M.A. in Information Management from the University of St. Gallen, Switzerland.

Dedication

To every marketer willing to fight against mediocrity, failure, and boredom with videos that thrill.

Authors' Acknowledgments

We would like to thank the many people who took time to provide their advice and input to us as we created the book you now hold in your hands. Specifically, we would like to thank the folks at Wiley who cared enough to make this book the best it could be, including Steven Hayes, Pat O'Brien, and Becky Whitney.

The authors would also like to thank those that contributed to the development and content of the book including Peter Economy, Verne Harnish of Gazelles, Rob Ciampa of Pixability, and Deborah Hrbek for her fantastic contributions to the legal chapter.

Kevin would also like to thank many who contributed to the development of this book including Barry Cohn, Michael Pool, Fran Biderman Gross, Cheryl Beth Kuchler, Mark Green, Keith Kupp, Jason Ferguson, James Goolnik, Mi Bewick, Nachshon Rothstein, Susan Older Mondeel, Emanuel Arruda, John Papaloukas, Joy Tutela, and most of all his partner in humorous living, his wife Van Van.

Matt would like to thank Stacee Mandeville, his partner in every way.

Bettina and Andreas would like to thank Pixability's customers and partners who gave us the insights into so many of the successful video marketing strategies you find in this book. Bettina and Andreas' biggest thank you goes to their parents, their little daughter Louisa who was such a good girl during the many hours they spent writing this book, and to Ann Thom, Louisa's nanny.

Publisher's Acknowledgments

We're proud of this book; please send us your comments at `http://dummies.custhelp.com`. For other comments, please contact our Customer Care Department within the U.S. at 877-762-2974, outside the U.S. at 317-572-3993, or fax 317-572-4002.

Some of the people who helped bring this book to market include the following:

Acquisitions, Editorial, and Vertical Websites

Project Editor: Pat O'Brien

Acquisitions Editor: Steven Hayes

Copy Editor: Becky Whitney

Technical Editor: Patty Russo

Editorial Manager: Kevin Kirschner

Editorial Assistant: Amanda Graham

Sr. Editorial Assistant: Cherie Case

Cover Photo: © iStockphoto.com / Cary Westfall

Cartoons: Rich Tennant (`www.the5thwave.com`)

Composition Services

Project Coordinator: Patrick Redmond

Layout and Graphics: Jennifer Creasey, Corrie Niehaus, Lavonne Roberts

Proofreaders: Lindsay Amones, Toni Settle

Indexer: Dakota Indexing

Publishing and Editorial for Technology Dummies

    Richard Swadley, Vice President and Executive Group Publisher

    Andy Cummings, Vice President and Publisher

    Mary Bednarek, Executive Acquisitions Director

    Mary C. Corder, Editorial Director

Publishing for Consumer Dummies

    Kathleen Nebenhaus, Vice President and Executive Publisher

Composition Services

    Debbie Stailey, Director of Composition Services

Contents at a Glance

Introduction 1

Part I: Creating Effective Marketing Videos 7
Chapter 1: Video Marketing from the Ground Up.................................... 9
Chapter 2: Integrating Video into Your Marketing 19
Chapter 3: Choosing Types and Styles of Marketing Videos................... 35
Chapter 4: Scripting the Right Message 47

Part II: Preparing for Production.................................. 69
Chapter 5: Producing a Marketing Video on a Budget............................ 71
Chapter 6: Finding the Perfect Location to Shoot 85
Chapter 7: Assembling Your Cast and Crew 99
Chapter 8: Making It Legal: Crossing the T's and Dotting the I's............ 117

Part III: Shooting Your Video 131
Chapter 9: Gearing Up 133
Chapter 10: Let There Be Light 149
Chapter 11: Sounds Good: Getting Great Audio 157
Chapter 12: Conducting the Big Shoot 169

Part IV: Editing and Polishing Your Video.................... 189
Chapter 13: Choosing Your Editing Software...................................... 191
Chapter 14: Planning First, Cutting Second.. 209
Chapter 15: Working with Music and Other Audio................................ 231
Chapter 16: Adding Titles and Visual Effects 249

Part V: Posting and Promoting Your Video 265
Chapter 17: Sharing Your Video on YouTube and Other Platforms 267
Chapter 18: Incorporating Marketing Videos into Your Website 287
Chapter 19: Promoting Your Video with Social Media........................... 303
Chapter 20: Using Search Engine Optimization and Paid Ads 319
Chapter 21: Measuring Results and Improving Your Video 337

Part VI: The Part of Tens 351

Chapter 22: Ten Video Marketing Don'ts 353
Chapter 23: Ten Nonmarketing Uses for Business Video 359
Chapter 24: Ten Video Marketing Resources 363

Index 371

Table of Contents

Introduction 1

Part 1: Creating Effective Marketing Videos 7

Chapter 1: Video Marketing from the Ground Up 9
Why You Should Consider Video Marketing.............................10
    Online benefits 10
    Emotional benefits 10
    Efficiency...11
Video Marketing as a Strategy 11
    Content..11
    Promotion 12
    Measurement..12
Applying Video Marketing Tactics 13
Creating Marketing Videos 14
Choosing Between Doing It Yourself and Going Pro 16

Chapter 2: Integrating Video into Your Marketing 19
Knowing Why Viral Video Isn't Always Virtuous....................20
Understanding the Viral Process..20
Identifying Communication Chokepoints 22
Marketing Internally with Video 24
    Aligning your team with video 25
    Maximizing your training technique 26
Marketing Externally with Video 28
    Generating leads and attracting buyers...........................28
    Assessing prospects and analyzing their needs 29
    Removing buying objections 30
    Building credibility 31
Developing a Video Marketing Integration Plan 31

Chapter 3: Choosing Types and Styles of Marketing Videos 35
Identifying Types of Videos...35
    Storytelling for impact 36
    Demonstrating through show and tell 37
    Capturing events..38
    Making use of animated video..38
    Only words and pictures: Is that really video? 39
Incorporating Video Styles..39
    Using humor effectively 40
    Being serious without the drama.....................................41

Informing with news-style video..42
Avoiding talking heads..43
Making testimonials meaningful 43
Creating a montage...44
Spicing It Up Creatively..44
Using archetypes to create recognition....................................45
Avoiding stereotypes that breed contempt 45
Making it fresh..45
Keeping it clean..46

Chapter 4: Scripting the Right Message 47

Sketching Out the Compelling Idea..47
Identifying the pain..48
Proposing a solution..50
Differentiating your approach..51
Creating the Concept 52
Establishing an emotional connection......................................53
Scripting with structural models 54
Urgency is in the eyes of the beholder 57
Calls to action..58
Ensuring an awesome experience for the viewer 59
Keeping it short, simple, and engaging 61
Storyboarding: The V in Video Is for Visual.....................................62
Scripting in Detail 64
Describing imagery and action 65
Writing dialogue...67

Part II: Preparing for Production 69

Chapter 5: Producing a Marketing: Video on a Budget...........71

Calculating How Much to Spend..71
Starting with a needs list..72
Determining the cost of the cast..74
Budgeting for the crew..76
Accounting for locations and permits.......................................77
Funding the costumes and make-up...78
Preparing the props...79
Buying and renting equipment...80
Borrow, Borrow, Borrow 81
Capitalizing on your internal resources....................................81
Trading with show business magic 83
Insourcing and Outsourcing the Process 83
Budgeting for Promotion 84

Chapter 6: Finding the Perfect Location to Shoot..............85

Scouting Out a Great-Looking Location......................................85
  Picking the perfect place 86
  Adding the right amount of light and noise.............................86
  Setting up a green room...87
Using a Familiar Place...87
  Shooting in your office 88
  Filming in your home...89
  Borrowing a location from a friend or family member..............89
Begging and Borrowing...90
  Asking local businesses 90
  Using a stranger's property..91
Heading Into the Great Outdoors 92
  Shooting in public places...92
  Shooting on sidewalks and streets...93
  Grabbing footage on the fly 94
Going Green (-Screen)...94
  Grasping the basics of chroma-key 94
  Respecting green screen do's and don'ts................................95

Chapter 7: Assembling Your Cast and Crew 99

Connecting with Your Audience..99
  Casting for communication 100
  Selling isn't acting...102
  Achieving believability...102
Opting for Professional Actors 104
  Weighing the pros and cons of casting professional actors 104
  Creating an effective casting notice 106
  Running a successful audition 107
Discovering a Diamond in the Rough...109
  Finding "natural" talent...109
  Coaxing Oscar-worthy performances from non-actors 110
  Casting an effective webinar 111
Casting behind the Camera 112
  Assembling a skeleton crew 112
  Deciding on a director..113
  Procuring the producer 113
  Securing a camera person 114
  Evaluating more crew positions 114

Chapter 8: Making It Legal: Crossing the T's and Dotting the I's ...117

Contracting Artists 118
  Choosing union or non-union...118
  Working with friends, relatives, employees, and others 119
  Owning the script and video 120

Obtaining Permission for Places 121
Using Copyrighted Material 122
    Invoking fair use... 123
    Recognizing the limits of parody 124
    Borrowing other people's music.. 124
    Mastering the use of trademarks 125
    Dissecting defamation.. 125
Protecting Your Own Productions 127
    Protecting your intellectual property 127
    Addressing liabilities and insurance 128
    Resolving disputes... 128

Part III: Shooting Your Video 131

Chapter 9: Gearing Up 133

Choosing Your Recording Media.. 134
    Opting for high definition or standard definition 134
    Capturing footage digitally 136
Having Hollywood in Your Pocket.. 137
    Understanding the pros and cons of tiny cameras 137
    Shooting with a webcam 138
    Using a smartphone camera 139
    Point-and-shoot: Getting video on your photo camera......... 140
    Shooting with pocket cameras 140
Shooting with a Traditional Camcorder 142
    Considering a camcorder... 142
    Shooting HD on a DSLR 143
Accessorizing Your Shoot 144
    Increasing the voltage with lights...................................... 144
    Knowing your microphone options..................................... 145
    Finding the right tripod... 146
    Making the most of monopods and steady mounts 146
    Ensuring an acceptable power level................................... 147
    Everything else you may need 148

Chapter 10: Let There Be Light 149

Lighting Up Your Video's Life 150
    Hard lighting or soft lighting 150
    Shooting in natural light.. 151
Applying Three-Point Lighting.. 152
    Light, the three-point way... 154
    I'm ready for my close-up 155
Pack Up Your Light Kit... 155

Chapter 11: Sounds Good: Getting Great Audio 157

    Sound Basics 157
        Wearing headphones.. 158
        Toning your room 158
    Recording Great Sound.. 158
        Using the in-camera microphone.......................... 160
        Clip on, clip off 161
        I call shotgun! 162
        Lowering the boom.. 164
    The Actor's Voice 165
        Diction and dialects.. 166
        The power of the pause 166
        Managing crowds... 167

Chapter 12: Conducting the Big Shoot 169

    Setting Up for a Shoot 169
        Getting organized.. 170
        Completing your checklists and "go-bag"............ 170
        Arriving on set.. 172
        Planning a realistic shooting schedule 173
        Practicing good habits before a shot 175
        Giving effective directions 176
        Maintaining continuity 178
    Shooting a Great-Looking Video 179
        Composing and dividing the screen 180
        Determining the best shot 180
        Moving and grooving the camera 182
        Matching your eyelines 183
        Following the 180-degree rule 184
        Shooting an interview... 185
        Shooting extra footage and B-roll 186
        Capturing the perfect take — several times................ 187

Part IV: Editing and Polishing Your Video *189*

Chapter 13: Choosing Your Editing Software 191

    Selecting Your System 191
        Choosing the platform.. 191
        Mac tools... 193
        Windows tools... 195
        Online tools 198
    Breaking the Ice 200
    Knowing How to Get Started 201
        Finding professional editing help 203
        Handling file formats, resolution, and conversion 204

Chapter 14: Planning First, Cutting Second 209

Determining Whether You Need to Edit 210
    Recognizing videos that need no editing......................................210
    Trimming your video..211
    Editing in-camera 212
Preparing for the Edit...212
    Shooting for the edit...213
    Understanding the ideal length of an online video.....................213
    Logging your footage...215
    Revisiting your script 216
    Collecting photos, sounds, and music 216
    Knowing what to do when you're missing material 217
Finding the Story 218
    Making a rough cut 218
    Switching it around..219
Mastering the Art of the Transition 220
    Knowing the types of cuts 221
    Finding the right rhythm..223
    Connecting the scenes 224
    Filling the gaps with b-roll 224
Polishing Your Video 225
    Fine-tuning your edit 225
    Adding bells and whistles 227
    Getting feedback 228
    Exporting the final video...229

Chapter 15: Working with Music and Other Audio 231

Understanding the Elements of Audio 231
Choosing Music for Your Videos 233
    Picking the proper tune for your audience 234
    Heading in the right direction musically 235
Knowing Where to Find Music 236
    Adding built-in music in video editing tools.................................236
    Incorporating stock music libraries 237
    Finding open source music..237
    Making your own music 238
Putting Music in Your Video 239
    Adding emotional impact...240
    Cutting your video to music 241
    Cutting your music to video 241
Recording Voiceover Narration...242
Adding Sound Effects 243
Mixing Your Audio Track...244
    Using tricks to make your audio sound better..............................246
    Ensuring audio sound quality on different types of equipment.....247
    Saving a botched audio track..248

Chapter 16: Adding Titles and Visual Effects **249**

Conveying Your Message with Titles..249
    Inserting opening titles and closing credits 250
    Specifying what to do next by issuing a call to action.................251
    Identifying speakers in lower thirds...252
    Explaining by using charts and diagrams...................................254
    Designing titles...255
Applying Visual Effects 256
    Moving between shots with transitions.......................................256
    Correcting color and applying filters 257
    Cropping, rotating, and zooming footage 260
Joining the Big Leagues: Motion Graphics and 3-D Animations 261
    Injecting dynamism and drama with motion graphics 262
    Producing 3-D animations on a budget 263
    Locating cool animations...264

Part V: Posting and Promoting Your Video **265**

Chapter 17: Sharing Your Video on YouTube and Other Platforms . . .**267**

Putting Your Videos on YouTube...267
    Creating a YouTube channel 269
    Uploading and tweaking your videos 271
    Managing playlists and favorites 273
    Adding annotations 274
    Understanding subscriptions..276
    Interacting with other YouTube users 276
Using Other Video Sharing Platforms 277
    Vimeo..277
    Viddler..278
    Dailymotion 278
    The rest 279
Posting Video for Viewing on Phones and Tablets 280
    Preparing your videos for mobile devices...................................280
    Understanding video formats for mobile devices 281
Streaming Live Content..282
    Recognizing what you can and cannot do 283
    Working with streaming providers..283
    Attracting an audience for your live broadcast...........................284

Chapter 18: Incorporating Marketing Videos into Your Website **287**

Knowing Where to Use Your Video..287
    Placing video on your home page..288
    Supporting web content with video 289
    Using video for e-commerce sites..290
    Increasing sales and conversions 291
    Separating video sections..292
    Working with video landing pages...292

Hosting Your Video 293
  Choosing between YouTube and a hosting service 294
  Selecting a video hosting service...295
  Using open source players 296
Using Video on a Web Page..297
  Styling your player..297
  Displaying an appropriate thumbnail picture..............................298
  Determining whether to use autoplay...298
  Inserting an embed code into a web page 299

Chapter 19: Promoting Your Video with Social Media 303
Gaining Visibility with Social Media..303
  Picking your social media battles...304
  Understanding where your audience lives online 305
  Identifying opinion leaders and influential channels 306
  Encouraging users to share your videos 307
Establishing a Presence on Facebook...307
  Boosting your business on Facebook 308
  Sharing video with your friends and fans 308
  Choosing YouTube or Facebook video 308
  Recording webcam videos on Facebook 309
  Uploading video to Facebook..310
  Editing and tagging a Facebook video 311
  Posting YouTube videos on Facebook...311
  Embedding video in your company Page 312
  Promoting video with paid campaigns 314
  Tweeting videos on Twitter...315
  YouTube is social, too...316
  Taking a look at other social marketing channels 317

Chapter 20: Using Search Engine Optimization and Paid Ads 319
Optimizing Your Video for Search Engines 320
  Picking the right title..321
  Writing effective description text 322
  Setting a target link..323
  Selecting effective search tags...323
  Choosing a thumbnail picture...325
  Adding closed captioning 326
Combining Traditional SEO and Video 326
  Using video site maps 327
Posting Paid Ads on YouTube 328
  Setting up a YouTube video ad 329
  Measuring your clicks 332
  Optimizing your targeting..332
  Creating a call-to-action overlay 333
Using Other Types of Video Ads..334

Chapter 21: Measuring Results and Improving Your Video **337**

Knowing What to Measure and Why 337
 Defining your goals 338
 Selecting the data you need 340
 Establishing a reporting rhythm 341
 Taking the proper corrective action 342
Using YouTube Analytics 343
 Tracking viewer numbers 344
 Examining traffic sources 345
 Analyzing user behavior 346
 Using Google Analytics to paint the full picture 347
Working with Analytics in Video Hosting Services 347
 Knowing what to expect from a premium service..................348
 Using specialized video marketing tools 349

Part VI: The Part of Tens *351*

Chapter 22: Ten Video Marketing Don'ts **353**

Don't Let Your Message Be Vague...353
Don't Put Too Many Messages in the Video 354
Don't Make Videos Long and Boring..354
Don't Forget to Prepare for the Shoot 355
Don't Ignore the Sound Quality 355
Don't Cast without Choices 356
Don't Think That Your Video Is Good When It Isn't........................356
Don't Omit Video from Social Media..357
Don't Ignore YouTube 357
Don't Make Only One Video 358

Chapter 23: Ten Nonmarketing Uses for Business Video **359**

Internal News Show...359
Simple Demonstrations...360
Training...360
Archiving 360
FAQ Videos 361
Teamwork Exercise 361
Company Contest 361
Feel-Good Videos 362
Internal Presentations...362
Music Videos for Your Company Band..362

Chapter 24: Ten Video Marketing Resources **363**

Video Gear: B&H Photo Video Pro Audio..363
Video Professionals: Mandy.com 364

Content Help: ROAR! Get Heard in the Sales and Marketing Jungle 364
Animation: Go!Animate, Xtranormal 365
Internal Video Production: H.R. Larious...366
Free Music: Incompetech 366
Video Seminars: ROARing Video 367
Industry and Educational Information: Web Video
    Marketing Council, Reel SEO 368
Social Media Integration: FanBridge, HubSpot, Prime Concepts 368
Promotion and Measurement: Pixability, Online Video Grader 370

Index.. *371*

Introduction

*O*ur suggestion to buy the copy of *Video Marketing For Dummies* that you hold in your hands (or that you have downloaded to your digital e-book reader) to help your business soar to new heights may seem self serving, but we believe that video marketing can help every business large or small and is no longer limited to Fortune 500 companies that carry out multimillion-dollar campaigns on network and cable TV. The explosion of online video, spurred by the boom in inexpensive video technology, allows any person, small business, or corporation to use powerful, visual storytelling to communicate effectively to its buyers, employees, and community.

We have worked diligently to ensure that *Video Marketing For Dummies* is the best and most up-to-date reference on the topic that's available anywhere — at any price. This book provides a comprehensive overview of the topics necessary for effective video marketing campaigns, presented in a fun and interesting format. We know from experience that video marketing can be an intimidating venture, and you can easily waste time worrying about what steps you need to take to make your campaigns as successful as possible. Don't worry. Relax. Help is at your fingertips.

About This Book

Video Marketing For Dummies is perfect for all levels of prospective video marketers. This book not only covers the different uses for a video marketing program but also provides scripting models and sample concepts that demonstrate how to create compelling content. If an important concept or development in video marketing exists, you can find it covered within the pages of this comprehensive book. In addition to help with scripting and production, you can find a variety of material to help you wade through the process of casting actors, choosing gear, using cameras, editing content, and sharing your video with the world, where it can "wow" your prospects.

How to Use This Book

Despite the obvious resemblance of this book to a big, yellow telephone directory, the proper way to use this book is not as a doorstop or a makeshift paperweight. You can use this book in one of two ways:

✔ If you want to find out about a specific topic, such as the basic principles of lighting design or protecting yourself legally, you can flip to that section and find your answers quickly. Faster than you can ask, "How do I post on YouTube?" you'll have the answer.

✔ If you want a crash course in video marketing, read this book from cover to cover. You'll be as prepared as you can possibly be for any video marketing eventuality.

This book is unique because you can read any chapter without having to read earlier chapters. You can read any chapter without having to read the next one in line, read the book backward or forward, or carry it around with you to impress your friends.

Conventions Used in This Book

When writing this book, we included these general conventions (which all _For Dummies_ books use):

✔ **Italics:** We _italicize_ any word you may not be familiar with and provide its definition.

✔ **Boldface type:** We **boldface** the keywords in a bulleted list and the steps in a numbered list.

✔ **Monofont:** All websites and e-mail addresses appear in `monofont`.

Pretty cool, huh?

What You're Not to Read

We believe that every word in this book is worth your time (and you probably aren't surprised). We realize, however, that you aren't likely to read every word. With that understanding in mind, we make it easy for you to identify "skippable" material by placing it into sidebars, those gray boxes in every chapter that contain information that's interesting and related to the topic at hand but not essential for your video marketing success. Other than that, you can go to town.

Foolish Assumptions

As we wrote this book, we made a few assumptions about you, our reader. For example, we assume that you're either seriously considering a career as a video marketer or that you're a marketer for an existing company that needs to add video to its arsenal of marketing tools, even if that company is your own. We also assume that you're ready, willing, and able to commit yourself to making awesome, compelling videos that generate an excellent return on your investment.

How This Book Is Organized

Video Marketing For Dummies is organized into six parts, each one covering a major area of video marketing. The chapters within a part cover specific topics in detail.

Part 1: Creating Effective Marketing Videos

To become a successful video marketer, you must open your creative mind to the uses and approaches that make video a special and powerful tool. Part I begins with a discussion of how the available technology is making video an affordable tool for many communication uses in businesses. In these chapters, we describe marketing video types, ways to integrate video marketing into your entire program, and the idea, scripting, and storyboarding process.

Part II: Preparing for Production

The way to save time and money when making videos is to plan efficiently. This part helps you understand the costs and suggests ways to reduce them without compromising the quality of your final product. We also help you cast actors and find locations. Most important, an entertainment attorney shows you how to protect yourself from liability by helping you understand all the legal pitfalls you may encounter — and even supplies a slew of sample legal forms to use.

Part III: Shooting Your Video

If you've ever wondered what it feels like to be on the set of a television production, now you can find out. Part III describes which video gear to buy and how to use it, and it explains how to ensure that your actors are seen *and* heard. We even walk you step-by-step through a video shoot.

Part IV: Editing and Polishing Your Video

Compiling all the footage from a shoot into a compelling story can be an all-consuming process. People have been known to enter an editing session and not emerge from it for several days. This part of the book demystifies the process of picking software and shows you how to add music and graphics to make your videos powerful and compelling.

Part V: Posting and Promoting Your Video

Making high-quality videos is only part of the process. You should use every tool at your disposal to attract viewers to your video and convert them to believers in (and, you hope, buyers of) your product or service. This part breaks down the best hosting sites, explains how to promote video via your website and social media site, and ensures that you have the tools and knowledge to measure and adjust your approach to draw the maximum response.

Part VI: The Part of Tens

Finally, we throw in "The Part of Tens," a quick-and-dirty collection of chapters, each of which lists ten (or so) pieces of information that every prospective video marketer needs to know. Some of the information covered in these chapters includes nonsales ways to benefit from video, common video marketing mistakes, and useful resources to assist you in the process. Look to these chapters when you need a quick refresher on video marketing strategies, techniques, and support.

Icons Used in This Book

To guide you along the way and point out the information you truly need to know, this book uses these icons along its left margins:

These tips and tricks can make video marketing easier.

Watch out! If you ignore this advice, the situation may blow up in your face.

Keep these important points of information in mind to become a much better video marketer.

This geeky-sounding jargon may not be critical to understand in detail, but may be helpful if you want to comprehend the mechanics.

Where to Go from Here

If you're considering a career as a video marketer — or if you were just handed a camera by your boss, who says that she needs a YouTube channel — you may want to start at the beginning and work your way to the end of this book. Simply turn this page, and take your first step into the world of video marketing.

If you're already engaged in video marketing and you're short of time (who isn't?), you may want to turn to a particular topic to address a specific need or question. The table of contents in this book describes the topics chapter-by-chapter. You can also find specific topics in the index.

Either way, we encourage you to experiment and enjoy.

Part I
Creating Effective Marketing Videos

"It was supposed to be a simple sleep potion. That's why you can't always trust the information you get off of 'Wiccapedia.'"

In this part . . .

We realize that you're eager to start posting videos and raking in the hits, but before you can begin filming, editing, and promoting, you need to find more information about marketing videos. In this part, we explore the different uses of video marketing in business and describe the benefits and opportunities you can expect. We lay out the different types of videos in the marketplace and show you how to integrate your existing marketing efforts with effective, humorous videos. Finally, we delve deeply into the step-by-step process of scripting and storyboarding a truly compelling message.

Chapter 1

Video Marketing from the Ground Up

In This Chapter

▶ Considering a marketing video

▶ Deciding on marketing video strategies and tactics

▶ Understanding the video production process

*V*ideo marketing is hardly a new form of getting your message across to prospects and consumers. Ever since television station WNBT broadcast the first television commercial for Bulova Watch Company, at $9 for a 20-second spot, on July 1, 1941 (before a Brooklyn Dodgers game), companies have marketed their goods and services using video.

Of course, the cost to produce and broadcast a television commercial has skyrocketed since then. Producing and distributing a commercial video message to the public via the traditional broadcast and cable television networks can now cost many millions of dollars. This high price has prevented many small businesses from distributing their marketing messages via video — until now. Thanks to the Internet, the YouTube site, and the reduced cost of equipment and technology, any company can now afford to create and distribute a video to its potential customers.

Everyone seems to be jumping on the video marketing bandwagon. But simply making and posting a video about your company cheaply and easily doesn't guarantee that the video you produce will automatically be effective or compelling. In this chapter, we tell you how to use video marketing for your business, differentiate between video strategy and video tactics, and determine whether to create a production unit in your own company or simply hire a professional video production firm to take on the task.

Why You Should Consider Video Marketing

After you create your own video, you can use it to communicate in ways that other marketing tools don't. Though video won't replace websites, direct mail, and trade shows as effective ways to generate and close business, it can enhance these other tools to make them more effective. You can use video to monitor consumer behavior and connect emotionally with your customers by using a variety of different systems that are both effective and economical for any company.

Online benefits

Most businesses now communicate online to some degree, and video is a powerful tool to support their online communication. Sites such as YouTube make video distribution and measurement cheap and easy. Video can help your marketing online in these four primary areas:

- **Behavioral analytics:** YouTube and other video hosting sites provide extensive viewer data that can give you deep insight into the behavior of viewers who interact with your videos.

- **Conversion:** Amazon, Dell, and other online retailers have publicly shared statistics showing that a posted video can increase the odds of a customer purchasing an item by as much as 35 percent.

- **Efficiency:** Software developers continually find new ways to integrate sites so that video messages can be easily shared and broadcast via social media networking.

- **Search engine optimization:** Bing, Google, Yahoo!, and other Internet search sites have made video a key factor in their search formulas. Posting an abundance of video on your website can move you higher in the search rankings — broadcasting your marketing messages to an even larger potential audience.

Emotional benefits

Video offers the opportunity to use sight and sound to connect emotionally with viewers via storytelling. Unlike reading material, video content communicates passively: The viewer simply watches and lets the story unfold. Outstanding video entertains and influences viewers by invoking a series of emotions that result from showing images that connect their hearts and their brains with your product or service.

Effective marketing practices bring efficiency to the sales process. Ideally, your marketing program helps attract customers who are predisposed to buy your product or service at a premium price. To increase the likelihood of a solid return on any investment you make in video marketing, never forget that the powerful emotions of fear and greed motivate buyers to take action.

Efficiency

The average person speaks at a rate of about 150 to 160 words per minute (WPM), which is half of this page. People read a little faster, at a typical rate of 250 to 300 WPM, or about a page of text in this book. That isn't much space to convey large amounts of information about your company's story or to describe a product or service in detail.

If the adage is true and a picture is truly worth a thousand words (we believe that it is), imagine the sheer volume of information that video can communicate. A simple 2- or -3-second video image can transmit tons of historical, emotional, and academic information simply from the imagery portrayed in the shot.

Because video has the potential to transmit large amounts of information, every detail is critical. As a video maker, you're now responsible for every image conveyed in every moment on the screen. Unlike editing a website or whitepaper, editing a video after you post it can be difficult (if not impossible).

Video Marketing as a Strategy

After you understand the power of well-made video, you'll undoubtedly want plenty more. But don't produce video haphazardly — an effective video marketing strategy requires forethought, planning, and consistency. In the following three sections, we cover the basic ingredients of developing a video marketing strategy.

Content

Your fundamental task when you begin video marketing is to choose the topics of your videos. Many companies start with a simple video that paints only a general picture of what the company does, which may satisfy the owners of the company (because it tells their story) but isn't necessarily effective in bringing marketing efficiency to the sales process.

To choose the content of your videos, focus on issues that are difficult to communicate via print or other marketing mediums. Detail every message you want to communicate with prospects, partners, and employees. The content of these messages provides good topics for video marketing. In Chapter 2, we suggest specific ways to identify the topics that will bring the fastest return on investment by video marketing.

Creating boring and irrelevant video is worse than creating no video. If you waste viewers' time, they will think less of you, your company, and your products and services. Strive to make the most interesting and relevant video possible every single time. If you show viewers that you respect their time, they will likely return the favor by watching your videos and maybe even buying what you're selling.

Promotion

You must use every tool in your marketing arsenal to draw viewers to watch. These marketing tools can help increase the number of views you receive:

- **Blogging:** Bloggers always look for compelling videos to include in their blogs and boost their own search engine results.

- **E-mail lists:** E-mail is still the most effective form of marketing for a consistent response. Send your videos to everyone you know.

- **Pay per view:** Target users who have a preference toward your product or service, and attract their attention for significantly less money than you would spend to broadcast a network TV commercial. Check out Chapter 19 for instructions on how to create effective pay per view campaigns.

- **Sharing sites:** Sites that repost videos, such as those featured on reddit or Stupid Video, can grab attention for your video and help it spread to more viewers.

- **Social media sites:** Post your video on your company's Facebook wall, and encourage your employees to follow your lead, or send an invitation to watch an exciting video for a quick blast of immediate viewership on Twitter. Be sure that your invitation on Twitter fits easily into its 140-character message limit.

Measurement

Using a powerful marketing tool doesn't benefit you if you don't measure its power. Though the result of your video marketing program can certainly be measured in part by increased sales, the measurements described in this list may paint a more informative picture:

✔ **Number of new prospects:** If your product or service has a long and complex sales cycle, video alone may not be enough to close the deal. Look at the statistics to see whether your video is expanding your market opportunity.

✔ **Demographic statistics:** Perhaps you believe that your product is perfect for customers from Generation X (generally, people born in the 1960s and 1970s), but, instead, those from Generation Y (born in the 1980s or early 1990s and commonly known as *millennials*) are responding to the video. Maybe it's time to rethink your strategy.

✔ **Geographical statistics:** Who knew that your service would be popular in Iceland? Maybe it's time to open a new office.

✔ **Time spent watching:** Modern technology helps you as a video maker see exactly when your pitch bores or offends viewers to the point that they stop watching.

✔ **Hours you save:** Calculate the number of hours you have spent repeating your sales pitch to customers, and then multiply that number by your hourly wage. The amount reflects the number of dollars a good video can save you before you make a single sale.

If an item can be measured, you can bet that someone, somewhere, has created a way to measure it. Be open-minded in examining all statistics related to your video marketing program, and learn all you can from them. You can find information on how to measure the efficacy of your videos in Chapter 21.

Applying Video Marketing Tactics

A strong video marketing strategy deserves strong action. You can add video to your marketing arsenal in several tactical ways. Chapter 2 describes many ways to integrate video with your marketing program — but first, consider adding these basic video tactics to your box of tools:

✔ **Run commercials:** Advertising is by far the most common and most effective use of video — even on the Internet. Identify the pain felt by your customers, and demonstrate why your solution will best solve their problems. Done well, these types of videos still show the highest and best return on investment.

✔ **Educate your public:** Whether you're teaching about your products or your industry, people search the web to learn. Educational videos give you a chance to show how smart you are and show why people should listen to what you have to say. Done well, these videos provide business process efficiency and can attract buyers.

✔ **Create a video blog:** Posts on your video blog, or vlog, are effective ways to attract people to your site and maintain their interest. Subject matter experts can use video in creative ways to teach and entertain an audience while also pushing their products or services. A video blog is a good way to update your constituency about news and events taking place at your company.

✔ **Host a webinar:** People love to learn, and a webinar is an efficient and effective way to teach. Whether you stream video live or record a live event for later broadcast, an educational and compelling webinar can attract hundreds of prospects and convert them to buyers.

✔ **Take advantage of video production activity:** The process of making videos can itself be beneficial to your company. Involving everyone in the scripting process forces them to carefully contemplate company messaging. The production process is useful for team building and for developing culture and leadership.

Video marketing is an active process. Everyone in the company can somehow participate. The more people you involve with your videos, the more people you have to enthusiastically promote them to the world.

Creating Marketing Videos

The video making process can seem intimidating at first glance, but order exists in the process. Your first time out, you'll undoubtedly spend extra time on understanding and executing the process, but the process becomes — trust us — faster and easier with every video you make. Follow these general steps to generate a compelling marketing video:

1. **Choose your audience.** Developing appropriate content is much easier when you know who your viewers are. (See Chapter 3.)

2. **Pinpoint your message.** After you know the *who,* you can figure out the *what.* Try to keep your message simple and concise. You can always make more videos if you have more messages to convey. (See Chapter 4.)

3. **Create a compelling concept.** You can't afford to be boring. If a topic doesn't excite you, it won't excite your audience either. (See Chapter 4.)

4. **Finalize the budget.** Less is more. Don't try to be George Lucas your first time out. Focus less on fancy effects, props, and locations and more on the story line. (See Chapter 5.)

5. **Draft a detailed script and storyboard.** The more detail you outline, the more easily you can meet — or exceed — your time and budget constraints. (See Chapter 4.)

6. **Brush up on your knowledge of any appropriate legal issues.** Protect yourself and stay out of trouble by knowing your risks and the law. (See Chapter 8.)

7. **Get your cast and crew together.** Involve in the production everyone you'll need to make and post your video. (See Chapter 7.)

8. **Gather your gear.** Now is the best time to buy fun "toys," such as cameras, microphones, and monopods. (See Chapter 9.)

9. **Scout out locations.** Look for the best places to shoot your video. (See Chapter 6.)

10. **Shoot the video.** The day of shooting is a day of fun on the set. (See Chapter 12.)

11. **Edit it.** Manipulate all elements of the video into a unified whole by cutting, combining, and rearranging its various elements. (See Part IV.)

12. **Refine and polish it.** Add music, titles, and graphics, for example. (See Part IV.)

13. **Broadcast it.** Distribute your video on the web. (See Chapter 17.)

14. **Promote it.** Show your video to everyone you know, and persuade them to pass it around to everyone they know. (See Part V.)

15. **Measure the response.** Find out whether you're getting the results you want, and learn, learn, learn how to make your videos more effective. (See Chapter 21.)

Of course, you can't always handle all these tasks alone. Video marketing is fundamentally a team experience, though it may often be a team that consists of only two or three people wearing several hats. This list describes the roles that must be filled in your video production:

- **Camera operator:** Controls the camera and gets the shots

- **Director:** Engineers the look and feel of the production by managing actors and crew members and, ultimately, deciding how to orchestrate all elements of the video

- **Editor:** Constructs scenes (including cutting unnecessary material) to achieve the director's vision

- **Graphics creator:** Uses Photoshop and PowerPoint and other graphics programs to create graphics

- **Lighting designer:** Ensures that lighting is bright, even, and appropriate

- **Producer:** Orchestrates the overall video production, including managing the budget, processing legal issues, and procuring hard-to-find objects

- **Production crew:** Helps gather props, apply make-up, devise costumes, make set changes, and serve coffee

- **Promotion manager:** Helps publicize the video to attract viewers to the finished product

- **Soundperson:** Holds the microphone and eliminates extraneous noise

- **Talent:** Can include experts, actors, or simply company personnel. Often, they perform roles outside their comfort zones (even to the point of looking ridiculous onscreen) for the sake of your company.

- **Writer:** Creates the concept and the script

Chapter 7 gives you insight into these people and how to get them to help with your project, even if you have no money to pay them.

Choosing Between Doing It Yourself and Going Pro

The video production process isn't for everyone. Your company, for example, may not have enough employees with the necessary time, talent, or desire to maneuver the process and develop systems for continually pumping out fresh marketing video. Hiring a video production company is an alternative to making videos in-house. If this idea appeals to you, consider a company's skill level in these areas before hiring one:

- ✔ **Acting:** Choosing a believable cast is critical to connecting with prospects. The company you hire must have a large pool of talent and be willing to hear your opinion about casting.

- ✔ **Budgeting:** The cost of hiring a production company is the primary consideration — prices can range from $500 to $500,000 for a single video. Shop around, and find the best quality for your money.

- ✔ **Editing:** Too many videos are now simply "mash-ups" of music and graphics, all moving too fast to make a true emotional connection. Look for seamless editing that enhances the story.

- ✔ **Finding locations:** You don't have to be in the same state (or country) as the production company, but it should have access to locations that project the appropriate company image.

- ✔ **Managing resources:** To create a quality video, the production company must have an adequate pool of acting, directing, and editing talent.

- ✔ **Storytelling:** A competent storyteller cultivates the most effective marketing videos, so the company you hire must be able to spin a good yarn. For example, many wedding videographers have jumped into the business video game.

- ✔ **Writing:** Either make your message explicit or find a company that can help you frame it into a compelling script. The worst online videos invariably result from a production company's use of the same boring formula it uses on countless other videos.

The best way to choose a production company is to watch its video products, review its budgets, and speak to its clients about their collaborative experiences. If you don't like the company's videos, don't assume that it's the client's fault. The production company is ultimately responsible for creating successful marketing videos, regardless of a client's direction.

Working with video professionals is not an all-or-nothing choice. You may be able to build an effective video marketing program by hiring a few key freelancers to shore up your organization's production weaknesses.

Animated alternatives

If you want to skip the production process or you aren't a team player or you simply lack the time and resources to hire a production company, you have alternatives: Visit www. xtranormal.com or goanimate.com to see how these sites have produced online software to help you create animated videos on your own, from your own desk. Both sites supply you with computer-generated characters that resemble humans in a variety of scenes so that you can generate any scenario you need.

Go!Animate lets you record the voices to match the characters, and Xtranormal creates computer-generated voices from the script you type. Both are somewhat robotic, yet videos on YouTube from both companies have well over 1 million views — which just goes to show you that it's less about the quality of the production than about the quality of the content.

Chapter 2

Integrating Video into Your Marketing

In This Chapter

▶ Answering the viral dilemma

▶ Identifying effective video topics

▶ Creating internal and external efficiencies

▶ Combining video marketing with other tools

*A*n exciting marketing tool such as video is often looked at as a panacea for many marketing issues. Though video is an amazing communication tool that's suitable for transmitting tons of information while creating emotional response, it has its best effect when it's integrated throughout your entire marketing arsenal.

Integrating video effectively into your marketing strategy requires planning and an understanding of the task you're trying to accomplish with your message. If you're focused on marketing your message internally, create video that fits with your culture and engages your employees in a positive manner.

Externally focused marketing videos need to be polished (even the ones that intentionally look unpolished). They should create efficiencies for your sales process while inducing prospective customers to buy your product or service. Video for the sake of having video simply wastes your time and that of your prospects. In this chapter, we address the question of whether to attempt to create a viral video, describe how to identify worthy topics for videos both internally and externally, and help you develop a plan to integrate video with your other marketing tools.

Knowing Why Viral Video Isn't Always Virtuous

The first topic that comes to mind for most marketers considering video marketing is videos that "go viral" — many a marketer now dreams of creating videos that tally zillions of hits and draw millions of buyers to their company's door, resulting in profits and accolades. Though creating this type of video is an admirable goal, first consider these important issues:

- **Few business videos go viral.** More than 48 hours' worth of video is uploaded to the YouTube site every minute, and fewer than 30 percent of these videos garner more than 99 percent of the traffic. Only about 1 million videos have more than 1 million viewers, and fewer than 50 videos have more than 100 million hits. Considering that business videos represent a small percentage of uploads — and that the most viral videos usually involve sex, scandal, or severe shock value — it stands to reason that the truly viral business videos are few and far between.

- **Broad-based businesses benefit from viral video.** If your business is local or has a small demographic, it will have difficulty justifying the cost and effort required to make a video purposely go viral.

  To a neighborhood store or restaurant, a million views may sound beneficial, but translating that number into physical dollars may not be as effective as waging a direct-mail campaign within your own neighborhood. Likewise, if you're a financial advisor working only with exclusive clients who make more than $1 million annually, a viral video is unlikely to reach your most profitable clientele. In fact, you may receive calls and e-mail from people who aren't your customers — which wastes your time.

- **No one can make videos go viral every time.** As with any other marketing approach, creating successful viral videos requires knowledge, creativity, and experimentation. Ad agencies charge millions to produce videos, and they distribute them in ways that they hope will go viral. Most fall short and see greater exposure by way of conventional channels, such as TV. Without a large following, lots of money, and a killer concept, getting a video to go viral requires a perfect storm of luck and timing. When it does, it's often too late to capitalize by attaching a marketing idea.

If you're committed to the holy grail of video marketers that is viral video, you need to first understand how it works and the factors at play.

Understanding the Viral Process

Though no perfect formula specifies how to make a video go viral, a recognizable pattern exists. If you truly want to take a shot at viral fame, follow these steps to increase from one viewer to millions:

Diet Coke and Mentos: EepyBird

One of the most successful marketing viral videos of all time originally had nothing to do with the two companies featured in the video. The original concept was not a marketing idea but was a simple experiment by a couple of friends — Fritz Grobe, a juggler, and Stephen Voltz, a former lawyer. They met at an international theater school where, at the suggestion of a friend, they dropped six Mentos candies into a two-liter bottle of Diet Coke, only to witness a geyser-like reaction.

For fun, they shot a video in one take of choreographed fountains using 101 bottles of soda and 524 candy pieces and released it on June 3, 2006. The video, a YouTube sensation, quickly went viral, and its popularity was reported on by mainstream media. The original video, which now has more than 14 million hits on YouTube, may have been seen more than 50 million times. In addition, copycat videos now account for *more* millions of views.

Certainly, this concept was beneficial to Coca-Cola, which saw a 5-percent sales increase, and to Mentos, which saw a 15-percent boost, but neither company had a part in creating the original video. In fact, when the two companies joined forces to sponsor their own EepyBird — the company (at www.eepybird.com) founded by Grobe and Voltz to develop other consumer product experiments and viral videos — video six months later, the result, though successful in driving traffic, paled in comparison with only 1.7 million YouTube views to date.

EepyBird has excelled in leveraging its videos into money for both itself and its clients, but only after the accidental, initial success that built its following. Therein lies the challenge for viral video marketers: How to reach the first 50 million views on purpose?

---

1. **Create and post a video that has the "WOW! factor."** Get creative, and make a video so amazing that someone other than you, your family members, and your co-workers are unbelievably impressed.

   Make the video shocking and relevant without crossing a line that may offend the customers you want to attract.

2. **Transmit via e-mail and social media to friends and mailing lists.** The larger the lists, the faster your video has the potential to spread. You can also pay for ads on Facebook, Google, and YouTube to boost its presence.

3. **Ask people to repost your video and e-mail it to their friends.** You can hope that people will comply because your video is remarkable, but you can always give them a financial incentive or another type of reward to pass it along anyway.

4. **Identify bloggers and news media who may find your video unique and will promote it even more.** Publicity is the play today to garner attention for a video that already has momentum. Some companies pay bloggers to repost their videos, so prepare to use your wallet if you wander down this path. You can even pay to have sites such as www.unrulymedia.com and www.seeding.com spread the word.

5. **Look for your video to take off on YouTube.** When your video accumulates more than 200,000 hits, YouTube may notice the traffic volume and feature your video on its home page. At that point, you should see the number of hits quickly jump to more than a million, and, you hope, drive business to your website (if you remembered to insert the URL into your video, of course).

The viral nature of the video depends on a combination of its compelling nature combined with fast growth in viewership. Both elements are incredibly difficult to engineer in advance, but high levels of traffic won't likely happen without outstanding content.

Maybe a viral video is right for your company, and maybe not. But you can get financial returns from your videos in plenty of other ways, even if the videos are seen by only a few people whom you already know.

Identifying Communication Chokepoints

Most companies want to confirm that they're receiving identifiable value from the time and money they spend on video marketing. The surest way to recognize return on investment (ROI) from a marketing video is to use it to solve a specific communication problem. It can be as simple as explaining the definition of a term or describing a specific action. Anything that obstructs your sales process from moving forward can be considered a *chokepoint* to be solved with video.

Most chokepoints have these characteristics in common:

- ✔ **Confusion:** Often your prospect doesn't understand a characteristic of your company or product. Perhaps you're selling a technical or complicated service. You may need to break it down into a series of simple ideas, each of which is worthy of a separate video. Because video can pack a lot of information into a short amount of time, videos resolving points of confusion can save you and your company time and money.

- ✔ **Redundancy:** If you have ever had to repeat yourself to a customer, you have experienced a chokepoint of redundancy. The reason you're repeating yourself is that your audience isn't comprehending your meaning the first time, or maybe even the fourth time, or the fourteenth. A powerful video can trigger both understanding and memory.

A humorous video can lock in the brain, as we explain in Chapter 3.

Material that you repeat often is worthy of being included in a video, even if it simply keeps you from sounding like an outdated broken record.

✔ **Inconsistency:** Whenever your managers are saying one thing, your salespeople are saying another thing, and your customer service reps are saying something else — all on the same topic — you're definitely dealing with a chokepoint. Over time, any company's message can become cloudy and inconsistent. And the more people you have in your organization, the more messaging resembles a child's game of telephone, where the message changes slightly every time it's passed along. Video marketing can efficiently provide an exact message with a good story to help everyone remember.

This step-by-step process can help you identify chokepoints in any company. Make someone accountable to involve the appropriate people from the sales and management departments, for example:

1. **Review all marketing materials.** Look for repetition and inconsistencies in your website, training materials, and collateral (the physical materials, such as brochures and cards, that you use for marketing).

2. **Interview your salespeople and customer service reps.** Find out what they're saying and where they're struggling with getting the message across. Assess which parts of their sales training they accomplish easily and where they have difficulty.

3. **Gather your management team in a room, and review the results of your assessments and interviews.** Then hold a brainstorming session with your senior executives that lasts from two to four hours. Schedule this meeting monthly (or at least quarterly) to ensure that you're proactively addressing any communications issues in your process.

4. **List your chokepoint concepts.** Use the first part of the meeting to share every possible chokepoint in the company, both internal and external.

   Don't eliminate items or try to use perfect wording on the list at this time — simply put every possibility on paper. You don't need to edit at this point.

5. **Simplify each chokepoint into a single sentence.** If the chokepoint is instead a paragraph, chances are good that it represents more than one chokepoint. Use language that a 10-year-old can understand, and state every chokepoint in a sentence of 15 words or fewer. (This technique not only ensures that you're clear and concise but also saves some much-needed trees.)

6. **Categorize the list.** The best way to address the issues on the list with video choices is to break them into groups. Categories may include Sales, Customer Service, Technology, and Maintenance. By grouping them, you can easily schedule and budget your video needs by department and priority.

Be objective about what's working and where problems exist. If your team experiences dissension over a potential chokepoint, the chokepoint likely needs your explicit attention, and you should consider a video. In the worst case, you add one more excellent video to your portfolio that will eliminate any possibility of confusion.

Chokepoints happen with both internal and external communication, and video can help in both areas. Make sure to include human resource managers as well as your sales and marketing people in the chokepoint discussions.

Avoid trying to solve too many chokepoints in a single video. Combining chokepoints can cloud your message and make your video less effective. Treat every idea independently, and help educate your audience on the specifics of a single idea. If your video is powerful and entertaining, your audience will likely want to watch more videos from you.

Marketing Internally with Video

Video marketing isn't simply a strategy for your sales and marketing divisions — it's also a way to apply powerfully efficient communication to every aspect of selling a message about your company. In fact, companies often spend more time selling internally than externally. Your company may have only a few concepts to convey to its customers. However, your employees may need to retain many hours of material that is continually changing. Video is an inexpensive way to convey messages in a memorable and meaningful manner that can be easily updated as necessary with the latest information.

What is a REIT?

A company in Canada presented ROARing Video with a challenge. The company wanted to communicate the benefits to small investors of participating in a large real estate investment trust (REIT). But most of the company's prospects failed to understand what a REIT is, let alone know how it functions. Kevin and Matt worked with company owners to identify ten different chokepoints in their sales process. After talking with its member service managers, Kevin and Matt uncovered difficulty in simply defining the term REIT itself.

ROARing Video created a series of entertaining 2-minute videos that humorously explain the definition of a REIT, how liquidity is handled, and the meaning of transparency in investing. The series proved popular with prospects and helped the member service managers explain other terms consistently. They often simply sent the videos to prospects, saving time and confusion.

Aligning your team with video

Motivating different types of people to do or say the right things in the right ways consistently is always a challenge. Left to themselves over time, most employees simply find the path of least resistance and develop their own patterns of behavior — which can lead to inconsistency and inefficiency in the workplace. Most companies function more effectively if their teams are aligned with common goals, purposes, and rules.

Video is a useful way to get all team members on the same page. A series of clever videos that intrigue and entertain is likely to be watched and talked about more than any written memo, and is likely to be remembered far longer than any verbal announcement. Address these key areas to achieve full marketing alignment with your team:

- ✔ **Value proposition:** Make sure that everyone in your company understands the pain you relieve for your customers, the solution you provide, and the way you differentiate yourself from competitors. If your video is compelling, your staff will be motivated to say the right things to the right people in the right way at the right time.

  For more on communicating a compelling value proposition, check out Kevin's book *ROAR! Get Heard in the Sales and Marketing Jungle* (published by John Wiley & Sons).

- ✔ **Core values:** Lots of companies have core values, but few employees remember them. Video is a useful way to demonstrate the emotional impact of your core values. Brief scenes showing the emotional repercussions of following your organizational "do's and don'ts" will help your crew remember to do the right thing — and avoid the wrong one.

- ✔ **Workplace rules:** Verne Harnish of www.gazelles.com suggests: "If your company isn't mocking you [playfully], you aren't repeating yourself enough." Why let your voice grow hoarse? The next time you tire of cleaning out the office fridge, make a quick, entertaining video, and let YouTube do the work of repeatedly telling people to take care of their own spoiled goods.

- ✔ **Human-resource issues:** Many companies' employee manuals are miles thick with all sorts of rules and regulations. In reality, few employees read the manuals, and human-resource managers have little time to police all those rules and regulations. People often feel uncomfortable discussing sensitive issues face-to-face. Video is a useful tool for showing how people should behave, and for describing the consequences when they behave badly. Check out www.HRLarious.com to see a company that creates fun and humorous human-resources videos.

- ✔ **Employee introductions to each other:** Fast-growth companies can add as many as 10 to 20 people per month. Not many people can remember all those names and faces, especially when they work on the other side of the building, across town, or, sometimes, on the other side of the globe. A video introduction can be a helpful way to familiarize employees with an expanding company, no matter where they're physically located. Simply shoot them introducing themselves, and let them add pieces of personal trivia that will make them memorable.

A simple channel hosted on YouTube, as suggested in Chapter 17, makes for an interesting "rogue's gallery."

✔ **Compliance:** If you're in a regulated industry, such as banking or the medical field, you must comply with a ton of regulations. The forms alone are enough to make your head spin. Video is an efficient tool for passing along important concepts that can save new employees from having to sift through mounds of pages just to tick the right boxes.

✔ **Company and industry news:** Companies often struggle to keep their employees informed of weekly changes and important notices. The bigger the company, the more difficulty it has in disseminating information to everyone.

Produce a simple weekly show featuring fun and exciting two-minute videos with news and stories. Kevin and Matt helped a company with this strategy and posted the show every Friday. By making videos humorous, and thereby making video viewing the highlight of the week, the videos registered 100-percent viewership.

Any good concept can be overdone. If your videos are boring and mediocre, they're also ineffective. Keep them fun and lively, and use an idea such as a news show to incorporate other elements from the list. In this case, you're marketing to your colleagues as your customers, so cater to their needs and interests to keep them engaged.

Maximizing your training technique

If a picture is worth a thousand words, a video must be worth *ten* thousand words of how-to training. Every company has to train employees to use a process. Creating a video library for training saves you time and money and maintains more consistency in your corporate learning than live training can.

Follow this simple step-by-step process to make your training videos powerful and memorable:

1. **Extract knowledge from the experts.** The most important task in training is providing the right information from people "in the know." The challenge is that the people in the know don't often articulate *what* they know. Find a subject expert, and interview that person to determine the key points to be shown in your video. Spend some time discussing which steps are crucial.

2. **Separate the process into manageable steps.** Any complex process is easier to learn when it's chunked down into a series of steps. If the steps are long ones, you may need a video for each one.

   Plan your training to be taught in chunks of three to five minutes.

3. **Identify the key interest point in every step.** If all steps are similar, a trainee may have difficulty differentiating them. Identify the one or two most important elements of each step in the process, and make it the focal point of each video.

4. **Create a memorable saying that differentiates the step from the others.** Any process with many steps is hard to remember, no matter how many times employees watch instructional videos. Make every video stand out on its own by finding a phrase or an action that's specific to the step.

   If you attach a song or a joke (even a silly one) to a step, you make the step much more memorable for the trainee. For maximum effect, coordinate the punch line to the action you want.

5. **Create a uniform look and feel to the series.** Making every video memorable is important, but you also need to tie it all together to distinguish each process.

   If your accounts receivable process is based on a horror film theme, for example, and your computer maintenance training series was shot in the style of an educational hygiene film from the 1950s, your employees will categorize the video series in their minds. They can then not only remember the information but also direct other employees.

The best training is meaningful and memorable. If you make the extra effort to create fun and entertaining training videos, you spend less time having to train people yourself or clean up after their mistakes.

Using the video making process to train brevity

The team-building effort of making short videos can be both fun and creative. Companies can also benefit from the way team members are forced to structure the script and storyline. Most people use considerably more than 1,000 words to communicate a simple idea to a co-worker or client. Because the typical video script of one to two minutes consists of fewer than 500 words, however, the video making process forces teams to carefully choose their words and frame their ideas.

Experienced employees working with new co-workers can usually find common language to fit short timeframes. Their effort still has impact, but not without thoughtfulness and intention. Have your teams create two-minute videos describing what they do and how they do it. You'll find that the experience will help them be consistent and more concise.

Marketing Externally with Video

Most people associate video marketing with business development, and for good reason. Video is now cheap to make and easy to distribute to people who have never heard of you. But video marketing isn't only about attracting customers — video resembles any other marketing tool in that it can add efficiency to these linear aspects of the sales process:

1. **Lead generation:** Gain attention and attract prospects.

2. **Customer assessment:** Clarify whether this customer is right for you, and reject any prospect who isn't a good match.

3. **Customer analysis:** Determine a client's wants and needs, which often aren't the same things.

4. **Prescription (or business model):** Specify what you have that can meet a customer's needs, and offer a price.

5. **Objection removal (or closing):** Identify whatever is preventing the customer from consummating the deal, and then eliminate the obstacle.

6. **Transaction:** Address customer *touch points* (the points in your process where you have contact with the customer) by specifically stating how you will deliver your product or service, helping them get benefit, and accept payment.

7. **Referral:** Encourage your happy customers to send their friends and neighbors to you.

8. **Repeat business:** Unless you're a surgeon or a bankruptcy attorney, you want customers to return and buy more of your product or service.

Every step in the sales process can be accomplished by your salespeople individually without assistance, but video can make the process easier and more efficient. You can help your sales team become more effective by specifying the task you're trying to accomplish in every area. Kevin has built a list of more than 100 questions to help you segment the specific actions of your sales process at every stage: See www.TheAwesomeExperience.com/100.

Generating leads and attracting buyers

Companies are always looking for new ways to attract customers. Brochures and networking alone are often ineffective, in addition to costly and time consuming. Also, many companies have difficulty getting their salespeople to say the same things (let alone the right things) when prospecting.

A compelling and entertaining video can communicate quickly and consistently the emotions necessary for attracting a customer who is predisposed to buy. If a video resonates with buyers, it acts as an efficient magnet that can suck needles from a haystack. A powerful video can generate additional brand awareness and clarify what your product does and for whom.

Video works for lead generation only if someone watches it. If your prospect list is small, the video is unlikely to magically end up in people's hands. If the video has amazing shock value that entertains, it may spread like wildfire. More often than not, however, it's your known methods of distribution that support the video's effectiveness for generating leads.

Assessing prospects and analyzing their needs

Salespeople spend a lot of time chasing potential prospects who aren't truly prospects. They like to think that everyone is a prospective buyer, when in reality they want to attract only people who truly need or want their product or service and, more importantly, are willing and able to pay for it. Video can help insert efficiency into the assessment-and-analysis process by compelling people to take action *only* if they're qualified buyers.

Using video to filter potential prospects saves you time and money. If the video clearly articulates the pain and solution of your value proposition (described earlier in this chapter, in the section "Aligning your team with video"), real customers should leap from their chairs to visit your website or call you.

Kevin's book *ROAR! Get Heard in the Sales and Marketing Jungle* (John Wiley & Sons) states a clear formula and provides instructions on how to lay out a compelling value proposition. You can download two chapters for free at www.AwesomeRoar.com.

A video that's clear about your offering should also repel anyone who isn't one of your best potential customers. Clarity saves you the time and effort of speaking to this group of people, because you aren't likely to close them on a purchase anyway. Still, if you make the video entertaining or informative enough, they may consider passing it along to someone who fits your customer profile, or at least sharing it with their social media networks.

The next time you're networking, conveniently forget your business cards. Instead, simply ask for the e-mail addresses of everyone you meet. By handing over their e-mail addresses, they're giving you permission to contact them, which you can do by sending an e-mail with a video link in it. If someone loves the video enough to e-mail you back, you know that you have a true prospect on the line. If no one responds, you can assume that people were simply being polite.

Removing buying objections

Not every customer is ready to buy after becoming aware of your product. Many salespeople have to complete the process of eliminating concerns, and some are better than others at closing customers. Often, salespeople are more adept at listening to themselves talk than at hearing the concerns of prospects. Why leave this crucial part of the sales process to chance? You can make a different video for each objection and let customers review them on your website before a salesperson ever gets involved. Here are some key areas of objection to address:

- ✔ **Inventory and services:** Video is a helpful way to show prospects that you have on hand what they want and what they need. A company selling furniture can create a short video showing every individual product from every angle and in every color. You can also break down a complicated service offering into several steps and create a short video outlining each phase. Not every prospect wants to peruse every single video, but if videos are handily catalogued on your website, basic questions can be answered without having to take up the salesperson's time.

- ✔ **Price:** Price is usually the number-one objection for most prospects — everyone would buy your product if it cost little or nothing. A simple video demonstrating how your product stacks up against competitors or showing how little your service costs per day in comparison to its benefits can help motivate price shoppers to open their wallets.

- ✔ **Value:** Prospects want to know that the product or service they're buying will be worth at least the amount they're paying for it (if not more). You can use video to demonstrate the more difficult segments of your offering and to convey its value faster and more easily than by simply speaking directly to them.

When making a video to remove objections, be sure to address the specific objection in the video. Let viewers know that you acknowledge their concern and are willing to address it. Letting people know that you're aware of their concerns about your product or service goes a long way in helping them lower their defenses against selling.

Good marketing videos incorporate objection removal into every aspect, whether they're specifically designed for that purpose or not. If your videos are on point and entertaining, prospects will want to do business with you and will most likely overcome their fears.

Resist the temptation to address all objections in one video. Trying to do it all often accomplishes nothing in the end. Instead, make a separate, short video for every objection and link them, for example, to a common page on your website where people can read the FAQ (a list of frequently asked questions) to quickly find the video that answers their question. You have the additional benefit of seeing which one is viewed most often, which gives you valuable information about how your customers think.

Building credibility

With the number of competitors now out there, new prospects want to know that they're dealing with honest and forthright people who can deliver what they promise. You must answer the questions in the following three categories to build credibility, and you can use video effectively to answer them:

- ✓ **Knowledge: Do you know enough to solve the prospect's problem?** In a video, you can share tons of content in a short amount of time. A library of videos on your product or service demonstrates your breadth of knowledge, and including subtle nuances shows that you have depth.

- ✓ **Understanding: Will you listen and comprehend the prospect's specific issue?** Simply stating that you're listening to someone is unlikely to make that person trust you. But demonstrating your listening process by presenting detailed stories that demonstrate your openness to your customers may prompt your prospects at least to take the time to give you a try.

- ✓ **Testimonials: Have other people had good experiences with you?** People rarely want to be the first to spend money on trying something new or untested. The testimonial is an important video tool for making people comfortable and letting them know that they aren't alone. Good testimonial videos are brief, and they're often best when you have a particular point to make rather than a general "I like this company" statement. The people giving the testimonials should be credible and have a trustworthy appearance.

Just as video can help build a good reputation, it easily can give a bad impression instead. Any blemishes or misrepresentations will forever be "out there" after you release the video online. Make sure that the video is honest, authentic, and inoffensive to those you're trying to attract, or else you may not be able to control the damage.

Developing a Video Marketing Integration Plan

Good things in business rarely happen by accident. Effective marketing requires a series of carefully constructed steps, integrated and executed with the purpose of moving a buyer to take action. This strategy requires planning and investment and enough time to get it right.

Most importantly, set a plan for your video marketing that incorporates all your other marketing efforts.

You can use the eight elements in this list to combine video with other marketing tools to create more of an impact with your marketing:

- ✔ **Your website:** Your website should contain your entire library of videos. They should be arranged in a way that makes sense based on the information on every page of your site. Chapter 18 helps you decided what to put where. Video is a key element of search engine optimization (SEO) and search engine marketing (SEM): Internet search engines return results more often from sites with video, and video helps to make your site feel more interactive. You can easily embed or install videos on your website. YouTube has simple tools for embedding, as detailed in Chapter 17.

- ✔ **Snail mail:** Plenty of direct-mail marketing still takes place. Whether you're sending letters or postcards, you should encourage readers to check out information in your videos online. By using a specific link printed in the mailer, you can easily track direct traffic to the video.

- ✔ **E-mail:** E-mail marketing continues to be the most effective marketing tool, especially when you consider the minimal cost to mail 1,000 e-mail messages. You can quite easily post a link to a short video in all your e-mail messages. Simply copy the link and paste it in the e-mail — you're ready to go. You can even add a small *thumbnail* (a miniature computer graphic) to the link and increase your click rates significantly.

  You can use a URL service such as www.bit.ly to create short, specific URLs for tracking e-mail response. E-mails are easy for people to pass around and share as well. For extra passive exposure, remember to insert a video link in your company signature.

- ✔ **Social media:** One effective marketing aspect of social media tools such as Twitter and Facebook is the capability to spread video quickly and easily. Most social media tools have a method for simply sharing a video. Their tracking systems are usually already built in, and most can share in just a few keystrokes. (We discuss how to incorporate these systems in Chapter 19.) If your video is truly powerful and strikes a chord, your community can spread the word for you.

- ✔ **Events:** Video is an excellent event-marketing tool. You can show videos at events that can entertain and create the right mood for those who participate, and a memorable video sent to participants after the event is certainly the gift that keeps on giving. An outstanding video can not only trigger emotional memories but also attract attendees to future iterations of the event. You can even use videos as party favors. Check out the later sidebar "Ship to shore" for an affordable and powerful event video idea.

- ✔ **Trade shows:** You can incorporate video into trade show marketing programs in many ways: Show a compelling video in the booth to help inform people about specific topics, or provide basic information while they wait for someone to help them. You can also integrate video into the design of the booth to ingrain your visual imagery and message.

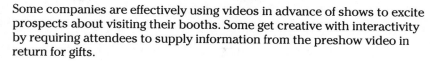

Some companies are effectively using videos in advance of shows to excite prospects about visiting their booths. Some get creative with interactivity by requiring attendees to supply information from the preshow video in return for gifts.

✔ **Seminars and webinars:** Every seminar you attend physically should become a video that can be broken up into clips, ready for posting on the Web. Many marketers post single-camera webinars and keep them on their sites for future viewers. Find ways to be creative. Talking heads and PowerPoint presentations can grow old fast, though relevant information and sparkling delivery help. The medium of video screams "Show me!" and the use of props and activity can make a webinar truly an event to talk about and ultimately pass around.

The downside of video in seminars and webinars is that it's all telling. If you speak poorly or you're careless with wording, you may create video that hurts, rather than helps, you. It's far better to record the material and edit it afterward if you aren't ready for prime time live.

✔ **Print advertising:** Be sure to integrate the look, feel, and tone of your collateral marketing materials — such as brochures, flyers, and premium items — with your video work. Consistency is a powerful tool in branding and messaging. You can effectively use your printed material to reference important video content by using links and QR codes (special images designed for smartphones), just as you can invite your prospects to ask for literature in your videos. The more you integrate, the more power you have in getting your message across. Check www.dummies.com/go/videomarketing for an example.

After you establish a strategy for combining video with your other marketing tools, budget the amount of money you're willing to invest in your overall plan. You also need to set a timeline for video releases that fits with the rest of your marketing program. Follow this step-by step-approach to build your integration plan:

1. **Start with your overall budget.** Video doesn't happen for free. Though it takes time *and* money, it doesn't have to be expensive. Borrow a little from every other marketing budget area to create your video budget, because you'll integrate video into those areas.

2. **Continually ask the video question.** Whenever you're discussing any marketing approach, ask your teammates, "How can video help us here?" You may be surprised at the ideas that come up.

3. **Establish a style guide.** Decide whether you want that YouTube feel or a polished, professional look. Every detail sends a message in marketing, and more polish doesn't always mean more business.

4. **Create a master calendar.** The best marketing plans are carefully coordinated for their timing. Video has a lot of moving parts in the production process. Make sure to give yourself ample time to adjust and coordinate with all your other marketing efforts.

5. **Internally address every detail.** You're responsible for every second that your prospect watches the screen. Someone who reads only 30 percent of your brochure or website still may buy. If the video loses someone somewhere in the middle, that person may not ever come back or even know how to find you.

6. **Review in a self-critical manner.** People often become excited about making a video and forget that it had a purpose beyond entertaining the people who created it. Make sure your videos are worth watching by their prospects. Save the self-flattery for your home videos.

Boring and irrelevant videos with poor messaging are worse than *no* video, so take the time to do it right rather than race to finish it fast.

Don't make your company memorable for all the wrong reasons. Video production takes time, and effective video marketing can take months to find the right messages and script them well.

Ship to shore

On a lovely October night on the Hudson River, two New York City entrepreneurs arranged a special boat charter for a small group of powerful NYC movers and shakers. Every passenger was instructed to show up as the person they wanted to be three years later and to speak and act as though they had already accomplished their goals. The hope of the hosts was that having everyone discuss their "accomplishments" would encourage them to help each other turn their goals into reality. The hosts wanted participants to remember the evening long after the boat had docked back in Chelsea, so they hired ROARing Video to record the experience.

Rather than simply post typical shots of the boat and mingling people set to music, Matt and Kevin planned a more creative approach. On arrival, all attendees gave video interviews about their accomplishments and their significance and the obstacles they overcame. Participants were also asked how they would celebrate reaching their goals. After the event, each interview was packaged into a one-minute video with attractive titles, photos of the boat, and inspiring music. The hosts sent every attendee a personal daily-affirmation video as a thank-you gift for participating. For the next three years, attendees can watch the one-minute video every day, grateful for the people who helped inspired them to reach their goals.

Chapter 3

Choosing Types and Styles of Marketing Videos

In This Chapter

▶ Determining the right type of marketing video for every situation

▶ Incorporating various video styles for the greatest effect

▶ Establishing an emotional connection

▶ Leveraging humor for memorability

▶ Creating impact creatively

*W*hen you have an engaging message to market, you want to make a video that leaves a lasting impression (a good one) on people who view it. The key advantage of video over most other types of communication is its ability to quickly create an emotional connection with the viewer.

The type and style of your video set the tone for how to write the script, choose whom and what viewers see, and develop the look, feel, and sound of the finished product. Making unexpected stylistic choices often has a greater impact than simply delivering what is expected.

This chapter explores the various types and styles most often used in marketing videos and helps you decide how to best use video to make your product or service memorable and move prospects to take action. You can find examples of these types and styles at www.dummies.com/go/videomarketing.

Identifying Types of Videos

A *video type* determines the structure of a video. The type is defined by the way it's cut and produced. It establishes how you will communicate the message and provides instruction for all the people involved in making the video. Select a type of video by considering these factors:

✔ **Purpose:** You should know why you're creating a video. When you understand the specific problem you're solving with your video, you can then focus on video types that will have the greatest impact on viewers.

✔ **Audience:** Will the video inspire customers, partners, employees — or all three groups? Knowing who your audience is and knowing what makes them respond are fundamental to choosing a video type that connects with them in a meaningful way.

✔ **Context:** You should know where, when, and how people are attracted to your video, and you should know what they're expecting when they click the Play button. Sometimes you want to meet expectations, but often you want to surpass them.

✔ **Distribution:** Your choice of where to distribute videos matters, too. The type of video that's created for interoffice use may not be appropriate for mass consumption on YouTube.

✔ **Time:** Time can be your friend or your enemy. Amazingly, four minutes of video can seem like a lifetime, whereas a compelling 15-minute segment can leave viewers wanting more. Video length can also be determined by production capabilities.

✔ **Budget:** The amount of money you can afford to spend on video styling can either open doors or close them. Some styles are more elaborate — boosting costs — and others are simpler to create based on readily available locations, props, and talent.

After you consider all these factors, you can select one of the many types of video that will move people to action in a powerful way.

Storytelling for impact

People love stories. They thrive on them. Stories allow you to put actions and words into context. When you're marketing a product or service, stories help you show prospects what you're about, without making them feel "sold." When a story is on target, a prospect identifies empathetically with its characters.

To prevent rambling (and obscuring your intended point), be sure that your stories are carefully constructed. Give your story a complete structure, which includes these elements:

✔ **The beginning:** Every video needs to start somewhere. The beginning establishes the context, characters, and expositions such as time, place, and circumstance.

✔ **The middle:** The middle contains the dramatic point of conflict or anticipation that engages your audience. It's where the action is.

✔ **The ending:** Ultimately, the conflict must be resolved, often with an offer of solution from your company.

To design a story that speaks to your audience and drives the action you intend, start with a clean sheet of paper and identify these required components of storytelling:

- **Setting:** Determine where the story takes place, and decide which important characters are involved. Viewers must be able to easily comprehend the location, the business process being addressed, and the company involved in the story so that they know what's happening.

  The video setting doesn't always have to be established at the beginning. Sometimes, revealing the setting at the end can have a greater impact. For example, viewers may react differently if a story they've just finished watching turns out to be a dream.

- **Protagonist:** This character drives the story. She nearly always has a purpose. The protagonist is the reason the story is happening. However, the person who drives the action isn't necessarily the character whom viewers identify as themselves.

- **Conflict:** Conflict establishes the emotional connection. Somehow, obstacles get in the way, and pain is created. When you coordinate the challenge of the characters to correspond with your prospect's pain, you make the emotional connection.

- **Resolution:** Ultimately, your prescribed course of action should end the story. Even if the purpose of a marketing video is only implied, it still must promote your product, service, or idea. The characters must be perceived as benefitting from your offering — or at least as perishing from never obtaining it.

One key difference between marketing videos and artistic videos is that marketing videos are designed to compel specific action from the viewer. A marketing video has a purpose beyond being entertaining and artful: Its story must make the point and drive the viewer to respond or retreat. Telling a story for the sake of the story itself may attract viewers, but not buyers. (This is not the time to let your inner Martin Scorsese take over.)

Demonstrating through show and tell

Many companies connect with their customers by showing them how to use their products effectively. A video may be useful for this purpose when text or pictures alone cannot adequately help viewers understand how to use a product.

Demonstration videos work best when they're short and to the point. Complicated demonstrations can be broken up into several shorter videos so that viewers can absorb one or two concepts at a time and easily search for problem areas.

Will it blend?

One of the most successful video marketing campaigns is at www.willitblend.com. To show the power of the Blendtec industrial-strength blender, the company created a series of fun videos to let viewers request items to be blended, such as super glue, golf balls, and glow sticks.

Blendtec viewership exploded when the company successfully blended an Apple iPhone and iPad. The videos have attracted millions of viewers, and more important, sold millions of dollars worth of blenders.

Capturing events

Event videos are used to record and summarize events and gatherings. Marketing videos from events usually include clips of speakers and activities. The goal of most event videos is to remind attendees of the value they received from attending. Event videos can also attract new prospects to the next related event on the schedule.

The challenge in creating event videos is to make them interesting and to connect with the emotion of the event. Often, event videos that simply play music accompanied by brief clips of meaningless images do little to make viewers respond.

Whenever possible, coordinate the theme of a video in a creative way to correspond with activities in the event. For example, hold a contest for attendees where the prize can be won only by those who watch and identify an element in the video that you send out two weeks after the event. This approach motivates people to anticipate receiving the video and look beyond the material to the key message associated with the item you want them to find. Ideally, viewers think about the event, and the benefits they derived from it, long after it has occurred.

Making use of animated video

In marketing, animation serves as more of a convenience than an art form.

Animation allows for the fast creation of complex visual imagery without having to endure the challenges of sets, props, people, and special effects. Whereas animation used to require a crew of artists drawing picture after picture, computer-generated animation now allows you to show almost any image you want by using a computer and a programmer.

Even home artists can get in on the act by trying an inexpensive, easy-to-use animation software program such as Go!Animate (goanimate.com) and

Xtranormal (www.xtranormal.com) which are discussed in Chapter 24. An animated video sets a tone of whimsy and allows for imagination to be shown in ways that would be impossible with live action, whether you're making animals and objects act like humans or showing your mom flying in outer space.

Only words and pictures: Is that really video?

PowerPoint presentations have become forever associated with sales and marketing. Unfortunately, many practitioners of this trade commit the ultimate PowerPoint crime: Stand in front of a group and read text from slides. As video becomes more popular, so does the similar trend of creating fancy motion graphics or words that move and simultaneously narrating them word for word or simply adding music. Though this approach technically qualifies as producing a video — you can post it on YouTube or your website and include a viewer — it doesn't create the same marketing benefits of an action-based video, because a PowerPoint presentation by itself generally falls short of establishing an emotional connection with the viewer by way of visual imagery.

Many video companies charge high prices for their words-and-pictures videos, touting the general benefits of video without specifically showing the difference in impact on the bottom line. Although a PowerPoint-style video may be easy to produce and gets your material on YouTube quickly, live or animated action helps your prospects relate to characters with depth and meaning. Your goal is to convey your message in a meaningful way and still be heard above the noise. As video marketers, we believe that actions speak louder than words.

If scant time or resources leads you to choosing a PowerPoint-style words-and-pictures video, you still have to communicate to your viewers in a compelling way. You must present words and pictures that truly matter in a way that engages people and speaks to their needs. Make your content readable and appealing so that viewers don't dismiss your message because of the medium.

Incorporating Video Styles

Video style is the tone or feeling of a marketing video. Unlike its type, which tells you how to construct the video, the style of a video determines the feelings that it creates. Filmmakers often use the word *genre* to describe a style. When we think of entertainment genres, mysteries, horror, romantic comedies, and adventure films come to mind.

The topic of film genre can be a useful guide to stimulating ideas on how you want your video to appear. Your video must first and foremost communicate your message to an audience that you're hoping will respond the way you want. Focus your efforts on the video's message, and use style to entertain while enhancing its memorability.

Using humor effectively

Knock-knock! Who's there? Iowa. Iowa who? Iowa lot of money for my marketing campaigns. This joke may not be the funniest one ever, but it serves well for exploring humor as an effective video marketing style.

Many video marketers focus on creating a professional image, which simply means making it look like it's expected to look. Sadly, this approach often results in boring and forgettable videos rather than helping to make the emotional connection that drives prospects to action.

More often, a marketer attempts to create a lasting connection by tugging at emotional heartstrings to create a small trauma in the viewer's mind. The marketer isn't trying to hurt you, but many of them believe that serious tragedy makes the video memorable.

Coming up with funny material that is neither offensive nor too casual requires forethought and objectivity. You have to plan jokes and be honest when they don't work. Still, humor is a worthy aspiration because it can accomplish tasks, as described in this list, that are seldom achieved by taking a serious approach:

- **Establish rapport.** Almost everyone loves to laugh. Inoffensive jokes can easily establish likeability and trust. A joke related to a difficult situation can disarm a prospect or client when you have to deliver "tough medicine." Relationships are often built on the experiences of shared humor — people tend to do business with people they like. And if they smile and laugh every time you're near, they will associate you with happiness. Combined with knowledge, humor enhances expertise, by demonstrating confidence and strength.

- **Trigger memorability.** Many marketers strive to create "Aha!" moments in customers' minds, such as when someone believes one thing and you turn his attention to make him consider another. These are the mechanics of the punch line to a joke.

  At the beginning of this section, we tell a joke to suggest a state to your brain and then quickly refer to it as a financial issue. The unexpected wordplay registers in the brain as humor, which triggers endorphins encoded for memory. That's why a childhood joke exists in your repertoire decades after you hear it.

> ✔ **Create alignment.** Effective jokes are based on shared experience, and humor works well when people understand communally the issues at hand. After a common problem is identified and a punch line created around it, insiders adopt the punch line as a trigger representing the issue. If no one remembers to turn off the lights when leaving, for example, a giant light switch painted on the wall makes people laugh and remember their responsibility without causing embarrassment.

Create humor in your video by using inside jokes. The challenge in using humor is quite simply that you have to be funny. Stand-up comedians train and practice and sometimes still fail on-stage. Humor works best when everyone understands the references. If you're creating an internal video for your company, you can capitalize on funny inside jokes around the office that mean nothing to outsiders but will have your employees rolling on the floor. Your industry undoubtedly has several inside jokes that would be understood only by those people who work in it every day. If your audience is culturally broad, making something funny to everyone becomes more difficult. To optimize and simplify a humorous approach in video, target the smallest community and use the insider's view to tickle their funny bones.

You don't have to use humor all the time, but if you want viewers to like and remember you in a consistent and productive manner, simply follow the words of the late, great Donald O'Connor: "Make 'em laugh! Make 'em laugh! Make 'em laugh!"

Being serious without the drama

There's a difference between a video that has a serious tone and one that's just dry and boring. Successful marketing videos create emotional connections by helping viewers identify with the struggles of the people or images on the screen.

A serious video should make the case for an important topic, in a way that establishes the urgent nature of the prospect taking action. The intensity of the drama needs to match the intensity of the urgency at hand. For example, a hungry college student may feel the urgent need for pizza, but a serious video emphasizing that plight in a way similar to a video about starvation in Africa would either feel inappropriate or be considered a comedic spoof.

The challenge in making serious marketing videos is that, ultimately, you're trying to sell something and the customer knows it. Outside of serious medical, emotional, or societal issues, most products and services aren't critical. If you push too hard and too often with serious content, a prospect can become numb or dismiss the urgency of your approach.

Before you take a serious approach, ask yourself these questions:

- ✔ Will the prospect believe that this issue is important?
- ✔ Will the prospect believe that this issue is urgent?
- ✔ Can the video story be presented realistically, without melodrama?
- ✔ Can the prospect use my action to resolve the issue?

If the answer to these questions is yes, a serious approach may be valid. Just be careful not to let the prospect think that you're crying wolf.

Informing with news-style video

The reason that TV news has been around forever is that it's effective. People simply want to be informed. News media companies spend millions of dollars every year cultivating on-air personalities and formats to keep you interested and entertained.

You can easily borrow from news-type shows to fashion a video that informs its viewers. Here are some examples of elements you may use:

- ✔ **The *Broadcast News* effect:** A good-looking, well-spoken anchor who says "This just in" can grab viewer attention right off the bat. Just make sure that the substance is worth the attention.

- ✔ **Newsreel footage:** Old-style newsreels no longer show up in movie theaters, but they can still be an effective approach in telling a marketing story. Making a story humorous by setting it in an earlier period can also add an element of fun.

- ✔ **Man on the street:** Street interviews add credibility because you're presenting supposedly ordinary people who are excited about your product or service. Edit carefully so that the video builds and supports your message clearly.

- ✔ **Talk-show segment:** Matt Lauer is still employed and for good reason. People enjoy a short feature about a single topic all wrapped up in a neat little package with an intro and an outro. (An outro resembles an intro except that it leads out of the story.)

- ✔ **One-on-one interview:** A good interviewer can pull an amazing story from your subject. This strategy may work well when you're presenting a CEO or another person who has responsibility for a project.

- ✔ **News panel:** Many cable channels use multiple screens to assemble a panel of experts to discuss an issue. A well-contrasted panel can bring energy and excitement to an otherwise flat topic.

Presenting a news-style format effectively gets your message across clearly. To have true impact, though, they can't be only informative — they must be entertaining as well.

Avoiding talking heads

All video marketers have something to say. A simple shot of a person saying it, however, doesn't truly take advantage of the power of the video medium. Unless you create a story that includes actors or animation, you probably can't avoid placing someone's face on the screen, though you ultimately want to use imagery to enhance the presentation.

Nothing in video is worse than "boring down the house." Someone who drones on directly into the camera without taking a break is certain to initiate someone else's nap.

Follow these suggestions to make talking heads more appealing:

- **Add titles and graphics.** You can add titles and graphics to the screen simultaneously to enhance what the speaker is saying. These elements provide additional information that people's brains can digest while their ears are listening to the speaker. The information may be humorous or supplementary.

  Chapter 16 gives you specific techniques for adding titles and graphics to your videos.

- **Add music.** Music has highs and lows, and it can affect the emotion of the video. The right music, scored underneath the speaker's voice, can add drama, excitement, and likeability to the segment.

  More details on how to find and include music are in Chapter 15.

- **Show two people discussing a topic.** Most people love to eavesdrop on a conversation, especially if it doesn't offend anyone. Gathering information that's passed from one person to another feels like you're getting the inside scoop. This technique can prevent people from feeling that the message is intended specifically for them.

Making testimonials meaningful

The testimonial is an excellent tool for video marketing. It offers the viewer a chance to see that other people like your product or service. Use the testimonial sparingly, and make the speaker speak and look credible.

A testimonial is effective only when it's brief and to the point. Your testimonial must address a specific aspect of your offering so that prospects clearly absorb new information. Simply showing five people who claim to enjoy your product or service has little effect. Prospects are smart enough to know that no smart marketer would ever show a testimonial from someone who didn't like the company.

Creating a montage

A *montage* is a compilation of live action, pictures, and graphics (and almost every other element we discuss in this section). By using video, you can pack a lot of material into a few minutes. A quick pace can make the montage video fun and exciting. Just make sure that the montage has a pattern that makes sense.

This list shows the order of elements in an effective sample montage:

- **Opening graphic:** Describes the video
- **Announcer:** Introduces the concept of your topic
- **Pictures:** Convey graphic images of a relevant topic
- **Announcer:** States the response to pictures and introduces a testimonial
- **First testimonial:** Proves that someone other than the prospect approves of your product
- **Additional graphics:** Enforce the testimonial in words
- **Announcer:** Introduces a second testimonial
- **Second testimonial:** Touts an additional aspect of your product
- **Announcer:** States the call to action
- **Final graphic:** Shows the call to action and provides website information

Spicing It Up Creatively

Video is an art, and art requires creativity. Marketers often get lost, however, in getting the message out and forget to add fun and creative elements. The easiest way to take a creative approach is to involve other people in the process. Shared experiences help make a video project speak more effectively to prospects and ensure that it pleases, rather than offends, prospects.

Using archetypes to create recognition

In video marketing, you have a short amount of time to help your prospect identify with your message. When you use an archetype, the prospect subconsciously fills in information about the character they're watching, leaving you with more time to communicate your information.

Archetypes is a fancy word for the types of people you know.

You may recognize the typical marketing archetypes in the following list. Notice how much information you already have in mind about these people:

- ✔ The concerned parent
- ✔ The executive
- ✔ The employee
- ✔ The entrepreneur
- ✔ The person who's technically oriented
- ✔ The curmudgeon
- ✔ The video game fanatic
- ✔ The members of a family

Understanding common assumptions about these archetypes allows you to create humorous scenarios where everyone can relate to other types of people.

Avoiding stereotypes that breed contempt

Though archetypes can help you connect with people, stereotypes can get you in trouble if you use them inappropriately. Cultural and racial identities come with built-in sensitivity issues that can create problems.

If you suspect that your material may be considered offensive, you're likely correct. Find a way to communicate your idea in a way that speaks positively about anyone who may be a prospect or a member of society.

Making it fresh

Because most marketing videos make use of easily recognizable scenarios, quite a thin line exists between the familiar and the cliché. Viewers have been bombarded by video messages since television commercials began in the 1950s. Everything that can be said in a marketing message has probably already been said many times already.

If it feels stale, it probably is stale. To break free from what's expected and freshen up the old ways, gather your favorite group of people and ask them to list ten ways in ten minutes to give your approach a new twist. Not every idea will be a blockbuster, but the fast pace kick-starts creative juices and encourages you and your friends to come up with one or two good ideas. A new twist on an old concept can often create more impact with the prospect than a brand-new idea can.

Keeping it clean

Society has unwritten rules (and, often, written laws) regarding profanity and sex. These unwritten rules have been changing with the advent of cable TV and the Internet, but they're moving targets. Your videos should present your product or service in a positive way. You can hint at a risqué concept without using foul language, nudity, or blatant sexuality.

Chapter 4

Scripting the Right Message

In This Chapter

▶ Sketching the concept

▶ Making it simple with script models

▶ Pursuing an excellent viewer experience

▶ Storyboarding for simplicity

*R*egardless of whether your video is a short introduction to your business or an extended description of your company history, it needs a *script* — the document that details every aspect of the video, including what people in the video say and do and where and how they say and do it. All marketing videos — including webinars, video blogs, and show-and-tell videos — benefit from scripting by ensuring that the video has structure, relevance, and continuity.

Scripting a video gives you a chance to show off your creative side while incorporating practicality and marketing skills. It's the part of the video marketing process where ideas are specified, judged, and expanded. The final script for the entire production is a blueprint that includes budgeting, casting, shooting, and editing the video.

Some people may be too intimidated to start with a blank page on the computer screen. It's one thing to imagine how a video will look and feel, and quite another to detail every word, picture, and action. Writing experience helps when scripting videos, but we happily share our experience so that you can easily get started in scripting. In this chapter, using a live-action video example, we show you how to flesh out the concept, follow structural models, make your video an awesome viewer experience, and document the script for sharing, in an organized manner.

Sketching Out the Compelling Idea

The key to making a successful marketing video is to make it compelling. Though you may believe that you're the next Steven Spielberg, your task isn't to win an Academy Award. The reason you make a marketing video is that you want it to compel viewers to do something. You may want them to buy from you, or even to simply consider a concept you're introducing. If the video doesn't connect with viewers emotionally, they're unlikely to be compelled to do anything other than click a link to move on to another web page.

Good marketing requires a solid understanding of your *value proposition,* which is *the* reason that someone would buy whatever you have to offer. It doesn't matter whether you're selling a product, a service, or an idea — you have to answer these three key questions or else your video will have little or no impact:

- ✔ What pain or related problem do you solve for the viewer?
- ✔ What is the objective solution?
- ✔ Why are you the best solution provider?

Answering these questions can help you build a compelling message that you can translate into an entertaining and compelling video. Without a clear and compelling message, the video may be entertaining but ineffective for marketing.

Identifying the pain

The first thing to remember when creating a successful marketing video concept is that the video is not about you. Many marketing videos fail to do their job because they fail to consider the mindset of the prospects who will watch it. These videos become vanity pieces instead. Believe us: No one wants to hear you drone on and on about yourself unless you're providing a direct solution to their pain.

Done well, video marketing is an effective tool for creating an emotional connection with viewers who are truly willing and able to buy. If you connect with their pain, they respond positively. Ideally, a prospect sees your video and exclaims, "That's me!"

Marketing videos work best to solve pain identified by *choke points.* Before you consider which actors, dialogue, and sets or locations to use, you have to flesh out a description of the pain you can solve for your potential customers, including how it looks, sounds, and feels. Only then can you represent their pain visually to help prospects see that you understand who they are and why they care about what you have to say.

Try this brainstorming exercise:

1. **List the problem.** Starting with a choke point, write a brief statement describing your pain. The statement should be narrowly focused, specific, and true. The broader the pain, the more difficult it is to create

video about it. For example, a tire company that says "Cars need tires" will have difficulty creating a compelling video idea based on only that statement. In comparison, a pain statement from a company focused on its all-season tire product, such as "The time and cost spent on changing tires or using chains only in winter is frustrating" leads to all sorts of empathetic imagery of customers enduring the hassle of adding chains during snowstorms or paying a mechanic every year.

2. **Gather three to five people in a room.** The creative process is always more productive when it's centered on dialogue. Set up a short, 30-to-60-minute brainstorming session with people who know your customers well, such as a selection of people from management, customer service, and sales. Encourage a diverse group of people to attend, including those who have a history of disagreeing with one another — healthy conflict is the best tool for uncovering the truth. If you can persuade an objective outsider to join the process, you may find that you don't understand your prospect as well as you may think.

3. **Have every person relate a story or an example of the pain you've solved.** After discussing the basic pain statement and validating its legitimacy, have every person give a testimonial, in rich detail, about a prospect who converted to your business. For fun, and to get into the right frame of mind, have people describe the scene as though they're pitching a movie, as in *"The scene opens, it's snowing, and Janet is standing around, looking at her wallet."*

4. **List all common details from participants' stories.** Have participants write down the common details they hear while listening to the stories, under the categories of *who, what, when, where, why,* and *how.* (See Table 4-1 for an example.) After everyone has compiled a list, the team can discuss the validity of the common answers — which form the basis of the concept. The other small details may prove useful for adding depth and color to the story in the video.

Table 4-1	Janet's Story
Category	*Detail*
Who	Janet, a working mom
What	She's preparing her car for the winter season.
When	December 2012
Where	Detroit, Michigan
Why	Roads are slippery and wet this time of year.
How	She's cautious and frustrated because she cares about her money and the safety of her children, which are conflicting needs.

5. **Consolidate the information into a short, descriptive paragraph.** The list you made is helpful in scripting, but for now you need a simple statement to test the idea and to act as a guideline for your concept, such as this example: *Budget-conscious consumers in snowy areas feel frustrated about being wasteful when they're forced to spend their time and hard-earned dollars on installing snow tires every year.*

This exercise uncovers the core of your message. Although lots of images come to mind in this process, trying to brainstorm video ideas at this point is counterproductive. The ideas may have merit but are likely incomplete. Resist spending more time with any video concept until you have fleshed out all the important messaging.

Keep handy a separate whiteboard, Word file, or bulletin board for future video ideas. Throughout the complete scripting process, great ideas may surface that are wrong for the particular video you're working on but are useful later. Often, some of the best new project ideas emerge inadvertently while working on another project. If you designate a storage place that you can easily find whenever you need it, you can take advantage of the creative bonus material by simply revisiting those ideas for future projects.

Proposing a solution

Ideally, your offering is the perfect solution to your prospect's pain, but pushing your brand on prospects too early can make prospects feel defensive, as though they're being given the hard sell. One benefit of creating video is that you *show,* rather than tell, people how to solve their problems. Establishing an obvious, objective solution as the answer to their pain helps prospects remain open-minded and eager to know more.

Being objective and honest while discussing the following questions about the solution you're proposing helps ensure that you aren't selling too hard or too soon.

- Is your solution the only one?
- Why is this solution obvious? (*Hint:* If you have to explain it, it isn't obvious.)
- What part of the pain isn't covered by your solution?

An excellent solution statement makes a prospect say, "Of course, that's exactly what I need!" An example from the earlier tire pain example is, *An all-season tire requires no changing, saving you time and money.*

You probably got it right if your prospect says, "Why didn't I think of that?!"

Differentiating your approach

After you go to the trouble to empathize with your prospect and help her feel enthusiastic about finding the solution to her pain and problem, you can let her know why she should come to you, and not to your competitors, for the solution.

Most companies believe that they differentiate from their competitors by providing good quality, service, or experience — but, truthfully, none of your competitors claims to have poor quality, no service, or little experience. If you want to lock in your customers' intentions and close more business by using your videos, tout a true differentiator — something that your competitors won't do or can't do without great effort or expense.

True differentiators have the following characteristics in common:

- They cannot easily be provided by everyone or anyone.
- They often take time to develop.
- They often cost money to develop.
- They're memorable.
- They require commitment.
- They're desirable.

Hash out these issues with your team to see whether your statements truly make you different or sound the same as your competitors' statements. The following statements are "red flags" that may help you understand whether your differentiators are truly different in a way that you can prove or are simply statements you've made that all your competitors also claim:

- "But we really are better at that."
- "Yes, but they're lying."
- "You'll see when you try us."
- "It's all about the relationship."

If you make any of these statements, chances are good that you have yet to develop clear differentiators that will wipe out your competition.

Differentiators don't have to be complicated. Our fictional tire company, for example, may say, "Our all-season tires come with a seven-year, no-hassle, roadside replacement guarantee." Obviously, if competing tire companies are offering roadside assistance for seven years, this statement doesn't help. But if the industry standard is five years instead and you have to bring the tire to the store during a snowstorm, the tire company has a serious competitive advantage.

Speaking to the right audience

Just because you have a compelling message doesn't mean that you can communicate it to every prospect in the same way. In his book *ROAR! Get Heard in the Sales and Marketing Jungle* (John Wiley & Sons), Kevin demonstrates a 3,500-year-old process, used at Passover Seders, for identifying the following four existing buyer types and persuading them to buy:

Wise buyers focus on making unemotional decisions based on facts to avoid making foolish purchases.

Cynical buyers have been taken advantage of, and they believe that it will happen again. After you earn their trust, they're the most loyal buyers because they believe that others will burn them if they leave you.

Simple buyers are straightforward and direct. They want only specific items, whether it's pricing or another specific need. They don't want to waste their time with you if you don't correctly address their immediate needs.

Disinterested buyers, or those who are unwilling to ask questions, are potential customers who are unaware of how your offering affects them. After you attract their attention, they convert to wise, simple, or cynical buyers.

Successful marketing videos are directed to at least two, if not all, of these buyers by following the following simple formula (outlined in Kevin's book title):

✔ Recognize the buyer type.

✔ Observe from their perspectives.

✔ Acknowledge their concerns.

✔ Resolve their needs.

Using this tool in your script development increases the impact of your video and produces better results. *ROAR!* describes all the tools necessary to apply this approach to your marketing message. It's a fun story, too.

 The statements in this pain solution, differentiation-structured value proposition (VP) provide much of the specific language necessary for effective scripting. Use the VP as a template to stay on track and on topic.

Creating the Concept

After you have a compelling message to communicate, you're ready to create a concept that transfers well visually to video. Good scriptwriting is all about layering. This list shows the necessary layered components:

✔ The message serves as the foundation.

✔ Characters bring the story to life.

✔ Structure carries viewers from beginning to end.

Creative aspects, such as humor and surprise, layered on top ensure that your entertaining video makes the rounds among business hopefuls.

A basic concept with a beginning, a middle, and an end gives viewers a sense of completion when watching your video, but that's just table stakes (your bet limit) when you're marketing to prospects. Creatively layering the video with information and technique also ties into emotional needs, so that your prospects are compelled to take action.

The most effective concepts are recognizable, yet they feel new and fresh, with surprises around every corner. These concepts speak directly to prospects while somehow feeling universally obvious. Good scripting sounds difficult, and it can certainly be challenging. The key to success is to continue rewriting and rethinking with your team until people are excited and about the brilliant ideas you apply in the piece.

Although we represent the conceptual and scripting process in a somewhat linear manner, it's quite organic. This process consists purely of creative brainstorming, and its stages may happen out of order, at all hours of the night, and in all sorts of places — including in the car, the shower, or the gym. Be open to the creative muse, and write down ideas as they occur to you. The process feels like a big, slushy mess until your idea starts to crystallize and becomes clear. Then continue to question until you're sure that you're pursuing the best ideas rather than the first ideas to occur to you. Note that scripting is only the beginning of the process, and that often, the final product takes its best shape only after you're in the editing process (which we discuss in Part IV).

Celebrating and enjoying the process help project excitement in your script, and, ultimately, in your production, but be sure that your excitement is on behalf of the prospects who you're marketing your message to. Because the process of making a video is a worthwhile accomplishment, novice video marketers tend to complete a video and then forget to scrutinize their work for effectiveness. Be critical of your work at every stage of this process. It makes for more entertaining and more effective marketing videos.

Establishing an emotional connection

The easiest way to connect with prospects emotionally is to use archetypes (discussed in Chapter 3). Some examples of these common types of characters who we all understand are the busy parent raising a family, the grumpy old relative whom you rarely see, or the overbearing boss.

You have only a short amount of time in which to make an impact on viewers and convey your message. Using archetypes in your concept gives viewers information and lets their brains, and their memories, do the rest of the work. By having in mind an archetype that shares the emotion of pain with a prospect, you can build a world around that person to communicate the message.

The use of an archetype moves you at least 50 percent of the way toward an effective marketing video concept. After you choose an archetype, however, answer these questions to determine whether your character connects emotionally and to help flesh out the character's depth:

- ✔ Does the archetype you chose for the main character represent your typical prospect?
- ✔ Are your prospects familiar with the cultural aspects of this particular archetype?
- ✔ Can this archetype represent your message effectively?

Videos that don't consist of live action, such as in blogs and webinars, can use archetypes effectively by way of images or storied references. Even basic demonstration videos can become more memorable by triggering emotional metaphors in viewers. For example, if your video explains how to use a piece of machinery safely, you may refer to learning to drive and then walk viewers through a safety checklist that's similar to double-checking their mirrors and seatbelts. Every bit of emotional context that you provide increases the memorability of your video.

In the tire company example, earlier in this chapter, we suggest an archetypical mother experiencing conflict while trying to manage money and her children's safety as winter approaches. This classic character is one whom most everyone can relate to in some respect, whether from their own experience or their mother's or wife's having been in a similar position. Some people may even be familiar with this archetype simply because they have seen a similar character many times in the media. This familiarity triggers basic emotions and helps make the concept easy to manipulate for great effect.

You can use archetypes for characters other than the main character in your video. The more archetypes you use, the more information you can transmit, and in a shorter period. In the tire company example, other supporting elements may be a tire salesperson, a spouse, and even the kids. After you choose the main character, make a list of possible supporting characters who may be able to help tell your story. Often, side characters carry the important marketing message that accompanies the story.

Scripting with structural models

Rather than arbitrarily creating a story from scratch, you can use simple structural models to integrate the message with the characters and create a script concept.

In all models, a touch of humor goes a long way toward making the story in the video entertaining and memorable. Many professional comedy writers use one of these two conceptual approaches to creating comedy:

- ✔ Put a silly person in a sane situation.
- ✔ Put a sane person in a silly situation.

Using either of these models boosts the level of humor and entertainment in your video.

Matt and Kevin use the following three simple concept models successfully to brainstorm videos at their company. After every description, we show sample models and humor enhancements to the tire company example:

- ✔ **Educational, or wrong way/right way:** (This model may stir memories of the "Goofus and Gallant" cartoon from *Highlights* magazine, which, depending on your age, you may have read while in the dentist's waiting room.) The video starts by showing the pain of someone performing a task incorrectly (the wrong way), and then it demonstrates why doing it the right way can make the result much better. You can enhance this model by using an educational film style from the 1950s and by adding effects such as an old-film look and exaggerated acting to make the video fun and unique. This concept works well in making internal videos when you need simply to demonstrate a task and the consequences of not doing it properly.

  - *Tire sample concept with a silly person:* The opening shot shows a woman who is viewing pictures of her children or strapping them into car seats. The announcer says, "Will you have to spend money for tires this winter? How will you manage?" The woman shrugs and holds up a sign that says, "Rent my kids for tire money" while waving wildly to the camera. The next shot, showing all-winter tires, pans out to the mother driving on a wintry road with her children. The announcer says, "No need to rent out your kids just to keep them safe on winter roads. Get all-season ABC tires, and you won't have to spend extra for winter safety."

  - *Tire sample concept with a sane person:* This scene opens on a shot of a tire store with a long line of cars with suitcases of money strapped to the top. People are anxious and frustrated. The announcer says, "If you want to avoid the time and expense of changing tires this winter, try our all-season tires," while the mother drives past with kids in the back seat who are smiling and showing off the family's all-season tires.

- ✔ **Simple story with a "gotcha" moment:** This model uses a series of short, detailed actions to tell a story, ultimately resulting in a "gotcha" moment of true surprise. To make the gotcha moment work, you must, as they say, "go big or go home." A little surprise likely has no effect, and the message is lost. Gotcha moments need to have catastrophic results or exaggerated outcomes. A long, slow build-up of normalcy and exposition in the beginning helps to make the gotcha moment stand out. Every scene should build intrigue by stimulating the viewer's curiosity.

- *Tire sample concept with a silly person:* In this video, the mother leaves the house after kissing her husband good-bye. It's snowing, so she has bundled up her kids. Next, you see her standing with them on an ascending escalator. After a seemingly long while, she reaches the top and ushers the kids into a giant monster truck in her driveway. A slide says, "Are you going to extremes to keep your family safe on winter roads?"

- *Tire sample concept with a sane person:* The scene opens showing a driveway of lookalike suburban houses and then cuts to details of men and women suiting up in the protective gear worn by hockey goalies. They all crawl into their cars simultaneously. One by one, the "goalies" leave their driveways and slip and slide down the icy hill. Next, the mother seats her kids in the car (in the same suburb), and you see a shot of her all-season tires. She drives comfortably down the hill, past all the sliding cars, many of which have by now slid off the road. A slide says, "The best defense is a good offense."

✔ **Crazy pain / rational solution:** This model focuses on the initial pain component by exaggerating it from the beginning. It differs from the simple story with a gotcha moment because the crazy behavior and exaggerations are apparent from the first or second scene of the video and because they build in every scene.

- *Tire sample concept with a silly person:* The scene opens with the mother working with her kids on money-saving tasks at their dining room table, such as clipping stacks of coupons as autumn leaves fall outside. She moves frenetically, and the action happens extremely fast as she demonstrates several activities to save money and time. A chart on the wall has a graph showing the amount of money and time saved and the goal of winter tires at the top. Viewers can clearly see that she is pushing her kids as aggressively as one of the sales mangers in the film *Glengarry Glen Ross.* Only after they meet their goal can she deliver their car to the mechanic to change the tires. A slide says, "Skip the high-pressure madness this year by buying all-season tires."

- *Tire sample concept with a sane person:* A woman visits a few different tire stores that all employ variations of a shady-looking mechanic trying to persuade her to pay for repairs at inflated prices. Shots are integrated with holiday themes that look scary or cheesy. The woman grows frustrated as every store she visits quotes ridiculous pricing or tries to sell her work she doesn't need. A slide opens and says, "Why not skip the winter tire craziness this year with all-season tires?"

The limit on provocative material: GoDaddy.com

With more than 2,000 employees, the well-known Internet hosting company GoDaddy.com manages more than 6 million customers and 34 million domain names and generates about a half-billion dollars in revenue. Contributing to the company's fame were its provocative commercials, shown on the Internet and during the Super Bowl, that featured celebrities such as race car driver Danica Patrick and, often, scantily clad models in provocative situations that have been known to create controversy among various conservative groups.

CEO Bob Parsons publicly claims a policy of determining what content offends these groups and then purposely creating videos to offend them. By doing this, he pushes those conservative groups to call attention to the videos, which increases sales. This sizeable company can afford to offend a few people, and its marketing choices have proven to be successful.

Parsons claims that his company's adult-oriented videos outdrive sales over its wholesome and funny videos by a ratio of 10 to 1.

Not all companies can risk offending their customers, like GoDaddy can. But if you're trying to attract attention, you have to be realistic about what drives traffic on the Internet: people having sex, cute dancing animals, and people getting hurt are, for some reason, the activities people want to see, as evidenced by the extraordinary number of viewer hits on those types of videos. If these categories can work with your message and your image, find a creative way to incorporate them appropriately into your videos, and you may benefit.

Any of these concepts can be an effective starting point for your video, and every one of them emphasizes a different aspect of the pain your prospects may feel.

Brainstorm all six variations of the conceptual models we describe, and then you can compare and contrast to see which one has the most appeal and impact. In the best case, you have six ideas for marketing videos, and you may have enough to create a series.

Urgency is in the eyes of the beholder

Creating an urgency to buy has long been an accepted technique of sales and marketing. Offering sales for a limited time only or stocking only a limited inventory is designed to make a buyer rush to action. Although infomercials still use this tactic successfully, much of the public is wary of this approach on all except recognizable brand items. On the Internet, authenticity is critical for long-term success, and creating a false sense of urgency can backfire by creating skepticism about your integrity.

Design videos around the substance of your product and service rather than around gimmicks. On the Internet, customers who have a true need can find you easily by using a search engine, and they will have already created their own sense of urgency by the time they find you. Your video is best served by emphasizing the urgency in the pain that already exists so that viewers can relate to it when they see your video.

In the tire company example earlier in this chapter, urgency is implied for those who are now shopping for tires or who sense that winter is on its way and need to prepare. Creating urgency beyond these two issues should be unnecessary. Answer the following questions to ensure that the issue of urgency remains in its proper perspective:

- Does your product or service truly solve an urgent need?
- What are the consequences if a prospect delays buying your product or service?
- Can you create urgency for your product or service without appearing slimy, pushy, or manipulative?

The best way to create urgency is in promotions that offer significant and meaningful value. The sacrifice you make in marketing videos for urgency is that they have a shelf life that fits only with the urgent nature of the offering. A promotion for Christmas 2014, for example, is useful only until December 26, 2014.

Calls to action

A *call to action* is a marketing term for a section of the marketing material that tells the prospect what to do now. The call may be as simple as "Call us today at 800-555-2323" or "Check out our website at www.greatcompany.com." Because of the way videos are distributed, the best calls to action remain simple and subtle. Your videos already automatically have implied calls to action, such as in these examples:

- If you e-mailed the video, you likely included instructions for contacting you.
- If you posted the video online, your website should have been in the title or description.
- The action of the video makes clear that contacting you is the best way to resolve the viewer's pain.

Using video as a marketing tool works best to overcome issues and establish emotional connections. Somewhere in the video, you should provide contact information for your business, or at least a path to resolve the pain of the viewer. But often the call to action may be subtle or irrelevant, or it may not be warranted. Perhaps you're simply using video to educate your prospects about a technical aspect of your product. The buyer who is simply seeking information doesn't necessarily feel positive about a blaring sales pitch at the end. If the video is emotionally compelling, the call to action should be subtle so that it doesn't put the prospect on the defensive.

An internal video rarely requires a call to action beyond the subject of the video itself. If an educational video explains how and why employees should use the office intranet, for example, the entire video is essentially the call to action. In this type of video, the call to action can be, and should be, simply stated as the title, such as "Use the Intranet."

Ensuring an awesome experience for the viewer

A good concept is simply a starting point for creating the script. Though the story and model provide the foundation for the video, it still needs additional layering to be truly compelling and memorable. Face it: You don't want prospects to have only a good viewing experience, or even an outstanding one. Ideally, you want viewers to have an *awesome experience,* which Kevin defines as the convergence of need, entertainment, and the unexpected, as described in this list:

- **Fulfill the need.** Aside from your compelling message, the main requirement of your prospect is trust. Unless viewers trust the source of the video, the message isn't considered valid and valuable.

  Trust in video marketing, as in most of the current realm of electronic media, is conveyed by way of authenticity. Prospects want someone who can resolve their problems, no matter what they are. Whatever solutions you provide in the video must be authentic ones that truly help, or else your video is nothing more than fictional entertainment.

  In the tire company example in this chapter, resolving the need means that you lend credibility to the company's claim that its all-season tire can be trusted for safety. Addressing this issue may be as simple as adding a graphic that says, "Highest-rated all-season tires by *Consumer Research Corporation,*" or a similar accolade that has already been achieved.

- **Make videos entertaining.** Every effort should be made to engage viewers and give them an enjoyable viewing experience — a person's attention span can shrink while watching a boring video. Consider every aspect to maintain the viewer's attention, including background, characters, music, and timing; every element should be a likable aspect that viewers can relate to. Even serious videos need to engage viewers in a way that makes them say, "That was worth my time, and I will watch it again."

  In the tire company example, you can incorporate several ideas for entertainment value by including bright and bouncy music that moves the action, in a festive holiday environment with humorous takes on the holidays. The richer the detail, the more engaging the video.

✔ **Nail down the effect by presenting the unexpected.** For true impact that viewers will remember and talk about, a marketing video should have the element of surprise. The more the surprise aspect is relevant to the product, the more effective it is.

In a humorous video, a good punch line automatically serves this purpose because it works only if it's surprising. But even dramatic marketing videos need something that creates an "Aha!" moment to trigger viewers' memories and makes them want to act on the video and (you hope) pass it along to others.

In the tire company example earlier in this chapter, this surprise moment would vary depending on the model approach you used, but it would connect to emphasize the emotional pain you're resolving. In the escalator example, also earlier in this chapter, the unexpected aspect is the break from normality of a mother and her children piling into a monster truck.

Of course, not everyone can create an outstanding marketing video every time they attempt it, but we're certain of one thing: If you don't attempt it, you'll likely never achieve it.

Incorporating a biting wit

Dr. James Goolnik, a prominent and successful dentist in London, England, is an aggressive marketer who hired a video creation company after realizing that he needed to incorporate video into his marketing arsenal. The company shot footage of Goolnik, his office, his staff, and dental options such as implants, bridges, and dentures. The footage was compiled into a brief video whose tone was generally professional — and boring. Though he knew that the video wasn't likely to attract new patients or to help him stand out from his competitors, he had already spent money on it.

After consulting with Kevin and Matt, Goolnik changed his approach. Together, they salvaged the original raw footage and chose to focus more narrowly on a common painful aspect of dentistry: the fear of dentures. Because almost everyone fears losing their teeth, this type of pain was easy to identify. People needed to know that they had alternatives to dentures, such as bridges and implants.

Kevin created a short scene that started with an attractive couple kissing. At one point, the woman pulls back, and you can see the man's dentures clamped to her tongue. She looks surprised and then screams as you see a shot of the man's toothless mouth and frightened face. The dentures drop to the table, and you see a graphic that reads, "Are dentures your worst nightmare? Ask us about better alternatives."

The remainder of the video shows Goolnik demonstrating why he and his staff are best equipped to deliver those alternatives using the footage from the previous video. This simple additional scene connects, in an extreme yet humorous way that is also memorable and sharable, with the emotional pain of people who have dental issues. After receiving a positive response to his video, Goolnik is now developing a series that addresses more fears in humorous ways. You can see the before-and-after videos at www.dummies.com/go/videomarketing.

Keeping it short, simple, and engaging

A great deal of heated discussion takes place over the optimal length of a marketing video. Studies within the Internet blogging community have shown that the average viewer doesn't watch a video for more than three minutes. We contend that this result has less to do with the attention span of viewers than it does with the inability of most marketers to produce compelling and entertaining content for more than three minutes.

Conventional wisdom says that most people will watch a video for as long as they're interested in it. Otherwise, no one would ever watch a 30-minute lecture or webinar. In short, the length of a video has less to do with how long people watch it than with the amount of interesting content it contains. Length has an impact, however, on *when* people watch your video.

People are busy, and they're being bombarded by tons of material. A short video is likely to be watched more quickly by more people because they don't have to invest much time to watch it. The following rule-of-thumb guide to most people's viewing behavior assumes that the video originated from a trusted source: Use this list of common video lengths to find the one that fits best with your marketing plan:

- **Four minutes or fewer:** Likely to be viewed immediately or within the hour. A video of this length doesn't distract much from a productive work day, and if it's from a trusted source, most people don't mind taking a break to check it out.

- **Five to eight minutes:** Likely to be viewed within three days because finding this much spare time in a busy day is a challenge. Often, viewers save the video and watch it shortly before leaving for home or while at home that evening.

- **Nine to 15 minutes:** Likely to be viewed between one week and a month after receiving it. A video of this length has to be truly important to warrant the time and concentration during the workday. The video may sit in the recipient's inbox until a lull in the workday.

- **More than 15 minutes:** Likely to be viewed from one month to a year after receiving it. Unless viewing the video is mandatory or likely to resolve an urgent issue, a video of this length sits until the viewer has leisure time to expend. Often, the viewer doesn't remember receiving it until cleaning out her e-mail inbox.

Of course, the more interest that prospects have in the subject matter, the more likely they are to watch a video sooner rather than later.

People are more likely to watch a video soon after receiving it if it is promoted as being hilarious and if it originates from a trusted source than they are to watch a video with a serious tone from someone they don't know. Most people love a laugh that breaks up their day.

Sometimes, you need a longer video to get your point across. Technical content often requires longer videos, but interested parties tend to watch them sooner. The longer you make the video, the longer you have to maintain viewers' interest. Any lull in the action can cause viewers to move away from the video and miss out on your call to action. Find creative ways to make the video shorter and more interesting.

One way to shorten a video is to reduce exposition, or detail. Often, you can convey your point by acknowledging implied elements on the screen.

For example, in the tire company videos, you may show your mother driving to a tire store in the snow, climbing out of the car, entering the shop, and announcing to the tire salesperson that Christmas is coming soon. Or, you can simply have your mom start at the tire store, wearing a coat with snow on it, with a Christmas tree in the background. The visual nature of video allows you to transmit tons of information in short bursts that take seconds instead of minutes.

Storyboarding: The V in Video Is for Visual

A *storyboard* is a piece of paper with boxes drawn on it that show how every shot in a video will be visually represented. Shots can be quite elaborate creations or simply rough sketches. The purpose is to outline each shot to see how to help the director, the camera person, and the editor put the video together.

Sometimes, the storyboarding process is used to flesh out the concept into more tangible action shots before scripting. Sometimes we storyboard first, and sometimes we script first. The storyboarding process may be easier for you to complete if you think more visually than just words on a page. It isn't the order in which you create the script or storyboard that's important — it's that both elements are fully complete and detailed so that you can create an effective schedule and budget for your video.

Although software programs can help you create storyboards online, we find that, for speed and ease of use, the pen is often mightier than the computer. If you insist on using an electronic means or you simply can't draw, the Celtx scripting software, discussed in the later section "Scripting in Detail," has a storyboarding feature and a free iPad app. Still, using software can be much more cumbersome and time-consuming than simply putting pen to paper and drawing some stick figures. Figure 4-1 shows an example of a storyboard for one of our tire company concepts.

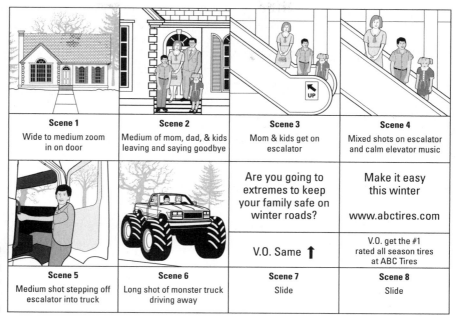

Scene 1	**Scene 2**	**Scene 3**	**Scene 4**
Wide to medium zoom in on door	Medium of mom, dad, & kids leaving and saying goodbye	Mom & kids get on escalator	Mixed shots on escalator and calm elevator music

		Are you going to extremes to keep your family safe on winter roads?	Make it easy this winter www.abctires.com
		V.O. Same ↑	V.O. get the #1 rated all season tires at ABC Tires
Scene 5	**Scene 6**	**Scene 7**	**Scene 8**
Medium shot stepping off escalator into truck	Long shot of monster truck driving away	Slide	Slide

Figure 4-1: A sample storyboard.

The storyboard helps you detail these actions:

- ✔ **Establish scenes and shots.** Each box in the storyboard represents a shot in succession. The figure loosely represents the composition of the shot and shows the placement of items and actors.

- ✔ **Determine action and dialogue.** Below every box is a smaller box in which rough dialogue or action can be stated. Arrows or other markings can be used in the main box to communicate the action.

- ✔ **Place graphics and voiceovers.** A box is used to show slides in the video. Graphics can be shown in either the big box or the little box.

A storyboard is a working document — a helpful way to quickly see how the parts of a video are assembled. Don't worry about making your storyboard a work of art. Just ensure that it accurately reflects what you want to shoot in the video in a way that other people can understand it.

A storyboard is best completed in pencil so that you can make necessary changes throughout the production process. A whiteboard can be handy for storyboarding in large groups and then simply taking a photo on your camera phone so that you can share it with colleagues. Either way, you'll make changes along the way, so use a method that can be easily modified.

The back of the storyboard is a useful place to jot down the needs of your production team. The list gives your production manager the details needed to set up the budget and production schedule. Many of these items are already detailed in the script, but this list helps you easily identify every item and refer back to them during the production and editing phases. You may want to fill in this information after you have completed the script or at least update it and ensure that it's complete. The list should include *cast, props, costume elements, music types,* and *sound effects.* For the storyboard in Figure 4-1, the list looks like this:

Cast	MOM - Marge Smith
	DAD - Steve Jones
	STEVE - Roy Marks
	JANE - Chloe Dunn
Props	LUNCH BOXES - 2
	BRIEFCASE
	PURSE
Costumes	WINTER CLOTHES
	SCARFS
	EARMUFFS
Music types	ELEVATOR MUSIC
	COUNTRY/ROCK FOR EXIT
Sound effects	WEATHER - WIND ETC
	MONSTER TRUCK REVVING
Locations	SUBURBAN HOUSE
	ESCALATOR
	MONSTER TRUCK

Scripting in Detail

A marketing video concept can easily be communicated verbally or simply in a written paragraph or two, but to turn an idea into production, you need a detailed script that tells everyone in the production process what action takes place and what words are spoken in the video. By using the written script, the producers, director, actors, and production crew can all figure out their roles in the production.

You can find several variations of formatting online for scriptwriting. To see a formal movie script model laid out, visit www.simplyscripts.com/ WR_format.html. Software is also available from several companies online. Our favorite, the simple and free software available at www.celtx.com, has lots of production tools. A more advanced, paid version is available if you are considering becoming the next Steven Spielberg of marketing videos.

To estimate the length of your script, assume that one script page equals roughly one to two minutes of video, depending on how much activity is taking place and how much detail you write into the action.

Describing imagery and action

Every element of your script needs to be detailed in a way that your actors know what to do and say. Certain ideas or concepts can remain open to interpretation, but try to record as much as possible on paper and then adjust the script in production. This way, the editor knows what's supposed to happen after receiving the raw footage. You need to describe these elements:

- ✔ **Location:** Fully describe the physical setting where the scene takes place. Pay careful attention to any details in the set or location that can help the producer find a place that matches the feel of the video.

- ✔ **Camera angles:** You may want to use wide shots or close-ups depending upon the effect you're trying to create. These need to be specified for each shot. Kevin and Matt created a fun video you can watch that demonstrates the different shots. You can see it at www.dummies.com/go/videomarketing.

- ✔ **Transitions:** Are you going to cut, dissolve, or fade into the next scene? Your editor needs to know what you have in mind. You should detail as much about the transition of every shot and scene so both the director and editor have a clear vision.

- ✔ **Activity:** The script specifies every action that takes place in the shot. It can be a small action such as having someone smile or big action that tells what everyone is doing in the scene.

- ✔ **Music and sounds:** This is the place to specify the type of music you want to set the mood, be it jazzy, classical, creepy, or humorous. All your sound effects also need to be incorporated in their proper locations as well as any voiceovers by announcers.

- ✔ **Slides and graphics:** Any slides with your company info or graphics that have titles overlaid on action should be specified in the script so editors know where to put them.

- ✔ **Props:** Your producer has to find every item that is held or used by an actor. Make sure it's clear in the script so she knows what to acquire.

Each of these items is represented in specific ways on the script page. A typical professional-looking script looks like this:

SCENE 1

MEDIUM: Scene opens on the front door of a suburban house.
It is snowing. The door opens and 2 Kids, Steve-8 and
Jane-6 come out excited and giggling. They hold lunch
boxes. As they leave the shot A mom is standing in the
doorway.

        MOM
    Be careful Kids.
    Jane, snug up your scarf.

Dad sticks his head out the door as Mom starts to leave.

        DAD
    Bye honey. You guys be careful
    out there.

        MOM
(She is smiling)
    Don't worry darling, we have
    it covered.

                        CUT TO

SCENE 2

MEDIUM: Shot from the side as Mom and the kids step
onto an escalator.

MEDIUM CLOSE UP: Shot of Mom and the kids riding the
escalator. Several shots ensue from different angles
for roughly 15 seconds. The kids look bored. There is
elevator music.

                        CUT TO

SCENE 3

MEDIUM CLOSE UP:

We see their feet step off the escalator and then
another shot of As the shot zooms out we see all three
step off the escalator into a car.

ZOOM OUT:

As we zoom out we see that they are driving off in a
Monster Truck.

```
WIDE: We see the truck"s taillights go down the street.

                                        CUT TO

SLIDE

Are you going to extremes to keep your family safe
on winter roads?

                                        CUT TO

SLIDE

Make it Easy this winter. www.abctires.com

          ANNOUNCER
(Off Camera)
      Get the #1 rated All Season
      Tires at ABC Tires.
```

Writing dialogue

Not every video has dialogue, but if your actors talk to each other, you have to write out what they're going to say and incorporate it into the action. The characters' names are set up in the center of the page with their lines below their name. You can use parentheses to give specific direction to them such as emotion or action like smiling or sticking out their tongue. Much of your compelling messaging may come from the dialogue so it's important to give lots of attention to the wording, making sure you're getting your message across clearly.

Too much back-and-forth dialogue can seem odd and unnatural, not to mention it can cause camera difficulties. Unless your script calls for a stylized approach that requires fast back-and-forth dialogue, it's best to keep the dialogue as natural as possible.

Test your dialogue as you write it. You can say it aloud with a friend, or play all the parts yourself. To really hear it, record it and play it back to see how it sounds. Often what seems good on paper can be very unnatural when spoken in real life. Hearing it aloud also helps fix word combinations that are difficult to say.

The script example shown earlier was created on this type of software, using the tire company example and the directions in this section.

Part II
Preparing for Production

The 5th Wave   By Rich Tennant

"I love the way you montaged Grandpa's
'Wanted' poster with Cousin Doug's arrest record."

In this part . . .

Making ideas come to life is a fun and exciting process, and you should be fully prepared for the thrill when the time arrives. In this part, we tell you how to budget for every aspect of a production and how to make it happen on a shoestring. We help you understand the pros and cons of working with union talent and how to scout locations. Finally, we provide you with insights and forms to protect yourself from a variety of legal issues, including copyright infringement, defamation, and liability.

Chapter 5

Producing a Marketing Video on a Budget

In This Chapter

▶ Setting a budget amount

▶ Saving through borrowing

▶ Outsourcing the production

*I*f you imagine your video production with celebrities walking on rain-soaked cobblestone in a European city to sell designer perfume or as another multimillion-dollar commercial that airs during the Super Bowl, you probably need to start liquidating your gold stockpiles or retirement account in order to pay for this vision. But as the price of video equipment falls — combined with some modest resources — the budget needed to produce a high-quality marketing video is well within the reach of even the smallest companies.

After you have a rough idea of the video content you're using, you can determine the production costs needed to create your masterpiece. You will likely discover that a few compromises are needed to turn your idea into reality without exceeding the budget. Even major Hollywood studios have to make ongoing decisions about where to spend money to produce the best possible product.

Finding the least expensive way to bring a unique idea to life is a healthy battle between creativity and creative budgeting, but that's part of the fun of making a marketing video. In this chapter, we discuss how much money you should spend on your video, how to lower your costs by using guerilla tactics, and how to put together your video production team. We also discuss the financial pros and cons of outsourcing an entire project.

Calculating How Much to Spend

The price you pay for video marketing can range from zero to an amount as high as your imagination and wallet can bear. Most national television commercials are produced by advertising agencies, whose average budgets for a single commercial range from $450,000 to more than $1 million. But even the expensive world of television advertising is changing rapidly, with high-profile commercials being shot on small budgets.

Cost and quality don't necessarily go hand in hand because you don't always get what you pay for. Many factors can affect the cost of a video, such as these examples:

- ✔ Actors
- ✔ Crew
- ✔ Locations
- ✔ Costumes
- ✔ Props
- ✔ Royalties
- ✔ Editing
- ✔ Promotion
- ✔ Equipment
- ✔ Music and sound effects

Although you can easily spend tens of thousands of dollars on a video, cost doesn't always equal quality. Always aim for the highest-quality product that's available at the lowest price.

In video marketing, the story and message are far more important than the production values of the video. A video that's beautifully shot but boring doesn't affect viewers as much as does a low-budget video that entertains and successfully communicates its message. Find inexpensive, inventive ways to tell your story and engage your audience. By keeping your video production costs low, you can maximize your return on investment (ROI) and have money left over to create additional videos.

Throughout this chapter, we base the video production budget around the concept of the script and storyboard (described in Chapter 4). This chapter discusses the primary budget obstacles in a script about a mother protecting her children from a potential vehicle wreck on winter roads by driving a monster truck. You can use the finished budget for this video, shown in Table 5-1, as a guide to the explanations in this chapter.

Starting with a needs list

Which elements you need in order to produce a video depend on the idea or concept you want to shoot. Your script and storyboard (covered in Chapter 4) should provide you with the basic information for outlining a budget. List every item that requires money, even if you eventually find a way to get it for free. This way, you're less likely to have unwelcome last-minute surprises.

Table 5-1	Sample Production Budget		
Line Item	**Quantity**	**Total**	**Worst Case Scenario**
Cast 'Mom'	1	$100	$150
Cast 'Husband'	1	$100	$150
Cast 'Child 1'	1	$100	$150
Cast 'Child 2'	1	$100	$150
Director / Camera Operator	1	$500	$650
Sound / Lighting Operator (including equipment)	1	$150	$300
Production Assistant	3	$30	$60
Editor (four hours)	1	$100	$400
Food (including plates, napkins, etc)	8	$80	$160
Costumes (scarves, hats, gloves)	3	$120	$200
Dry cleaning ('Husband' suit)	1	$15	$25
Location costs	2	$0	$350
Props (lunchboxes, briefcase, purse)	3	$0	$35
Director's Chair (gift for our truck owner)	1	$10	$20
Contingency		$250	$500
TOTAL		$1,655	$3,300

 The first thing to look for in your concept is any obstacle that can potentially bust the budget. Then you must determine whether the obstacle is surmountable. If your video features a realistic, slow zoom into the cockpit of an orbiting space shuttle where viewers find Brad Pitt at the controls, you may need to mortgage your home. Early in the budgeting process, you should identify issues and come up with creative ways to achieve your vision — or rethink your idea.

Chevrolet and the Super Bowl

To find out whether it's possible to create a high-quality video and not spend a million dollars, the Chevrolet car company (through Mofilm.com) held a contest named Chevrolet Route 66. Aspiring video marketers from 32 countries submitted 400 scripts and 198 films to compete for a commercial spot in Super Bowl XLVI in 2012. The winner, 26-year-old Zachary Borst, was an unknown video creator whose winning entry, *Happy Grad,* was shot on a budget of less than $500.

The key to his success is that his video is well written and well executed. In it, a high school graduate mistakenly assumes that his parents' graduation gift to him is a new Camaro sports car — rather than a dorm-room refrigerator. His talented friends and family helped him create the video, with the agreement that if he won, they would be paid from his $25,000 prize money. The largest expense was renting the bright yellow Camaro for the day.

Certainly, Borst's video has good production quality, but its story, acting, and editing make the commercial effective. Not everyone can create this level of video quality at this low price, but hiring a production company with this kind of talent can certainly prevent you from having to spend the $250,000 to $1 million per commercial that Chevrolet normally spends. From the company's perspective, the contest was a huge success. The ads generated more than 32 million total views online during the three weeks from December 22, 2011, to January 14, 2012. In addition to awarding prize money, nearly 110 million television viewers saw the ad on Super Bowl Sunday — not too shabby. Check out the winning video at www.goatfarmfilms.com.

Determining the cost of the cast

Hiring the cast for your video doesn't need to be expensive. Talented actors in many cities will often happily work your video — simply for the experience or for a little extra spending money. No matter how much you pay the cast, provide them (at minimum) with food and drink during the shoot. A cast member who requires a unique look or an uncommon skill makes casting more difficult.

Start with a *casting breakdown,* which is a list of names and brief descriptions of every character. Even though you may easily remember what the cast members should look like, you may want to send the breakdown to someone else who can help you find actors. In a sample script, the breakdown looks like this:

- ✔ **Mom:** A suburban housewife in her 30s who is protective of her children
- ✔ **Dad:** A suburban father in his 30s who works in an office
- ✔ **Child 1:** Under 10, male/female, attends elementary school
- ✔ **Child 2:** Between 12 and 14, male/female, attends high school

Union actors and crew are likely be outside the scope of your budget. (See the nearby sidebar, "The cost of union talent.") Although you can use inexperienced actors for your video, you should seriously consider hiring actors who know what they're doing. Even small towns often have experienced or semiprofessional actors — you simply need to find them. Start by contacting a nearby theater or drama school. Most organizations that work with actors are happy to pass on casting details. You can read more about casting in Chapter 7.

Many local laws regulate how child actors can be employed on video shoots. These laws may simply limit the working hours in a day or manage complex regulations that require paperwork to be filed for every child who's employed. Contact your city or state film office for more information.

If you're working with non-union actors, the wages you pay are whatever amounts you agree to. Many non-union actors are happy to have the exposure and, depending on their experience and the demand for their services, will work for fees ranging from $25 to $250 per day with no residual fees.

The cost of union talent

Most small companies simply cannot afford to hire union talent for their videos. The Screen Actors Guild (SAG) and the American Federation of Television and Radio Artists (AFTRA) — organizations that govern contracts for actors — specify how actors can work and how much they're paid, as reflected in these numbers:

 ✔ The minimum-scale pay, or *session fee*, for a union actor is $74.025 per 1 hour of production work.

 ✔ An 8-hour day, therefore, earns an actor $592.20. The first 2 hours of overtime earn an actor 1½ times the hourly rate, and every hour after that earns 2 times the hourly rate.

 ✔ After the session rate is established (for example, one day), you have to pay residuals for as long as the commercial runs on the Internet.

 ✔ For the first 21 months, the residual amount is 7 times the session amount, or $4,145.40, plus an additional 15 percent to be paid to the pension fund.

These specifications make your cost per actor $4,767.21. Because it's extremely difficult to make a video truly disappear from the Internet, you have to continue paying the actor a minimum of $4,761.21 every 21 months until you can document that the commercial is completely unavailable.

In addition, SAG and AFTRA require that when one union actor is used, every actor on the project is paid union scale regardless of whether they're also union members. A 4-person commercial that takes 1 day to shoot therefore costs $21,768.21 for the first 21 months and then $19,044.84 for every subsequent 21-month period.

If the video "goes viral" and has staying power, your cost after 5½ years is $59,857.89, whether or not the commercial brings you business.

These numbers are only for actors. Unionized crew — which may be required cooperatively — adds to the bill. When considering union talent, decide whether a single union actor is truly worth the $60,000 to tell your story.

Budgeting for the crew

The *crew* consists of everyone you need in order to shoot and produce the video — a primary production crew and a postproduction crew. You need to budget for every member of both crews.

You may be able to fill many crew roles yourself or with colleagues. This list of basic production crew members shows a range of non-union daily rates for experienced people, which may vary based on region:

- **Director:** $500 to $5,000
- **Camera operator:** $200 to $1,500
- **Sound operator:** $100 to $1,000
- **Lighting tech:** $100 to $1,000
- **Production assistants:** $20 to $150

You may need several production assistants. Often, people help just to be part of the fun.

For postproduction, you also need an editor. If no one in your company has video editing experience or wants to learn, hire a freelancer. A qualified non-union editor can charge between $25 and $200 per hour. You should figure roughly three to five hours of editing time for every minute of finished video.

To find quality crew members for a low price, look for people who are just starting their careers and who are seeking experience. Their fees should be much lower than if you were hiring highly experienced professionals.

Find out whether a film school or communications department at a local college has students looking for experience. Young people can be even better educated about film and editing techniques than older professionals because they've grown up using the software that now comes standard on most computers. They may be able to bring in other people as well, such as cast members. Students should still be offered a modest fee for their work, but you may "hire" them for free if you can arrange an internship through their schools.

After you choose the crew members who best fit your video, you need to agree on the fee. Start with offers that are a little less than your budgeted amounts. For example, if a camera operator is budgeted for $500, make an initial offer of $400. Doing so may allow you to be under budget, but it also allows some room if the crew member demands a little more than your first offer.

You work long days and, often, long nights with your cast and crew, so be sure to budget for drinks, snacks, lunches, and dinners. You'll likely have a large line item in your budget for doughnuts, pizza, and Chinese food. Believe us: The better fed everyone is, the happier they are and the better they work. And don't forget items such as plates, napkins, water, and sugar for the coffee.

Accounting for locations and permits

The shooting locations you choose can affect your budget significantly. In Chapter 6, we discuss how to determine which locations are right for you. If you're shooting on private property, negotiate the cost with the owner. Some popular filming locations may charge for the privilege, but you can often get a free location — either because the owners are excited to have a film crew around or because you have offered to give the owners some footage for their own use.

If you can't find a space for free, you can still keep the budget low. Small private apartments or office spaces can usually be found for less than $1,000. If you want to hire a popular restaurant, find a time when its owners are less busy and when a free room may be available, or visit after hours. A medium-size commercial establishment can range from $1,000 to $2,500 for a full day of shooting.

Take care of the private property you pay for, and always leave it in the condition you found it in order to avoid extra repair costs.

If you're shooting on public property, most city and state governments require you to obtain permits to film if the shoot meets one of these conditions:

- ✔ It takes place inside public property.
- ✔ It uses professional equipment such as lighting, industrial equipment, or generators on public property.
- ✔ It disturbs traffic or pedestrians.

Most cities are generally friendly to filmmakers and video makers because they commonly believe that filmmaking promotes their cultural image. Even New York City requires no permit if you're shooting only with handheld cameras. The permit fees in some cities can range from a few hundred to a few thousand dollars, depending on the size and scope of your project. Most cities also require a liability insurance policy of around $1 million if you're granted a permit. The cost of this policy for your production varies, depending on the location and specific activity involved, but you can figure a cost of anywhere from a few hundred to a few thousand dollars.

To find out whether you need a permit to shoot, contact the film office for your city or state government, which you can easily find by searching online. Most governments have a film office web page where you can download permit applications and research fees and insurance requirements.

It's make-believe, not a documentary, so don't think too literally about the location you need. If your scene is set in a hospital but you can't afford the cost of shooting in a real-life hospital, try using a doctor's office. Even adding rails (and sound effects) to the bed in a regular bedroom can be a convincing substitute for a real-life hospital. You can always narrow the shot and use simple decorative items such as pictures, candles, or books to turn an otherwise blank space into an office, a restaurant, or a library.

In the monster-truck video example in this chapter, you can likely shoot on the private property of the truck owner. Also, you're asking a friend to help you enter the office building that has an escalator you can use in the evening. The amount of your budget for locations on this video is zero.

Funding the costumes and make-up

Most videos require no fancy costumes or make-up. If your video requires a gorilla suit or a Mike Tyson facial tattoo, you can ask a local costume and make-up shop for help. A costume shop usually offers a hire rate so that you can rent the costume rather than buy it outright.

For a high-budget video, allow for at least $300 to $500 per cast member for costumes and make-up. Period videos, set in different eras, such as in the Wild West or in the Shakespearean era, can run you more than $500 per cast member for every day of shooting.

A medium-budget video may call for someone to wear the uniform of a police officer or a doctor. These costumes usually aren't expensive, but unless the local sheriff is your pal, you may need to rent them. An average rental is about $50 to- $100 per day, depending on the costume and where you're shooting.

Search online for local costume shops, which usually carry make-up as well, or use some of these popular stores, which have costumes available year-round:

- ✔ **Hollywood Toys & Costumes, Los Angeles:** www.hollywoodtoysand costumes.com
- ✔ **Ricky's NYC, locations throughout New York City:** www.rickysnyc.com
- ✔ **Costume Express, order online for same-day shipping:** www.costume express.com
- ✔ **Party City, locations throughout the United States:** www.partycity.com

The (low-budget) monster-truck video example shows a normal-looking family so that you can get away with using normal everyday clothing and make-up. The video takes place in the snow, so if the cast can't provide their own winter clothing, you may need to purchase scarves or gloves from a discount store.

The cost of three scarves, three hats, and three pairs of gloves is about $120. You can ask the cast to provide jackets and pants. The husband character is filmed only indoors and doesn't need winter clothing, but he is asked to provide a simple suit and to pay for dry cleaning. You may want to ask the cast to provide their own clothes and make-up, but state clearly that you aren't paying an additional fee.

If the cast wears their own clothing, it can become damaged or stained. Agree in advance about reimbursing the cast for replacement items or dry cleaning if anything unexpected happens. Dry cleaning can run from about $5 to remove the stain from of a pair of pants to more than $30 to clean a fancy dress.

Preparing the props

Properties — or *props,* as they're commonly known — are the physical objects in the script that are necessary to set the scene. Props are usually small, handheld items that add to the reality of the video. A typical video may need a few small items to spruce up the set and a larger item or two to set the scene. Most small props can be found around the home or office.

Extravagant videos often call for big-money props. Special effects can also add to the expense. If you want a car to crash through a plate of glass being carried across the street, you need specially made breakaway glass, made of hardened, candy-like sugar water, which can cost thousands of dollars. If you need only a few breakaway bottles for a bar fight scene, you can order a case for $200 or less.

The 48-hour scramble

Good, fun training in making marketing videos is the subject of *The 48 Hour Film Project* (www.48hourfilm.com). Matt and Kevin decided in 2011 to use this project as a way to help them make videos inexpensively and fast. They made a spoof of Shakespeare's *A Midsummer Night's Dream* in New York City. The whole production had to be planned, written, shot, and edited in 48 hours. Sadly, they missed the deadline by seven minutes, but the video has been well received. You can see it at www.dummies.com/go/videomarketing.

Matt and Kevin had only a few hundred dollars to spend on the film and encountered some interesting challenges, including how to turn the actor playing Puck into a satyr with furry legs and horns. Thank heavens the project began in October, when plenty of costume stores were open. They found cheap plastic horns and a furry dog suit, and the combined cost of Puck's costume was only $50. After applying a little make-up and tape, a character's horns stuck to his bald head. They also cut up a dog suit to make legs and accepted the fact that a fantasy video would have characters that looked a little odd anyway.

They learned that creativity can successfully be applied throughout the process to tell a good story, regardless of time and budget.

Before production begins, make a list of every prop you need and research the cost of items that aren't readily available. Virtually anything you need can be found on the web, but you need to estimate the cost of shipping as well. Add a contingency line item to your budget to cover any unexpected prop expenses that inevitably crop up during production.

The low-budget, monster-truck video example needs these items:

- ✔ **Two new lunch boxes:** $10 apiece; $20 total
- ✔ **One briefcase:** $15; found used at thrift store
- ✔ **One purse:** $0; owned by cast member
- ✔ **Artificial snow:** $380, to hire snow machine and fluid bottle

The lunch boxes, briefcase, and purse should be easy to acquire inexpensively or even for free, but fake snow is quite expensive. Waiting for an authentic snow-fall is unrealistic, so you have to be creative again. At the beginning of the video, you can add a short voiceover of a weather forecaster saying, "Be careful in all that snow out there this morning." This statement sets the scene for viewers to know that snow is covering the roads, and you never even have to show the snow.

Buying and renting equipment

You can find tons of information in Chapter 9 on the kind of gear you need to add to your video, but this section addresses the capital costs as well as incidental needs for the production.

Considering the current low cost of video equipment, buying your own is a realistic option. You can easily outfit a complete production team for as little as $3,500, and then you have what you need for this shoot and for any future video productions. This list of essential video production equipment includes cost estimates:

- ✔ **Camera:** You can shoot high-definition (HD) video on a camera that costs only $200. Even better, however, $1,000 buys you a camera that is top-of-the-line for this type of video production. You may want two or three for studio work.
- ✔ **Sound:** An elaborate sound system can cost thousands of dollars, but you can find a good sound recorder and a few good microphones for well under $350.
- ✔ **Lighting:** Light kits come in all shapes and sizes. A few scoops and bulbs from a hardware store will suffice for a lesser version that costs less than $50. If you want to go pro, expect to pay around $500.
- ✔ **Tripod/monopod/sound boom:** Put your cameras and sound equipment on something stable — $300 is enough to stabilize any production.

- ✔ **Chroma-key:** A green screen, or chroma-key, system can help you visit any location on Earth without your having to travel there by providing a screen, usually colored green, that can be replaced in editing by any image, such as a mountain range or bullfight. Decent chroma-key systems range from $500 to $3,000. (See Chapter 6 for an in-depth description of chroma-key systems.)

- ✔ **Miscellaneous:** You need multiple batteries, chargers, media cards, and other items, such as a gear bag in which to store it all. A thousand dollars buys you all you need to be prepared for any shoot.

- ✔ **Editing system:** You can easily get fancy with editing, but a basic MacBook Pro laptop computer includes iMovie software to get you started with a one-stop purchase. You pay $1,600 to cover your trip to the Apple Store, though you may want to go big-time and spend $4,500 for the fully loaded 27-inch iMac. Additional software can run you another $500 or so. We discuss editing in more detail in Chapter 13.

You'll find no shortage of "gearhead" toys that you can buy to make creative videos. Many items, such as camera dollies, can be improvised with items such as skateboards. Save some money until your videos make you enough money to invest in more equipment.

Borrow, Borrow, Borrow

And now, we present the secret to scraping by on a modest video budget:

- ✔ Borrow
- ✔ Borrow
- ✔ Borrow

These three *B*s are meant to remind you that you can leverage the glamour of video production to persuade people and companies to loan you the items you need in order to produce your video. By ensuring that everyone working on your video keeps these three *B*s in mind, you also help prevent overspending by others. Everyone wants to share the spotlight with you, so let them!

Capitalizing on your internal resources

You may have friends or company colleagues who want to volunteer their time on your video marketing project. Including fellow employees as cast members for internal videos is especially smart — not just because it saves money but also because staff members enjoy watching themselves and their colleagues in videos. The company benefits from having its message communicated widely, and from the positive environment that videos create when everyone takes the time to enjoy watching them.

Tap in to the people on this list to find actors or crew members, and to procure any locations or props you may need:

- ✔ **Colleagues:** If you're making a business video, involving people from your company makes it fun and more likely that everyone will spread the word to promote your finished product.

- ✔ **Friends:** If you haven't asked your friends for a favor for a while, now is the perfect time to do it. You may know someone with the perfect look, or maybe your friend does. Leave no stone unturned.

- ✔ **Family members:** Now you can return the favor for all those embarrassing videos of you that your parents shot when you were young. Family members are great choices for older actors and extras.

- ✔ **Business partners:** Your vendors and suppliers have a vested interest in your business doing well, and they probably wouldn't mind having an opportunity to help you succeed. Let them review your needs list, and you may be surprised at what they're willing and able to come up with to help you reach your goal.

In the monster-truck example, the biggest challenge is likely getting a particularly essential prop: the monster truck. The vehicle is essential to this video's concept, but finding one for your video without paying large sums of cash isn't an easy prospect. Try the following step-by-step approach to procuring challenging needs — such as a monster truck:

1. **Search:** Google is definitely your friend when you want to search for hard-to-find needs. Use the web to determine whether monster trucks are located in your area. If you can't find one reasonably nearby, consider alternatives. The concept of the video is that the mother goes to extremes, so you can probably get away with using a semitruck, a dump truck, or a snowplow. These may be easy to find in your area.

2. **Offer:** Make your company's services available in exchange for using the truck for a day. Ask only reasonable favors of the owner, and find ways to make loaning the truck convenient for the owner. The video script doesn't require the truck to move, so let the owner know that you can move the shoot to the truck's location — saving the cost of paying for gas and a driver and preventing wear and tear. Remember that you need someone to unlock the door of the truck to get the right shot of the family climbing inside the vehicle.

3. **Compensate:** Always give the person who loans you something an item or service of value in return for their expense, time, and trouble. Even if you can't pay money, come up with innovative barter ideas that give value in exchange for their help. In the example, you may offer to shoot a few minutes of extra footage of the monster truck that the owner can use to promote himself and the truck. If you create a win-win situation, you should have no problem getting everything you need to make your video. Just be sure to schedule enough time to keep everyone happy.

Trading with show business magic

Leverage the show business magic of making videos by persuading people to support you in exchange for the chance to experience a piece of the magic. This list suggests some things you can do for *angels* (as these supporters are sometimes called) who offer goods or services:

- ✔ **Treat them like VIPs.** Invite supporters to visit the set to watch the video being made, and perhaps even provide them with their own director's chairs. (They cost about $10 if you search online.) You can stencil the name yourself by using a can of spray paint.
- ✔ **Put their names in lights.** Run credits at the end of the video, and add a list of people to thank. Give them titles, such as executive producer, if they were helpful. (That's what they do in Hollywood!)
- ✔ **Put them in front of the camera.** Cast them in major roles or, if that isn't appropriate, as walk-on talents who are visible only in the background.
- ✔ **Deliver gifts.** Give them a DVD copy of the video in a case that has been signed by the cast and crew. An extra DVD case and some markers should cost less than $2.

Insourcing and Outsourcing the Process

Of course, the easiest way to complete your video is to simply hire a production company to do it. Unfortunately, hiring a production company is also in most cases the most expensive way. Cost is a major factor in deciding whether to hire an in-house or outsourced video production. Keep in mind that you can outsource only certain aspects of the production process, such as writing, directing, editing, or working the camera.

Consider these issues when you're judging outside video production service providers:

- ✔ **Quality:** The people you hire can provide a level of professionalism that meets or exceeds the look and feel you require for your video.
- ✔ **Business acumen:** Video professionals who are unfamiliar with your industry or business may have difficulty helping you communicate your message effectively. Avoid the assumption that an entertaining video is an effective marketing video.
- ✔ **Style:** Find a video professional who can create a video in a style that's consistent with your company's image. Some professionals shoot only in their own style, and they lack the flexibility you may need on your shoot.
- ✔ **Capability:** If you're looking for animated video, pick a company with colleagues who know specifically how to make animated videos. The same advice applies to live-action videos: Focus your precious time and money on finding professionals who can make the type of video you want.

Hiring a video professional can cost hundreds or thousands of dollars for a project, and the cost varies depending on region, demand, and experience. Many production companies charge between $5,000 to $30,000 for a complete production. Interview carefully, and remember that you don't always get what you pay for.

Budgeting for Promotion

The moment your video is complete, you want people to see it. Part V of this book details many different ways to get your video noticed by thousands of people (or millions, if you're lucky). You most likely need to spend money to get the video in front of your prospects. How much money you spend to promote your video depends on these factors:

- ✔ **The number of videos you have:** Managing a slew of videos can be difficult when you use a simple platform such as YouTube. Video management software from companies such as Pixability can make it easier for a reasonable cost.

- ✔ **How you integrate video into your overall marketing plan:** If your video is only one element of an entire campaign, calculate the cost of the supporting materials and the technology necessary to integrate the video into your website.

- ✔ **The size of your target market:** If your target market consists of no more than 200 people, contacting prospects and getting the video into their hands are fairly inexpensive. A prospect list of thousands or millions of people, on the other hand, requires strategy and effort — and a serious amount of money — to have a reasonable percentage of the target list see it.

- ✔ **The size of your e-mail list:** It can take an e-mail list of 20,000 or more people to see a significant response from a marketing e-mail. You may have to buy lists and subscribe to a service for large e-mail blasts of your video.

- ✔ **Your social media capability:** If you have a ton of Facebook and Twitter followers, promotion is simple with compelling content. Otherwise, you may have to hire social media experts to get the word out.

- ✔ **Your willingness to buy placement:** More people can see your video when you purchase placement on YouTube and Facebook. Prices for this strategy can range from $50 to $500 per day, depending on the size of the audience you want.

Build the video around your marketing strategy rather than the other way around. Video is a tool that can save you far more than it costs, if you plan strategically.

Do it right, do it well, and then do it inexpensively.

Chapter 6

Finding the Perfect Location to Shoot

In This Chapter

▶ Creating a set in your home or office

▶ Shooting away from home base

▶ Using a green screen

*W*hether your video takes place in an office setting or in a mysterious café halfway around the world, its location is the key to telling your story the right way. Creatively, you must choose the strongest setting for your video's story. And, more practically, you must also find a locale that not only looks believable but also lets you shoot with as little interference as possible from the outside world.

This chapter shows you how to find great-looking locations for your video, for cheap or (even better) free. We describe which elements are fundamental to setting up a location for your shoot that runs as smoothly as possible, whether you're in a controlled environment, such as your home, or out in the wilds of the real world. Finally, we cover the basic instructions for using that wonder of the digital film age: the green screen.

Scouting Out a Great-Looking Location

Location scouting is the industry term for finding the perfect place to shoot and ensuring that you can shoot there. This step is important in preparing to film your video because an appealing location not only helps tell your story but also allows your cast and crew to work quickly and comfortably.

An ideal location is low on headaches and provides you with lots of *production value*, the effect of spending lots of money when you didn't.

Picking the perfect place

Look over your script and list all your locations. Whether you have a single locale, or 20 locales, be sure that all of them are not only appropriate but also interesting and memorable. A strong, unique location sticks in a viewer's mind and helps portray the true purpose of your video — your message.

As you write your script, keep in mind these important guidelines regarding locations:

- ✔ **Be ambitious.** Don't let the lack of a budget inhibit your imagination. If a scene works best in an art museum or a rock concert — or the White House — go ahead and add it to your list. You can think of creative ways to "fake" a location or change it slightly to wherever you end up shooting. Rather than try to spice up a boring setting, dial down an ambitious setting to a more realistic level.

- ✔ **Be specific.** Setting a scene in an office or a house may provide clues to your character. Are you neat as a pin or extremely messy? Ultramodern or old-fashioned? Cold or cozy? The human eye picks up on little details and tells the brain how to feel about the characters. In *The Odd Couple,* we definitely know whether we're in Felix's room or Oscar's, simply by looking at whether the bed has been made.

- ✔ **Rewrite to fit the locale.** If you have access to a truly unique location, you can also retool your script to incorporate the benefits it offers. A building with unusual architecture, an office with a spectacular view, a lobby waterfall — all are memorable features that can help make your video one of a kind.

Adding the right amount of light and noise

When you're scouting a location, make sure that a potential spot has an authentic-looking backdrop for your scene and also has ample light and a minimum level of outside sound. A dimly lit room dulls not only the look of your scene but also the viewer's interest. In addition, a noisy locale, such as a busy workplace, a large room with an echo, or a neighboring freeway or construction site can provide huge audio problems.

Here are some suggestions to look for:

- ✔ **Favorable weather conditions:** To determine what to expect, visit the location around the same time of day that you intend to shoot.

- ✔ **Acceptable lighting conditions:** Bring a camera and shoot some test video of the location to show fellow crew members what the site looks like in its natural state. Then you'll know whether to add extra lights or change locales instead.

> ✔ **Appropriate sound levels:** Try talking in the test video at the same distance from the microphone as the actors will be positioned.
>
> ✔ **A suitable number of electrical outlets:** Make sure you have plenty of them, especially if you plan to use lights.

Setting up a green room

Shooting a movie is a bit like throwing a party: You have a suitable location and a list of guests — in this case, the actors and crew — and you must ensure everyone's comfort. A *green room,* which is an asset on any shoot, is the "holding" area, where cast and crew who aren't involved in the current scene wait to be called into action, chat quietly, and (you hope) memorize their lines.

A green room must be neither green nor a room. It can be a patio, a hallway, or even a parked SUV. Here's a list of green room requirements:

> ✔ **A suitable location:** The green room must be located far enough from the shoot that talking doesn't intrude on the scene.
>
> ✔ **A safe storage area for personal items:** Examples are bags, phones, and laptops.
>
> ✔ **An electrical outlet:** You need an area where people can charge their camera, light, and cellphone batteries.
>
> ✔ **Food, glorious food!** A well-fed crew is a happy crew. Whether it's sandwiches, salads, or snacks, feed everyone and make sure to have on hand plenty of water and that paramount commodity known as coffee.
>
> ✔ **A bathroom:** Never shoot without one nearby.

Using a Familiar Place

There's no place like home, especially when you're shooting a video. Using your own office or home, or looking within your circle of family and friends, for a location is a smart move because it gives you full control of the set while shooting. You can rest easy knowing that you don't have to deal with strangers' property; in fact, the only danger is being *too* relaxed — you still have a video to make!

Use the elephant!

On one shoot, the authors of this book found themselves facing, of all things, a life-size elephant replica. The video was rewritten to incorporate this surprising element and became a memorable hit, with the crowd buzzing over the topic of the video — literally, "the elephant in the room." You can check out the video at www.dummies.com/go/videomarketing.

Shooting in your office

Because this book talks about creating marketing videos, the subject of your own video is most likely your company. It may even feature the Academy Award–winning talent of your staff. In that case, of course, you should just shoot it right in your office. Shooting a video can serve as a fantastic exercise for company efficiency. Simply ensure that the shoot doesn't interfere with your workday, or vice versa.

Here are a few suggestions for making a successful video shoot at work:

- **Decide whether a weekday or the weekend is a better choice.** This decision is entirely up to you and is dependent on the nature of your business. Shooting on a weekend ensures fewer distractions but also requires staff to come in on their day off (which can create either a relaxed atmosphere or a rebellion). Treat a workday shoot as a special event at your workplace, in the same way you would treat a company-wide meeting or workshop.

- **Notify staff ahead of time.** The more advance warning you give, the more you pave the way for a smooth shoot. Staff can schedule meetings and phone calls accordingly or move pressing business out of sight if necessary.

- **Be inclusive.** A video shoot is the type of team-building exercise for which some companies pay top dollar. A fun, problem-solving activity that everyone can assist with — whether it's setting up a shot, rounding up props, or encouraging an outstanding performance from a nervous staff member — provides tons of opportunity. Keep everyone involved and interested in what's happening, and you'll get cooperation and great-looking video in return.

- **Turn off all mobile phones!** We say it a few times in this book because a few folks always leave their phones turned on. A staff member may even be tempted to take a call during a shot. Incoming calls and "important" text and e-mail messages are sometimes unavoidable during the workday, but try to keep them to a minimum. Your business is unlikely to collapse if your staff holds off on calls for a few minutes.

Filming in your home

Shooting a video in your own home feels a little like working in your pajamas: It's comfortable and familiar, and you're the master of your domain. But your own home probably has more distractions in it than does shooting at Disneyland. From your own family members and neighbors to your barking dog, a few things can knock you off track and force you to lose time.

Treat your home location exactly as you would treat any other location: Provide a green room, keep track of your equipment, and be mindful of waiting time. Even when a video is shot in your home, your cast and crew must still trek to the "workplace" and spend time waiting and working at someone else's property.

Give your neighbors a heads-up about your shoot. Provide extra parking space for visitors, and minimize the noise level, especially later in the day. And, of course, provide the essentials: food, water, coffee, and a bathroom.

Borrowing a location from a friend or family member

Perhaps a good friend or a close relative offers her office or home to you for your shoot. What a wonderful gift! Now the trick is not to permanently torpedo that relationship because of a mishap or misunderstanding during the shoot. Borrowing the space of someone you know is a terrific way to nab the perfect location, but it can also turn into a mess if it isn't handled properly.

When a friend or family member offers his home or office for a shoot, a plan that seems simple and workable in a conversation by e-mail or phone can turn into a logistical nightmare in reality. A two-hour shoot that you envisioned may turn into a seven-hour marathon, your "set" may be needed suddenly for a meeting, or someone may trip over a wire or lose the key to the bathroom.

Before showing up at a friend's office or home with a small army of crew members, a ton of equipment, and a long list of demands, follow these suggestions:

- ✔ **Make a list of items you need.** List a space to shoot, a green room, an accessible bathroom, and anything else, within reason, that you can think of. E-mail the list to your friend, and make sure that she reads it. Then double-check it. People often seem to think that film shoots are simple events, when in reality they're complicated and require hard work. (It's fun work, but it's work.)

- ✔ **Set a realistic timeframe.** We respect this rule: Determine the length of time you need, and then double it. A two-hour shoot? Make it four. If you don't need to nail down the timeframe, consider it a bonus. Having to specify a hard deadline to vacate the site can be a helpful motivator to get the job done quickly.

✔ **Make a plan for setting up and breaking down.** Factor in time on both ends of your shoot to prepare and then to get out, leaving the place exactly the way you found it.

✔ **Bring your own coffee.** Bring food and water, too. Treat the location shoot as a camping trip. Avoid taking advantage of your friend's hospitality. Bring everything you need, and take it all with you when you leave.

✔ **Bring a power strip.** Or bring two. Outlets may be in short supply, and you don't want to risk powering down someone's computer while fussing with the wall socket under his desk.

✔ **Say "thank you."** Say it often, and mean it. It goes a long way toward creating happy working relationships.

If you prepare properly and give your friend or family member a realistic idea of what to expect, the result is a fantastic shoot where all parties walk away happy (though you should a nice restaurant dinner as a thank-you gift).

Begging and Borrowing

In the film *The Great Escape,* James Garner played a World War II prisoner with an intriguing code name: The Scrounger. He could literally get hold of any item someone needed — from lumber to nylons — all from within the confines of a prison camp. Luckily, in making your video, you don't have to deal with a situation as severe as a prison camp (though you may at times feel like you're waging a war). You still sometimes have to scrounge for what you need, especially at locations. Borrowing a space can be a delicate art, and you can become a master in a short time. (Chapter 8 covers the legal aspects of using other people's homes and workplaces.)

Asking local businesses

The good news for location scouting is that much of what you need is in your community. If you need to shoot a scene in a restaurant, a cozy bookstore, or a crowded bar, the chances are good that if you walk in and ask nicely (especially if it's a venue you've frequented), the owner will let you use her site. In a testament to human nature, people are usually willing to help, and they're also dazzled by the statement, "We are making a movie." Use these five powerful and magical words responsibly.

As in every other situation involving someone else's property, inquire thoughtfully and make sure that the business owner or manager knows exactly what to expect. Visit the person days or even weeks ahead of your shoot, and initially go alone. Don't bring a mob. Your goal is to convey professionalism and friendliness, not to disrupt in any way the well-being of the business. In short, go in early, go in solo, smile easily, and ask politely.

Bear in mind that shooting at a stranger's business during operating hours is a different ballgame from shooting in your own office. You likely have no green room, no power strips jammed with plugs, no extra lights, and maybe even (gasp!) no coffee. In this quick-and-dirty form of *guerilla filmmaking,* you get what you need in as little time as possible.

Shoot your scene, at full voice and energy level, as quickly as you can, and then become practically invisible the rest of the time. Shoot with a skeleton crew, with either you on camera (and a good microphone attached to your clothing), or you, a camera person, and a maximum of two or three actors.

To get a local business on your side, offer a trade, such as an appearance within the video (free publicity) and thanking the business in the list of credits (if you have one) or on your website. Also, if you're shooting in a bar or restaurant, you can sit down and have a meal on the spot. Patronizing a supporter's business is a smart move.

Though "big-box" stores — those huge, corporate-owned megastores — may seem attractive for location shoots, you likely can't shoot there. Many stores have corporate policies against any type of filming in them, especially by other businesses. When you ask a question at a mom-and-pop business, you're likely to speak to the top dog. At a big-box store, however, you're dealing with members of local management, who have to triple-check their approval with the higher-ups and a wall of attorneys. Rather than waste your time becoming entangled, go local.

Using a stranger's property

Just as when you walk into a business and boldly ask to shoot a video there, a stranger's personal property — the person's house, yard, boat, porch, or whatever — should be handled professionally. Again, go alone to inquire, and then lay out the full scope of the environment you want to shoot in and estimate realistically how long you think it will take. The more helpful information you can share with the property owner, the more at ease he will feel with your shoot.

As with shooting in someone's office, plan to provide everything you need, including food and water. Bring in as little as possible, and finish as quickly as you can. Restrict your movement to the space in which you're shooting, if possible, and maintain continual communication with the property owner about the schedule.

These three terms should serve as your mantra while shooting on a stranger's property:

> ✔ **Speed:** Work quickly and efficiently.
>
> ✔ **Invisibility:** Maintain a low profile when the camera isn't rolling.
>
> ✔ **Transparency:** Keep the property owner in the loop on your progress.

Heading Into the Great Outdoors

After being stuffed into all those offices and crowded spaces, you may want to grab a breath of fresh air — and bring your video crew along with you. In this section, we talk about *exterior,* or outdoor, scenes.

Exterior locations add production value to video scenes. Whether you're in a park, in the woods, on the street, or in front of a business, you're capturing the real world, and it's immediately authentic-looking. If you look around enough, it can also be memorable.

Shooting in public places

Laws differ among states, but you can generally shoot video freely in public places, unless they're specifically prohibited. Keep in mind the difference between a group of 3 or 4 people shooting outdoors with a single camera and mic and a 15-person crew with all sorts of bags and equipment that can block traffic. (Though this chapter covers the logistics of shooting in public spaces, the legal aspects are covered thoroughly in Chapter 8.)

The keys to producing appealing outdoor video are efficiency and discretion — shoot fast and respect the people around you. In fact, follow these rules for shooting outdoors:

> ✔ Practice your scene, and quickly get it right.
>
> ✔ Shoot the scene twice.
>
> ✔ Wrap up your shoot and move along.

Public parks are ideal places to shoot because you have lots of varied space to choose from and a certain degree of privacy. If a mundane indoor conversation at a desk can be moved to a park bench or the edge of a waterfall, for example, you vastly increase the video's production value.

Certain places are definitely off limits for commercial video. Monuments, museums, privately owned parks — all these locations are likely to ask you to shut down and move on if you try to shoot there.

Sound is the biggest challenge in shooting outside. Buy a good microphone, and have someone wearing headphones ensure that sound is being picked up. If you rely on your camera's built-in mic, you may end up capturing not only your subject's sound but also every other sound around you — wind, tweeting birds, noisy trucks, and the guy on the bench nearby who's singing pieces from last night's opera performance. A good *shotgun* microphone (a camera-mounted microphone that records wherever the camera is pointed) can eliminate many extraneous noises.

Do not show a person's face in your video without the person's written consent, even if it's only in the background. People inevitably wander in and out of your shoot, but whenever someone is prominently featured, simply stop shooting and either wait or move a few feet away. (For more information on the legal issues of filming strangers, refer to Chapter 8.)

Shooting on sidewalks and streets

Shooting real life on the street definitely lends lots of value to your video. You can do person-on-the-street interviews or show characters hailing cabs, driving away, entering buildings, or following (or running away from) someone — they're all kinds of great-looking situations.

On a crowded street, plaza, sidewalk, or parking lot, your main challenge is shooting while other people are walking through your shot. Remember that it's their space, too. These rules are important to follow:

- **Be private in public.** Find a spot where you can shoot with a degree of privacy, and shoot fast.

- **Avoid talking to strangers.** When people wander up and ask about your video, their interest is genuine and touching. Unfortunately, it's also a time-waster. The longer you're shooting in a crowded public place, the more difficult it is to shoot what you need and move on. Smile politely, say thanks, and get back to work!

- **Post a guard.** Have a crew member quietly and politely ask people not to cross your shot during a scene. Most people will comply. If you encounter a fussy pedestrian, let the person pass and try again.

- **Avoid shooting trademarked signs.** Avoid messy legal woes by not blatantly showing the logo of a business. If you position the camera creatively, for example, you can simply show the word *Bank* rather than a famous big-name logo.

Grabbing footage on the fly

In *The Terminator,* Arnold Schwarzenegger approaches a car and breaks its window. In this low-budget shoot, director James Cameron had no permit to shoot the scene, so his crew used a guerilla-style strategy: They parked the car on the street, and after Arnold broke the window, they all ran off. If police officers had observed this scene, an extra scene would have appeared in *The Terminator* — an officer writing a ticket.

At times, you may want to grab a quick shot somewhere with no time scheduled for permission or planning. More than ever, be efficient and discreet. Follow these quick tips for grabbing footage on the fly:

✔ Use the minimum number of people possible.

✔ Determine what you want to shoot and how to do it.

✔ Shoot your scene as quickly as possible and move on.

Be respectful of the location and the people around you.

Going Green (-Screen)

So you had too many cups of coffee and got a little out of control when writing your script and dreaming up shooting locations. That explains why some scenes are set at the Great Pyramids, the Eiffel Tower, and the moon. Before you press the Delete button on these "out there" ideas, consider shooting with a green screen.

Green screen effects are in tons of movies and TV shows nowadays. From the amazing vistas in *Lord of the Rings* to your local weatherperson standing in front of a map, green screening opens up the possibilities of a location like nothing else can. *In green screen* shooting, the subject is filmed standing in front of a physical green screen, which is later replaced with a new background to produce the effect of the subject being in a specific location. The green screen seems to produce true Hollywood magic, but like most magic, the illusion is built on hard work and technical skill.

Grasping the basics of chroma-key

Green screen is a popular nickname for the process more properly named *chroma-key compositing,* or simply *chroma-key.* All chroma-key processes operate using these basic steps:

1. A subject is filmed against a flat, colored backdrop.

2. In postproduction, the colored background is *keyed-out,* or removed and turned to black.

3. A new background is inserted over the black, giving the illusion of the subject being in that location. Suddenly, your character stands atop a pyramid or walks on the moon!

In filmmaking terms, *compositing* is the layering together of two or more film images into one. The process dates to the 1930s, where it dazzled audiences with such movie spectacles as *The Thief of Baghdad. Blue screen* and *mattes,* which are special photographic layers, were used to create scenes such as a flying carpet soaring over a city or, later, spaceships zooming toward the *Death Star.* Most of the elements involved were physical, and the work was slow and painstaking, with layers of imagery filmed repeatedly to mix all the elements together.

With the advent of the digital age, the chroma-key process allows computers to do much of the heavy lifting, taking over the layering work and allowing for crisper, cleaner special effects with almost no limitation on what's possible. Best of all, chroma-key has allowed consumers a chance to play George Lucas and create their own special effects, right in their own living rooms.

These days, the most common type of chroma-key backdrop, and the one most easily available to consumers, is the green screen — usually a section of cloth or muslin mounted on a sturdy frame or hung on a wall. Green is the popular color in the digital age for chroma-key because it's far from human skin tone and because modern camera sensors are highly attuned to it (though blue is still a popular alternative).

Respecting green screen do's and don'ts

For the kinds of videos this book covers, green screening can be a creative and fun choice that lets you place your actors against any background you want. However, green screen is also a major time-waster because it's still a complicated and detailed process during postproduction. Before embarking on the green-screen process, weigh the time you would spend getting it right in postproduction versus the value you may achieve from using green screen in the first place.

If you decide to take the leap and go green (or blue), here are the items you need:

✔ **A green or blue backdrop:** You can buy one from a retailer that sells specialized chroma-key backdrops or entire kits with support structures and lights. You can also use a solid-colored sheet or fabric that's close to industry standard shades.

✔ **A camera tripod:** Your camera must be locked down and motionless during green-screen shots.

✔ **Proper lighting:** You need a generous amount of light for the backdrop itself. The key to using chroma-key is bright even lighting for the green screen, as shown in Figure 6-1.

✔ **Chroma-key editing software:** Simpler programs, such as iMovie, can't handle this advanced software. Both Final Cut and Adobe Premiere have excellent chroma-key capabilities, however. (Both are discussed at length in Chapter 13.) You can find numerous books and online guides for mastering the basics of chroma-key editing, including step-by-step instructional videos on YouTube. Just search at your favorite search engine, and you'll find plenty of resources from which to choose.

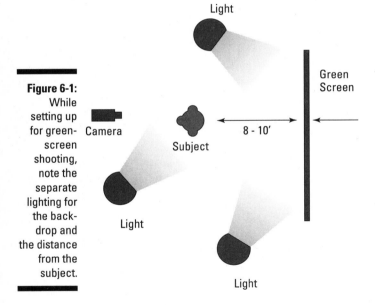

Figure 6-1: While setting up for green-screen shooting, note the separate lighting for the backdrop and the distance from the subject.

To avoid trouble, follow these tips for green-screen shooting:

✔ **Avoid shadows on the backdrop.** Your green screen has to be presented to the camera as a single, even color. When your subject is casting a shadow, or if the backdrop has large wrinkles, these darker areas are tough to erase — or, in chroma-key jargon, *key out* — in the editing process. Treat the backdrop as a separate subject with its own lighting.

✔ **Keep the camera still by using a tripod.** Remember that you're inserting a separate background behind your subject, and the background remains still during the shot. If you shoot the subject handheld or pan or tilt the camera, you create movement — and the weird-looking effect of a moving subject on a still background.

✔ **Dress your subjects appropriately.** Don't let anyone wear the same color as (and not even close to) the backdrop. A green shirt against a green screen "disappears", and a disembodied head will remain (though it's a useful way to achieve the floating-head effect).

✔ **Keep your distance.** Position your subject eight to ten feet from the green screen to prevent the shadow from being cast on the backdrop and to prevent any movement from causing the backdrop to billow. Also avoid reflecting the bright green color on the subject and giving him a partially erased, keyed-out transporter effect directly from *Star Trek*.

✔ **Be sure that the green screen fills the camera frame's background.** If the green color doesn't quite reach the edges of your camera frame, you have to adjust by zooming or physically moving the camera. Otherwise, you see a strip of the wall on the edges of the shot.

Chapter 7

Assembling Your Cast and Crew

In This Chapter

▶ Casting professional actors

▶ Working with non-actors

▶ Finding a qualified crew

*T*hough videos are made with the help of items such as fancy cameras, expensive lenses, and state-of-the-art software, they're essentially made by *people* — the most important tools in your video arsenal. High-tech equipment can make your video a good one, but using talented people — in front of and behind the camera — makes your video outstanding.

If you've never dealt with casting and directing actors, their world may seem mysterious to you. This chapter breaks down the mystery by describing the qualities to look for in an acting performance. It also helps you boil down the essential qualities you want from actors so that you can give helpful direction and get the best possible performance from them.

A talented film crew that works well together is essential to your video's success. The business adage of everyone on your team "being on the same page" is never more critical than during the monumental task of creating a video from scratch. We show you the important roles behind the camera and tell you how to find the best players to fill them.

Connecting with Your Audience

Perhaps you've met someone with whom you felt an instant connection — someone who made you immediately think, "Wow! This person is on the same page as I am. We understand each other, and I want to spend more time together." This human connection causes a good feeling, and it describes the effect that great actors have on people who connect with their performances.

Great actors can (figuratively) reach through a movie screen, TV, or crowded theater and connect with you, without having ever met you personally. You instantly feel for these people, and you see things from their perspective and want to see what they do next. This powerful achievement is the reason that great actors are master communicators. (And you certainly want master communicators in your video.)

Casting for communication

Suppose that you're holding an audition to cast the roles in your video. You watch as a series of actors read the lines from your script. As you watch, you immediately start picking out the actors you like. This initial reaction is a gut feeling, a subconscious reaction in which your brain tells you which performances work best before you can even think about it. The subconscious part of your brain is a decent casting director.

Your subconscious reaction to an actor's performance boils down to a good actor's ability to masterfully communicate the external qualities and inner life of a character to the audience.

Good actors spend years training to master their ability to communicate. This list describes the qualities to look for in actors when you're casting a video — the person must

- **Be the right "type" for the role:** The person should come across as a believable embodiment of the character on the page.

  Type refers to an actor's physical look and general demeanor. It also refers to the way viewers fit an actor into familiar *archetypes,* or universally understood characters. When you first lay eyes on an actor, that person comes across as a boss, a soldier, a bad guy, a seductress, a mother, or a clown, for example.

- **Be able to connect with the audience:** Does the actor's performance immediately jump out at you and engage your interest?

- **Possess a strong acting technique:** For example, the person must be able to take direction, make adjustments, and repeat a performance multiple times.

The world contains as many types as it contains people, and you should always keep an open mind when casting your roles, especially in regard to race and gender. The petite actress you've written off as a mouse may stun you when you realize she's the perfect ruthless CEO for your video. When actors play *against type* in this way, many memorable performances emerge.

The ability to connect with the emotions of an audience is an actor's most powerful weapon. The performances you remember — the ones that stick in your head for years — are the ones in which the actors connect with the audience.

In *The Shawshank Redemption,* Morgan Freeman is an instantly likeable and sympathetic character (though he's a convicted murderer) who guides viewers through the movie's twists and turns with humor and heartbreak, until they're rooting for him to have a happy ending. He connects with viewers by way of his human qualities of honesty and vulnerability, and they are putty in his hands. Nice job, Morgan.

Even when a movie character is awful and cruel, however — such as Heath Ledger as the terrifying and unpredictable Joker in *The Dark Knight* — viewers can still connect with that person, not because they too are awful and cruel, but because an actor can create a character so over-the-top scary, yet completely honest and *compelling,* that they connect with him out of sheer fascination.

This connection isn't made from some mysterious, arcane actor magic. Instead, it's made as a result of an actor honing the three most important communication tools:

- ✔ **Body language:** This term covers everything below the neck. Good actors are at ease with their bodies and are *grounded:* They convey confidence, flexibility, and readiness for whatever comes next. If you freeze-frame a scene, you should be able to tell how the actor feels about a situation based on her body language.

- ✔ **Vocal quality:** Actors' voices should be clear and articulate and loud enough to register with the microphone (and the other players). Actors should speak at an appropriate pace for their characters, with the ability to add nuance that makes their line readings believable yet memorable.

- ✔ **Facial expression:** It's the main weapon in an actor's arsenal in film and video because the camera spends a lot of time close to it. Facial expression doesn't mean lots of facial movement — quite the opposite. Great film (and video) performances are made of subtle facial expressions, and the most crucial area is the *eyes.* The proverb "The eyes are the window to the soul" is absolutely true: The human brain is wired to connect to the eyes of other people as conduits of their thoughts and feelings. (Take a look into Morgan Freeman's eyes, and you'll know that it's true.)

The subtleties of body, voice, and face are the reasons that casting directors videotape acting auditions, and the reasons that you should, too. The camera catches little details that make for great performances.

An actor's *technique* consists of that person's set of skills, allowing her to achieve the performance you require, to change the performance if necessary, and to repeat it over multiple camera takes. (Always prepare for several takes.) An actor's look and ability to connect may help her get hired, but her technique helps her keep the job. The ability to imitate a feeling or character type isn't enough at that point. Great actors can take direction, make it work in their performances, and repeatedly hit their marks. Some actors can audition well, and maybe even give you one good take, but fall apart when asked to adjust or repeat a moment in a scene. Avoid this situation because it burns up time on the set and leads to general frustration all around.

When you audition an actor and you like her performance, try asking her to repeat it. Add a change, such as pausing once or twice or speeding up the delivery. You can also add an action, such as using the words on the page to prevent the person who is being spoken to from walking out the door. You're not waiting for the exact performance you want because actors also need time to prepare for roles, but you can get a solid grasp on their technique.

Selling isn't acting

Suppose that you're watching a cheap, late-night car ad on TV. The salesperson yells and waves his arms about the sale you're missing and how you should rush down *now,* at 3 a.m., and drive away with a deal. You can't hit the Mute button fast enough to make the person go away. What turns you off (other than the bad suit)? Your first instinct may be the salesperson's pushiness. After all, most people don't like being aggressively "sold to." But the negative feeling that viewers experience comes from the salesperson's perceived insincerity. He's working too hard to convince you, which means that you don't trust him — or his suit.

As an audience, people react negatively whenever an actor seems to be working too hard to convey an emotion or a character tic. "Hamming it up," which disengages viewers, is a sign of not reading the audience correctly — a mistake for an actor or a salesperson.

Some salespeople, of course, are skilled at what they do. They can speak to potential customers with genuine charm and passion and an honest belief in the products they sell. These people are good at what they do because they win people's trust. Good actors gain people's trust as well. We aren't necessarily implying that your top salesperson should try his hand at acting in your video — selling isn't acting. Though an actor and a salesperson possess similar skill sets in certain ways, acting differs in its ultimate goal: to portray a fictional character in a way that makes the character appear to be a flesh-and-blood, living human being. The creative and emotional requirements of acting are different kettles of fish from the salesperson's job of gaining trust and closing a deal.

Achieving believability

After you cast your actors and begin working together, you enter a process of collaborating with them about their roles. This experience can be rich and rewarding, with your actors looking to you for guidance and information and with you seeing them bring your fictional characters to life.

Before your shoot, the role may consist of little more than some dialogue and a few actions on a piece of paper. At this point, you can discuss the following important issues with your actors, possibly a few days in advance, to help fill in gaps and flesh out the character:

✔ **The character's goal:** You may have heard the old cliché "What's my motivation?" It's the same as the goal, and it's crucial to every performance. The character is in your scene for a reason — one that means the difference between life and death, such as "saving the company," or a simple one, such as "eating lunch in peace." Whatever the goal is, it should be important to your character.

✔ **The character's actions:** After you set the goal, how does the character go about pursuing it? Find active words and terms that characters can use in relation to other characters, such as *convince, win over, deceive, bond with,* and *reassure.* Though your characters' actions can change throughout the script, their goals should always remain the same.

✔ **The character's back story:** You don't have to create an extensive biography, but adding some history in relation to the scene is helpful. Ask questions such as, Has the character ever been in this situation? Is this the first time? Does the character have longstanding relationships with the other characters?

✔ **The character's attitude toward other characters:** Determine whether the character acts superior or inferior or as an equal toward other characters.

✔ **The character's appearance:** If you and an actor have a strong sense of the character she's playing, she must be dressed for the part. Make specific choices, such as neat, sloppy, sharp, outrageous, or conservative.

Avoid creating overly detailed character backgrounds. Some acting schools teach actors to create extensive biographies for their characters and to fine-tune, in great detail, every aspect of their characters. This process can be a tremendous waste of time and exhaust your cast with too much information. A few specific choices about a character goes further than a ton of useless detail, by keeping them focused on the important task — the scene at hand.

Talent is the glitter, technique is the glue

You may believe that *talent,* the all-encompassing term that describes a natural ability, is what acting is all about. Talent definitely exists — you've witnessed it in every good performance you've ever seen. When someone states that an actor is special or an actor has *it* (whatever *it* is), you're seeing his natural talent.

Similar to a singer who could hit a high C as a kid, or a rock star who could play the guitar without lessons as though she were ringing a bell, some actors can just pick up a script and blow away viewers, seemingly with no effort.

But the idea of an actor using nothing but pure talent is a myth. Talent alone isn't the quality that gets the acting job done. It's technique and skills, developed through hard work, that make the difference. And these are qualities you can seek out and measure.

The collaborative work that you and your actors complete not only helps everyone better understand the characters but also serves as an excellent "icebreaker," as you get to know one another and learn how to work well together. Everyone then has a stake in making your script work, which leads to a positive experience during shooting.

Opting for Professional Actors

The old saying "Ninety percent of directing is casting" means that if you hire the right actor for a role, the hard work is done for you. The actor understands what the role requires and after getting the character up on its feet, brings it alive in ways you have likely never imagined. Hiring the right actor for a role is a dream situation for you because you can rest assured that your story and content have a greater chance of affecting an audience.

Choosing to bring in professional actors (or *talent,* which is the industry term) can put this ideal situation within reach. These people can introduce a few challenges, too, which should factor into your decision.

Weighing the pros and cons of casting professional actors

When you cast a professional actor, you bring in a specialist — an outsider who is providing expert help. This complete stranger (to you), despite knowing nothing about your business or product, brings a skill set that allows her to quickly understand a new situation and adopt a character's point of view. You may even find that the actor sells your business on camera better than you can.

Depending on where you live, you can usually find a pool of local talent. Big cities such as New York, Los Angeles, and Chicago are teeming with actors of every size and shape. Places such as Austin, Baltimore, and Seattle have first-rate, smaller acting communities. And most midsize towns have theater communities, with talented actors who occasionally make TV and radio commercials. The professional talent is out there — it's your job to find it.

A few benefits of casting professional talent are described in this list:

  ✔ **They have professional work habits:** Good actors don't bring only talent to the table. They show up on time, they know their lines, they seek to understand their characters' motivations, and they don't make unreasonable demands. A good actor treats an acting role as a real job (because it is) and is generally a joy to work with.

- ✔ **They can memorize scripts:** Actors are often asked, "How do you memorize all those lines?" The answer is usually that they repeat their lines endlessly, or at least until they can virtually say the lines in their sleep. Most actors don't think twice about the difficulty of memorizing lines — they consider it part of their job.

- ✔ **They're versatile:** Professional actors can make small adjustments or huge changes on the fly, giving you a wider array of choices for performances.

- ✔ **They have good timing:** Nothing can substitute for the ability to hit a dramatic pause or land a punch line — or both in the same sentence. Professional actors can find "beats" in a script and give you unexpected moments that make your scene "sing."

- ✔ **They look good:** More than simple beauty, physical attractiveness can obviously be a bonus when casting actors, though attractiveness isn't always about good looks. Character actors with distinct, unique looks can possess tons of charisma and magnetism that win over audiences.

You can, however, also encounter challenges to working with professionals:

- ✔ **Pay:** Professional actors are *professional,* and they should be paid for their services, just as you would pay any other specialist. The notion of the starving artist working purely for art or for her portfolio simply disappears in a commercial project, such as making a marketing video. Be prepared to pay them, typically at a flat rate for a day's work. (Keep in mind that less-experienced actors may accept smaller payments in return for the experience and exposure your video gives them.)

- ✔ **Unions:** The Screen Actors Guild (SAG) and the American Federation of Television and Radio Artists (AFTRA) are the watchdogs of the film, TV, radio, and (to a degree) Internet world. An actor who is a member of either organization may have to be paid by contract (and paid well). If you aren't willing to play by union rules, your carefully selected actors may have to walk away from your production.

- ✔ **Agencies:** New York City and Los Angeles are full of agents handling actors and taking a cut of their pay. But even towns such as Cleveland have special talent agencies that may require a sizeable fee for access to their talent pool. These agencies can find you actors, but you have to pay the price.

Your decision to work with professionals may be simply a financial one. If you have a bigger budget, you can definitely cast from the professional world. If you're on a tighter budget, you can still look for non-union talent (some great actors are in this category) and get the performance you need. You can also look to amateur actors, whom we describe later in this chapter, in the section "Discovering a Diamond in the Rough."

Creating an effective casting notice

When it's time to search for actors, your best bet is hold auditions by way of a *casting call* — an invitation for actors to audition for your project. In actor-heavy towns such as New York City and Los Angeles, you can advertise the call online at Backstage (www.backstage.com), the biggest acting industry trade publication. You can also post on numerous websites where actors pay a subscription fee to view casting calls.

One of your best bets is craigslist (www.craigslist.org), which features its own casting section, where you can post for around $25 per notice.

Wherever you advertise your casting call, craft an informational casting notice, which is your chance to let the world know about your production and the specifics of your casting needs. Because it's also the first point of contact between your production and your prospective actors, try to make a good impression. Treat it no differently from any other job posting — make your casting call professional, informative, and succinct.

Your casting notice should contain, at minimum, these elements:

- ✔ **Project title and the type of video you're casting:** Identify your video as an external video, industry event video (for a trade show, for example), or internal video for company use.

- ✔ **Union membership status:** Specify whether you're looking for union or non-union actors or whether you're open to either.

- ✔ **Shooting dates and location:** Before you start casting actors, you should have an accurate estimate of when and where you'll shoot.

- ✔ **Breakdown of roles:** You must specify what types you're looking for, such as age range, gender, or race (if necessary for the character). A short description is helpful.

  Be specific about necessary skills, such as singing, dancing, or speaking a specific language.

- ✔ **Payment amounts and other details:** You don't have to state a number — just mention whether the roles are paid. (If you get involved with unions, you have to deal with pay scales.) Also mention whether food, transportation, and a copy of the video are part of the deal. All these details make your project look more attractive to your potential cast.

- ✔ **Submittal guidelines:** Request head shots and résumés, and include your e-mail address (you may want to create a separate e-mail address, to save your inbox from the potential clutter). You can also ask for a link to a demo reel, if it exists. Some actors have their video highlights posted to YouTube or Vimeo, and you can get an idea of how they look and sound, as well as see their acting abilities.

A proper casting notice reads like this:

Busy Bee, Inc., seeks cast for short Internet video. Non-union only. Shooting February 2-4 in NYC. Seeking — Dave, male, 40-60, CEO of large corporation; Amy, female, 20s, young go-getter; maitre d', any age or gender, snooty restaurant host, French accent required. Pay, food, transportation, and DVD copy included. Send head shot, résumé, and demo reel link to `Casting@ BusyBee.com`.

During the submission process, separate truly professional actors from those who are less serious and likely unreliable. An actor without a professional-looking head shot and résumé should be taken off your list. These items, which are considered industry-standard calling cards, should include or describe an actor's

- Contact information
- Physical statistics (height, weight, hair, and eye color, for example)
- Film, TV, theater, and voiceover experience
- Formal training experience
- Special skills, such as singing, dancing, language accents, martial arts, gymnastics, or ninja moves

  (An actor's skills are sometimes unusual.)

Running a successful audition

You post your casting notice, and your inbox becomes flooded with submissions. After you sort out the best picks and toss the rest, it's time to hold your audition, one of the most rewarding and nerve-racking experiences an actor can face. To run your audition properly, follow these guidelines.

Setting up the space

The first step in running a successful audition is to set up a usable space. Follow these suggestions for setting up your space correctly the first time:

1. **Choose between an open or closed audition.** In an *open call,* you post the audition time, and actors sign up for a spot. If you audition *by appointment only,* you see only the actors you choose — when you choose to see them.

2. **Meet and greet.** Assign someone to greet actors as they arrive at your audition, check them off your attendance list, and gather any head shots they bring with them.

3. **Schedule with space.** Schedule auditions about 10 to 15 minutes apart, which allows actors 5 to 10 minutes apiece, and *stick to the time limit.*

Ask actors to arrive at least a half-hour early to give everyone enough time to look over the scene they're reading.

4. **Create a holding area.** Designate an area where actors can wait beforehand to look over their lines and psyche themselves up for their auditions.

Conducting the audition

It wouldn't be an audition, of course, without the audition. Follow these suggestions when you reach this critical part of the audition process.

1. **You sit, they stand.** Seat yourself (and anyone who's helping you) behind a table while the actors stand for the scene. You can take notes on what you're seeing, plus you'll gain a better sense of how they hold themselves and move, and the actors remain active, not passive.

2. **Film it.** Set up a camera to capture the audition for review. Have actors "slate" themselves by providing their names and contact information on camera

3. **Chill out!** Keep the atmosphere friendly and relaxed. The more comfortable your actors, the more natural their performances.

4. **Observe everything.** Write down whether actors showed up on time, dressed professionally, showed some personality, and said, "Thank you," for example. It's a great way to gauge their work habits.

5. **Let the actors prepare.** Ask them to arrive at least a half-hour early, to give them time to look over the scene they're reading.

6. **Designate someone to be the reader.** The *reader* acts out the scene with the actor during the audition and gives him someone to "play to." The reader should be interested in the scene, but not showy — no grabbing the spotlight, please. The reader should read the entire scene from the side of the stage, giving the actors the stage to themselves.

7. **Give direction.** After an actor's initial reading, provide a little direction to see how they absorb it. (It's another chance to see how well they work.)

Following up with actors

After you decide which actors you're interested in, you'll want to get in touch. Follow these steps:

1. **Notify the best actors.** After your audition, notify the actors you want to see again. Give them an idea of aspects of their performances or the script you want them to emphasize for the next audition.

2. **Hold callbacks.** A *callback* is a smaller audition (usually on another day) of the best actors you've evaluated. You can even try pairing actors in a scene to see how they play together.

When you settle on the perfect actors for your video, contact the other actors from your callback to thank them for their time and talent. This action not only soothes wounded egos but also boosts your reputation as someone worth auditioning for.

Discovering a Diamond in the Rough

You may decide not to cast professional actors, either for budgetary reasons or because you want to cast in-house with your own staff. If you're making a video for internal use, your target audience is your own company. You can derive a lot of value from casting familiar faces, and you certainly leave room for humor when you poke fun at situations within your business.

Using amateur talent can be rewarding in a lot of ways, but it obviously presents its own set of challenges. The following sections tell you how to find the best natural talent and how to get the most from their performances.

Finding "natural" talent

When you start looking at people from your professional or personal life as possible actors, you have to adopt a director's eye. The next time you interact with them, for example, try picturing whether that person can believably carry off a role. Watch and listen as they talk to other people, study their facial expressions, and observe their body language. Don't worry: You aren't stalking them. This is simply how great directors make discoveries of untapped talent.

 When casting from within your own business, you may find a great deal of natural talent. These people have personalities and public speaking abilities that you're familiar with. You may have an early idea of who can play specific roles in your video, and approach them. You may even consider crafting the roles in your script to fit the personalities within the ranks of your business.

To find natural talent, look for people who have these three traits:

- **A knack for performing:** In the office, this person may deliver spellbinding presentations and win over clients. In casual gatherings, she may be the life of the party, telling jokes and stories and holding court like a seasoned entertainer. She may carry herself with self-confidence and easily connect with everyone around her. These charismatic traits make the person compelling to be around, and it also makes her a natural choice for the first non-actor to look at for your video.

✔ **The right look:** Determine whether this person can pass physically for the character. (See the archetypes discussed earlier in this chapter, in the section "Casting for communication.") As always, be flexible about race and gender.

✔ **Reliability:** Ask whether this person can step up and deliver the performance you need or whether he'll freeze up on camera? Determine whether he's easy to work with and can take direction without complaint.

Sometimes, natural performers want to do things their way — or no way. You may find a better actor in someone who is more dependable and avoids showboating.

To recruit non-actors, especially people who may feel shy or overwhelmed about being on camera, reassure them that you *know* they will perform well in the video. People can easily become self-conscious, and if you're confident that they're right for a role, you must instill that confidence in them.

Coaxing Oscar-worthy performances from non-actors

Professional actors have the training and experience to hit their marks and deliver the performances you need. Non-actors lack this background experience, and may feel lost in front of the camera, asking questions such as, "Where should I stand?" "Where should I look?" "How quickly should I speak my lines?" It's enough to bring on an anxiety attack, so prepare your counterattack by tricking people into giving great performances.

Here's a list of tricks to use while directing non-actors (feel free to try them out with professionals, too):

✔ **Keep them relaxed.** People who are tense show it in their faces and voices, which prevents them from giving standout performances. Keep the situation light, stay positive about every take (even the bad ones), make jokes, provide water and coffee, and generally boost their confidence. As a director friend our ours likes to say, "Tell them they look pretty."

✔ **Use gaffer tape.** Use the tape to make an X ("the mark") on the floor to indicate where actors are supposed to stand in a scene. Actors who move to this mark a scene are "hitting their mark." If someone is looking off camera, you can have a fellow actor stand in the right place. Or, if someone is looking at an imaginary spot offscreen, put the X on the wall where his eyes should land.

✔ **Keep them busy.** Give actors activities — completing paperwork, looking into bags or purses, pouring drinks, putting away stray items — to take their minds off the camera and dispel their self-consciousness.

✔ **Give them goals.** Use statements with important-sounding verbs. "Convince them," "warn somebody," and "motivate your colleagues" are all familiar actions that people perform in everyday life.

✔ **Suggest an imaginary "as-if" circumstance** to stimulate their creativity and draw out a better performance. Your directions can be physical ("as if it's cold," "as if your chair is uncomfortable," or "as if you've spilled coffee on the floor and are trying to hide it") or emotional ("as if you're waiting for a phone call about a promotion," "as if you just found $200 on the ground," or "as if you were bad-mouthing the character who just walked in").

✔ **Write out cue cards.** Memorizing lines is the hardest part of acting for most non-actors (and a few pros, too). If you're shooting a scene in which an actor is speaking to someone off camera but is having trouble remembering lines, simply hold the script off camera approximately where the other character's eyes would be located, and let your actor continue reading. It isn't an ideal solution, though it may relax the person enough to complete a good line reading.

✔ **Break it up.** Break the scene into back-and-forth shots between your characters. You can break longer passages of dialogue into bite-size chunks for every shot.

Non-actors sometimes ask whether they can "hide" the script in front of them during a scene, perhaps taped to a wall or nestled among the paperwork on a desk. Your answer should be No, to avoid non-interaction with their fellow actors and their eyes pointed downward for the entire scene. Someone may even be tempted to turn a page of the script in the middle of a dramatic moment.

Casting an effective webinar

Web-based seminars, or *webinars,* are wonderful tools for holding conferences, workshops, or presentations. Connecting participants from just about anywhere via the Internet eliminates the logistics of physically bringing people together and allows interactive seminars to be conducted from a single location. However, even with the ease of conducting a webinar, one important factor remains: The presentation must be clear and compelling. The presenter's public speaking skills are essential, and with the elimination of the built-in energy of a live audience experience, they have to know how to work well in front of a camera. This list describes the essential elements of an effective webinar host:

✔ **Speak clearly.** A webinar is still a public speaking event, not a video chat. Speaking with volume, clarity, and good diction helps make your presentation strong and effective.

✔ **Look at the camera.** Keeping your eyes on the camera forces eye contact with the audience and helps the audience stay better focused on what you have to say.

✔ **Keep it slow and steady.** Good presenters are good teachers, and those teachers should take their time in making their points because they have no in-person audience to gauge whether their information is sinking in. Rushing through a presentation can cause a web audience to tune out.

✔ **Keep it simple.** A webinar that has fewer strongly scripted and presented points is more powerful than one that's overloaded with information. If you have a wide variety of topics to cover, divide them into several presentations.

✔ **Practice, practice, practice.** Rehearsing is always a good idea, and webinars are easy to work on — simply videotape yourself giving your presentation and watch it afterward. Show it to a few colleagues, too. You'll find areas for improvement before your web audience ever sees you in action.

Casting behind the Camera

You're a brilliant visionary, and that's why you've begun a video project to show off your talents to the world. Or, you're a normal person struggling to make a tightly scheduled production come together. Either way, you need help assembling a talented crew to complete your video.

Filmmaking is an ensemble effort. Every time you hear Steven Spielberg or Martin Scorsese receiving heaps of praise for their films, you should know that a few hundred talented folks helped them. Your production will involve only a fraction of their undertaking, but you can still use crew members who are as passionate and dedicated as you are. This section outlines the main crew positions behind the camera, explains what they do, and describes the skills they need.

Assembling a skeleton crew

As when you use non-actors, you may be forced to use a crew that has little or no experience in making a video. Do not be daunted by this scenario. If you understand the nature of the roles in a video crew, and if prepare extensively, you can stumble through your first video production with relative ease.

Keep a few things in mind to ease the task of assembling a crew when you shoot a lower-budget video:

✔ Modern cameras are so light sensitive that you probably don't need much extra lighting. However, good lighting makes a video look professional.

✔ If you use a shotgun microphone (see Chapter 11) mounted on your camera, you eliminate the need for a soundperson.

✔ If you're directing your video, you can also be your own camera person and shoot the scene yourself.

The first crew decision you make for your video is which role *you* want to take — most likely, director or producer. These roles allow you to guide the production. Directors tend to maintain creative control, and producers run the logistics of the production.

Deciding on a director

In the movies, the director is the only person whose name (sometimes) appears above the movie title, along with the names of the leading actors. The reason is that the director literally calls the shots by deciding where the camera should be positioned, setting up every scene, working one-on-one with actors on their performances, and making the whole production come together.

Good direction requires that you guide every action that happens during a shoot — and that you keep an eye on how it all looks in editing, decide which shots may be needed to make a moment work, and make changes on the fly whenever necessary. Good directors work well with actors by putting them at ease, giving clear and specific direction, and setting the tone for the entire shoot. The job requires highly developed technical skills and skills for working with people.

If you feel that you best understand the content of your script, and if you're comfortable choosing shots and working with actors, the director's chair is the spot for you. The director has the most powerful role in a shoot — the one who gets to say "Action!" or "Cut!" and the visionary who answers to no one (except for the producer).

Procuring the producer

The director may be "the big cheese" creatively, but the producer ultimately is the even bigger cheese. In Hollywood, the producer picks the project, hires the cast and crew, and, most importantly, finds the financing and writes the checks. Though the role of a producer is sometimes unclear (even to producers), a capable producer is truly invaluable. The producer assembles, or "produces," all the elements that combine to create a film production.

In your video, the producer should be considered the supervisor of the project, responsible for following the budget, procuring the location, scheduling the cast and crew, acquiring props and costumes, printing scripts, providing food and drink for the ensemble, and ensuring that the director sticks to the schedule.

Though the producer doesn't physically perform every job in a film, this person must ensure that every job gets done. ("Get it done" should be every good producer's motto.) If you believe that you can turn the chaos of a video shoot into order, or if you know someone who can, you've found your producer.

Securing a camera person

The proper title for a camera person on a movie set is the director of photography, or DP. The DP doesn't simply fiddle with lenses and buttons — in fact, on many shoots, the DP doesn't even do the shooting. Working with the director, the DP decides where to position the camera, which technical adjustments to make to the camera, and what type of lighting is necessary. The connection between light and the sensitive instruments behind the lens are the elements that make a movie look good, which is why these elements need their own director.

On your shoot, you don't need an *artiste*. You need a good camera person — someone who can make your scenes look their best and who can determine not only the proper camera angles but also break down individual shots. This person may see things you didn't notice when you put your video on storyboard, such as the need for an extra close-up or how to break a single shot of two characters into a dynamic series of back-and-forth moments.

A camera person's eye should be trained at all times on the camera's LCD monitor — to see what the video will look like, to catch actors who "drift" out of the frame, to ensure that microphones are hidden, and to determine whether the lighting is too dim or too bright. The camera person should be able to look at a scene on a shoot and picture how it will look eventually onscreen. Like a painter or photographer, a camera person needs a good *eye*.

A good camera person also need a *steady hand*. Someone who's shooting with a handheld camera, for example, must be able to keep the actors in the frame, with no excessive camera shake or panning. A camera person doesn't follow the action as much as she anticipates it, to keep the scene looking smooth and seamless.

Evaluating more crew positions

A shoot using a simple three-person crew — a director, producer, and camera person — can make a good video. The director can even perform double-duty as the camera person. If you have enough money in the budget, however, or a number of people who are eager and willing to help, these five additional crew positions can make your video even better:

✔ **Soundperson:** If you shoot with a boom mic, you need a soundperson. This person's job (while wearing headphones) is to point the microphone closely to the actors who are speaking and to check for clean recordings every few takes.

✔ **Gaffer:** The gaffer works with the camera person and the director to set the mood for the scene and to light the actors appropriately. (Feel free to surprise your friends with this knowledge the next time you watch movie credits together.)

The supersticky, incredibly useful tape that gaffers use for taping down light stands, attaching pieces of equipment, or making a quick fix to a broken camera or light part is known as *gaffer tape.*

✔ **Continuity:** The scenes that comprise a film or video are usually shot multiple times, out of order, over exhaustingly long days. Your trusty continuity person ensures that everything looks consistent from shot to shot and tracks details from the script, to avoid, for example, accidentally shooting a night scene during daylight hours. Detail oriented to a fault, this person keeps the audience engaged in *the story,* and not on the lead character's red shirt that was green in an earlier scene.

✔ **Hair and make-up:** This person has one of the most important crew roles for actors, responsible for giving every character an appropriate hair style and applying **make-up** to minimize the effect of unforgiving camera lenses and bright lights. The person in this role is also responsible for ensuring that actors maintain a consistent look over the course of a long shooting day.

✔ **Production assistant:** Anything goes in the role of production assistant, or PA. A PA is sometimes known as a *gofer* because he "goes for" (looks for and gathers) whatever items the director needs. Running errands is the main task of the PA (who, obviously, should be reliable, flexible, and energetic), though you can also assign innumerable smaller jobs. The PA may locate equipment, move scenery, position cables to prevent actors from tripping over them, and (of course) serve coffee.

Chapter 8

Making It Legal: Crossing the T's and Dotting the I's

In This Chapter

▶ Using people legally

▶ Legally using locations

▶ Respecting copyrights

▶ Protecting your rights

*T*he focus of video marketing is to gain customers, not to have lawsuits filed against you. Commercial video making has rules and regulations that can affect how you shoot, edit, and promote your video. As a result, legal concerns must be part of your creative process. Considering which people or locations may appear in a video — and under what permissions or what intellectual property must be respected — shapes your creative choices.

This chapter outlines how to protect yourself, your organization, and your investment by following through on the legal side of creating video. We provide sample legal documents that were prepared by the New York entertainment attorney Deborah Hrbek, Esq., as well as our own, detailed insights on managing and resolving legal disputes.

Though this chapter provides information regarding the laws and practices that affect you in the course of making commercial video, none of the authors is an attorney, and no part of this chapter contains legal advice. Rather, we point out the sorts of legal issues that commercial video makers should be aware of, and we discuss them from a practical, layperson's perspective. Consult your own lawyer to see how any of the points we raise may apply to your situation.

Contracting Artists

Anyone working on a video can easily be considered an *artist,* or *talent.* From the person who holds the microphone to the one who suavely announces your product, all are artists who are providing their talents and services. And whether they're paid or unpaid, unionized or non-union, skilled or unskilled, they all have had a hand in creating this piece of commercial art. You must therefore consider every person's individual contributions and ensure that you have the proper legal documentation in place to protect your work and yourself from any issues that may arise.

Choosing union or non-union

Some actors, writers, and crew members belong to unions. You can find unions for actors, unions for screenwriters, unions for film and television employees, unions for directors, and many more. Formed many years ago to protect workers in the entertainment industry from being exploited, unions specify issues such as pay, hours, perks, and credits. They can also determine the number of union members that you must hire for your production and the amount you're required to pay members of the cast and crew.

To determine whether union talent will work well for you, consider these two issues:

- ✔ **Budget:** Hiring union talent can be expensive. Though union members in the entertainment industry often have extensive professional experience, no one has found proof that price or union membership directly correlates with the abilities or experience of an individual artist. However, if you have a large budget, consider enlisting union talent in front of the camera — and behind it. Talent with name recognition already belongs to unions and will cost you union scale even if they're your friends.

- ✔ **Location:** Most cities and towns don't have an abundance of union talent to choose from because not much film or video work takes place outside of New York City or Los Angeles. Ironically, Los Angeles and New York City also have large talent pools of non-union actors and crew members composed of people trying to break in to the industry.

Union proponents may tell you that their artists are the best professionals and therefore cost more to hire. Their statements may or may not be true — you have to judge for yourself. If you choose to use union members for your production, you must adhere to union requirements or risk retribution for both you and the artist. All four primary unions that represent these artists provide useful information on their websites explaining how to do business with their members:

✔ **The Screen Actors Guild (SAG),** at www.sag.org, represents primarily actors who work in film, movies, and commercials.

✔ **The American Federation of Television and Radio Artists (AFTRA),** at www.aftra.org, represents actors in the various entertainment media.

✔ **The Writer's Guild of America (WGA),** at www.wga.org, protects screenwriters' rights.

✔ **The International Alliance of Theatrical Stage Employees (IATSE),** at www.iatse.org, provides protection for all members of the stage crew, including film technicians and editors, in the United States and Canada.

Any union member you hire must adhere to the rules and policies of the union he belongs to, and any union member who breaks the rules risks penalties and punishment from the union. Even if the person agrees to different terms with you as the producer, the union must approve these terms in advance. After you decide to hire a union member and sign a union agreement, you're committed to following union terms for all the talent in the production. If you decide to violate the union's terms, you will most certainly be called to arbitration, sued in court, or subjected to a fine.

When you engage a union member as talent or part of your crew, you generally have to use the standard form prepared by the union in question. The sample forms on the website (www.dummies.com/go/videomarketing) are designed for use with non-union crew and performers. From the beginning, clarify compensation, individual obligations and responsibilities, screen credits, and other important issues. Don't let people problems — union or not —cause production problems.

Working with friends, relatives, employees, and others

People you know often act in your videos — they're easily available, and they usually want to participate in the fun. You may also try to add to your production the people you see on the street when you're shooting in public. Doing so can give your production a more spontaneous, real-world look and feel.

Everyone involved in a production needs to be aware of the use and purpose of the video, and every person whose image or appearance is included (even in the form of a photo or drawing) must formally agree to your use of their likeness. To confirm that they understand, agree, and consent to the way you intend to use the footage that you shoot and in which they appear, all participants should be required to sign a document to verify that they understand the following terms:

✔ They will be filmed.

✔ They will not be paid (unless you have in fact promised to pay them) regardless of whether the filmmaker profits from the film.

✔ The film may be edited and distributed without any approvals by the participant.

The law makes exceptions in cases where filming someone is newsworthy to the community, but that exception almost always applies to journalism, not to marketing.

Anyone who appears in your video must sign a *participant release form* (or *appearance release* or *appearance waiver)*, which is essentially a formal acknowledgement of the person's informed consent to be filmed and included in the video. You can download a sample form from `www.dummies.com/go/videomarketing`.

Everyone you film in a production must sign an appearance waiver. When shooting in public areas, don't believe the common misconception that you can simply post a sign advising people that their presence in the area signifies their consent to being filmed — your claim won't likely hold up in court.

Carry releases with you at all times so that participants can sign on the spot. (Carry extras, too, so that you can give a copy to those who sign it.) If signed releases aren't returned to you during the shoot, you must get consent after the shoot, blur or edit out the appearance altogether, or risk litigation. Chasing down signatures after the shoot can be difficult, blurring looks unprofessional, and no one wants to end up in court. So, without a doubt, requesting and receiving release signatures immediately are always your best options.

Owning the script and video

Video marketing is a collaborative process, but this collaboration can lead to arguments over ownership. Technically, the script of your video belongs to whoever wrote the script. The same concept applies when you're shooting video: If you ask your next-door neighbor to hold the camera, for example, the footage she shoots may legally belong to her.

With nothing in writing to document, clarify, and establish ownership, the copyright belongs, by default, to the photographer (even though the physical footage does not). You can't use the footage, therefore, without the copyright holder's permission.

To maintain your ownership of a video and its script, everyone involved in your production must sign an independent contractor agreement. You can download a sample from `www.dummies.com/go/videomarketing`.

This *work-for-hire* arrangement requires writers and camera operators, for example, to turn over ownership of their work products to you or your organization in exchange for agreed-to payments. Then you own the rights to the end product.

Failing to formalize a written agreement about the script leaves you open to copyright infringement litigation. In addition, a court may prevent you from showing your video — TV stations and Internet service providers (ISPs) may refuse to show it, and insurance companies may reject your application for liability insurance. (For more information about liability insurance, see the later section "Addressing liabilities and insurance.")

If you fail to properly document ownership before your script is complete, you have two options:

- ✔ Buy the script from its author, using a script and copyright assignment that makes you the owner. You can download a sample form from `www.dummies.com/go/videomarketing`.

- ✔ Negotiate with the author to give you the exclusive right to use the script in your film in exchange for compensation (usually, money).

Obtaining Permission for Places

People aren't the only entities you need permission from before you shoot: The location you choose may also require you to obtain a permit, as in the types described in this list:

- ✔ **Public:** Many city and state governments require shooting permits to generate money for themselves and to help them plan for potential disruptions or disturbances caused by your production. If you disrupt traffic, for example, and you lack the proper permit, you can be fined. Research your local government rules before you start filming.

- ✔ **Commercial:** Offices, malls, stores, restaurants, hotels, and other types of commercial spaces are private properties, and you need an owner's legal permission to shoot there. Most will allow you to shoot, however, if you simply ask.

  Commercial signage may cross the line of trademark infringement. See the later section "Mastering the use of trademarks."

- ✔ **Private:** Even if a friend allows you to shoot in his office or home, it's still private property and you must get the proper permission. A location release should reduce the risk from the most common types of complaints. You can download a sample document from `www.dummies.com/go/videomarketing`.

Guerilla video making

Because many cameras and phones can now shoot high-definition video, video makers sometimes shoot *guerilla* video on private or public property without permission. This covertly shot video, however, shows lasting evidence of the violation if problems from the secret shoot crop up later. Consider the risk versus the benefit for your company when you embark on a guerilla activity that can harm your reputation or expose you or your company to legal risk.

Wherever you shoot, leave the area exactly as you found it. Respect the people and property involved in your shoot, and make cleaning up fun for all participants. The next time you need a place to shoot, you're more likely to get permission.

Using Copyrighted Material

The most often discussed issue in online video is, by far, copyright infringement. Any item that you use in a video without permission from the owner can lead to issues of copyright infringement or potential lawsuits (or the *worst* punishment for certain folks — being banned from YouTube forever).

These common items are subject to copyright law and may require permission from the owner before you can use the material in your film:

- ✔ Video
- ✔ Movies
- ✔ Music
- ✔ Photographs
- ✔ Screen shots
- ✔ Artwork
- ✔ Writing
- ✔ Trademarks or brands
- ✔ Celebrity likenesses

If you're making a commercial video designed to generate profits, the rules are more stringent than for personal or artistic videos that may be allow you to draw freely from the public domain. Familiarize yourself with copyright law to help keep your attorneys focused more on contracts and less on litigation.

Invoking fair use

The *fair use* legal precedent, upheld by the U.S. Supreme Court, allows people to use another person's copyrighted material for purposes of commentary, education, or parody. The criteria for fair use, however, are blurry and open to interpretation. As the U.S. Copyright Office points out, "The distinction between fair use and infringement may be unclear and not easily defined. There is no specific number of words, lines, or notes that may safely be taken without permission. Acknowledging the source of the copyrighted material does not substitute for obtaining permission." For more information about the U.S. Copyright Office, see the later section "Protecting your intellectual property."

The criteria for fair use determination can be found in the 1976 U.S. Copyright Act (17 USC §107):

> *Notwithstanding the provisions [requiring permission of copyright holder], the fair use of a copyrighted work, including such use by reproduction in copies or phonorecords or by any other means specified by that section, for purposes such as criticism, comment, news reporting, teaching (including multiple copies for classroom use), scholarship, or research, is not an infringement of copyright. In determining whether the use made of a work in any particular case is a fair use the factors to be considered shall include:*
>
> 1. *The purpose and character of the use, including whether such use is of a commercial nature or is for nonprofit educational purposes;*
>
> 2. *The nature of the copyrighted work;*
>
> 3. *The amount and substantiality of the portion used in relation to the copyrighted work as a whole; and*
>
> 4. *The effect of the use upon the potential market for or value of the copyrighted work.*

The fact that a work is unpublished shall not itself bar a finding of fair use if such finding is made upon consideration of all the above factors.

Check out the Center for Social Media at `www.centerforsocialmedia.org`. Of all the useful web resources on the subject of fair use, this site has the best resources and best practices for understanding how to stay within fair use guidelines. You can even read and follow a specific code of conduct to keep you out of trouble.

A common misconception is that the fair use exception doesn't apply to commercial videos. In fact, making a profit doesn't in and of itself eliminate fair use as a claim. Every situation is considered on its own merits. Very little case law exists in this specific area of making industrial/marketing videos; however, it makes fair use in this context a risky defense until the courts make more decisions.

The unhappy birthday

Believe it or not, the song "Happy Birthday to You" is not in the public domain. The song was originally written in 1893 by Mildred J. Hill and Patty Smith Hill. Through a series of extensions, the copyright on the song now extends through 2030 and generates roughly $2 million annually for its owner, Time Warner Corporation. It isn't paid every time a parent sings the song to a child, of course, but any entity using the song in a product or program must legally pay the company a license fee that ranges from a few hundred to a few thousand dollars. Despite this arrangement, some researchers believe that the chain of title on the song is questionable and that it now resides in the public domain. But until Time Warner ceases to pursue alleged violators for royalties, singing "Happy Birthday" in your video comes at great cost or great risk.

Recognizing the limits of parody

Making fun of someone or something in the public eye is considered *parody*, which is protected by the First Amendment of the United States Constitution as a form of free speech. Parody — a specific justification for the claim of fair use — allows television shows such as *Saturday Night Live, The Daily Show, The Colbert Report,* and *Tosh.O* to show video clips in their for-profit productions, even without permission from their owners.

Parody doesn't always constitute fair use under the law. Making fun of your competitors may also expose you to other legal risks, such as defamation, discussed later in this chapter, in the section "Dissecting defamation."

Borrowing other people's music

Music is likely the primary copyright infringement issue in making video. Unless you want to pay for license fees to a major artist or record label, most of your iTunes portfolio is off-limits to your video. The music industry regularly hunts down offenders on such websites as YouTube and Facebook, forcing them to take down the videos. Fortunately, you have alternatives:

- ✔ **Make your own music.** If you play an instrument or you're adept in using the Garage Band program on a Mac, you can make your own music. To brush up, check out *Garage Band For Dummies,* written by Bob LeVitus (John Wiley & Sons). You can also hire musicians to record music for you. Just be sure to get signed releases from everyone who jams on the gig.

- ✔ **Pay a music service.** A number of stock music providers on the web will sell you all kinds of music for your video. Some charge by the song, and others let you subscribe monthly. License fees can range from a few dollars to a few hundred dollars. Two of the more reasonable resources are at www.Pond5.com and www.Iphotostock.com.

✔ **Use open source music.** This music is either in the public domain, such as very old recordings no longer protected by copyright, or other music that's offered royalty-free by aspiring artists who simply want their music to be heard. Our favorite open source music source is at incompetech. com, which we describe in more detail in Chapter 24.

Mastering the use of trademarks

A *trademark* gives the right of ownership to any sort of artwork or writing that's connected to a particular product or service: its brand name, logo, unique symbol, or description — whether it's a slogan or a written description. Even if a trademark isn't officially registered, you cannot legally use any element that's trademarked to someone else (often indicated by the trademark notice ™ or ®) without the permission of the trademark owner. This statement is true even if the trademark appears only as an insignificant element of your video.

Ironically, in big-budget movies, brands pay big money for product placement. But if a video from a smaller operation has a can of soda or a bottle of liquor in a shot, the producer is likely to receive a cease-and-desist letter from the owner of the trademark.

You can be sued if you violate trademark infringement law. The law punishes violators by making them pay extra money to trademark holders or, in some cases, by serving injunctions to prevent videos from being shown. If a brand is worth protecting, its owner likely has the funds to take you to court.

Don't spend more than you must and then risk unnecessary litigation. Rather than violate trademark law, make up a fake brand or at least hide the brand name from the camera or blur it during editing. The website of the United States Patent and Trademark Office (www.uspto.gov) contains a lot of useful information about trademarks and copyrights.

Dissecting defamation

No matter how tempting or potentially profitable it may seem to slam your competitors in a video, doing so may expose you to a lawsuit. Legally, you aren't allowed to harm the reputation of a person or a business by way of either of these two methods:

✔ **Libel:** To defame in writing, such as in a document, but may also refer to the script or another type of written information that's used in a film or video.

✔ **Slander:** To say or record someone making a statement that harms a person's reputation. To count as defamation, of course, the statement must be made to someone other than the person being discussed. (There's no law against making a simple insult.)

Only these viable defenses allow you to say nasty things about others publicly and then prevail if you're sued:

✔ **Truth:** If the information is true, it's an accurate reflection of the target, and it cannot possibly do damage to the person's actual deserved reputation.

✔ **Opinion:** If you share an opinion and you specify that it's only your opinion, not a fact, you may have a defense to a defamation claim.

✔ **Fair comment, or public interest:** The First Amendment allows for free speech in open discourse about public figures, actions, and activities — regardless of whether the discourse is truthful. (This defense helps super-PACs during election years.)

To avoid issues of defamation, simply focus on your company's strengths rather than on your competitors' weaknesses. Comparison can sometimes make for compelling video, however, and you should not avoid comparison if you can keep it legal. Check your facts thoroughly, and represent them accurately. If you face a defamation issue, removing the video and issuing an apology can go a long way toward defusing the problem.

YouTube or EveryoneTube?

Because YouTube — owned by Google — is the largest online distributor of video, pay special attention to its rules on copyright infringement. YouTube has done its best to stay current with fast-changing laws and to create policies that protect copyright holders without slowing down and restricting the artistic expression of its users.

The YouTube policy is rather simple: Post what you want. If someone complains, your video is flagged, and you have the opportunity to respond. If you're found to be violating someone's rights, you're forced to take down the video. When you accumulate more than three violations, you're forever banned from YouTube.

Some rights holders have entered into an agreement to share with YouTube, as a form of compensation, the advertising revenue from their videos. They can also choose how they want their videos to be protected, such as using the Creative Commons Attribution license to grant permission to others to reuse their videos.

To truly understand your various options and their consequences, check out the Copyright Center on YouTube by going to www.you tube.com/t/copyright_center or scrolling to the Copyright link at the bottom of the YouTube home page (www.youtube.com).

Protecting Your Own Productions

Your video is your property, of course, and as much as you may want to ensure that the rights and assets of others are protected, you're entitled to your own protection. Whether you're protecting yourself from litigation, liability, or infringement, take a proactive approach to preparing for the worst and hoping for the best.

Protecting your intellectual property

Protecting your own intellectual property is important for you and your company. You have only one way to ensure that your material remains *your* material — register a copyright.

Technically, you don't need to officially register your copyright with the government in order to own the intellectual property rights to your video. However, formal registration is the *best* way to prove that you own the video and the *only* way that entitles you to sue others who violate your copyright.

The "poor man's copyright" is a myth. Mailing a document to yourself or filing a copy with a writer's guild or an attorney is insufficient protection.

The U.S. Copyright Office is the office of public record for copyright registration. Properly registered material is deposited at the Library of Congress, which notifies the public that you're the original creator of whatever item you're registering. To copyright your video, submit an online application at www.copyright.gov (click the Registration button in the row of buttons at the top of the page), and attach a digital copy of the footage you want to protect. The filing fee is $35. Just do it.

To give notice of your claim on the ownership of the copyright in your film, simply add the copyright symbol (©), followed by your name or company name and the year you created it and including the phrase *All rights reserved.* The purpose of the copyright notice is to let others know that you own the video and that you expect to be asked for permission before anyone tries to sell, license, reproduce, or use your material. Insert the copyright symbol, date, and name in the footer of every page of your written material. Also insert the symbol, date, and name on a title slide at either the beginning or end of the video.

You cannot legally copyright an idea, but you can copyright the words or video you use to express that idea. Even if you have a great idea, if someone wants to write or demonstrate it differently than you did, they have that right.

Addressing liabilities and insurance

Unless you have superpowers (and even if you do), trouble will likely strike at some point during your production. Taking action before problems arise is simply smart business, and in the end, it affords your video its best chance for success. Insurance offers protection in several areas:

- ✔ **Errors and omissions (E&O):** Protects you, the videomaker, from accidentally violating a copyright. Also, if you plan to find a distributor to send out your video, you're usually required to buy insurance before one will agree to do business with you.

- ✔ **Production:** Covers you for incidental damages that happen during production, such as when a camera breaks or a stage lights bursts.

- ✔ **General liability:** Protects you from legal action taken by members of the cast, crew, or passersby if any of them is accidentally injured during production. It also protects you from damage to property that may occur in the locations you choose.

If you can't afford insurance, consider having all parties sign an *assumption of risk and waiver of liability.* This document helps protect you from the consequences of someone getting hurt while performing any action — such as walking or running or leaping from buildings — that may place them, or their property, in harm's way. The document doesn't prevent you from being sued (eliminating attorneys from the earth is the only way to make that happen), though it may help settle lawsuits faster. You can download a sample of this document from the website: www.dummies.com/go/videomarketing.

Resolving disputes

In a typical lawsuit (or *traditional litigation),* both sides hire lawyers, sue, and battle it out in the courtroom. The lawyers attempt to negotiate a settlement agreement based on the parties' respective legal rights, which, if an agreement is reached, is often "so ordered" (that is, turned into a court order) by the judge in the case. If the parties cannot agree to settle, the judge makes the final decision, and it costs everyone a bundle.

You don't need to go to court every time you're in a disagreement about intellectual property. You can use one of the following methods to resolve disputes. These methods of *alternative dispute resolution* (ADR) are becoming more common because litigation in court is stressful and expensive:

- ✔ **Arbitration:** This increasingly more common process resembles litigation, except that it's less formal and, often, cheaper if independent arbiters are selected. Arbitrators aren't judges; they're attorneys or industry professionals whose decisions are binding and not subject to appeal.

✔ **Mediation:** Courts routinely refer parties to mediation, which is increasingly common in commercial matters because of its cost savings, in an effort to aid settlement. Mediation that takes place before a party files suit or enters arbitration proceedings can be even more effective. Mediation between colleagues can help amicably resolve ownership issues, disputes over the way video is used, disputes with writers or camera operators, or other parties involved in the suit. Mediation can be conducted while a video is being made (to try to save the project) or after the relationship breaks down (to clarify the parties' rights in the final product.)

✔ **Civil collaborative law process:** All parties hire attorneys who are trained in mediation and other techniques to assist them in reaching a settlement based on their interests rather than based simply on their legal rights. Settlement takes place out of court, and if negotiations break down, all parties must hire new attorneys for any litigation or arbitration proceeding that may follow. Everyone in the suit has a financial incentive to reach an amicable settlement.

Another choice you have is to decide whether any idea is truly worth the cost, time, and resources involved in a dispute with lawyers. If not, you may be better served to come up with a new idea and move on.

Part III
Shooting Your Video

The 5th Wave   By Rich Tennant

"Where's the audience track? You know, where I can put in coughs, throat clears, and drink orders?"

In this part . . .

Now is the time to unleash your "inner Spielberg." In this part, we introduce you to all the gear you need for shooting great-looking video. We delve into the detailed aspects of lighting (so that actors are visible) and sound (so that they're heard, too). Last but not least, we take some time to consider every aspect of a video shoot, including camera angles and continuity.

Chapter 9

Gearing Up

In This Chapter

▶ Picking a recording media

▶ Choosing the right camera

▶ Adding lights and microphones

▶ Accessorizing your camera

The best part of video preproduction is getting to play with the "toys" — the camcorder, recording media, lights, microphone, and other accessories that transport your video from the realm of scripts, budgeting, casting, and endless meetings to the big screen, or at least to the big computer screen.

Moviemaking has become quite a democratic affair. The ability to shoot a film formerly belonged solely to movie studios — and to anyone rich enough to afford the expensive, complicated, and heavy equipment. Over the years, consumers have gained access to cheaper, smaller equipment, from the good old days of Super 8 film to the first bulky video cameras. After the digital revolution began, the quality of consumer video equipment advanced rapidly to the current era of high-definition (HD). Now an average consumer can buy an HD camcorder that can achieve near-cinema quality in video.

Of course, the average consumer can also now choose from a sea of cameras, each laden with baffling numbers and abbreviations describing terms such as *megapixels, resolution,* and *hard drive size* — though few consumers know what all those numbers and letters mean. Additionally, the price range of camcorders is all over the map: from pocket-size cameras for less than $200 to the more advanced *prosumer (pro*fessional con*sumer* — a fusion of professional-level and consumer grade) behemoths for $2,000 or more. You may wonder about the true difference in these choices — and which one to buy.

"The right tool for the right job" is the motto of this chapter, as we guide you through the various levels of cameras, from low end to high end, explain to you what those numbers mean, help you pick the right camera for your video project, and — even better — prevent you from spending too much money. We even list the accessories that help your camera do the best possible job.

Choosing Your Recording Media

After you shoot some great-looking footage, you need somewhere to put it. From the beginning, cameras have needed a form of media on which to record footage. Cameras have come a long way from the days of using expensive celluloid film; a few short decades ago, you shot footage on film and sent it to a lab, and then you waited while it was processed — all the while crossing your fingers that your movie wasn't out of focus. Digital cameras let you watch your footage immediately to ensure that you got a good take or even to delete mistakes or unwanted footage.

Of course, because electronics companies compete for your dollar, a myriad of different types of recording media are available. You have to choose not only a camcorder brand and style but also a method of recording footage. Choice is a wonderful thing, but it can also induce headaches. The following two sections simplify the process a little.

Opting for high definition or standard definition

High definition (HD) is an eye (and ear) catching buzzword to describe a certain type of electronics product. People who hear this term feel assured that whatever piece of equipment it represents must be part of the cutting edge, whether it's a big-screen TV or a toaster. (Okay, not yet, but *someday.*) What exactly does *HD* mean?

Whether you're capturing a recorded image on a camera or watching it on a screen, its *resolution* (how much detail the image can hold) becomes important. In digital media, the resolution is measured in *pixels,* the smallest unit of measurement used for the information in a digital picture. When you look at a digital image, you see a carefully arranged series of computer code (rather than film images, which are the result of the reaction of light and certain chemicals).

Definition describes the amount of resolution in an image, in terms of *aspect ratio,* or the size and shape of the collected pixels in an image. Until the first few years of the 21st century, digital camcorders recorded in *standard definition,* which generally has an aspect ratio of 720 x 480, or 720 horizontal pixels by 480 vertical pixels (also known as 4:3). Around 2007, as high-definition TVs and TV shows became commonplace, camera makers began to market HD video cameras for consumers.

3-D or not 3-D?

As increasingly more three-dimensional, or 3-D, blockbusters are released, the movie industry tries new ways to draw its audience away from the stiff competition offered by cable TV, DVDs, and streaming movies. And now that 3-D technology has made its way to living rooms everywhere, 3-D HDTVs are becoming more available and more outrageously expensive. Naturally, 3-D consumer video cameras are also being sold so that regular people can play James Cameron and dazzle their friends and family with a cinematic experience. Should you shell out the big bucks and join the wave?

Our answer is "not yet." Though 3-D can be exciting and certainly represents the cutting edge of modern filmmaking, it likely isn't what you need for your marketing videos. You need a special system to show off your cutting-edge video, and buying a 3-D camera also requires buying a 3-D home theater system (including the goofy-looking eyewear you need for viewing 3-D video).

In addition to requiring an outlay of your cash, your video has little chance to benefit from 3-D. Your audience can't watch it online in 3-D, and any dazzle it can add to presentations can also be achieved by using a high-quality HD camera and great direction and acting. It still represents an expensive storytelling gimmick, one that hasn't yet scaled down to the Internet video market. Computer makers may eventually produce 3-D monitors and mobile devices, or computers and home entertainment systems may continue to meld into a central magic box that completes all the necessary tasks. For now, save your money and focus on benefitting from the HD camera you already own.

High-definition (or *high-def* or *HD)* cameras capture footage at a higher resolution than do standard-definition cameras, at either 1280 x 720 (commonly referred to as "720p" or 16:9) or 1920 x 1080 (either "1080p" or "1080i"), which is the highest resolution available in modern camcorders. The *i* in *1080i* signifies the *interlaced scan,* a technique in which a camera records alternating lines of video resolution to create a single image; the *p* in *720p* and *1080p* represents the *progressive scan,* in which a camera records every line of video resolution without alternating. Both techniques are available in video camcorders. Progressive scan, a more modern technique, looks better than interlaced scanning when displaying fast movement, such as the kind found in sporting events.

HD cameras have more pixels on the screen than standard definition does, and they therefore add more information to your picture, which produces crisper images that have vibrant colors and fine detail. The term *full HD* describes the highest possible resolution — 1920 x 1080. When you watch a football game on an HDTV and believe that you can almost touch the Astroturf in person, you know that you're looking at a mountain of pixels in full HD.

If the camera you use offers the option to shoot in either high definition or standard definition, shoot in high-def.

Bear in mind these two statements when shooting in HD:

- **HD video consumes lots of storage space.** Producing more pixels per image requires more bytes of storage, so don't be surprised when you fill your media storage quickly. The general rule of thumb is that one hour of shooting in 1080i (or 2 hours in 720p) equals 8GB of storage.

- **You don't always need all available pixels.** There's a big difference in resolution between a 52-inch HDTV and a 15-inch laptop screen. Shooting in 1080p or 1080i definitely displays more pixels onscreen, but the pixels are intended for the larger TV or monitor. The human eye, including those of your potential audience, can't detect the difference between 1080p, 1080i, or 720p on a computer monitor. If you're aiming for an Internet market and you're looking to minimize storage space, you can scale down the resolution a notch and still produce great-looking HD footage.

Capturing footage digitally

One of the first things to consider when buying a camera is how to capture and store your footage. Digital technology basically does the same thing in all its forms — turns images into computer-ready files that are easily transferred.

This list describes your video storage options, in order of our preference:

- **SD card:** (The letters *SD* stand for *s*torage *d*evice, not *s*tandard *d*efinition.) This tiny, plastic card is the common storage unit for both video and point-and-shoot cameras, with the capability of storing, simultaneously, a mix of video, photos, and audio. A decent SD card is cheap and easy to find, and you can easily swap it in and out of your cameras or upload its information to a computer.

A camcorder that has two SD card slots switches to the second card whenever the first one fills up. The drawback is that this type is tiny and easy to lose. (One of the authors of this book is, at this moment, wondering what became of one of his cards.)

Buy a few midsize cards (8GB or 16GB), and swap them out as they fill up. You can buy larger cards (32GB or 64GB), but you increase the risk of losing more footage if one goes missing or bad. Also, always ensure that your SD card has a class rating of 6 or higher. The higher the class rating, the faster the card reads and writes information to your camera and computer.

- **Internal flash drive:** This large SD card, which is built in to a camcorder, is another good choice. A flash drive reads and writes data with no moving parts. Camcorders that have either 16GB or 32GB flash drives are common, and some even have a hybrid of flash memory and SD card slot, allowing you to continue recording even if your drive fills up. The drawback is that the in-camera drive requires you to plug the entire camera into your computer to upload footage and empty the hard drive. It's a simple process, but you have to stop shooting while you upload.

✔ **Hard disk drive (HDD):** "Bigger means better" is the idea, with cameras housing computer hard drives (including spinning discs that write information at fast speeds) at larger sizes. Common hard drive sizes are 40GB and 60GB, which is much more space than you're likely to need for a single video, so you can shoot it all without having to swap out cards or upload.

Don't drop your HDD camera (or any camera, for that matter). If you do, you may damage its sensitive hard drive. You then must have the camera repaired — and you risk losing any footage that's stored in it. Pass on buying an HDD camera. Too many unpredictable elements on a video shoot can lead to the loss of your footage.

✔ **MiniDV tape:** Until recently, this was the most popular and commonly used type of digital media. The tiny tape stored digital footage, both SD and HD, with stellar image quality, and it was inexpensive, reusable, and easy to label and store.

MiniDV tape must be uploaded in real-time — so you have to wait while the tape plays all your footage. Also, major manufacturers no longer make MiniDV-ready cameras. MiniDV, like the VHS tape, is a former industry standard whose time has come and gone. You can certainly still shoot great-looking HD footage on MiniDV, but you're essentially looking to the past.

Having Hollywood in Your Pocket

We authors remember the first VHS camcorders to hit the market back in the 1980s. Revolutionary at the time, they were also heavy and cumbersome, similar to carrying a shoebox full of bricks. (Ah, memories!) Modern high-end cameras, especially broadcast-level rigs, are still heavy and cumbersome, but nearly all consumer camcorders can now fit into the palm of your hand. Some can even fit in your pocket.

Understanding the pros and cons of tiny cameras

As a result of living in an age where the nuts and bolts of a video camera (lenses, sensors, electronics that run everything) have become ever smaller, you can now buy tiny, extremely portable cameras that you've seen only once, in James Bond films. In addition, a tiny camera can now be built in to almost any common device (cellphone, computer tablet, or laptop, for example), turning it into a miniature video camera, some of which shoot in high-definition.

But is miniature technology any good? The answer depends on where you're shooting and how you'll use it. We see tiny cameras this way:

> Though miniature technology is astounding, it suffers from a loss of capability and overall quality as camera size scales down.

Mini-cameras fall short of their larger siblings in these four areas:

- **Limitations in lens size and sensor size:** These parts of a camera (the most important parts) read images and light and convert into pictures. When a camera is extremely small, as on a phone or laptop, it has less ability to capture detail, and lower-light conditions become a true problem.

- **Tiny audio components:** A small camera has, obviously, a small microphone and, like a camera lens, can capture less detail. In addition, because small microphones have less range, volume and quality are lost at longer distances.

- **Unacceptable zooming levels:** The zoom control on a pocket camera, when available, tends to be limited and choppy. Zooming lends itself to larger cameras, where their larger buttons let you control movement more smoothly. Avoid zooming on most pocket camera models.

- **Footage compression:** Most mini-cameras save footage as MPEG-4, or MP4, files. This popular digital video format is perfect for YouTube (where it uploads fast and plays smoothly) and for easy sharing via e-mail. Because it's a *compressed* format, it can compress an 800MB video file into an 80MB file that looks great when played on a computer. However, a video in this format doesn't look good when its size increases, so your YouTube video may look blurry on a big-screen TV.

Shooting with a webcam

The next time you're working on your laptop, be aware that they may be watching you! We say this only because most modern laptops are supplied with built-in webcams, not because we think they're out to get you. (We aren't even sure who "they" are.)

Your laptop camera is a miniature marvel (the size of a fat pinhole, with a built-in microphone nearby) that places a tiny broadcast studio in your lap.

This type of camera is the perfect device for communicating by way of Skype, web conferencing, or video blogging (or *vlogging*). YouTube is overflowing with user channels containing video that was shot on webcams.

A webcam excels at only one task when you're creating video: YouTube-level vlogging. This device is an excellent way to communicate with an audience in an informal, you-are-there style. The rougher edges of the video quality can add charm and a sense of accessibility to your content. It's a good type of camera for a company's YouTube channel, for example, where updates can be delivered to an audience or questions can be answered in an informal friendly way.

Using a laptop as a video camera, however, is a bad idea. In addition to its low video quality (the picture is blurry compared to true HD, and as soon as something moves in the frame, you see lots of blur and wobble), it simply isn't built for active shooting. One slip that causes a fall, and you lose both the camera and the computer.

Using a smartphone camera

If you own an iPhone or another type of smartphone, you may be aware that it has a working telephone in it. It's buried in there somewhere, among the angry birds, the e-mail and texting apps, and the camera for shooting videos and photos.

The smartphone has replaced many objects in people's daily lives. We use ours as an alarm clock, a radio, and a flashlight, for example. And, of course, we use it as a camera. Smartphone cameras are growing more capable in every new version that's released, packing in more megapixels and adding 720p, and sometimes 1080p, video, giving their users less reason to carry regular cameras to events.

One item that a smartphone camera doesn't replace, however, is a real video camera, at least for business videos. The easiest proof we can offer is to recommend that you shoot a scene first with your phone and then with a standard camcorder. A smartphone is useful for casual shooting, but the limitations of its lower-quality lens, optics, and audio should rule it out of any serious consideration for shooting video. Use a smartphone to shoot your wrap party, not your company's video.

The next time you use your smartphone to shoot video, turn your phone on its side, to avoid shooting skinny pictures that have black bars on both sides. Most people instinctively shoot video on their smartphones using the same orientation for making a call, with the sides — which are longer than the top and bottom — held vertically. If you look at a wide-screen TV set or computer screen, you can see the shape your video should match.

Point-and-shoot: Getting video on your photo camera

Nearly all modern point-and-shoot cameras have video recording capacity, shooting 1080p and 720p video in addition to their regular still-photographic capabilities. The difference between this type of camera and the mini-camera (described earlier in this chapter, in the section "Understanding the pros and cons of tiny cameras") is that the point-and-shoot comes supplied with good lenses and sensors that capture movement with more clarity and work decently in lower-light conditions. The small size and high-quality video of the point-and-shoot make for a good combination, with solid models offered by major brands, including Canon, Sony, and Nikon.

The point-and-shoot also has limitations, with users often at the mercy of automatic settings (though certain higher-priced models feature manual controls) and tiny sound. Again, it's a decent choice for lower-end video, but not for a full-out production. If you're spending money on a higher-end point-and-shoot, you may as well buy a midrange dedicated video camera.

Shooting with pocket cameras

The Flip camera was the next big thing when it hit the market in 2006. A pocket-size wonder that shot 720p HD to a flash drive and plugged directly into any computer USB port, it was similar to the iPod's resemblance to other MP3 players — the slick, high-quality top of the mini-camera mountain was perfect for the YouTube generation.

Then a few years later, Cisco bought Flip's maker — Pure Digital Technologies — and, to the dismay of Flip's many fans, pulled the plug on the Flip, claiming that the pocket camera market would be rendered useless by the increasing sophistication of smartphone cameras. The party was over, yet the Flip still sells. At the time we wrote this book, the Flip was still available — and it remains one of the best-selling pocket cameras. In the meantime, Sony, Panasonic, and Samsung have all continued to produce their own versions of the Flip, some with improved features.

The main selling points of pocket cameras, whether Flip or its competitors, are described in this list:

✔ **It's portable:** The Flip and its knockoffs can't be beat for their size and shape, and they slide right into your pocket. The most recent models have emerged with an even more slender design.

✔ **It's easy to use:** Flip cameras took a page from Apple and gave users a user-friendly control system with a 3-inch LCD screen and a minimum of buttons to shoot and scroll through footage. The Sony Bloggie has recently expanded the size of its LCD screen to occupy most of the back of the camera.

✔ **It has HD video capability:** The Flip shot good-looking video in 720p, and its competition has upped the ante recently, to 1080p.

✔ **It easily uploads footage:** Pocket cameras come with USB connectors that pop out and plug in to any computer, allowing instant uploads and, in some cases, charging.

✔ **It's inexpensive:** With a price tag of less than $200, the amount of bang you receive for the bucks you spend on this camera is hard to beat.

✔ **Adequate (rather than outstanding) picture:** You definitely can shoot crisp, clean HD video by using these cameras. But movement tends to blur and wobble the image, and they aren't made for low-light situations.

✔ **Automatic settings:** You get what you get. In most cases, you likely don't want to fiddle with camera settings anyway. But if you want to adjust the focus or light levels, most pocket cameras lock you into using automatic settings.

✔ **Mediocre sound quality:** Most cameras follow the Flip's lead, with a tiny microphone on the front of the camera that picks up all nearby sound. A subject who is more than a few feet from the camera competes with every other sound in the area. An exception is Kodak's discontinued Zi8 model, which featured a small microphone jack that allowed for plugging in an external mic.

✔ **MP4 compression:** For the most part, this video format is still the standard for pocket cameras, and, though it's a great format for YouTube and the Internet, it doesn't scale well to larger screens, the way true HD does.

✔ **Wait time:** Most pocket cameras use internal flash memory — when you fill the camera with footage (usually about an hour's worth), you have to plug it in to your computer and dump the footage to your hard drive. In addition, because certain pocket-camera models run on internal rechargeable batteries, whenever you run out of power (quickly in some models), you have to plug them in and recharge.

The pocket camera was designed to give the casual user an excellent video experience for shooting events and B-roll (secondary) footage and for video blogging. Though you can use a pocket camera to shoot video of decent quality, aim instead for an awesome experience by using a camera that does more than simply get the job done.

Shooting with a Traditional Camcorder

This class of video cameras, larger and more complex internally than pocket cameras, offers the best options for shooting video, with full HD, excellent sensors, audio input options, and, in some cases manual control over focus and exposure. Even though this grade of camcorder is still surprisingly small (most can fit into your hand), they still pack a ton of fancy features.

Considering a camcorder

Shopping for a camcorder can be a dizzying experience. You can find dozens of models with various features, and the most baffling part is their extensive price range — you may find one camcorder priced at $200 while a similar-looking model retails for $1,200, for example.

As it turns out, performance and features account for the price difference. Consider these price differentiators for camcorders:

- **Lens:** The lens is the most important part of any camera because that's how light finds its way to the sensors inside and are then converted to pictures. Lower-priced cameras have simpler, cheaper (often plastic) lenses with an automatic focus that provides a basic, slightly flat picture. Higher-end cameras have lenses (often made of high-quality optical-grade glass) with a longer focal length, manual focus, and, in some models, interchangeability with other lenses.

- **Sensor:** The biggest differentiator in camera quality and price, the sensor handles light sensitivity, allowing you to shoot great-looking images at any light level and to control the vividness of colors. It's the *quality* of the sensor, rather than its size, that makes the difference.

- **Optical zoom:** *Optical zoom* refers to the physical zooming that takes place through the camera lens, whereas *digital zoom* refers to the process where one part of the camera image is enlarged, often leading to a blurry shaky mess. Optical zoom is what you're looking for, and higher zooming power requires a more expensive camera.

- **Image stabilization:** This function decreases the amount of shake that takes place when you hold the camera in your hand. It's offered as either optical image stabilization, in which the lens itself physically adjusts itself to correct shake, or as digital image stabilization, where the camera sensor digitally corrects the shaky image.

✔ **Audio option:** Does your camera have a microphone jack out and a head jack in for monitoring sound with headphones? Allowing an external microphone to plug in vastly increases audio quality. Basic-quality cameras have ¼-inch RCA jacks, whereas certain high-end models feature XLR plug-ins, for professional-level microphones.

✔ **Manual exposure control:** Though you may not be ready to use exposure creatively, higher-end cameras give you some control over the amount of light that enters the lens.

The more control you have over the picture and sound quality of a video camera, the higher (generally) its price tag. The good news about camcorders is that most of them produce excellent HD video. You can spend from $300 to $500 on an high-quality camera, but for $500 to $800, you can buy a first-class camera that gives you a degree of creative control over your images.

Beyond the $800 amount, you begin to move into the territory of *prosumer* cameras, featuring a cross of professional-grade and consumer features, range in price from about $1,000 to $5,000. This type of camera has a wealth of manual controls and advanced sensors to justify its price tag. It's quite an expensive toy, but the beautiful images it produces are tough to beat with a lower-end camera.

Stick with a major brand name when you buy a camcorder for your marketing videos. Canon, Panasonic, and Sony — the top makers — offer the best features for decent prices.

Shooting HD on a DSLR

In recent years, a small revolution has taken place in the digital camera market. The high-end digital single-lens reflex (DSLR) camera was suddenly exploited for its video capabilities. Beginning with the Canon 5D Mark II, this traditional photographic camera began to feature 1080p video recording capability. Its interchangeable lenses and large sensors could easily be used to achieve a textured "film look" with a shallow field of focus, putting it on par with much more expensive HD cameras for a much lower price, usually between $900 and $5,000.

Both Hollywood and the British Broadcasting Company (BBC) took notice of the DSLR, and it has since been used in numerous TV shows and film productions, including an episode of *House* that was shot with the Canon 5D. The DSLR certainly hasn't taken over the consumer digital camcorder market by adding full 1080p video capability, but it's increasingly becoming *the* choice for video professionals and hobbyists alike, and we'll inevitably see its production usage grow. (Two of the authors of this book, Kevin and Matt, shoot their professional marketing videos on a DSLR camera.)

To create the kind of videos we describe in this book, buy a model other than a DSLR. It's a phenomenal camera for hobbyists or for people who have some video experience under their belts and want to expand their filmmaking skills. But because of its advanced nature, we don't recommend it as a first step into the world of video. Only after you invest a serious amount on using a camcorder should you feel free to jump into the DSLR craze.

Accessorizing Your Shoot

An outstanding camera is only one element of your video making equipment arsenal. Consider adding the following additional types of equipment. Doing so only expands your capabilities and gives you greater tools to enhance your creativity.

Increasing the voltage with lights

Most modern camcorders can shoot fairly well in low light, but only being able to see the subject you're shooting may not be enough to make your video look good. Lighting your subjects, and perhaps giving them a bit of dramatic or glamorous flair, can truly make your scenes come to life.

We cover everything you need to know about lighting in Chapter 10. For now, these basic options can shed some light on your videos:

- **Light panel:** This attachable, battery-operated LED panel sits atop your camera. It usually comes supplied with a dimmer switch and is ideal for throwing ample light on subjects in the foreground. You can also mount the light panel on a *light stand* (a tripod for lights) so that it serves as a backlight for your subjects. You can find a good light panel for about $50 at www.amazon.com.

- **Clamp light:** Available in any hardware store, this work light uses either a standard bulb or a halogen light. (Halogen heats up the room, so you may want to stick with standard bulbs.) Clip one to a chair, a table, a door, or even a ladder to add a general wash of light to a dimly lit scene. You can also point a clamp light at an actor for a dramatic effect. It isn't a professional movie light, but it can serve you well for less than $10 per bulb.

✔ **Light kit:** A light kit consists of two or three lights (typically fluorescent), light stands, and often, a reflector, such as an umbrella that sits behind the lights or a *soft box* system that diffuses the light and eliminates hard shadows. A light kit is a good investment, and after a little practice time, you can master the basic 3-point lighting technique to use repeatedly in your shoots. You can find a good light kit for slightly less than $200 to more than $500. Amazon, B&H, and TubeTape all carry good kits for reasonable prices.

Knowing your microphone options

A video camera records video *and* audio. Capturing clear, crisp audio is every bit as important as shooting a great-looking picture. However, most cameras don't have as many options for recording sound as they do for recording video. We explain your audio options in depth in Chapter 11; for now, these are your primary choices:

✔ **Use the in-camera mic.** This choice, the simplest, can get the job done.

In-camera mics record sound from every direction, so unless your set is absolutely quiet, your actors have to compete with every other sound in the vicinity. Recording with the camera mic outdoors is even more of a challenge because your actors will likely be drowned out by street sounds.

✔ **Plug in a wired external mic.** This choice is a good one, especially in scenes with little physical movement or in interviews. A *lavalier* mic is a plug-in mic that can be clipped to an actor's clothing for excellent sound pick-up. When you have characters who need to be in motion, you need to switch mics.

✔ **Attach a shotgun mic.** A shotgun mic sits in your camera and records straight ahead, in a narrow direction, at whatever subject you're filming. Wherever you shoot, that's what you record.

The shotgun mic is likely the most practical option for outdoor shooting because the subject is heard well over nearby street sounds.

✔ **Record sync sound.** First record sound on a separate audio recorder, and then sync it with the actors' lip movements later. This method is used in most every professional production — it captures quality sound, but is a painstaking, time-consuming process. Don't choose this method for shooting the type of video we describe in this book because it takes too much time and involves a great deal of editing technique.

Finding the right tripod

A tripod is a necessity, whether you're a beginning camera operator or a seasoned pro. Handheld camerawork calls for a steady assured grip, and even then, camera shake can spoil the shot. A scene that calls for little or no camera movement requires a tripod. Even if your scene needs a basic pan or tilt effect, you may be better served by using a tripod. Though you can find them in different sizes, including tabletop versions for your cameraphone, we describe models for standard-size camcorders.

Incorporate these four primary characteristics when you pick a tripod:

- **Maximum height:** You need to know the height of the tripod when it's fully extended. We recommend a height of at least 60 inches for a video shoot.

- **Load capacity:** You aren't likely to use a heavy camera, but it's good to know how much weight your tripod can bear. Many basic models can hold at least 15 pounds.

- **Material:** If you have to choose between plastic or aluminum, we advise you to pick the sturdier, more dependable, aluminum.

- **Removable mount:** To help you mount a camera with ease, a tripod usually has a mount that you can pop off, screw into the bottom of the camera, and then pop back on.

The tripod head can be moved by adjusting the knobs around it. Loosen them to allow for a fluid pan or tilt, and tighten them for scenes with no camera movement. Whenever you extend or collapse a tripod, ensure that the camera isn't attached.

Making the most of monopods and steady mounts

A monopod is typically a telescoping pole with a camera mount on one end. It's a one-legged version of the tripod — you can't use it for mounting a camera so that you can walk away from it, though it can be a useful ally in shooting. A monopod greatly reduces camera shake by moving the camera from the camera operator's hands to a steady platform. A monopod can also smooth out camera moves, such as pans or tilts, and it provides the means to shoot high-angle shots by extending the camera operator's reach.

A monopod acts as camera *stabilizer* — a camera mount that separates the movements of the camera from the camera operator — typically, by using a counterweight. If you've ever seen a movie in which the camera seems to glide along smoothly as it tracks a character, you're probably seeing the most famous camera mount in Hollywood: the Steadicam, which is a stabilizer attached to a body harness. It was invented in the 1970s as a means of providing smooth, shake-free camera movement. Now it's used in movies, TV shows, and sporting events — the Steadicam is even used at every NFL game (and it's even available for the iPhone, for about $150).

You can achieve the marvelous, smooth glide of a Steadicam by using one of a number of camera mounts that are on the market. A monopod offers a basic form of stabilization. Other stabilizers, by brands such as Manfrotto and Steadicam itself, retail anywhere from $60 to $600. A number of fairly easy do-it-yourself kits are available to help you build a homemade stabilizer. If you spend a few minutes browsing YouTube for videos of consumers showing off their camera stabilizers, you'll see how easy they are to use, and you'll see the type of amazing camerawork they can add to your video.

Ensuring an acceptable power level

You're shooting the big scene of your video. All the actors are hitting their marks, and the scene is playing beautifully. It's a moment of triumph — until you see the flashing red light on your LCD screen. The battery in the camera is about to die, accompanied by your perfect take. You have to interrupt the actors in order to swap batteries. Sound tragic? Imagine this scenario becoming worse when you realize that you failed to charge your spare battery!

Cameras drain battery power. Some cameras devour it like candy, and you can easily become powerless on the set. Though this behind-the-scenes nightmare happens to the best of us (including the authors of this book), you can avoid it by following a few easy steps:

1. **Have at least three batteries on hand for your shoot.** Having two batteries ensures that you have a single backup, but having three gives you peace of mind because you always have one fully charged battery that's ready to go.

2. **Charge all three batteries before you shoot.** It's part of the night-before ritual that we discuss in Chapter 12, and it's a good, healthy habit.

3. **At your shoot, set up your charger immediately.** Make it your first task after you arrive. Plugging in one battery immediately is your second task.

4. **Keep an eye on the battery level during the shoot.** When the battery level dips below one-quarter full, swap it out for a fresh battery.

5. **Continuously charge one battery, and keep a fresh one ready.** Rotate batteries, and you'll never have to worry about losing a scene because you lack battery power.

Everything else you may need

Browse the website of any camera or electronics store, and you're bound to find even more accessories that you may decide you can't live without. You may want to include these five items in your camera kit:

- ✔ **Padded camera bag:** This bag is the first and best protection your camera has from the big, scary world. Find a bag that fits your camera snugly so that it prevents shifting but allows you to pack batteries, cards, chargers, and other accessories.

- ✔ **Cleaner kit:** Your camera can pick up dirt and smudges, and the lens can betray the occasional fingerprint. Inexpensive lens cleaner kits and static-free wipes are available to keep everything clean and looking new.

- ✔ **Dual shoe bracket:** If you have a light panel and a shotgun microphone and you want to mount them both atop your camcorder, this type of bracket, available from several makers, lets you attach your light and mic — turning you into a one-person movie crew.

- ✔ **External hard drive:** If you plan to shoot lots of footage, maybe on more than one project, buy a 500GB to 1TB external drive for uploading and storing raw footage. A portable drive works well if you're moving between locations. Top brands include G-Drive, Western Digital, and Seagate.

- ✔ **Folding hand truck:** Used by professional videographers, this item is the easiest way to transport equipment in and out of locations. It keeps everything neat and saves you from enduring unnecessary back pain.

Chapter 10

Let There Be Light

In This Chapter

▶ Choosing your lighting options

▶ Shooting in natural light

▶ Mastering three-point lighting

▶ Building your light kit

---

*L*ighting a video is important because your audience needs to see what's going on. Beyond that task, understanding how lighting works, and how to set the mood, can add to your final product the perfect look that hooks viewers from the moment they click the Play button — and makes them want to continue watching.

Good lighting can add depth to video scenes. Using a flat image, you can create the illusion of distance between the actors and the background. You can control the mood by contrasting shadows and light, and you can endow the colors of the scene with a warm or cold temperature. More importantly, you can give your final product a professional look that separates it from the crowd of amateur-looking YouTube videos. The best part is that you can do it for a relatively low cost. Think of lighting as "eye candy" that can help make your marketing effort a success.

This chapter covers the basic principles of lighting — achieving the look you need in a few simple steps and adding effects that can help you create a memorable video that stands out from the rest of the pack.

The old expression from the movie business, "Hurry up and wait," refers primarily to how long it can take to light a scene. Lighting is typically the most time-consuming task in shooting video. The first few times you handle lighting, you may eat up precious minutes, but you'll pick up speed as your skills increase. In the meantime, schedule a little extra time into your shoot. If you're "burning daylight" (if the clock is ticking), don't go overboard with fine-tuning. Get a nice, even light and move on.

We've put color examples of concepts for this chapter on the web site. You can download them from www.dummies.com/go/videomarketing.

Lighting Up Your Video's Life

A lot of options and choices are available to light your scene. You can use the available light in the locale where you're shooting or spend a decent chunk of change for a professional lighting kit — or you can find a solution somewhere in the middle.

To determine what kind of lighting you need, you must first determine the mood of your video. While there are subtle variations, these are the most common choices:

- **Natural:** Using available light to give your scene a realistic look
- **Comic:** Usually brightly lit to match the humorous tone
- **Dramatic:** Shadows added to underscore the serious tone
- **Suspenseful:** More shadows and a greater contrast of light and dark
- **Warm and fuzzy:** For tender moments, a softer touch

Hard lighting or soft lighting

In any shooting situation, ask yourself which type of light you want to use as a source:

- **Hard:** Crisp, direct illumination from your light acts almost like sunlight.
- **Soft:** *Diffused,* or spread out, light gives a gentle, even feel to your subject.

For the type of video you're generally likely to make, soft lighting is the winning choice. It's used in most Hollywood productions because it ensures a more natural look that doesn't draw the audience's attention to the lighting itself. Though you can always make a creative choice to use hard lighting for certain scenes, soft lighting most often serves you best.

Diffused light can originate from several places:

- **Direct light:** Bounced off a reflector (or *bounce board),* a cloth disc the size of a Hula-Hoop with silvery fabric on one side catches the light and throws it back at wherever you point it.
- **Diffuser:** Use a white, translucent cloth attached to the lights by clips or even some reliable clothespins. (A film shoot is about the only place you'll find more clothespins than you use on the standard clothesline.)
- **Softbox light:** This type of light is contained in a large, hood-shaped housing with a white, diffused filter. You can buy one as part of a lighting kit (which is slightly more expensive than buying the light alone) for an easy, powerful lighting solution.

✔ **Umbrella reflector:** When you attach a reflective umbrella to a light, you can point the light at the umbrella to produce a pleasant, diffused effect. The umbrella reflector is a favorite of photographers.

✔ **Do-it-yourself diffuser:** On the other end of the scale, a white poster board or square of foam core makes a good reflector. You can use pieces of cheesecloth to filter the light for a softer look to produce a good, natural-looking light.

Shooting in natural light

Natural light refers to the type of light that's normally available at a shooting location. Using natural light assumes you aren't using lighting kits, light panels, bounce boards, or any of the lighting options we discuss in Chapter 9. You may encounter these types of natural light on a shoot:

✔ Direct sunlight

✔ Indirect, or reflected, sunlight

✔ Fluorescent lights in an office

✔ Lamps

✔ Candlelight, for a more intimate or mysterious feel

Natural light is the easiest lighting to set up, whether you're indoors or outdoors.

Indoor lighting

If your script takes place in the workplace, shoot in your own office, where the abundance of fluorescent lights gives everything a uniform, well-lit look. Problem solved.

Fluorescent light can give human skin a slightly greenish, unhealthy look. Also, the uniform lighting inside the office can lead to a "flat" look to your video. To see what we mean, look at the typical homemade YouTube video: The lighting on everything within the frame looks the same, which literally flattens your perception of the image. If you're aiming for a decently lit scene, this flattening effect is likely acceptable; if you want your scene to have a little more lighting "oomph," however, flat lighting limits your options.

To shoot indoors with regular indoor lighting, follow these guidelines:

✔ Avoid placing your subject in front of a window. Position the subject against a wall, facing the light. If you have to shoot by a window, draw the blinds or curtains.

✔ Position the camera between your subject and the window.

✔ Use the sunlight from the windows as the main light (or *key light*), and position a lamp (the *fill light*) to the side of the subject to fill in any hard shadows.

Outdoor daylight

For shooting an outdoor scene, simply move your video outdoors and shoot under *the* oldest (and cheapest) lighting source: the sun.

The sun gives life to Planet Earth, but is the bane of film crews everywhere. Shooting in bright sunlight outdoors can give your video a harsh, overly contrasted look with lots of shadows, as shown in our web examples, especially in the eye socket (not to mention squinting actors). Plus, you have to keep in mind the whole matter of the revolving Earth The sun appears to move continuously. In one shot, the sun is in front of the actors, and in the next shot, it's behind them. And then it hides behind a cloud!

To shoot video outdoors in natural light, heed these guidelines:

✔ **Position subjects so that they aren't facing into sunlight.** In addition to the annoyance of squinting, facing the sun leads to lots of shadows and a washed-out look.

✔ **Use a reflector to eliminate shadows.** Have a crew member hold the reflector.

✔ **Shoot on an overcast day or at dawn or dusk.** Your camera (and your subject) will love the even look of the light.

Never shoot directly into the sun with a standard camera lens. Hard, direct sunlight can damage the delicate sensors in your camera — and worse, the delicate sensors within your own retinas. To help prevent problems in cases where you simply must shoot into the sun, special lenses and filters are available for this type of light.

Backlighting

Shooting against a bright background — with the sun behind you or against a window— can cause the sensors in your camera to overexpose, leading to your subject morphing into a shadowy figure while the background changes to the same degree of white as you find on a supernova. On the left, an actor is backlit by a sunny day outside the window; on the right, he's lit evenly, with the window light hitting him directly. You can download an example from the web site at www.dummies.com/go/videomarketing.

Applying Three-Point Lighting

Three-point lighting, which is the most basic and common type of professional lighting, is a videographer's friend. It provides even, warm illumination on a subject while minimizing shadows. You've seen three-point lighting in movies, TV shows, commercials, and news reports — virtually anywhere that calls for solid, even lighting.

Naturally, three types of light are involved in three-point lighting:

- ✔ **Key:** The main light is used to provide the greatest level of illumination on your subject. A 500-watt bulb works well.

- ✔ **Fill:** The secondary light fills in the shadows created by the key light. The fill light can have about half the intensity (approximately 250 watts) of the key light.

- ✔ **Back (or "kicker"):** The kicker shines from behind, adding a "rim" of light to the subject's head and shoulders. It also has about half the power (about 250 watts) of the key light.

Three-point lighting accomplishes a neat trick: It "pops" out a two-dimensional image, giving it a third dimension. (This effect isn't the same as the 3-D process you see in big-budget movies.) Three-point lighting gives your shots a sense of depth — your eye can make out distances between your subject and the background.

Figure 10-1 shows an overhead illustration of the three-point lighting layout. The position of the camera and the subject are marked, along with the positions of the key, fill, and back lights.

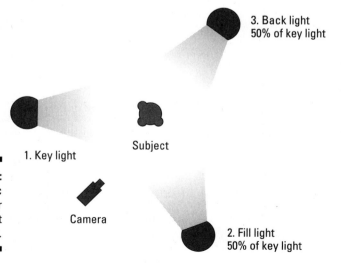

Figure 10-1:
The basic layout for three-point lighting.

Light, the three-point way

If you're ready to play with lights, follow these four steps to give your scene an even look with some added dimension:

1. **Determine where the subject and the camera are positioned.** This advice is a good rule of thumb for every lighting setup. The lights should accent the action on the screen, not the other way around. After the director and the camera person (both of whom may be you) have decided where to position the subject and the camera, set your lights.

2. **Set the key light.** The key light should be to the left of the camera, at an angle roughly 15 to 45 degrees in relation to it. In other words, if the camera is at noon, the key light is between 1:30 and 2:30. The light should be elevated so that it shines on the subject at about 45 degrees. (This strategy may be difficult in certain spaces, so just do your best.) Though the light should shine into the face of your subject, you should experiment to avoid creating harsh shadows and weird angles.

3. **Add the fill light.** The fill light should be set on the opposite side of the camera, also at an angle that's between 15 and 45 degrees relative to the camera's position (between 9:30 and 10:30). The light should be about the same height as the key light. Experiment until you have eliminated the major shadows from your subject's face. Some shadows will remain beneath the subject's nose and chin, but nothing too dramatic.

4. **Position the back light.** The back light doesn't light the background — it lights your subject from behind. The ideal place for the back light is directly behind and high above your subject. You can make the light stand out of the frame of the shot and still position the light so that it shines on your subject's head and shoulders. The light shouldn't be drawing much attention; maintain only a rim of light outlining your subject and adding a slightly magical glow.

After you position (and reposition) the lights, step back and look at your creation. Better yet, look at it through the viewfinder of your camera. You should see a shot that looks evenly and warmly lit, with a sense of depth to the frame that gives it an engaging and professional look.

Congratulations! You've just mastered three-point lighting. In this setup, you can light any simple scene easily and make it look great. After you've grown comfortable with it, you can begin to experiment: Change the heights of the lights, move the back light around, and switch sides for the key and fill lights. Watch how you can create shadows and even change the shape of your subject's face. You can be quite creative and versatile with this basic layout.

Kiss and make up

Make-up can be an important part of good video lighting (for men and women alike). In addition to hiding blemishes or imperfections, just a touch of powder can eliminate reflective shiny spots, especially on foreheads and noses. Nowadays, specially designed make-up is used in high-definition (HD) video. The camera sees everything, so don't overdo it, either.

I'm ready for my close-up

Three-point lighting is perfect for video interviews. The challenge lies in shooting in someone else's space — an office that can be cramped and tough to light, for example. The same rules apply for setting up three-point lighting, though you may be forced to move all your lights closer to each other.

Shoot with a soft light, using diffusion on your lights. This strategy complements your subject nicely. Be sure to still use your back light, even if you have to cram it over to the side, behind the subject. The kicker (the back light) gives your subject depth and warmth.

 If a lack of space is an issue, you're better off losing the fill light and moving the diffused key light around to compensate. You can substitute a reflector for the fill light to eliminate unwanted shadows. Between the soft lighting and the halo-like glow behind the subject's head, that person will thank you later for making him look good.

Pack Up Your Light Kit

A good light kit has everything you need to adequately light a scene. A complete light kit has everything you need for any occasion.

Your light kit should have these elements in it:

- ✔ Three lights
- ✔ At least six bulbs of proper intensity (three for your shoot and three backups)
- ✔ Three light stands

✔ Three heavy-duty extension cords (at least six feet apiece)

✔ An electrical power strip

✔ A roll of gaffer tape

✔ Heavy-duty work gloves

Lights become *very* hot.

✔ A hard case or padded bag to transport all these items, especially if you're breaking down and transporting your lights to other locations.

Additionally, you should include these helpful (but optional) accessories in your light kit:

✔ A reflective bounce board

✔ Diffusers

✔ Gels (at least the basic red, yellow, and blue)

✔ A bag of clothespins

✔ Sandbags to stabilize your light stands

Chapter 11

Sounds Good: Getting Great Audio

In This Chapter

▶ Choosing the right microphone

▶ Directing your talent for better sound

▶ Managing ambient noise during your shoot

*B*elieve it or not, sound in movies was once considered an oddball gimmick. When studios first contemplated adding sound to silent films, many industry people dismissed it as a passing fad. Then the first "talkie" made a fortune, and the era of sound was upon us.

Because video is a visual medium, sound can be overlooked in planning a production. But good audio is a crucial part of any film, TV show, or marketing video. Try watching your favorite video with the sound turned off: You will see that it's nearly impossible to follow the story and that those great-looking visuals have a lot less punch without great-sounding audio to go with them. *Sound is half the video experience.*

Luckily, all modern video cameras come with a built-in microphone, so your videos will always automatically be recorded with sound. But options exist for creating higher-quality audio and making your video sound as good as it looks. This chapter explores your options for getting great audio in a number of different settings and describes how to control the quality of sound of your talent and the noise within your shooting environment.

Sound Basics

The audio in your finished video is made up of four elements:

✔ The "live" sound in your scene, which includes dialogue, the sound of objects, and *ambient* sound, or the natural background noise of where you're shooting

✔ Voiceover or narration over scenes or credits

- ✔ Music
- ✔ Sound effects

You naturally encounter the first element — the live sound in your scene — during your shoot; the other three elements are introduced during the editing process. Keep in mind what sort of music or sound effects will be inserted into your scene later. For example, knowing about a sudden blast of dramatic music or the sound of an explosion helps the director and actors play their scenes accurately and to their full potential.

Wearing headphones

If your camera has an audio-out jack, plug in headphones and wear them while shooting. This way, you can always hear the exact sounds that your microphone is recording. Larger, cushioned headphones are better for this job than earbuds because the headphones can block most ambient noise and allow you to hear the sound that your microphone is recording. Earbuds allow in a certain amount of outside noise, and they're more likely to fall out of your ears, which can spoil a shot.

Before a day's shooting, test the audio on your microphone and camera while wearing headphones. Shoot a few seconds of someone talking, and then play back the clip to ensure that your microphone is working and that no buzzing or static from a loose connection or an outside source is present. Shooting with a dead microphone is an all-too-common mistake that can give you a nasty surprise when you watch your footage later and realize that it has no sound. (We speak from experience.)

Toning your room

This classic Hollywood trade secret can come in handy: In every location during a shoot, record 30 to 60 seconds of silence or *room tone.* By *silence,* we mean no talking, no creaking chairs, no footsteps, and no cellphone beeps or other sounds. The ambient noise of office work, street traffic, or chirping birds is the type of noise you want. Why? Because later, during editing, you may want to cut out bits of unwanted sound, such as when your colleague sneezed off-camera during a dramatic moment. Replace the sneeze with the room tone, and you have yourself a perfect-sounding scene.

Recording Great Sound

If you search for *microphone* at your favorite search engine, you can quickly discover many different types of mics, and they're supplied with a ton of dense-sounding industry terms, which can be overwhelming for the novice sound engineer. You have many options for recording sound — from built-in, no-fuss, on-camera mics to professional audio recorders that record sound as a separate entity to be combined with video during editing. You decide which type of microphone will work best for your particular video application and the result you want.

Regardless of which microphone you select, its basic recording principle is the same as any other: Your mic turns sound vibrations into electronic signals that are recorded on a form of physical media, including record albums (remember them?), cassette tapes, videotapes, DVDs, and modern digital cards and hard drives.

In choosing a mic, the first thing to consider is the kind of scene you're shooting: a scripted scene involving dialogue, an outdoor crowd scene, or a presentation over loudspeakers, for example. Knowing what type of audio you're recording can help you choose the right tool for the job.

The *pickup pattern* on a microphone is one of three types (shown in Figure 11-1), which represents the direction from which the mic receives sound signals:

- ✔ **Ominidirectional:** Picks up sound from all around the mic. Choose this one if your sound originates from several directions, such as in a crowd situation.

- ✔ **Unidirectional (or cardoid):** Picks up sound mostly from one direction, primarily directly in front of the mic. A handheld mic is often unidirectional. Choose this mic type for miking a single person or a musical instrument.

- ✔ **Shotgun (or hypercardoid):** Picks up only the sound directly in front of it. You usually find this type of focused, unidirectional mic on top of a camera.

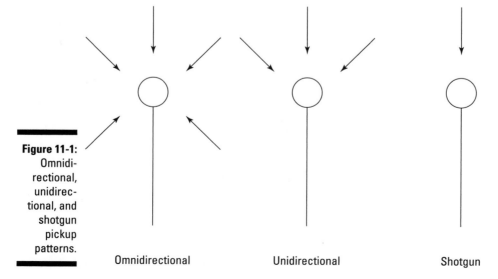

Figure 11-1: Omnidirectional, unidirectional, and shotgun pickup patterns.

Omnidirectional   Unidirectional   Shotgun

Using the in-camera microphone

Whatever type of camera you're working with, from a pocket-size Flip camera to a high-end, professional camcorder, you're also using a working microphone that records audio tracks directly on your video footage.

If you aren't sure where the in-camera mic is located, take a moment to look for it. It's typically a small hole or grid on the front of your camera, as shown in Figure 11-2.

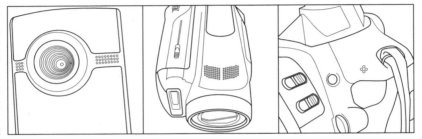

Figure 11-2: Typical locations of the built-in microphones on different camcorders.

The in-camera mic is omnidirectional, capturing sound from nearly everywhere around the camera. For its size, it's downright powerful. And, it's included with your camera, so it saves you money. If you're shooting on a shoestring, or even half a shoestring, the in-camera mic gets the job done. It's a decent choice also for recording events such as speeches, sporting events, and concerts.

For the type of videos we discuss in this book — scripted, message-focused marketing videos — the built-in mic isn't likely the proper tool for your needs. It presents several challenges to recording quality audio for your video:

- ✔ **It has substandard quality.** The in-camera mic is limited in its ability to capture clear and accurate audio. Built to be convenient, it can't record the same high-quality, focused audio that a good external mic can record. The bottom line is that it works in a pinch but doesn't produce sound as well as other options do.

- ✔ **It records _every_ sound in a scene equally.** The in-camera mic picks up the sound of actors talking, and the traffic racing outside, and the sniffle of the guy standing in the corner, and your camera humming, and every creak and bump when you move. That's too much audio!

- ✔ **It's the same distance from the subject as you are.** The greatest drawback of using a built-in mic is that the farther you move the mic from your subjects, the more the volume and clarity of the sound you're recording drops. To record a conversation and shoot it from across the room, consider buying an external mic — unless you want to ask your actors to shout.

Clip on, clip off

If you're filming a sit-down interview or a (mostly) stationary speaker, one mic makes the perfect accessory for your subject's business attire: the *lavalier* microphone. This clip-on mic attaches easily to a tie or collar or lapel for close-up sound with hands-free operation. Figure 11-3 shows your wired and wireless options.

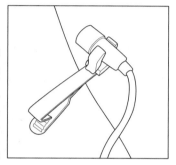

Figure 11-3: A "wired" lavalier microphone and a wireless version.

The *lavalier* (or "lav" or *body mic)* is a popular choice for segments featuring "talking heads." Roughly the size of a paper clip, and sporting a small alligator clip, it can be attached close to the subject's mouth to produce clear, uniform sound without picking up background noise. You can make the lavalier invisible by nestling it among the subject's clothing and then easily shoot on your own, without other crew members present. If you're traveling and have your camera and lavalier with you, you can easily set up a professional-looking — and professional-sounding — interview. The lavalier truly makes for a pocket-size video studio.

You have two lavalier choices:

- ✔ **Wired:** A wired lavalier is the most affordable and the easiest type to use. A thin cable is typically attached to a ⅛-inch miniplug. After you attach the mic, simply run the cable to your camera and plug the cable into the mic jack. Most available cables are long enough to accommodate the correct distance between your camera and your subject. If not, extension cables are available from your local electronics store.

- ✔ **Wireless:** The mic itself is the same as the wired version, except that the cable runs into a small *transmitter pack.* The pack can be hidden on the subject, either in a pocket or attached to a belt. The transmitter sends the audio to a small *receiver,* which has a miniplug that connects to your camera.

A wireless lavalier gives you more freedom from cables running across the floor but has its share of challenges also. The sound it provides isn't always as good as sound from a wired lavalier, and sometimes the transmitter picks up outside interference, such as radio signals. Also, you should charge the transmitter batteries before every shooting day because the transmitter eats up battery power *fast*.

Here's the best way to place a lavalier mic:

1. **Place the subject where you want him positioned in the camera frame.**

2. **Position the mic about six to eight inches from the subject's mouth.**

   A spot on the person's chest usually works best.

3. **Attach the mic clip to an article of clothing.**

   Make sure that the mic has a clear line to the subject's mouth — that's where the sound is coming from, after all.

4. **Check the audio level by having the subject speak normally while you're using headphones.**

   Check the volume level, and make sure that you hear no unwanted sound, such as the subject's breathing or the rustle of clothing.

5. **Readjust the mic's position, if necessary.**

The small size of the lavalier makes it easy to hide in locations other than on clothing. Similar to "bugging" a room in a spy film, you can clip the lavalier to a chair or to the edge of a book, embed it in a plant, on place it on a car's sun visor for a driving scene — anywhere you can still ensure a clear line of sound from your subject.

I call shotgun!

For your video needs, we recommend the shotgun mic exclusively. The reason is simple: It excels at delivering quality audio with minimal hassle. The *shotgun* mic (see Figure 11-4) is a focused, unidirectional microphone that picks up the sound directly in front of it, with little ambient noise.

Dress for audio success

An interview subject can help your production by wearing the proper attire for attaching a lavalier microphone. Ask her to wear clothing that allows the mic to be attached with a direct (but hidden) line to her mouth.

Jackets and ties provide the best clip-on spots. A mic can also be tucked underneath the collar of a shirt, blouse, or sweater, as long as the sound isn't muffled in any way.

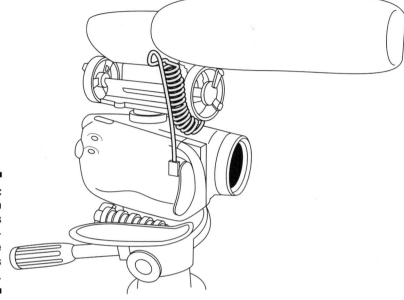

Figure 11-4:
The shotgun mic records sound wherever the camera is pointed.

Think of a shotgun mic as an audio "straw," single-mindedly sucking up only the sound you want.

The beauty of using the shotgun mic is that it attaches to the top of the camera. Wherever you then point the camera lens is where you're recording sound. This strategy is useful when two or three people are talking in a scene — if you're at a distance where you can see all three, you capture a quality recording of their audio.

The shotgun mic is also a helpful way to shoot dialogue in crowded conditions. If you want to record a few words from your CEO during a company party but you don't want to deal with a handheld mic and cable, use a shotgun mic — and consider your mission accomplished.

You can also use the shotgun for decent sound while shooting outdoors, where ambient sound can easily drown out dialogue. For outside conditions, ensure that your mic has a good *wind screen.* You place this foam (or faux fur) cover on a mic to block the sound of wind. Most shotgun mics already have wind screens, but you may want to upgrade to faux fur. To see how the mic stands up, test it with its wind screen attached on a windy day.

The shotgun mic is so reliable at picking up the sound directly in front of it that any sound to its sides is mostly excluded. The farther your actors are to edge of the mic, the less sound it records. If a character sits in a chair while another is moving around the room, your scene may suffer a drop-off in volume.

This problem has two solutions: Restage the scene so that all characters are within range of the mic, or detach the shotgun from the camera to turn it into another favorite Hollywood audio tool: the boom mic.

Lowering the boom

The *boom mic* is the number-one choice for audio recording in the world of film and television. This microphone, mounted on the end of a *boom pole,* is typically wielded by a crew member who's known as a *boom operator.* The boom mic, which can be found on the set of nearly every film and television production, offers these advantages to the world of marketing video:

- ✔ You can use a shotgun mic in place of a boom mic.
- ✔ A boom mic can reach much closer to the action than a shotgun mic can.
- ✔ The boom mic provides excellent sound quality and tremendous flexibility for staging scenes.

The boom operator holds the boom pole in a "sweet spot," where she catches the best audio, as shown in Figure 11-5. The boom mic is often positioned over the tops of the actors' heads, where the pole can be moved from one character to another as they talk. Or the pole can be held at the side or bottom of the scene. The key to using a boom mic is placing it close to, but just outside, the edge of the camera frame.

Figure 11-5:
A boom
operator in
action.

For your boom kit, you need a few items:

- ✔ **Shotgun mic:** Buy a quality mic — don't cheap out!

- ✔ **Boom pole:** Though this item has a large price range (more than $1,000 at the high end), you can find one for less than $200 — or even roll up your sleeves and build a do-it-yourself version with a telescoping painter's pole for less than $50.

- ✔ **A 25-foot length of ⅛-inch audio cable:** The cable should be more than long enough to reach the camera and allow the boom operator to move around a bit.

- ✔ **Headphones and (optional) extralong ⅛-inch cable for the boom operator:** The boom operator (or "op") monitors the audio on headphones to attempt to find the best position to hold the boom pole. Otherwise, if you monitor the sound from the camera, you'll find that you're directing the boom operator's position.

For sit-down interviews, you can mount the boom mic on a microphone stand and walk away. Do not touch the pole while shooting because the mic picks up the sounds of your hands thumping or shifting along the pole. This setup can also work in a scripted scene where an actor is stationary. But if the scene requires more than one actor, or if actors move around, get yourself a boom operator.

Operating a boom is a ninja-like art: The mic must be positioned as close as possible to the camera edge without being visible, and it must catch the audio from whoever is speaking within a scene. The challenge is that if the camera moves, the boom operator must move in tandem with it — in addition to the upper-body workout that results from holding a pole over actors' heads for several minutes at a time. Worse, the boom operator must work *silently,* with no audible footsteps or pole noises. Always *rehearse your scene with the boom operator* so that she can work with the camera operator to perfect her "boom ninja" skills.

The Actor's Voice

Another tool in your audio arsenal is provided for free by your actors: their voices. If you've cast professional actors, you end up — ideally — with people who have vocal training. Professional actors treat their voices as instruments, recognizing them as not only vital parts of their craft but also as potential moneymakers. (Listen to the distinct voices of Morgan Freeman, Judi Dench, and Jack Nicholson. Their one-of-a-kind voices helped make them famous.)

Whether you're dealing with seasoned or first-time actors, you can get the most from the mouths of your talent in a few ways, as described in the following sections.

Diction and dialects

William Shakespeare, no slouch himself in producing one or two quality scripts, had some good advice 500 years ago for video actors: to speak their lines "trippingly on the tongue." In other words, he suggested good *diction,* or the proper enunciation of the words in a script. Your actors need to practice diction in order to get your message across. Even unscripted interviewees can stand to use good diction.

Our discussion of diction in this book covers several areas:

- ✓ **Volume:** Actors should speak loudly enough for the mic while still sounding believable. (Our experience tells us that nearly every actor can stand to be a bit louder.)

- ✓ **Clarity:** Determine whether actors are speaking unclearly, such as pronouncing words incorrectly or dropping sounds off the ends of their words. Most of us do this when we're speaking casually. Make sure that actors practice pronouncing the trickier words in your script. No one should sound like Mary Poppins, but every word should be clearly understood.

- ✓ **Pace:** Make sure that your actors aren't speaking too quickly or too slowly. Many people tend to rush through sentences when they're excited or stressed — which is exactly how actors will feel with the camera on them. Take time to rehearse the scene, and find an appropriate speaking pace.

- ✓ **Vocal energy:** Not to be confused with volume, *vocal energy* refers to the quality of an actor's voice, such as whether he's speaking with passion and animation or in a tired monotone. Because the camera is fairly close, actors don't have to speak the way they would to a crowded auditorium, though their voices should possess energy and make the dialogue sound authentic and believable.

Everyone speaks in a *dialect,* or regional accent. There's no universal, unaccented way to speak. A dialect can add huge amounts of believability and variety to a performance and truly drive home the content of your video. A dialect that's too strong, however, especially if an actor seems to be struggling with the lines in a script, can also detract the audience from engaging in your video. The key is to ensure that the words in your script are striking the audience as clearly and effectively as you need.

The power of the pause

People who speak to large groups or, worse, in front of a camera tend to barrel through their lines in an effort to reach the end of the script as soon as possible and stop speaking. Because they simply forget to *pause,* they're missing out on the most powerful audio tool available.

A well-placed pause carries a lot of weight. For a brief moment, suspense hangs in the air. The words you've just heard settle for a second, and then you hear more. A pause used by actors can add drama, dimension, and structure to the words they're saying.

Work with actors to find two or three spots to pause the dialogue. Don't overdo it, and don't make a pause last forever. Make sure that it's real, however, where the speaker can take a breath and feel in control of her words, not the other way around.

Managing crowds

Keep this Hollywood secret between us and you (and everyone else reading this book). Watch a crowd scene in a movie or TV show — a restaurant or bar scene is perfect. Notice how you hear the main characters speaking clearly while the crowd around them is quiet. How do the creators *do* that? Yes, mics are being used, but the bigger trick is that the *crowd is completely silent during filming.* All their talking is pantomimed, and the sounds are later added by editing.

Hollywood uses stock crowd sounds, which is why (if you're paying attention to these sort of things) you sometimes hear the same voices on different TV shows. When you're shooting a crowd scene, stock crowd sounds are available for different group sizes, and you can find the one that best suits your scene.

You can also direct the crowd to simply speak more quietly than normal. Depending on how many people you're working with, this suggestion can be an easy solution or a tough one to manage. The key is to get a great sound level from your main actors while retaining a believable amount of background noise. Remind crowd members that they're adding to the authenticity of a scene and offer to throw a party after the shoot is complete.

Chapter 12

Conducting the Big Shoot

In This Chapter

▶ Preparing for a shoot

▶ Directing actors effectively

▶ Finding great-looking camera angles

▶ Shooting footage that makes editing easier

The big day has arrived! All your hard work — from brainstorming and writing to hiring the right cast, crew, and equipment — has come to fruition. You're ready to stride onto the set as the big-shot director or producer, riding crop in hand, and yell "Action!" It's all a breeze from this point, right?

Not quite. A video shoot can be an incredibly high-pressure environment, with too much to do and too little time to get it done. You must perform an amazing juggling act that keeps the cast, crew, camera, script, set, props, costumes, and all those inevitable but unplanned events all moving forward to get your video "in the can" by the deadline.

The good news is that a video shoot can also be one of the most creative and rewarding experiences you'll ever have. When all the elements click and you see that outstanding performance or fantastic camera angle, you'll feel a sense of deep personal satisfaction and pride that you nailed it. When the shoot is going well, the payoff far outweighs the pain.

This chapter explains how to prepare for the shoot — from developing a checklist the night before to setting up on the big day. We lay out the steps involved in every good camera take, and we list the little details that every first-class director must keep an eye on so that you can capture the outstanding footage you need.

Setting Up for a Shoot

Directing or producing a video is similar to running a marathon — you must be rested and ready before you can go the distance. The night before you run 26 miles, for example, you don't want to begin wondering whether you should have bought new running shoes. Similarly, the night before the big shoot, you want to be as prepared as possible. The more you prep, the smoother your shoot — and the better you sleep the night before.

Getting organized

Buy a production notebook to make your film or video production extremely well organized. We recommend a good old-fashioned, three-ring notebook, the type often carried by schoolchildren. It's the perfect one-stop spot to store all your shoot-related information, and it will soon become your new best friend.

Stock your production notebook with these items:

- ✔ **Dividers:** Add instant organization, and make the items you need during the shoot easy to find.

- ✔ **Pens and pencils:** Pens are the first thing you lose, so be sure to have more than one.

- ✔ **Blank paper:** You may need scratch paper or sheets of paper to illustrate shots.

- ✔ **An envelope:** Store the receipts from your expenditures.

Completing your checklists and "go-bag"

After you have a production notebook (described in the preceding section), store these items in it:

- ✔ **Script:** Your copy of the dialogue to be used in the shoot should always stay with you so that you can make notes, change the dialogue, or stay abreast of scenes that have been shot.

- ✔ **Call sheet:** This is a list of your cast and crew's arrival times on set. If you expect them to arrive at different times, keep track of their schedules.

- ✔ **Cast and crew contact sheet:** This list of contact information (such as e-mail addresses and phone numbers) is the easiest way to ensure that participants can contact each other.

- ✔ **Schedule:** A schedule is useful when a number of cast or crew members are arriving on the same day and you want to better schedule the shoot, by determining which scenes to shoot and when, and when to let everyone take a break.

- ✔ **Talent releases:** Keep the legal paperwork ready so that you can request the necessary signatures to use the cast's likenesses in your video. (For more information, see the section in Chapter 8 about getting legal.)

✔ **Storyboard:** This series of panels shows the individual shots within a scene. Keep the storyboard handy to show your crew the shots you want. (You can read more about storyboards in Chapter 4.)

✔ **Prop and costume list:** Double-check this list after the shooting day ends to ensure that all items are returned to the appropriate person or place.

✔ **Script breakdown:** List cast members, props, costumes, and types of shots for every individual scene, and specify whether the scene is an interior or exterior scene.

✔ **Cast breakdown:** This reverse version of the script breakdown lists actors and the scenes in which they appear. Creating this list helps you schedule the shooting order of scenes.

Though the script breakdown and cast breakdown may be unnecessary for a simple shoot, if you have multiple scenes and actors, consider the breakdowns as insurance against losing important elements of the shoot. (We've seen actors released from a shoot for the day only to find that they were still needed for another scene later the same day.)

The night before your shoot, complete these tasks:

✔ **Charge all batteries.** Power up all related devices, such as your camera, lights, laptop, and cellphone.

✔ **Clear out any reusable media.** If your camera records video to SD cards, format them (otherwise known as erasing them) and clear some space. If you're shooting on tape, ensure that you have more than enough to shoot on.

✔ **Double-check your equipment.** Quickly test your camera, lights, and microphone. Ensure that every item works and that the all equipment and accessories are available.

✔ **Pack props and costumes.** Don't wait until the morning of the shoot to pack everything!

✔ **Make copies of the script.** While you're at it, take the extra step of labeling every copy individually for your cast and crew.

✔ **Stock up on cash.** Withdraw cash from a nearby ATM so that you can purchase food, water, extra batteries, last-minute cab rides, and any other necessities you may need for the shoot. This is where the receipt envelope comes in handy.

✔ **Confirm call times.** Call, text, or e-mail all participants to ensure that they know when and where to show up.

While you're charging batteries and anxiously awaiting the last of the cast to confirm their call times, turn your attention to another vital element of the shoot: the *go-bag.* Simply fill a gym bag, large backpack, or (our favorite) rolling suitcase with the following essential items, and then you can take this film production survival kit with you anywhere:

- ✔ **Batteries and chargers:** Store any batteries that aren't already installed in your equipment, and add any extra AA or AAA batteries you may need.

- ✔ **Extension cords:** Bring along at least two heavy-duty cords.

- ✔ **Power strips:** Bring two of these also.

- ✔ **Gaffer tape:** Heavy-duty tape has a million uses.

- ✔ **Lights and mic:** As long as these items fit in your go-bag, add them.

- ✔ **Tripod and monopod:** Even if these items don't fit in the bag, pack them as part of your preparation ritual.

- ✔ **Laptop (and optional external hard drive):** These devices are likely to have separate cases, but you should make them part of your preparation ritual too. You may need them for transferring footage among cards on the set.

Take a moment to look over everything you've packed. You've created a production notebook, double-checked equipment, charged batteries, confirmed schedules and locations with your cast and crew, and made for yourself the world's best go-bag. You're ready to go, so take a deep breath, and get a good night's sleep.

Arriving on set

Whatever call time you've given your cast, plan for your crew to be on-site at least one hour earlier. Even if the hour is more time than you need to set up, having enough time to get ready without feeling pressured starts the shooting day on the right note. Besides, you'll quickly fill that hour.

When you arrive at your video location, first review the day's schedule with your on-site contact, who should offer any assistance you need. If you follow our advice in Chapter 8, you already have approval to shoot at this location, so be polite and professional, and proceed with setting up your space.

Every shoot requires these three distinct spaces:

- ✔ **Shooting area:** This area should be ready for use when you arrive on the set so that you can begin setting up camera angles and lighting. Be polite but firm about claiming your space, and remove any items that don't belong in the scene.

✔ **Equipment area:** Designate a quiet corner in which to store equipment, props, and costumes and to serve as a charging station for batteries.

✔ **Green room:** Give your cast and crew (and perhaps certain equipment) a place to relax — and stay out of the way — between takes. In an office space, for example, a conference room is the perfect spot, but you may have to take whatever you can get. The green room is also a good spot for setting up an alcove to serve coffee and water to your cast and crew.

After you determine the boundaries of your space, you can set up the following equipment in it:

✔ **Charging station:** Plug in a power strip, and set up your camera's battery charger (and the chargers for light batteries, if you're using them).

✔ **Data station:** Plug in your laptop and external hard drive so that you can periodically "dump" footage. If you're shooting a lot of footage on memory cards, high-definition video fills a standard card quickly. Even if your memory cards don't fill up, you should back up your footage regularly. (Plus, this decently sized screen lets you watch footage while you're on the shoot.)

✔ **Camera, tripod, lights:** After you unpack these items, you can start setting up the first shot. Check the natural ambient light in the room by looking at the camera's viewfinder to see what adjustments you need to make. Experiment to find the camera angles that work best.

When the cast begins to arrive, you can start the production: Situate cast members in the green room, have them sign the talent release, give them a few minutes to get coffee and food, and then start getting them into costume.

Planning a realistic shooting schedule

When you watch a short scene in a video, you may believe that creating the scene was a simple task. And if the video is no good, it probably was a simple task. Virtually anyone can flip a switch on a camera and ask an actor to speak. Finding a unique and memorable way to shoot a scene takes time to prepare and pull off — even for simple scenes — and this amount of time has to be figured into your shooting schedule.

Two forces are at work in every film and video shoot: the creative need to make the production special and the technical need to complete the production as quickly and inexpensively as possible and still look good. These needs are equally important. If you can't complete the shoot on schedule, you'll have nothing to show, but if you rush to complete the video with no regard for creativity, what's the point in even making it?

We would love to boil down the standard schedule to the simple mathematical formula "*x* number of shots divided by *y* setup time equals *z*," but scheduling simply doesn't work that way. (Besides, math is not our forté.) To come up with a realistic estimate of the time you need, consider these factors:

- The number of shots your production needs
- The length of each shot
- The amount of time you need to realistically set up, shoot several takes, and break down the set

Shooting usually takes longer (often, *much* longer) than most people anticipate. The technical setup can be complex, and actors may need a few takes to nail their performances. If you're working with non-actors, you may want to add an extra 30 to 60 minutes to their scenes, just in case it takes longer to get the performance you need.

These guidelines can help streamline the shoot:

- **Spend no more than five minutes setting up a shot.** A five-minute limit keeps the setup process lean and mean. You should have enough time to adjust the lights and position the camera. Obviously, some shots require more time than others, but when you're working on a deadline, time magically passes faster than normal.

- **Shoot scenes out of order.** Few film productions shoot scenes in the exact order they'll appear in the finished product. Usually, the shooting schedule is created by determining which resources (such as locations, actors, props, or lighting) can be reused in other scenes. Those scenes are then filmed consecutively.

  By shooting out of order, you can schedule certain actors' scenes one after the other and then release the actors when they finish, leaving fewer people to manage as the day progresses.

- **Shoot "big" scenes first.** If you're shooting a crowd scene or another type of complicated shot, get it out of the way early in the day. Your cast and crew will be more energized, and you'll have that worry out of the way as the day wears on and pressure grows to wrap up the shoot.

- **Experiment.** Once, anyway. If you want (or a cast member wants) to try a radical idea, just to see whether it works, do it. But shoot the scene as specified in the script, too. Don't get *too* creative at the expense of the clock.

- **Cut freely.** If you find that your schedule is overstuffed, pull out your script and storyboard and cut some shots. Not scenes, mind you, just shots. We generally encourage you to shoot scenes with multiple shots (called *coverage,* which we address later in this chapter, in the section "Determining the best shot"). If time is running out, be prepared to change the shot list.

✔ **The fewer people who are on the set, the faster you can shoot.** The more people who watch a scene, the more your shoot can turn into a party rather than a production. When something strange or funny happens on the set (and suddenly everyone is laughing or chatting and no longer working), you have to play the role of benign dictator. Firmly, but with a friendly smile, ask all bystanders to clear out — pronto. When you have a camera, you wield power!

Practicing good habits before a shot

Your camera is set up, your actors are in place, and all eyes are on you. You're ready for the first take of the day. What do you say and when do you say it? You can actually set up a smooth productive workflow by using a series of commands to move through each shot within a scene.

Draw from this handy list of words and phrases to communicate with your cast and crew — and to help them to communicate with you:

✔ **"Quiet on the set."** When you let everyone know that you're about to "roll camera," the only audible sound should come from whatever is happening in front of the camera. Side conversations, coughing, and mobile phones can all spoil a take, and you should have zero tolerance for them.

✔ **"Roll camera."** When your actors and crew are set, cue the camera person to start shooting.

✔ **"Camera rolling."** The camera person should reply to "Roll camera" with this phrase after shooting begins. If you're doing the shooting, just say "Camera rolling."

✔ **"Sound rolling."** Someone who is listening to sound separately on headphones says this phrase to indicate that the audio sounds good.

✔ **"Action."** Finally! This famous cue tells actors to start the scene and lets everyone else know to remain quiet. Wait a few seconds after the camera and sound are rolling to say it.

✔ **"Hold."** If a sudden event (such as a passing police siren) interrupts a shot, call "Hold" to let everyone know to stop what they're doing until the interruption ends. Then call "Action" again.

✔ **"Cut."** After a scene ends, wait a few seconds to say this famous cue so that the crew continues shooting video and recording sound until the moment you say it.

After a few tries, your cast and crew will have the order and rhythm of these cues down pat, and your set will quickly sound professional (as long as an actor doesn't announce, "I'll be in my trailer.")

On a clean and orderly shoot that moves along smartly, the director is the *only* person to call "Action" and "Cut." As in any other business, a movie shoot requires someone to be in charge and call the shots. If everyone starts chiming in, the production slows to a crawl.

Every take of a shot should have *handles* on it — a waiting period of a few seconds before you say "Action" and after you say "Cut." This way, an editor (who may be you) who works on the scene in postproduction has a clearly defined segment of video to work with. "Action" and "Cut" are also cues for them.

Don't press the Record button immediately after calling "Action" or "Cut" (a mistake typically made by novice filmmakers). This bad habit leaves the editor with a scene that is potentially missing its first and last seconds — a huge amount of editing time. (Applying a cool transition effect, such as a dissolve or a fade-in, during the editing process is then impossible.) Also, actors shouldn't break character until you say "Cut." As they finish their lines, they should remain in place until you stop shooting.

Shooting for at least three full seconds before and after a scene is generally a good standard. Your video will benefit from it, and your editor may even send you flowers!

Giving effective directions

A good director pays attention to two tasks while working with actors: giving actors inspiring helpful guidance to shape their performances and moving actors around within the camera frame. The latter task is particularly important because an actor's performance is divided into scenes and shots and the actor likely performs scenes out of order (by shooting the final scene first, for example). Actors have to hit their marks and participate in repeated takes of the same moment. Only a skilled director can negotiate these challenges.

Luckily, most actors want direction, especially considering the challenges that film acting presents. Actors look to directors to take charge and steer them through the video production process. Even before you provide brilliant direction to actors, you should establish a *solid relationship* with them — even for the short duration of your shoot.

To foster a working actor-director relationship, follow these guidelines:

 ✔ **You gotta have trust.** Start by establishing rapport with your actors. If you've only just met, take a minute to greet them and make them comfortable on the set so that they're relaxed and feeling that they can trust you. Chat with actors about their careers (often one of their favorite subjects) or whatever other topic comes up. A few minutes spent breaking the ice with your actors can reward you with a cast that feels a personal stake in making your video as good as possible.

✔ **Let actors ask plenty of questions.** Your actors may want information about your business, the purpose of the video, or about the script. Answer their questions as best you can, and don't hesitate to say, "I'm not sure. Let's figure that out together."

✔ **Validate your actors' feelings and suggestions.** An actor may show up on the set with absolutely opposite ideas of how to approach the character in the script. Even if an actor is 100-percent wrong, don't mention it — simply say, "I hadn't thought of it that way, but that's a good idea. Let's try it both ways." You can always shoot one take of the opposing version and then get back on track. The result is an actor who feels like part of the creative process.

✔ **Always remain positive.** If an actor gives a subpar performance, always make a positive statement, such as "Good job." Then ask for an adjustment, whether it's making eye contact with a fellow actor, trying a new action, or "dialing it down." Never call out an actor in front of the cast and crew. He'll feel defensive and embarrassed. If an actor isn't giving you what you need, take that person aside and discuss the best way to work it out.

Part of your job is to be a cheerleader for your talent so that they feel confident in front of the camera.

If you're reading this book, you likely haven't directed many business videos — indeed, you may have never directed anything.

Whatever the level of your directing experience, these tried-and-true directing techniques can help get you the performances you need:

✔ **Block scenes.** *Blocking* refers to charting an actor's specific movements throughout a scene, such as entering a room, taking a seat, standing up, moving to a window, or a combination of actions. People rarely do nothing but stand around in real life, so give your talent some movement and watch them come alive.

✔ **Ask actors to perform an action.** An *action* is a direction (containing a verb) around which actors can easily base their performances within a scene.

All these directions can be completed: "Stop him from leaving," "Convince her that she's making a mistake," and "Avoid telling the truth."

"Reflect on your regrets" cannot.

✔ **Give actors the business of activity.** You don't want performances — you want believable characters. *Business* consists of physical activities that can be conducted within a scene to prevent actors from just standing around, looking awkward and self-conscious. If a character is in a workplace, for example, have the character work. If a character is relaxing, that's an activity, too.

✔ **Dial it down.** Remember that film and video acting is a far cry from theater acting because a theater actor must ensure that attendees in the balcony can see her performance too. A film and video actor, on the other hand, must reach only as far as the nearby camera lens. For example, a camera picks up tiny details, especially face and eye movements, that an audience member cannot. Ask actors who are giving theater-level performances (exaggerating their voices or the movement of their faces or bodies, for example) to make them smaller. Otherwise, you end up with a "hammy" performance.

Use a rating system to request the acting level you want: "Your acting is a 9 now, but we need only a 5." Most good actors can scale a performance up or down to remain believable.

✔ **Run those lines.** Memorizing a script is quite a challenge for some actors. Break longer lines into a couple of shots for them so that they can get a better grasp on their lines. Be aware that the reverse also happens — an actor who knows his lines *too* well may give you an over-rehearsed performance.

The key to making dialogue work well is to know not only the words in the script but also the motivation behind them, or *why* the actor is saying the words. You want the words in your script to have a natural-sounding *cadence* (rhythm). Have actors run their lines in different ways — and ask them to truly *listen* to the other actors in the scene — to see what motivates them to speak.

✔ **Conduct line readings.** In a *line reading*, you speak a line in exactly the way you want the actor to speak it. This practice is generally frowned on artistically because some actors feel that they're simply parroting your words. However, this approach is sometimes appropriate — an actor who is truly stuck may even ask you to demonstrate what you want. We recommend using a line reading as a last resort. Consider it the nuclear directing option.

For more tips on getting believable on-camera performances from your cast, check out our helpful and humorous video at www.dummies.com/go/videomarketing.

Maintaining continuity

Continuity is the purely technical requirement of maintaining a consistent look and action in every shot, including the background and lighting of the set and the actors' costumes, hair, and (most frequently) movement. A mobile phone that's held in a character's right hand in one shot and shifts to the left hand in the next shot jars the audience out of the moment.

If continuity mistakes happen to you, you're in good company. Many successful Hollywood movies are full of continuity mistakes. Throughout *The Wizard of Oz,* for example, the length of Judy Garland's hair and dress changes several times. If that type of huge production can slip up, your video can, too.

A simple way to keep an eye on actors' positions between shots is to call "Hold!" (refer to the list in the earlier section "Practicing good habits before a shot") and quickly set up for the next shot. You can also show actors an earlier take so that they can position themselves to match their own movements. If your characters are drinking from a glass, for example, make the liquid level consistent from shot to shot (to prevent the audience from wondering how the glass was seemingly refilled). If you're shooting over several days, take a photo of your actors in full costume so that they can match their looks for the next day.

Continuity has an additional meaning for actors. It refers to their characters' mental and emotional states from scene to scene. When you're shooting scenes out of order, matching these states from the previous scene can be challenging. As a director, it's your job to keep actors on track from scene to scene by reminding them of their previous circumstances, such as where they're coming from, what has just taken place, and where they're headed. You can even draw a timeline for reference. Actors should see the big-picture view of their entire performances *and* their scene-to-scene progress.

Shooting a Great-Looking Video

To say that camerawork is a technical process, and not a creative one, is a mistake. Film and video are visual media, and the camera resembles a paintbrush. A huge dose of creativity determines where to place the camera. If you look at the camerawork of Alfred Hitchcock, Steven Spielberg, or Peter Jackson, for example, you see one stunning memorable image after another. This section tells you how to use your camera effectively, from choosing angles and specifying movement to framing scenes and capturing extraordinary imagery.

To illustrate the techniques we describe in this section, we use the following familiar scenario to show how to use the camera and the *frame* (the rectangular image you see on a movie, TV, or computer screen) to better tell a story: When a young child plays ball in the house and his mother warns him to move outside, he ignores her request and instead breaks an expensive vase. Oops! The child's unhappy mother confronts him.

Composing and dividing the screen

Composition is the process of creating a picture that helps to effectively tell a story within the camera frame for each shot. Just as a photo needs composition to possess more visual power, a moving picture needs composition to help tell the story more powerfully.

The *rule of thirds* (a visual arts composition guideline) divides a rectangular picture, such as a camera frame, into nine smaller rectangles of equal size — three across and three down. Though this concept originated in photography and painting, it has its place in film and video production.

Using the rule of thirds to position the subject one-third of the way from the edge of the frame (rather than in the center of the frame) makes the picture stronger and more interesting visually.

Because the rule of thirds also applies to framing the background of an image, you can create beautiful, symmetrical images in outdoor shoots by positioning the ground across the lower third of the frame and positioning buildings and trees and the sky in the upper two-thirds of the frame.

The rule of thirds is an artistic concept related to the way the human brain interprets imagery. It simply makes images "look better."

In the example, you can create tension in the shot (again, because of the way the brain processes images) by moving the camera so that the child is one-third of the way from the edge of the frame. When the child tosses the ball, you see the nearby empty living room, full of breakable objects, and you start to anticipate the ball flying from his hands and into Aunt Bertha's expensive Ming vase.

If you have a photo camera, try this experiment for capturing a better, stronger image. Frame the subject in the center of the shot, and take a picture. Then move the camera to frame the subject approximately one-third of the way from the edge of the shot, and compare the photos.

Determining the best shot

Your selection of camera angles, or *shots,* is limited, technically, only by your imagination, though you should master the basic principles before trying any fancy tricks. This section explains the building-block shots you see in most film and TV productions, and most scenes are built using a combination of these shots. In Hollywood, *coverage* is the practice of shooting a scene from various angles.

When you start shooting video, take these types of shots first:

✔ **Master:** The master shot is the foundation of your coverage. It shows everything — every important element of your scene. Place the camera far enough away to capture all the action, and shoot the entire scene from beginning to end. You can always cut back to the master shot to remind the audience where the characters are located in relation to each other.

✔ **Medium:** The medium shot moves in to show characters (or a single character) in an area from roughly just above their waists to a little over their heads. The medium shot is commonly used because it shows facial detail but still conveys a sense of the bigger picture.

✔ **Close-up:** In the close-up shot, the camera moves in tightly on a subject's face or on an object, such as the bouncing ball in the example in the earlier section "Shooting a Great-Looking Video." The close-up is a powerful tool to show lots of facial detail and to build tension and emotion in a scene.

✔ **Extreme close-up:** In this type of shot, the camera (obviously) moves in even more tightly on a subject to show lots of detail. A shot of a character's eyes or of fingers drumming on a table or of a doorknob turning slowly shows an intimate level of detail to drive home a particular moment. Though an extreme close-up is rarely followed by a master shot (it's too much of a leap for viewers to make from small to large), you can follow it with a close-up or a medium shot.

These steps show one way to break down the scene in the bouncing-ball example:

1. The master shot shows a child tossing a ball in the living room. The shot is framed to show the child positioned one-third of the way from the edge of the frame. You can hear his mother say, "Don't play ball in the house!"

2. Cut to a medium shot of the child watching the ball move up and down. He smirks and says "No problem, Mom."

3. In the master shot, the child throws the ball high into the air. Uh-oh.

4. A close-up shot of the child shows the watching the ball begin to descend.

5. Cut to a close-up of the child's hand reaching for the ball — and missing it.

6. An extreme close-up shot shows his eyes widening as you hear a vase shatter.

7. Cut back to a medium shot of the child looking at the floor, horrified.

8. A close-up shot of the broken vase shows the ball lying in the middle of the glass shards.

9. Cut to a close-up of the child as he gulps and his mother scolds him.

10. Return to the master shot, as the child turns to face his mother and blurts, "It wasn't my fault!" while she crosses her arms angrily.

These steps break down a scene, moment by moment, into shots that underscore the emotion of every beat of the scene. We won't win an award for this scene, but we can probably make an audience feel tension (and make them laugh at the child's excuse). That's how you "paint" a scene with your camera and the camera frame. Kevin and Matt have created a humorous video to illustrate these shots at www.dummies.com/go/videomarketing.

 In any scene you shoot, keep your shots smooth and steady. In the age of point-and-shoot video cameras, people have a tendency to start the camera rolling and then point it at various characters in a scene, in one long take. They often attempt this all-over-the-map approach with a shaky hand so that the scene ends up looking like an earthquake just occurred. Unless you're shooting *The Great Quake of the 21st Century,* we recommend that you simply place the camera on a tripod. If your scene involves a lot of camera movement, shoot it with a smooth steady hand.

Moving and grooving the camera

Anyone can put a camera on a tripod, turn it on, and shoot the scene before them in a single shot. But this style amounts to simply recording a scene, which is boring, rather than true directing, which uses the different shot choices that are available to tell a story, controls what an audience is seeing from moment to moment, and moves the camera to achieve great-looking images.

You can choose from a few basic camera moves:

- ✔ **Pan:** Simply move the camera from side to side, along the horizon. If the child in the bouncing-ball example (refer to the earlier section "Shooting a Great-Looking Video") enters a room, spots the ball on a table, and walks to it, you can follow his movement by panning from the doorway to the table.

- ✔ **Tilt:** Move the camera laterally, along a vertical plane. In the example, you would tilt the camera from the child's hand grabbing the ball and then lifting it to his chest as he looks at it mischievously.

✔ **Track:** In this tricky-but-fun shot, you simply follow the subject throughout the scene. You can track the child from an outdoor starting point, keep him at a distance, and then follow him right up to the ball. The tracking shot, which is used in lots of Hollywood films can be an effective way to show off. (A famous three-minute tracking shot from *Goodfellas* follows Ray Liotta's character through the hallways and kitchen of a nightclub.)

You can pan and tilt by using either a handheld camera or placing it on a tripod or monopod. You can track on either a handheld or a monopod. We recommend a monopod for tracking shots because the camera shakes less when it's mounted. To add a slick touch to your video, work out a brief tracking shot of one character.

Matching your eyelines

An *eyeline* is the invisible line leading from the eyes of a character on camera to a person or an object that the character is looking at off camera. The cut that you make to the next shot showing the off-camera person or object must be placed within the second shot where the brain would expect it to be. If a character is looking upward, for example, you should then cut to the object that the viewer sees, placed above the camera. If the character's eyeline and the object's position don't match (if they look down at an object that you then see hanging over their heads, for example), the audience becomes disoriented and disconnects from the scene. The eyeline makes a subtle but crucial difference when cutting between two people who are speaking to each other within a scene.

In this section, we explain how to add two medium shots to the bouncing-ball example from the earlier section "Shooting a Great-Looking Video." One shows the mother furrowing her brow at her child, and the other shows the child lowering his head after being scolded. For these two shots, you can shoot the actors in this scene separately or even on different days because they don't appear in the frame together in this particular moment. Above all else, you have to match the eyelines of the mother and her child.

Suppose that the child looks up at his mother towering over him and then you cut to a shot of her face. Rather than look downward at him, as your brain expects, she instead looks directly across the shot at an object at the height of her eyes. Your brain would automatically connect the two shots to make you wonder what she's looking at (another person in the room, for example). Because she's the taller of the two, her eyes should aim downward at him, at a spot that's as close to the same spot in the frame where his eyes were looking up in the previous shot.

A character who looks off-screen at another character should be looking at the spot where the other character would stand. If you *reverse* the shot (to show the other character), the second character's eyes should be focused on the spot where the first character is positioned. An eyeline that's shot incorrectly confuses viewers and causes them to "check out" of the scene. Any well-made TV show or film has examples of shooting proper eyelines. In one with incorrect eyelines, you cannot determine where characters are oriented in a scene.

To ensure matching eyelines, position an off-screen actor behind the camera so that the on-screen actor can look at that person and deliver her lines. Encourage actors to stand immediately off-camera, even when they aren't part of a shot, to help make eyelines match. It also helps a cast member with her performance to speak directly to their scene partner, even if the partner is standing off camera.

Following the 180-degree rule

The 180-degree rule is a critical guideline in how scenes are shot in a film or video. When you watch a movie in which two characters are speaking and the cut moves from one to the other, you're likely seeing the *180-degree rule* in action: It establishes the spatial relationship between characters or objects within a scene, specifically when the scene cuts between shots of them. Most viewers aren't aware of the 180-degree when it's followed; but when it isn't, viewers can become disoriented or confused about where characters are standing or sitting in relation to each other.

To use the 180-degree rule to construct a scene, imagine a straight line running down the middle of the characters, as shown in Figure 12-1. To avoid disorienting the audience, choose *one side* of the 180-degree line on which to shoot all your shots, and don't cross the line. Understanding this concept can be confusing, so we walk you through an example.

Rather than show each actor individually, such as in the bouncing-ball example in the earlier section "Shooting a Great-Looking Video," you can use the popular Hollywood technique known as the *over-the shoulder* shot. For a shot of the child in the example looking up at his mother, you place the camera over her left shoulder and aim it at the child so that part of her left shoulder and hair frame the shot of his face.

Cut back to the mother looking crossly at her child. If you place the camera over his *right* shoulder, pointing up at the mother, who is towering over him, his right shoulder and hair frame the shot of his mother looking cross. Then you cut back to the first shot over her *left* shoulder, of the child looking remorseful.

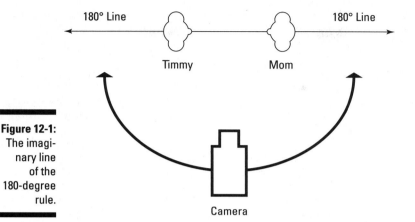

Figure 12-1:
The imaginary line of the 180-degree rule.

In the example, we stay on one side of the line, over the mother's left shoulder and over the child's right shoulder. If we had moved from her left to his left, we would have crossed the line and confused the audience, because they wouldn't know where the characters were standing in relation to each other.

In another example, you see a shot of a train flying down the tracks, moving from right to left in the frame. Cut to a person waiting for the train, and then cut back to the same train, except that now you've crossed the tracks and you're shooting from the other side. The train is now moving from left to right! Your brain believes that it's another train, heading directly for the first train, and suddenly you've made a disaster film!

The 180-degree rule has one exception: If the camera is moving, you're allowed to cross the imaginary line if the shot itself moves across it. Then the audience will understand why you switch sides in the next shot.

Shooting an interview

Shooting an interview is a fairly easy task. In the world of marketing videos, you'll likely shoot sit-down interviews.

Follow these steps to shoot a simple but professional-looking interview:

1. **Set up two chairs.** One is for the subject, and one is for the interviewer (who may be you). The subject should be seated.

2. **Set up your camera on a tripod.** Place the tripod to the side of your chair, facing your subject.

3. **Frame the subject.** Use a medium shot, moving upward from mid-torso or slightly closer.

4. **Light and mic your subject.** This topic is covered in Chapters 10 and 11.

5. **Have your subject look at you, not at the camera.** Looking into a camera lens tends to make a person self-conscious. You can conduct an excellent interview that has a conversational flow by having the subject speak to you. The camera serves to record the conversation you're having.

A person who is verbose the first time he answers an interview question may want to answer a question a second time, after having the opportunity to find the best wording for his answer. To avoid being heard asking the interview questions, you can edit yourself out, by having the subject repeat your question within the answer, as in this example:

You: "How long have you been the president of Smith Industries?"

The subject: "I have been president of Smith Industries for 40 years."

Encourage your subject to answer as simply as possible, always including the question within the answer, and you'll have a professional-looking, easy-to-edit interview that you can replicate with different subjects.

Shooting extra footage and B-roll

Watch any political thriller (especially one with Harrison Ford or Morgan Freeman as the commander-in-chief), and you're bound to see an impressive shot of the White House while ominous music plays in the background. Did you know that the shot wasn't filmed by the movie's director? It may not have even been filmed by anyone working on the movie. That shot of the White House is a classic example of an *establishing* shot (that shows you where you are) and is a member of the family of B-roll footage.

B-roll footage is supplementary, alternative footage that accompanies a documentary or TV news story. For example, in an interview with the president of Smith Industries, during an especially dry segment, you can *cut away* to show the Smith Industries factory floor or show workers picketing the president's office.

You can shoot and use B-roll to support the main storyline in your video. Film anything related to your business, or to the storyline of your video, and *intercut* (cut back and forth) it with your main (or *A),* storyline.

Story Comes First

When discussing video production, it's easy to lost in tech talk about equipment, technique, scheduling, and so on. But there's one element that trumps everything else. This should drive every decision you make about your video: Always tell a good story.

This is a simple but crucial attitude that should form the basis of every part of your production. For all the equipment, people, scripting, messaging and number-crunching that go into making your video, it all boils down to you telling your audience a good story. If you were at a party or dinner, and had an amazing tale to share, how would you tell it? How do you strip it down to just the best parts, leaving out the fat? How would you keep the audience on the edge of their seats, wanting to know what happens next? And, how do you get a reaction out of them, whether a laugh, a gasp, or, in the world of video marketing, a new customer clicking to your website?

Think of the movie Die Hard. When it came out, expectations were low – a B-grade action movie starring Bruce Willis, a TV actor. Yet it made a mountain of money, and begat sequels and its own genre: one man (or woman) versus the baddies. More importantly, it elevated action movies from cheeseball status to a new level of legitimacy. And all because of some of the best storytelling ever seen onscreen. It has a central character you root for, an unforgettable bad guy, juicy dialogue, suspense, humor, and even some genuinely moving moments. (Plus explosions. It's an action movie, after all.) Best of all, it gave the audience a fun experience while treating them like they were smart.

The best way to keep good storytelling in mind during your shoot is to put yourself in your audience's place. Imagine a complete stranger, someone that you want to engage, watching your video for the first time. They don't know anything about your company. Imagine they're also smart and that they'll click away from a bad or boring video. Your job: hook them and keep them hooked. And you have the incredible power of visual storytelling at your disposal.

It's a big responsibility, but also a wonderful position – you're in control of the audience experience. The story is yours to tell, and the reactions are yours to enjoy. A story-driven attitude will make it easier to decide where to put the camera, how to direct your actors, what dialogue to include, what lines to cut, and how to edit it later.

B-roll can be shot quickly, using your camera's internal mic. Shoot lots of footage until you find shots that blend well with the main part of your video. You can also shoot establishing shots of various buildings or areas where your scenes take place.

Capturing the perfect take — several times

Whether you're shooting a scripted scene or an interview, you probably won't get the perfect take the first time every time. Someone may flub a line or slam a door off-screen, a dog may begin barking, or a sudden rainstorm may interrupt a romantic picnic scene. Or, the "magic" just isn't happening right away, and your actors need a few takes to warm up and discover the best way to play the scene. In any case, if you have to do it again, shrug your shoulders, yell "Cut," and prepare everyone for another take.

Shooting multiple takes can be demanding because actors have to repeatedly speak the same lines and hit the same marks. However many takes you shoot of a scene, the acting always has to seem fresh. One way to achieve this goal is to let the actors vary their line readings slightly on every take. You can always revert to an earlier take if you don't like the revised version.

After you capture an excellent take, shoot a *safety* take immediately afterward. This extra version ensures that your editor has two good takes to work with, just in case something goes wrong with the footage during the postproduction process.

Part IV
Editing and Polishing Your Video

The 5th Wave   By Rich Tennant

"This should unstick the keys a little."

In this part . . .

Editing a marketing video requires patience, objectivity, and, sometimes, many late nights staring at your computer. In this part, we help you pick the right editing software, and then we explain how to use it. We show you how to add music and how to add attractive graphics, titles, and effects to make your marketing video stand out from the crowd.

Chapter 13

Choosing Your Editing Software

In This Chapter

▶ Choosing between a Mac and a PC

▶ Editing tools for your system

▶ Getting professional editing help

▶ Making sense of video formats and resolutions

*E*ven the simplest, modern editing tools are powerful applications. If you want to edit your own videos, expect to spend some time learning how to use your tool of choice. If you've ever worked with Word or PowerPoint, for example (from the Microsoft Office suite), you may recall that you spent some time learning how to use that program. Let's be honest: Most people discover new features and new ways of doing things in these programs all the time.

Choosing the right tool to edit a video can save you a lot of time. And a useful tool doesn't have to be expensive. In this chapter, we look at all the options that are affordable for growing businesses.

Selecting Your System

Editing programs are similar. They're sophisticated tools for content creation with a lot of powerful features. The best way to approach them is to first read about the basics, or you may take a class to get started. Then just dive in and complete a project. Most people become comfortable using their chosen editing tool during the first few hours.

Choosing the platform

The first item to choose in selecting an editing system is the hardware. Most people use the computer they already have, but if you happen to be in the market for a new system anyway, it's worth the time to consider your video editing needs.

Though Windows-based PCs still dominate the market, Apple's Mac computers have become more popular over the past few years. Because the Mac is particularly popular with the creative crowd, many people believe that an Apple computer is best for video editing as well. Though there's some truth to it, the difference isn't as big as it used to be.

Deciding whether the type of computer truly matters

The good news is that you can edit videos on virtually any modern PC or Mac. Your choice doesn't matter much; you can find some of the best editing programs in either computer family. But Macs and PCs have strengths in different areas.

Macs tend to be a bit easier to use and crash less often. The selection of video tools and related software, such as programs for sound and image editing, is excellent. Though most Mac-based programs are more robust and reliable than their PC counterparts, the differences aren't huge.

The Mac's biggest advantage for marketers is that it comes preinstalled with iMovie, a strong, entry-level editing application. iMovie's combination of ease of use and power is still unmatched in the PC world. If you have a Mac or are considering buying one, this excellent program helps you get started with video editing.

One strength of the PC world is its huge selection of different system configurations and editing applications. If you have specific needs, you're more likely to find the perfect solution in the PC world. On the other hand, more complexity is involved in making a PC-based editing system work perfectly simply because many different components come from different vendors. In contrast, Apple sells a complete solution that works out of the box but offers fewer specialized options.

If you already have a modern PC or Mac, just go with it and don't worry too much about your system configuration. You will find a solution that works for you. If you run into bottlenecks, you can always tune your system later.

Determining how much horsepower you need

Video editing is one of the most demanding types of applications you can run on a PC or Mac. Editing programs need a lot of CPU power and storage space.

How much horsepower you need depends on the sophistication of the tasks you have in mind. You can do some basic editing even on older laptops. But most people nowadays want to edit high-definition (HD) video, apply visual effects to their videos, and even work with multiple audio channels. If you want to do this kind of work on an older PC, you need a lot of patience — you may spend hours staring at your screen, waiting for your PC to finally render your clips with the latest effects you've just applied.

To edit videos efficiently, work with a modern computer — a system that's less than 2 years old. A good editing system should also have a number of other features:

- ✔ **A modern dual-core or quad-core CPU:** More speed is always better.
- ✔ **At least 4 gigabytes of RAM:** More is better, and it saves time.
- ✔ **A hard drive with 500GB of space or more:** Video files are typically large, and your disk fills up quickly. Alternatively, buy an external drive with a USB 2.0 or FireWire connection.
- ✔ **A hard drive that has, ideally, a rotation speed of 7200 revolutions per minute (rpm) or faster:** A slower disk still works, but you need a bit more patience.

Though you no longer need a super-tricked-out, high-end system for video editing, having a faster computer saves time.

Mac tools

The selection of editing tools on the Mac is somewhat smaller than on the PC, but that isn't necessarily bad news because of the high quality of Mac-based programs:

- ✔ **Apple** itself provides two industry-leading editing applications:
  - *iMovie:* Entry level
  - *Final Cut Pro:* Professional level
- ✔ **Adobe,** the market leader in creative software, offers a full line of tools for the Mac.

iMovie

If you have a Mac, you already have iMovie. This powerful, little editing application comes preinstalled on every new Mac.

Upgrade to the latest version of iMovie, if you can. If your version is older, you can buy the current edition on the Apple App Store for about $15, or on DVD for $49 (together with the rest of the iLife suite of programs). It's more than worth the price.

iMovie covers virtually everything you need for normal video editing, and it comes supplied with helpful templates for impressive titles and neat visual effects.

The main drawback of iMovie compared to professional-grade applications is that it can deal with only a single video track and a single track of background sound. You can use background music and a voice-over narration track at the same time, but using more elements isn't possible. This restriction isn't a big deal for most videos, though it can be limiting on ambitious productions.

A good companion product for iMovie is Garage Band, which comes preinstalled on Macs as well. It lets you put together soundtracks for your videos and provides some useful background music tracks that you can use immediately.

Final Cut Pro

Final Cut Pro is the professional-grade editing application from Apple that covers most capabilities that an editor needs. It's used by many professionals, including such legendary editors as Walter Murch (*The Godfather, Apocalypse Now*).

In 2011, Apple released Final Cut Pro X, an entirely new version of its product that received mixed reviews from professional editors. Though it's much faster and easier to use, it lacks some of the more exotic features that editors in the TV and movie industry expect. Don't worry: Most people don't even notice these small drawbacks.

For business users, Final Cut Pro X is a major upgrade step from iMovie. Its user interface is quite similar to iMovie, and old iMovie projects can be imported directly. The additional power of Final Cut Pro X blows away its younger sibling, but at $299 it's still affordable. It offers much more flexibility, such as unlimited video and audio tracks, many more visual effects, a feature-rich footage management system, and sophisticated audio editing. Figure 13-1 shows the program's rich user interface.

Figure 13-1: An editing project in Final Cut Pro X.

If you're going with Apple editing programs, start with iMovie, and then upgrade to Final Cut Pro X when you run into limitations.

Adobe Premiere

Apple's primary competitor on the Mac platform is Adobe and its Premiere editing programs.

Premiere Elements

The entry-level Adobe editing program is Premiere Elements, an application designed for consumers and business users. At $99, it's quite affordable.

The advantages of using Premiere Elements over the free Apple iMovie program are that it

- ✔ Supports multiple video and audio tracks

    The additional power is useful if you edit more complex projects, such as footage shot with multiple cameras simultaneously.

- ✔ Offers a more sophisticated way to organize large collections of raw footage

- ✔ Provides more flexibility in dealing with photos and other images

- ✔ Can generate DVDs and Blu-ray discs directly from the editing application

Premiere Pro

Premiere Pro, the Adobe program for professional video editors, offers all the same professional features of Final Cut Pro X. Some editors like it better because

- ✔ Its user interface is a little more optimized for the way big-time professionals traditionally work.

- ✔ It has broader support for the file formats that professional-level cameras produce.

- ✔ It integrates (as part of Adobe Creative Suite) particularly well with the other products in this package, such as Photoshop and After Effects.

At approximately $800, Premiere Pro is significantly pricier than its competition. In terms of features that a business user may need, you may find it difficult to justify the additional cost versus Final Cut Pro X. But if you're already familiar with other Adobe products, or if you need some of the specific features that Premiere Pro offers, Premiere Pro can still be a good choice. If you already own other versions of Adobe Creative Suite, cheaper upgrade options are available.

Windows tools

Dozens of editing programs of all sophistication levels are available on the Windows PC platform. In this section, we look at the most popular ones.

Windows Live Movie Maker

Much like iMovie on the Mac, the free editing tool Windows Live Movie Maker covers basic video editing needs. It lets you quickly import footage and pictures, arrange and trim clips, add music, and apply basic visual effects and titles.

The current version of Movie Maker runs only on PCs running Windows Vista or Windows 7. You can download Movie Maker for free at the Microsoft website: www.microsoft.com/download. Previous, more limited, versions were part of the Windows XP operating system and should already be preinstalled on older PCs.

Movie Maker is a helpful way to get your feet wet with video editing. Most people working on advanced video projects quickly run into its limitations, such as having only one background audio track, one video track, and limited visual effects. Furthermore, its particular way of handling the start and stop points of clips isn't ideal for precision editing.

Adobe Premiere

The people behind Photoshop also provide their video editing program, Premiere, for Windows PCs. The Premiere version you need depends on your goals.

Premiere can work with multiple video and audio tracks, which allows for the easy arrangement of footage and complex narrative structures. That's an important advantage over the free Windows Movie Maker.

Premiere Elements

Premiere Elements is a strong editing application for consumers and business users.

Compared to the free Windows Live Movie Maker, Premiere Elements packs in a ton of features that let you edit your videos in a much more sophisticated way. It organizes footage more intelligently, it can stabilize shaky footage, and it comes supplied with a huge selection of transitions and visual effects. It can even handle green-screen effects and animated graphics.

At $99, Premiere Elements is an appropriate choice for people who want to do advanced video editing and also want to avoid the cost and complexity of the pro-level tools.

Premiere Pro

We discuss Premiere Pro, Premiere Element's larger sibling, in the earlier Mac section "Premiere Pro." The Windows version is largely identical, and it's a highly respected tool for professionals. Premiere Pro can make a lot of sense for people who get started with Premiere Elements and soon need more power for advanced projects.

The particular strengths of Premiere Pro are its

- ✔ Broad support for different file formats
- ✔ Fast performance
- ✔ Wide selection of third-party, visual effects plug-ins

Professionals also like the sophisticated workflow options and countless output formats that Premiere Pro supports.

All this performance comes at a price: Premiere Pro alone costs $800, but you can also buy it as part of Adobe Creative Suite, which costs about $1,700 and adds After Effects, an animation program, as well as Photoshop, the well-known image-manipulation software.

Sony Vegas Movie Studio

Sony's aggressively priced Vegas Movie Studio HD program is an interesting alternative to Adobe products, positioned between Premiere Elements and Premiere Pro. At a list price of only $99, it offers features that are comparable to some of the best editing programs on the market. If you're looking for the most bang for your buck, Vegas is worth a serious look.

The biggest drawbacks to the Vegas Movie Studio HD program are that

- ✔ It doesn't have with the same broad support base as its more popular competitors.
- ✔ It doesn't integrate as well with popular applications such as Photoshop.
- ✔ Its user interface is more old-fashioned than that of the competition.
- ✔ Not many third-party effects are available.

Avid Studio

Avid is generally considered to be the company that invented modern video editing on the PC. The company is the market leader in high-end production tools for movie studios and TV stations. When you turn on your TV or go to the movies, you're likely watching material that was edited on Avid software.

Avid also offers consumer-grade tools, such as Avid Studio. This product (formerly Pinnacle Studio) is significantly more sophisticated than Premiere Elements. It boasts unlimited video and audio tracks, animated titles, broad format support, sophisticated audio editing, and a ton of professional-level special effects.

The $170 price for this feature set is reasonable, and the product even comes with a green-screen backdrop and software for Blue-ray disc authoring. Avid Studio is a good choice for people who want to do frequent, sophisticated editing and are willing to endure a bit of a learning curve.

CyberLink PowerDirector

Another tool competing with Premiere Elements is CyberLink PowerDirector, priced similarly to Premiere Elements at $99. The PowerDirector feature set is comparable to other products in this market segment, but its performance tends to be somewhat faster, and its user interface is nice and clean.

The drawback to using PowerDirector is its somewhat weaker media organization functionality, which can be a problem for people with a lot of footage. But thanks to its speed, it's one of the best programs on the market.

Online tools

Increasingly more software is moving online, or, as the IT industry likes to call it, into "the cloud." Many people already use web-based e-mail, online word processing and spreadsheets, and even online bookkeeping software.

Video editing is tougher to move online because video files are generally huge. One hour of high-definition (HD) video footage can occupy as much as 12GB of storage space or more, and files of this size are time-consuming to transfer to cloud-based services.

Still, online tools can work well for small video projects with only limited amounts of footage. If you want to put together a brief clip, online tools can help you avoid the hassle of installing and learning to use a full-blown editing program.

YouTube editing tools

The online video market leader YouTube provides a wide range of nifty tools that can help you put together a short video quickly.

The YouTube Edit Video feature is available as a button next to every one of your YouTube videos. It isn't a full video editing program, but it's a handy way to quickly optimize existing videos. The Edit Video button lets you

- ✔ Trim long clips.
- ✔ Stabilize shaky footage.
- ✔ Apply basic effects.
- ✔ Apply free background music tracks.

Read Chapter 17 for details about the Edit Video feature.

Another, entirely different, tool is the YouTube Video Editor (see `www.you tube.com/editor`). This simple editing program lets you

✔ Trim and assemble your existing YouTube clips.

✔ Apply background music and transitions.

✔ Add basic titles.

Think of the Video Editor as a limited version of a program such as iMovie or Windows Live Movie Maker. Figure 13-2 shows the Video Editor's easy-to-use interface. If you only want to assemble a video from a small number of clips, it's a useful little tool. It's also a nice way to get started with basic video editing.

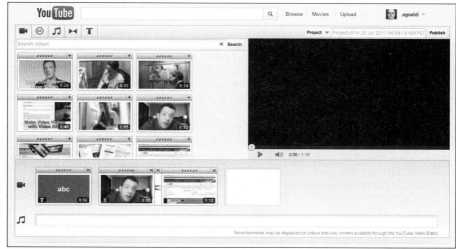

Figure 13-2: The YouTube online video editor.

In addition, YouTube works with a number of partner companies to offer several more sophisticated, online editing tools: `www.youtube.com/create`. These tools, which are free to try on basic projects, typically charge for more advanced features.

The following tools make sense for businesses:

✔ **One True Media:** This tool tries to make editing simpler by sticking to a step-by-step procedure that walks you through the process of putting together a video. It works well for small and simple video projects, but is somewhat cumbersome for more serious editing and for fine-tuning videos.

- **Stupeflix Video Maker:** Based on a number of predefined templates that let you quickly put together pictures and short video clips in a good-looking, collage-type video, Stupeflix Video Maker helps you produce quick results, though it's fairly limited for real business videos.

- **WeVideo:** This full-featured, online, video editing program, which works a lot like iMovie, offers a flexible and fast editing timeline and many features, such as multiple audio tracks, that you would normally expect in professional video editing applications. WeVideo is likely the closest thing to a full-blown video editing application in the cloud.

Animoto and other automated services

Because making a video is time-consuming, several software makers have tried to create automated ways to edit videos.

The popular service Animoto (`www.animoto.com`) lets you assemble, from your pictures and video clips, attractive video collages full of special effects. The amount of work you need to invest in this task is minimal. You choose a style template, select the pictures and videos you want to add and a music track, and you're done. Animoto can even pull down your pictures from Facebook, Flickr, and other image-sharing sites.

Several other services work in the same way: Magisto, Muvee, Stupeflix, and more. They all offer similar features but differ slightly in the richness of their style templates.

Letting a machine do all the editing work for you sounds tempting, but in practice the results are quite limited for the purposes of marketers. Ask yourself whether you would let a machine write your marketing text or design your collateral. Probably not. You know that the results wouldn't be satisfying. The same concept applies to video marketing: Video editing is all about storytelling, and a machine can't understand and tell a story. Good marketing focuses on differentiation and standing out in a crowd. Using the same standard template as everyone else doesn't let you do that.

The clips generated by Animoto and its competitors may look nice on a superficial level, but in most cases they don't make the grade for marketing purposes. Use these services to put together nice collages of your vacation pictures, but don't expect them to work for you business needs.

Breaking the Ice

Like most creative skills, video editing is both fun and challenging. Though the tools you need in order to engage in it are becoming increasingly simpler, they still require you to invest some time to learn how to use them.

Knowing How to Get Started

At first, the business of editing video may seem confusing and somewhat scary. The process has many technical expressions to understand, many software features to use, and many concepts to grasp. The best way to deal with this complexity is to simply dive in. The first steps in video editing are fairly easy, and you can build your skills step by step.

Reading books and watching DVDs

As a starting point for editing video, you may want to read a book about your editing software of choice. A book can help you understand the basic concepts that your editing application is built on, and it can provide a quick overview of all its features. In addition, good books have step-by-step guides for more advanced features.

Several books in the *For Dummies* series explain how to use some of the most popular editing programs, and we highly recommend them.

Apple and Adobe products generally have the biggest selection of good instruction books available, though some of the less-popular editing applications aren't covered as thoroughly. Before you decide on a particular editing program, look at what kind of information and support are available for it.

When you buy a book about your editing software, make sure that it covers the version you have. Programs can change quite dramatically from version to version, and a step-by-step guide for the previous edition is largely useless for the editing application you have.

Courses also are available on DVD. These audiovisual guides are helpful for your first steps and to quickly find out about the overall process of editing. But DVDs are largely useless for step-by-step instructions, so in most cases you probably should find a book and a DVD about your editing software. The amount of time you can save is easily worth the money you spend.

Every modern editing application comes supplied with a built-in Help function. Modern Help systems are fairly well structured and provide you with context-sensitive support about the more advanced features of your editing software. It's typically the quickest way to find a basic level of help when you're stuck.

Taking classes

Because video editing software is fairly complex and continually changing, taking a class is a useful way to get started with the help of an expert. Good classes not only walk you through the features of editing software but also teach you how to use the software in the context of a real-life video project. A class is typically a much more effective way to see how to use a program (or general editing software).

Here are a few options for classes:

- ✔ ROARing Video (Kevin and Matt's company) offers full-day workshops that walk you through the entire process of creating a compelling business video. They teach everything from story creation to editing. Check the website `http://roaringvideo.com` for schedules.

- ✔ Some film schools, art schools and community colleges offer video production courses and workshops to the general public. It may be somewhat time consuming to find the right class in your area, but you can gain access to highly qualified film school instructors at an attractive price.

- ✔ If you're on a Mac, your local Apple store can help you get started. Apple offers workshops related to its software products; one-on-one sessions (available via the One To One program, which costs $99 for an entire year) for focused expert support; and even support programs designed for small businesses.

Attempting your first test project

After some preparation, there's no better way to get up to speed in video editing than to simply try it. Select a topic for a test project, and try to put together a simple video about it.

If you have some video footage from your last vacation or family event, that's a good place to start, because your family can then enjoy a watchable, well-edited video. Or if you want to dive right into marketing-oriented videos, shoot some quick footage about your business and use existing pictures.

Avoid overthinking your first project. Your goal isn't to produce a masterwork of cinematic storytelling — it's to explore the features of your editing tool and experience the basic process of editing.

Your first project should follow these guidelines because you find these elements in most serious video projects:

- ✔ Import, view, and organize multiple clips of raw video footage.
- ✔ Use pictures and graphical elements, such as a logo, in your video.
- ✔ Experiment with different title styles.
- ✔ Try variations of background music to see how music can influence the mood of a video.
- ✔ Explore basic visual effects, such as transitions between scenes.
- ✔ Record a voiceover narration track.

Make a short video first, maybe a couple of minutes long.

Finding professional editing help

Professional video editors go to school for years to learn their craft. Even talented amateurs are unlikely to ever reach the level of artful storytelling that a professional editor can provide. Besides, video editing is time-consuming. A professional can produce a good snippet in a fraction of the time you need.

If you want to achieve the highest quality while still seeing a result quickly, consider using professional help in the editing process. Professional editors know how to use their tools in their sleep, understand how to best structure a video to get the story across, and know many tricks that make a video shine.

When you work with an editor, listen to her advice. Some of the best editing tricks and practices can sometimes seem counterintuitive to the layperson. For example, many people believe that videos benefit from the addition of tons of fancy visual effects, but experienced editors know that these gimmicks often distract from the story that a video is trying to tell. Convey your marketing goals as clearly as possible to your editor, but trust her with translating these goals into the language of video.

Choosing a video editing service

To find turnkey ("do it for me") editing support, look for companies that specialize in editing videos for you. Some also provide professional videographers, if you need one, but they can work with existing footage in any case.

In contrast to freelance professionals, editing services provide you with much more structure and help in achieving the result you want. Though freelance editors and local video production houses specialize in the editing process itself, good business video editing services have marketing experts and online specialists on staff as well, to will help you get the most benefit from your video marketing initiative. The service company looks at *all* aspects of your project, not just the purely video aspects.

Andreas' and Bettina's company Pixability offers a service for businesses that produces polished marketing videos and helps publish and promote them online. Customers can upload their own footage, or Pixability can provide a camera crew. A professional editing team then creates one or more videos for you, depending on your marketing goals. Finally, Pixability's online marketing experts support you in publishing your videos to all relevant channels, and they provide you with software to help you promote your message and track your results. For details, go to www.pixability.com.

Working with freelance editors

Many video editors work as freelancers. They sign up for large productions at TV stations or film production companies, but between large gigs, they often have time to do smaller projects.

The best place to find freelance editors is online. You can find editors on craigslist (`http://craigslist.org`) in the TV/Film/Video jobs section. Other helpful websites are at `www.mandy.com`, `www.elance.com`, and `www.odesk.com`.

When you post a job ad, be sure to describe your project as precisely as possible. Video editing is quite a diversified field, and an overly simple ad, such as "Seeking video editor for marketing project," invites many responses unrelated to the ones you're looking for. Describe the kind of video you want to make, how long you want it to be, what material you already have and which special requirements (for example, animated graphics) you have. Though most freelance editors have their own equipment, to avoid misunderstandings, specify clearly that you providing no infrastructure.

Editors work for vastly different hourly rates, depending on their skill and experience level. Taking the cheapest route typically isn't a good idea because less experienced editors tend to work more slowly. You may be able to negotiate a fixed price for the entire project, but this strategy requires you to specify exactly what you want. Always leave room in your budget for unforeseen changes — a good number is 10 to 15 percent of your total editing budget.

The big question is, of course, how much money to include in your editing budget. If you're making a relatively basic, and short, marketing video from an intermediate editor, expect to pay a few hundred dollars, to as much as $1,000, for editing. If you want an expert editor who can create special effects and who has advanced editing skills, your budget can stretch into the low four figures. The higher number of elements you have and the more footage you have, the higher your costs.

Before selecting a video editor, always ask for a demo reel. Serious editors have online demos that highlight their previous work. Don't be dazzled by fancy special effects; look for a style that would work for the kind of video you're planning. Someone who normally cuts only music videos may have difficulty adapting to a style that's more suitable to a corporate video.

Handling file formats, resolution, and conversion

Video used to be supplied on magnetic tape. Though it was available in several formats, such as VHS and Betacam, figuring out what you had was fairly simple. The digital world has brought about a dramatic cost reduction (video professionals no longer have to own a VCR for every cassette format), but it also brought about more complexity. Dozens of different digital video file formats are now used in the industry.

Fortunately, modern editing programs handle much of this mess for you. Almost all editing tools handle the most common dozen or so formats. But if you work with video footage shot by someone else, you still may occasionally encounter an exotic format. That's why you should understand the basic principles of using video file formats.

Sorting out the file formats

Digital video produces extremely large files. These files would be even larger if not for the heavy compression that's applied to the original video signal. Video compression uses some fancy calculations to squeeze high-quality moving pictures and sound into files that are as small as possible. To give you an idea, your video files would be between 5 and 50 times larger without compression.

The compression process is managed by a coder/decoder, or *codec*. This piece of software squeezes the video into a smaller digital format when it's recorded and decompresses it again when it's being watched. Because a codec typically isn't compatible with other codecs, you can't watch a video recorded via codec A on a device that supports only codec B.

Some of the most popular video codecs are

- ✔ Apple ProRes
- ✔ Digital Video (DV)
- ✔ H.264 (a more modern version of MPEG-4)
- ✔ MPEG-4
- ✔ Windows Media (WMV)

The data generated by these codecs is stored in a file that contains additional information, such as the title and description of the video, synchronization markers that sync audio and video, subtitles, and more.

You see these file formats, or *container* formats, on your PC or Mac. These container formats and their file endings are the most popular:

- ✔ Flash Video (`.flv`)
- ✔ MP4 (`.mp4`)
- ✔ MPEG (`.mpg`)
- ✔ QuickTime (`.mov`)
- ✔ Windows Media (`.avi` or `.wmv`)

Don't let yourself become confused: Container files can contain **several** different codecs. For example, a QuickTime file can contain a video in Apple ProRes, DV, or H.264 format. Each format can be matched with a number of audio codec formats, such as AAC, AIFF, or MP3.

In other words, if someone asks you for the format of your video files and you respond "AVI" or "MOV," the person doesn't know much more about the format than before he asked. Any container file type can contain any of dozens of different codecs.

The only way to determine what you have is to open the video file in a player application, such as QuickTime Player or Windows Media Player. Then use the menu command that shows you details about the file. In QuickTime, it's Window⇨Show Movie Inspector. In Windows Media Player, it's File⇨Properties.

Figure 13-3 shows you what a typical detail description looks like. Under the Format label, you can see which video codec (H.264) is being used and see how the audio track is encoded (Linear PCM). These details are important if you want to work with someone to process your video files.

Figure 13-3:
Format
details of a
video file in
QuickTime
Player.

Understanding frame rates, resolution, and data rates

Video files have a number of characteristics that determine their picture quality and size. Mixing files with different characteristics in the same video project is difficult, so you should know what you have.

Figure 13-3 shows these important details about the video file:

 ✔ **Resolution:** The picture size of the video. The traditional TV resolution is 720 x 480 pixels. High-definition resolutions are either 1280 x 720 pixels (referred to as *720p*) or 1920 x 1080 pixels (*1080i/p*). Mixing resolutions in the same video project is possible, but footage must be scaled to the target resolution, which can be time-consuming and affect picture quality.

✔ **Frame rate:** Specifies how many individual pictures (frames) per second the video contains. The standard is 30 frames per second, but some formats have 60 frames or 24 frames. Occasionally, you see odd-looking numbers for frame rates, such as 29.97 or 23.98. The reason is that the American TV standard uses these slightly reduced frames rate for obscure technical reasons, though they're roughly equivalent to the rounded-up number. Mixing frame rates in the same video project is possible using the latest video editing applications, but doing so requires a lot of computing power and can lead to unwanted effects.

✔ **Data rate:** Most video codecs can compress video to different degrees. A strong compression rate produces smaller files but reduces picture quality. The data rate shows how much data per second the video file consumes. The higher the data rate, the higher the quality. But the number also depends on the resolution of your video file. The higher the resolution, the higher the data rate must be, in order to provide adequate quality. For example, a high-definition clip with a resolution of 1920 x 1080 pixels that's compressed using the H.264 codec looks quite good at a data rate of 25 megabits per second. The same clip at a data rate of 5 megabits per second still looks good but loses quite a bit of detail. At a data rate of 1 megabit per second, everyone can immediately spot the lesser quality.

When you export video files from an editing program, you can often choose the resolution, frame rate and data rate. Don't change the resolution and frame rate, however, because you may lose quality in the necessary transformation process. Specify a relatively high data rate for your master output file. You can always further compress a video file later, but you can't make up for the quality hit caused by using a smaller data rate.

Converting formats

Modern editing programs can work with most widely used video file formats. However, if you use footage in a more exotic format — material provided by someone else, for example — you may encounter roadblocks. Your editing application may not be able to work with unusual formats directly.

In this case, convert these files to a more standard format by using a video conversion program. Your editing program or DVD creation software may even have one already.

You can find many free or inexpensive conversion programs. If you have to deal with an exotic video file format, the time savings are definitely worth the price. On Windows PCs, AVS Video Converter and Any Video Converter Pro are good choices. On the Mac, AVCWare Video Converter and Wondershare Mac Video Converter are recommended products.

You may even be able to avoid paying: The free programs MPEG Streamclip (`www.squared5.com`) and HandBrake (`http://handbrake.fr`) run on both platforms and should solve most conversion problems. Though they may be slightly more difficult to use, they typically get the job done.

Chapter 14

Planning First, Cutting Second

In This Chapter

▶ Sharpening the focus

▶ Creating the story

▶ Polishing your video

*E*diting is the art of telling a story using video footage, pictures, and sound. Many people think of film and video editing as "cutting out unwanted scenes," but that's similar to saying that writing text consists of only omitting unwanted words.

Hollywood has many stories about the importance of outstanding editing. For example, the first cut of the original *Star Wars* movie was rumored to be quite bad — test audiences hated the film. George Lucas, the director, switched to another editing team who recut the film completely under tremendous time pressure. The movie soon became one of the biggest successes in Hollywood history, winning an Academy Award for editing, among many other awards.

On its most basic level, *editing* consists of assembling the best scenes into a coherent film. It sounds simple enough, but often the story of a video changes entirely (or is even simply uncovered) during the editing process. The final edit has many layers: pictures, dialogue, sound, music, special effects, continuity, rhythm, and pacing. In a good edit, all these elements fuse to tell a story that captures the audience.

Editing is often called *the invisible art* because the best editing isn't noticed by the audience.

Even when you plan a video shoot meticulously, surprises and changes take place during editing. An idea that seems outstanding at first may not work in the final video. On the other hand, unexpected moments of excellence may show up in your footage to give your video an extra boost.

Editing can make or break your video. This chapter tells you how to approach this essential process. We use the Apple iMovie editing software in our examples, though other editing programs work similarly.

Determining Whether You Need to Edit

Thanks to digital technology, you don't always need to use a full-blown editing program (such as the ones we describe in Chapter 13) to make your video presentable. In some cases, you can squeak by with much simpler tools to come up with usable marketing content.

Recognizing videos that need no editing

Some types of video can stand on their own with no significant amount of editing. You can prepare these types of video for publishing with a minimal amount of trimming:

- ✔ **Talking-head:** A talking-head video shows a person simply speaking into the camera to make an announcement or to explain a concept or an issue. This technique isn't terribly interesting visually, but it can be effective if the speaker has interesting material. If your talent can complete the statement in one take, you typically don't even need to edit.

- ✔ **Speech and presentation:** Sometimes, you can tape a representative of your company or an outside expert presenting a relevant topic at an event. You can typically use this footage without editing if the presentation is brief.

    Presentations on video tend to be less interesting than the ones you see in person.

- ✔ **Simple product demonstrations:** A salesperson, or even a CEO, may be able to give a killer product demonstration in only one take. Sometimes, a charismatic salesperson can be more convincing than a slickly produced product video. A competent camera person can show details of the product by zooming in or moving the camera.

A simple product demonstration video, which tends to not look fancy, works best for loyal customers who already know that you sell quality goods or services and who want to know more about your new products.

Even in videos that need no editing, you may want to add intros and outros — for example, with your logo at the beginning and a call to action at the end. You can do this with online editing tools, such as the YouTube video editor (described in Chapter 13). Some online, video marketing tools, such as the Pixability Caffeine software, provide functionality that automatically adds intros and outros to existing clips, saving you editing time. Hosting providers, including Brightcove and Wistia, let you add intros and outros to hosted videos by using either the *pre-roll* or *post-roll* feature, but this strategy doesn't work if you want to post videos to YouTube or other public sharing sites.

Trimming your video

Clips often tend to be too long. If you want to use a one-take video, you can simply trim off unwanted pieces at the beginning and the end. Fortunately, trimming a clip on your computer is fairly easy. The best tool depends on the platform you use:

 ✔ **On the Mac:** Mac users already have QuickTime X, a preinstalled media player that has basic editing features.

   If you want to trim a clip, open the video file in QuickTime X, and then choose the Edit➪Trim command. A timeline showing the entire clip appears. Drag the yellow handles to mark the start and end of the clip, and then click the Trim button. The resulting clip can be saved or exported for use on YouTube or on your website. Figure 14-1 shows how to use the trim function in QuickTime X.

Figure 14-1:
The trim function in QuickTime Player.

 ✔ **On the PC:** PC users can select from a variety of video processing tools that provide the trimming function.

   An easy way is to use Windows Movie Maker (described in Chapter 13). This simple editing application is free, and it works well if you want to trim only a few clips.

 ✔ **On a smartphone:** To record video, you may be able to trim on the spot. The Apple iPhone has a built-in trimming feature. To access it on the iPhone, shoot the video, press the Pictures icon on the iPhone home screen to open the camera roll, and then select the Camera Roll album. When you click the video, you see the timeline at the top. As in

QuickTime, you drag the yellow handles to mark the start and end of the clip and then click the Trim button when you're done.

Save the trimmed video as a new clip, or else you lose the rest of your footage.

Some simple video programs even let you assemble multiple clips into a longer clip. For example, QuickTime X lets you add a clip to the end of the current clip by choosing the Edit⇨Add Clip to End command. On a PC, use Windows Movie Maker and simply drag and drop the clips to the storyboard. This method works for assembling two or three clips, but don't expect it to replace an editing program. As soon as you want to move beyond the simplest trimming level (and save time in the end), invest in quality editing software.

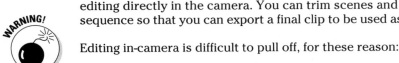

Editing in-camera

For short and simple videos, you may be able to edit *in-camera*, by shooting scenes in the exact order and at the exact length you need in the final video. This technique requires quite a bit of preparation: Determine the exact story-line, the shots you need, and their sequence.

For additional assistance, some digital video cameras let you perform basic editing directly in the camera. You can trim scenes and even change their sequence so that you can export a final clip to be used as a presentable video.

Editing in-camera is difficult to pull off, for these reason:

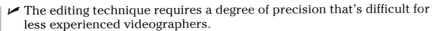

- ✔ The editing technique requires a degree of precision that's difficult for less experienced videographers.
- ✔ Errors are difficult to fix.

Shooting digital footage is cheap, and modern editing programs are easy to use, so you have little reason to even use the in-camera editing technique, unless you're under an extremely tight deadline.

If you work with a smartphone or a tablet, you can perform basic editing tasks using apps such as iMovie for the iPhone or iPad. This method quickly becomes tedious, however, so don't try any fancy editing tricks.

Preparing for the Edit

An efficient, effective editing process is all about preparation. And that preparation starts with shooting your footage.

Shooting for the edit

The low cost of using a modern digital camera eliminates any concern about shooting additional footage. That's why people tend to shoot way too much footage, which makes the editing process more time consuming. On the other hand, an essential shot may be missed in the hustle and bustle of the shooting day, making the editor's life much more difficult.

Keep the editing process in mind whenever you shoot video. Shooting short and simple videos may even remove the need to do much editing.

To shoot footage that makes editing easier, follow these guidelines:

- ✔ **Go on location with a well-prepared shot list.** This list briefly describes every shot you want to take. If you prepare a storyboard (as we explain in Chapter 4), you can use it as the foundation.

- ✔ **Don't leave the shooting location without checking your shot list and ensuring that you got all the shots you wanted.** Reshooting is much more expensive than adding another few minutes to shoot the missing scene.

- ✔ **When shooting a planned and scripted scene, start the camera briefly before the action starts, and stop it a few seconds after the scene ends.** Leave at least three seconds of space at both ends, and don't let the camera run needlessly. Following these suggestions saves you time later, when you're sifting through footage.

- ✔ **When shooting documentary footage of an event that you can't fully control, err on the side of shooting too much footage and letting the camera roll.** Missing an important scene is more painful than sifting through a lot of footage later.

- ✔ **Shoot a sufficient amount of b-roll footage.** This supplemental footage of surroundings or the location itself is valuable during the editing process. (We discuss the b-roll later in this chapter.)

Understanding the ideal length of an online video

An edited video is always shorter than its original footage because you select the scenes you truly want to use — which begs the question, "How long should an online marketing video be"?

The correct answer is "It depends." Many people believe that the attention span of an online audience is short and that videos for online marketing therefore should be less than three or four minutes long. It isn't a bad rule of thumb, but the ideal length depends on what your video is trying to achieve.

Research from the Pixability Online Video Grader (www.onlinevideo grader.com) shows that the most popular business-oriented YouTube channels don't stick to the three- or four-minute rule. The best video marketers use a wide range of video lengths, starting at short 30-second clips and progressing to educational pieces that are 20 minutes long. Figure 14-2 shows differing lengths for both successful and less successful channels.

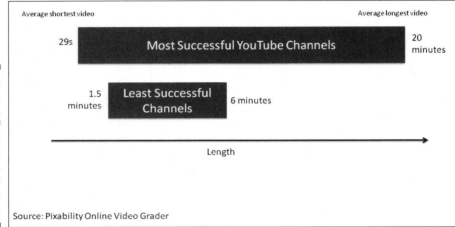

Figure 14-2:
The average video lengths of successful and less-than-successful YouTube channels.

The proper length for your video depends on its goals and on the mindset of your audience. Think about where your target audience stands in the buying process. To grab viewers' attention, you have to send the right type of message and at the right time:

✔ Somebody who already likes your product, and who wants to know its details in order to evaluate it, is happy to sit through a long product demonstration.

✔ For somebody hearing about you for the first time, even 60 seconds may be too long.

Don't be boring, and don't waste your audience's time. You can easily fall in love with your own video and make it longer than necessary because you simply can't get enough of it. As a rule, make it as short as possible. Every scene in your video should have a good reason to exist.

Logging your footage

After you return from a shooting location, follow these general steps to log your footage — the most important step in preparing for the editing process:

1. **Download the footage to your computer.** Using a modern camera, this process can be completed quickly — just copy the digital video files from the camera. Shooting on tape is more time-consuming because you have to let the tape run so that your editing program can capture all footage digitally. Refer to your camera's instruction manual to find out how.

2. **Import the footage into your editing program.** You may already have completed this step if you downloaded the footage using your editing software, but in other cases, you first have to import the footage manually.

3. **Organize your clips.** After you have a bunch of clips that cover different parts of your project, start by organizing them to better see what you have. Group clips that are related to the same scene. Editing programs offer different methods to help, such as folders or "bins" in which you can store clips, labels and "tags" that you can assign to clips, or "events" that group related clips. Figure 14-3 shows clips organized into events in iMovie.

Figure 14-3: Groups of clips, organized into events.

4. **Watch your footage.** Review all your clips to determine what you have. If you have a lot of footage, there's no way to avoid this time-consuming step.

5. **Remove unwanted material.** If you have clips that are clearly unusable, remove them immediately. Don't delete them — just store them in a folder labeled Junk in your editing program or in your computer's file system. Some editing programs can "reject" clips, by hiding them from your clip list while storing them in the system. Store even unwanted clips in a safe spot because sometimes a clip that looks like junk now can come in handy later.

6. **Take notes.** The best way to find your footage quickly during editing is to take the time to take notes about every clip. Add a few simple words about the content of the clip and its level of quality. Most advanced editing programs even let you take notes directly in the program so that you can later search for keywords quickly.

If you have interview clips or talking-head clips and you want to find a sound bite later, take more extensive notes about the topic discussed in a particular clip.

7. **Mark the best clips.** If you have multiple takes of a scene, mark the one you think is best. Many editing programs let you use a special Favorites functionality, or you can simply make a mark in your notes. Also mark b-roll footage that you think looks good, and make notes of the best sound bites in interview clips.

Logging your footage may seem like a tedious and time-consuming process, but investing time in it pays off later. During editing, you can waste a lot of time hunting for a particular clip that you somehow recall but didn't mark properly.

Revisiting your script

After you're familiar with the footage you've shot, review it systematically with your script in mind. Now it's time to find out whether the footage lets you tell your painstakingly crafted story. (Chapter 4 explains how to write a good script.) Check for these elements:

- ✔ **Usable (if not excellent) footage for every scene in your script:** Careful logging of your footage pays off now because it's impossible to remember the details of innumerable clips of raw footage.

- ✔ **Filmed material that may not be in your script but can add value to your video:** Sometimes, actors engage in brilliant improvisation, or interview partners say something brilliant and unexpected, or you capture a heartwarming moment on camera. Think about how to fit these particularly remarkable scenes into your storyline.

- ✔ **Additional assets you may need:** Even if you have footage for everything, you may need additional material such as music, sound effects, visual effects, or photos. Make a list of the elements you want to add.

Collecting photos, sounds, and music

Video footage isn't the only element of an edit. You may want to use these elements, too:

✔ **Background music:** Most videos need some type of music. Chapter 15 explains how to find and select music tracks.

✔ **Additional sound effects and a voiceover narration track:** These elements can often enhance a video. See Chapter 15 for details.

✔ **Titles:** They are important to introduce your video and add additional explanations. See Chapter 16 to find out how to create and use titles.

✔ **Additional visual elements, such as photos, diagrams, or even animations:** These elements may help to convey your message. Chapter 16 has more details about these types of assets.

If you cannot take footage of an important subject in your video, photos can often help to bridge the gap. Photos don't have to look static, if you use movement to show different parts of them. You may be familiar with the work of the documentary filmmaker Ken Burns (*The Civil War, Baseball, Jazz),* who uses historical pictures extensively in his films. His masterful method of panning and zooming over photos, which even bears his name (the *Ken Burns effect),* is now a feature in many editing programs.

Knowing what to do when you're missing material

Even if you plan your shoots meticulously, something almost always goes wrong. You may not be able to shoot a particular scene because of bad weather, or you may simply forget to shoot a scene in the hectic rush to wrap up a busy shooting day. Don't worry much if you fall into this trap — it happens even to seasoned professionals.

We've just described the worst case. Frequently, you realize, while watching footage, that you have no usable material for a particular scene. The talent's hair may look different in two separate takes that are supposed to follow one another, or the light may look quite different, or you may discover an object in the background that makes the take unusable. The audio may even sound terrible, or you may find questionable bug remains on the lens. It all happens.

You can deal with these problems in a number of ways:

✔ **Reshoot the scene.** This solution is the best but most expensive option. Reshooting a ruined scene is still fairly easy to do for simple types of videos, such as interviews or product demonstrations. But if you produce a scripted video, reshooting is typically a stretch because reassembling the entire team, re-creating exact scenes, and filming everything so that the new material fits in with the old is extremely time consuming.

✔ **Use editing tricks.** You can use a whole bag of tricks to save a botched scene. Differences in light can often be saved by adding color correction. A gap in continuity can frequently be remedied by making a well-placed cut to a different perspective. Audio problems can sometimes be repaired with filters, additional sound effects, or overdubbed dialogue. When you watch even very expensive Hollywood movies carefully, you discover these tricks. Everybody uses them.

✔ **Change the story.** If you can truly find no way to save a particular scene and to do a reshoot, consider changing your video's story so that you can survive without the missing piece. This strategy often sounds more difficult than it is.

Viewers don't know what your original story was, so as long as you make the new version flow naturally, nobody will notice.

Finding the Story

If you planned your video carefully (see Chapters 2 and 3), you may believe that editing simply involves the mechanical process of assembling all the pieces. But storylines often change considerably during editing. Great-sounding ideas in the script and attractive scenery during the shoot don't guarantee a quality finished video. Viewers may not comprehend that one clever joke you were so proud to write, or maybe a cast member turns out to be unlikeable onscreen.

Editing is all about finding out what truly works for your video, and more often than not, you will change many elements of your video. It's completely normal, and it happens to all kinds of productions. A big-time Hollywood director sometimes even cuts from the final film the entire role of a highly paid actor if it just doesn't work.

In some types of videos, you uncover the entire story only during the editing process. For example, when you film an event, you may not know in advance what will happen. The role of the editor is to find the interesting bits in all that footage and to arrange them so that a story comes to life.

Making a rough cut

The first step in determining what your video will look like is to make a *rough cut,* in which you line up all the good footage to figure out what works. A rough cut is typically much longer than the final product, and it doesn't contain many of the elements from the final video, such as titles and visual effects.

To make a rough cut, first log your footage, as explained earlier in this chapter, in the section "Logging your footage." Then follow these steps:

1. **Review your storyline in sequence.**

   Tackle every scene separately.

2. **For every scene, find the best takes that you marked during logging.**

3. **Mark in and out points for every clip to trim it to the part you want in the video.**

   Don't worry much about the exact timing. It comes later.

4. **Insert the clip in your editing program's timeline, in any order you want.**

   Figure 14-4 shows what a rough cut looks like in an editing program. It's just a sequence of clips with no further treatment.

5. **Repeat this process for all scenes to assemble a sequence of clips that tells your intended story.**

Figure 14-4:
A timeline with a rough cut in an editing program.

When you watch your rough cut for the first time, it probably looks bumpy, overly long, and <ahem> rough. Your goal is simply to figure out how well your material works when it's assembled.

If it's possible in your editing program, make a safety copy of your first rough cut, of either the timeline or the whole project. This copy may come in handy later in the editing process, when you don't see the forest for all the trees and you need a fresh perspective. Making a copy can also be a helpful way to find raw clips quickly if you have a lot of footage.

Switching it around

The great thing about modern editing software is that you can experiment by moving clips and entire sequences to find the best combination of clips and scenes. Be careful: You can easily get lost in the experimentation process. First consider why you would want to change something, and if you have a truly good reason, do it.

Try some of these suggestions:

- **Use different versions of the same take.** Sometimes, a take that you think is best when you watch it in isolation no longer works well with the rest of the material. If you're unhappy with a take, try using a different take of the same shot to see whether it improves the entire scene.

- **Drop clips or entire scenes.** Shorter is typically better in editing. If you feel that a particular clip or an entire scene doesn't add much value to the video, drop the clip entirely and watch the video without it. If you don't miss it much, your audience will likely never miss it.

- **Change the order of scenes.** Particularly in documentary-style and educational videos, scenes don't necessarily have a natural fixed order. You can also change the sequence completely for dramatic effect. For example, if you sell lawnmowers and you want to show how your latest model performs, you can grab your viewers' attention if you first show the pristine lawn that results from using your product and then demonstrate how your product was responsible.

Editing is storytelling, but stories don't always have to flow linearly. Early in your video, specify to your audience that you have something interesting to say. Learn from the pros: James Bond movies, for example, don't start with a boring explanation of the villain's latest evil plot, but rather with a high-octane action scene that grabs the audience's attention immediately.

If you've ever watched an artist paint a picture, you know that she works for a long time on a tiny detail and then steps away from the easel to take in the entire picture in context. Do the same with your video: After you work on one scene, take some time to watch the whole thing, or at least a bigger portion of it. Take notes about what you like and don't like. You will often find that a solution that seemed workable in isolation doesn't work well in the context of the film as a whole.

Mastering the Art of the Transition

A rough cut is all about finding the right way to tell a story with your video. In a written document, the rough cut would be the equivalent of the outline and first draft. But there's more to editing: Just as you would refine a written text for style and powerful language, refine your video edit with better timing, transitions, additional material, and refined cuts.

Working on these elements is the style aspect of video editing, and it makes all the difference between a video that's barely watchable and one that excites viewers.

Knowing the types of cuts

A *cut* in film editing connects two shots. One shot ends and the next one begins, and between them is a cut. The word *cut* comes from the act of physically cutting celluloid film in traditional movie editing. Today, in the age of digital editing, no cutting is taking place, though the name stuck.

Your rough cut probably uses plain hard cuts exclusively, but as you start refining your video, you may want to consider using other types of cuts to help advance the story and make the viewing experience more sophisticated.

Different types of cuts serve different purposes. Depending on the effect you want to achieve, use one of these cut types:

- ✔ **Hard:** This is the most basic (and by far the most frequently used) type of cut. One shot ends, and the next shot starts immediately. Both the picture track and the sound track are cut at the same time.

- ✔ **Transition:** One shot flows into the next with some kind of visual effect. The simplest form of transition is the *dissolve,* which softly transitions one picture to the next. You can use many different types of other transitions, some of which can look quite fancy. Chapter 16 explains the different types of transitions in more detail.

    Use transitions to suggest a special relationship between two shots, such as a scene transition.

- ✔ **Slow cross dissolve:** This type can be used between shots as a softer replacement for hard cuts. If you want to edit to slow music and achieve a soft, flowing pace, the dissolve is a useful technique.

    Figure 14-5 shows what a cross dissolve between two shots looks like in the context of a video. On the left, you can see the timeline with the vertical bar that shows which part of the video is playing. On the right, the preview pane shows the two shots that the cross dissolve combines.

- ✔ **L or J:** Change the picture track and sound track of your video at different times, not at the same time, as with hard cuts. A good example is an interview partner starting to talk while viewers still see the previous shot. Then, after a few seconds, the picture cuts to include the interviewee. *L cuts* change the picture first, and *J cuts* change sound first. They're also frequently used in dialogue editing to show the reaction of one person while another is speaking.

Figure 14-5:
A cross dis-
solve cut.

Figure 14-6 shows what a J cut looks like in an editing program — in this example, iMovie. Notice that the audio track on the second clip starts earlier than the picture does. Viewers already hear the person speaking in the second clip while the first clip is still playing.

Figure 14-6:
A J cut in
the iMovie
precision
editor.

✔ **Jump:** Cut from one view of a person or an object to another one that's only slightly different. You should generally avoid using the jump cut, but it can be used occasionally for dramatic effect. It's also used in interviews or talking-head videos to shorten a statement or to add visual variety. For example, the person who's speaking can be shown in a medium shot while you cut to a slightly tighter shot for the next sentence.

Many beginners in video editing overuse fancy transitions. Modern editing programs are supplied with dozens of different transitions, and spicing up a video with all that eye candy is tempting. But don't forget that most viewers are more impressed by good storytelling than by overused special effects. A good rule of thumb is that 95 percent of your cuts should be plain hard cuts. If you use more than a few transitions in your video, you're probably overdoing it.

Finding the right rhythm

Videos have a particular rhythm and pace to them. Every cut marks a point in time, and these points together form a rhythm, such as the drum beats in music. Though most viewers don't perceive this visual rhythm consciously, it influences strongly how they react emotionally to the video.

You can easily see the importance of rhythm and pace on the extremes of the spectrum: A music video typically has a lot of fast cuts — sometimes several per second. On the other hand, a documentary series on PBS often moves slowly, with some scenes allowed to play out over several minutes.

The appropriate rhythm for your video depends on what you're trying to achieve and who your audience is. The frantic editing pace of a contemporary action movie doesn't work for a comedy piece or a product explanation video. On the other hand, a pace that's too slow can be perceived as boring.

To find the right rhythm for your video, think about a piece of music to match it. Many videos need background music anyway, so finding music that conveys the atmosphere you want can help you find the right pace easily.

After you have an idea about the rhythm you want to achieve, revisit your rough cut. You will likely need to trim many of the clips to establish the right pace. But in other cases, a particular scene may turn out to be too rushed and need more "air." Because most editing programs show you clip length visually on the timeline, you get an immediate overview of clip length in relation to each other. Figure 14-7 shows an example.

Figure 14-7:
A timeline
with clips
of different
lengths.

Expect to make several rounds of improvements to your rough cut to find the right timing for your video. During this process, you may discover that you need to shift scenes around some more. Editing is an iterative process where you approach the final result in multiple steps.

When your video is a piece of comedy, editing plays a major role in establishing the appropriate comedic timing. Much like a comedian uses pauses and a changing tempo to deliver jokes in the most effective way, comedic editing needs to be carefully timed. Check Chapter 3 for more tips on how to add humor appropriately to your videos.

Connecting the scenes

Videos and films consist of different scenes. A *scene* covers an action that takes place at the same location and at the same time, and scenes typically consist of multiple shots that cover different perspectives — all of which is a fancy way to say that a scene is simply a group of shots that belong together.

For example, a profile video describing an industrial company may start with a scene that introduces the company, showing its building, its factory floor, and its employees at work. The next scene may be a quick word from the CEO, and the scene after that may introduce the latest product introduced by the company.

You can often use the following editing techniques to help viewers understand when a scene ends and the next one begins:

- ✔ **A transition, such as a slow fade or a wipe:** These special types of cuts separate scenes more visibly than a hard cut. Though the cuts within a scene are typically just plain hard cuts, a transition suggests that something special is going on, such as a jump in time and place.

- ✔ **An establishing shot:** This wide shot of a location shows viewers where the next scene is taking place.

- ✔ **The title:** Showing a title chart or subtitle with a location name is a clear method of introducing the next scene.

- ✔ **A change in music:** When one piece of background music ends and another starts, viewers assume intuitively that a new scene also starts.

 You can use these scene-separating techniques in combination. For example, a scene may end with a fade to an establishing shot for the next scene while the music is changing at the same time and a subtitle shows viewers where the next scene is taking place.

Filling the gaps with b-roll

The term *b-roll* describes supplemental footage that can be used to provide additional context for the viewer or to fill gaps in the main storyline. We talk about how to shoot b-roll in Chapter 12. Having plenty of b-roll is always a good idea because it makes an editor's life easier.

Use b-roll in your video in these common scenarios:

- ✔ Illustrate what a speaker or interviewee is saying by showing the subject of the explanation.

- ✔ Add a bit of rhythm and visual polish to an otherwise long and visually boring scene.

- ✔ Separate scenes in a scripted video to give the viewer "breathing room." Many TV series use a few pieces of b-roll between scenes — for example, in shots of the city where the story is taking place.

- ✔ Hide cuts in an interview or another continuous scene. If you have only one perspective of an interviewee, shortening the interview is difficult. Cutting directly looks jumpy and indicates that you've omitted material. If you cut instead to a piece of b-roll while the interviewee is still talking, you can easily mask the cut.

- ✔ Disguise small flaws in the footage. Did the camera suddenly shake in the middle of the interview, or did the subject move briefly out of focus? No problem — simply use a bit of b-roll to hide the mistake.

If you use b-roll only to disguise mistakes, your use of it may become too obvious. Use b-roll frequently to make your video more interesting and varied. But also avoid using b-roll that has nothing to do with the subject and doesn't add true value.

If you missed out on shooting b-roll or you have to use someone else's material that didn't come with b-roll, you can either use photos that may match the subject or even use a stock footage library to try to find footage that works with your subject. Large stock websites such as Getty Images, iStockphoto, and Shutterstock now also offer video material. Professionals use these libraries all the time to bolster their footage collection, and you can too.

Polishing Your Video

After you refine your rough cut into a well-timed, well-trimmed video, it's time to apply the final layer of polish. A bit of further fine-tuning makes the difference between an acceptable video and one that looks truly professional.

Fine-tuning your edit

Videos can benefit from a number of relatively simple steps you can follow to improve certain aspects that viewers may not even consciously recognize:

1. **Tweak your cut timing.** If a cut seems even a little bit "off," spend some time fine-tuning it. Even placing a cut a frame or two earlier or later can make a difference. Figure 14-8 shows the precision editor in iMovie that lets you tweak your cuts precisely. Most other editing programs have a similar feature.

Figure 14-8:
The preci-
sion editor
in iMovie.

2. **Add music.** You may have already worked with music during earlier editing steps, but now is the time to finalize your background tracks.

3. **Clean up the audio track.** Most audio tracks can use some additional work. Be sure that the levels are correct and consistent throughout the video. Viewers don't like viewing one scene that's too loud followed immediately by one that's barely audible. Some editing programs have the Normalize Audio function, which optimizes audio levels automatically. Also, hard audio cuts rarely sound good. You can add a dissolve transition to the audio track while still applying a hard cut to the picture track. See Chapter 15 for more audio tips.

4. **Use color correction.** Though scenes should have a consistent look between shots, video cameras sometimes pick up different color schemes. The color-correction feature in most editing programs can help fix this problem. Color-correction also lets you give your video a unique and more interesting look. Read more about this topic in Chapter 16.

Figure 14-9 shows a fully built timeline with transitions, music, a voiceover narration track, and titles. Take a minute to notice where b-roll is used (in city shots), how scenes are held together with straight cuts, and how cross-dissolve transitions are used between scenes. If you look at the audio track, you can see that the voiceover narration starts in the middle of one scene and continues seamlessly to the next scenes. Also notice the title sequence at the beginning (the black box) and the call to action at the end.

Figure 14-9:
A fully built
editing
timeline.

Adding bells and whistles

You can add a number of elements, as described in this list, to complete your video and make it look more interesting:

- ✓ **Titles:** A video should have a good title sequence, and editing programs offer a variety of different templates. Try a few different styles to see what works best.

- ✓ **Sound effects:** A well-placed sound effect can make certain scenes much more interesting. We aren't talking about explosions or alien ray gun sounds, but about basic background tracks or sounds that match the visible content on the screen. Sometimes, your original background sounds for a scene aren't good, and you can use canned sounds to replace them. Some editing programs come with small libraries of sound effects, and you can find more online.

- ✓ **Visual effects:** Most editing programs have effect filters that change the look of your footage completely. Though you should always use these effects sparingly, they may occasionally help make your video look more interesting.

- ✓ **Visualizations and animations:** Many marketing-oriented videos benefit from visualizations that better explain a product. If your budget allows for it, you can even work with a professional to produce a fancy 2D or 3-D animation. These *motion graphics* can make your video look quite sophisticated.

We talk more about music and audio in Chapter 15, and we discuss visual effects in Chapter 16.

You can experiment with bells and whistles in the earlier stages of the editing process, though you typically should wait until the end of your editing process before trying to use them fully. They're typically time consuming to apply, and if you change your edit afterward, you may have to do unnecessary work.

Getting feedback

On the big premiere day of many Hollywood movies, hundreds or even thousands of people have already seen it. Movie studios use test audiences to determine whether a movie works or they have to change material by editing.

You should do the same: Don't wait for premiere day (if you have one) to solicit feedback. Ask people you trust to give you honest feedback well in advance — possibly, in the early stages of the editing process.

To inspire meaningful feedback, follow these steps:

1. **Try to find test viewers who are as similar as possible to your future audience.** Your best friend or your mother probably enjoys your video anyway, but she likely isn't part of your target market.

2. **Reproduce the circumstances of the final audience when you show your video to your test audience.** If the video is designed to be published online, show it on a computer screen in a YouTube-size player, not on your 55-inch, big-screen television set. A video looks and feels completely different on a big screen than on a tiny computer player.

3. **Don't explain.** You may be eager to point out all the crucial elements of your video, but you probably shouldn't do that for your target audience, either. Telling the test audience too many details influences their judgment, which negates the purpose of the feedback round.

4. **Show your video, and don't comment.** If the video isn't finished yet, don't mention it to your audience. See whether they notice. Just pretend that you aren't present.

5. **Ask test viewers for their feedback, and just listen to them.** Resisting the temptation to provide explanations is difficult if you hear criticism or if people don't understand something, but don't comment now.

6. **Ask a few neutral questions, and don't lead the "witness."** Ask questions along the lines of, "What would you think about our company after watching this video?" or "Where would you go to buy our product after watching it?" The answers to these questions can help you determine whether you've properly conveyed your message to the test audience.

7. **Take extensive notes.** Even better, record the feedback on video (after asking test viewers for permission).

8. **After the session, review your notes.** Then you can decide what you want to change about your video.

Use your best judgment to figure out specifically what you want to change about your video based on the feedback you receive. An opinion is just an opinion, and your test audience may have a particular perspective that other people don't necessarily share. Making changes is time consuming and may cost money, so balance the desire for perfection with your budgetary and time constraints.

Ideally, you can watch the reactions of your test audience in the same room, but if that isn't possible, solicit their feedback online. Upload your video to YouTube, specify Unlisted permissions, and send the link to test viewers for comment. Ask them to provide written notes or, better, to tell you about their thoughts in a brief Skype call.

Exporting the final video

When you finally finish editing, you export the video from your editing program so that you can use it later.

Typically, you should export multiple versions of a video because you can use the final product in different ways:

✔ **Export an archive copy with the highest possible quality that your editing program offers.** You can always decrease, but not increase, quality (and therefore file size). That's why you should store a high-quality copy, in case you want to create other versions later.

✔ **Produce smaller versions of the video with lower resolutions for uploading to online platforms or for DVD production.** Most editing programs have export presets designed for these purposes.

Some editing programs let you directly share video on websites such as YouTube or Facebook. Sharing this way is convenient, but if you notice a mistake after uploading the video, removing the video again is messy. Normally, exporting video to your hard drive is safer — watch it one last time, and then upload it manually to gain more control over every step.

Many people struggle with making computer backups. But hard drive crashes happen, and laptops are stolen. Your painstakingly produced video is one that you want to keep in multiple copies in different locations. Considering how much time you invest in creating the video, it's probably one of the most expensive items you can make on your computer, so investing a few more minutes to safeguard your video files is more than worth the time you spend. Get an external hard drive and copy your video files to it, and then store it away from your office or house. Losing an edited video that you've spent 5 or 10 or even 100 hours working on equals heartbreak that you shouldn't risk.

Chapter 15

Working with Music and Other Audio

In This Chapter

▶ Making beautiful music

▶ Adding narration

▶ Mixing and applying the audio

*U*nless your video is destined to be shown with its sound turned off, you have to consider its sound design (as experts refer to it) before the video is complete. Sound does much more than simply supplement pictures — the choices you make for adding music and sound effects have a huge emotional effect on the viewer. In this chapter, we look at ways to find and use music, and ways to use other sound effects to improve your audio tracks.

Understanding the Elements of Audio

We suspect that you've already noticed the music in a movie thriller becoming quite dramatic just seconds before the suspected killer turns the corner to stab the victim or the sound in a science fiction film becoming *loud* whenever aliens begin an attack. If you try to watch an exciting movie with the sound turned off, you will immediately notice that much of the excitement of watching instantly disappears. The reason isn't simply that you can't hear the actors — it's also that your emotions were being triggered by the music and the sound effects that accompany the film.

John Williams and the epic soundtrack

To see how music can deeply influence the emotional mood of a movie or video, watch a film that's accompanied by music composed or conducted by John Williams. You may have heard of some that showcase (and benefit from) his rich and remarkable work: *E.T., Jaws, Indiana Jones, Jurassic Park, Home Alone, Schindler's List,* and films from the *Harry Potter* and *Star Wars* series, among others.

A movie accompanied by a John Williams soundtrack rarely has a moment without music. Apart from his recognizable melodies, much of his music is subdued and understated — it's in the movie simply to support the story from the background. This style is also the best way to add music to your marketing videos: Make it low-key and subtle, and provide an occasional "musical moment."

Whenever you create a marketing video, you have to make choices about the sound design of the video in order to trigger the same kinds of emotions in your viewers. Consider these guidelines:

- **Maintain natural sound.** Natural (or *ambient)* sound is the audio that's recorded while shooting a video, including all dialogue and background noises. Most videos intended for marketing need additional music or narration combined with the video's natural sound.

  Natural sound can be quite important to certain marketing videos. For example, when Kennametal, a manufacturer of metalworking tools, needed to show how its milling tools worked under real-world conditions on the shop floor, it eliminated music from its videos so that prospective buyers could hear the shavings fall during milling. In other cases, natural sound is extremely distracting and should be omitted. For example, if you're showing off your facilities and an extremely loud machine distracts the viewer, it then makes sense to not use the natural sound.

- **Add voiceover.** Sometimes, the best way to convey the message of your video is to have it narrated, using the *voiceover* technique: Viewers hear a recorded voice tell your story, without seeing the person who's speaking. Most documentary movies and TV news stories use voiceovers. You can hire professional voiceover talent to use in your videos.

- **Apply sound effects.** Familiar sounds trigger reactions in viewers. For example, a honking horn immediately triggers the thought of a traffic jam without having to show a traffic jam visually. Used sparingly, sound effects can drive home important points in your message.

- **Determine the music.** Even if you want the music in your videos to be mostly unnoticeable, you have to choose the style you want to use.

Choosing Music for Your Videos

You may wonder why music is even necessary in a video that isn't destined to sell a pop singer's latest album. Music determines a lot about the perception of your message because viewers make split-second, subconscious judgments about the content of your video depending on the type of music you choose.

In contrast to music videos, the music in your marketing video is meant to complement the message you're trying to convey. Music isn't the focus of a video — it's there simply to add color.

You must understand the difference between music you pay royalties to use and royalty-free music. Most of the music that you hear on the radio or buy online is copyrighted and can be used in videos only if you pay royalties to its record label — often an expensive strategy because you must pay for every use of a copyrighted music track. Record labels sometimes even charge more, depending on how many views your video attracts. And, "borrowing" music and hoping that you won't get caught is *not* an option. Your videos containing copyrighted music can be banned automatically from sites such as YouTube.

The easiest way to save time and expense is to use only royalty-free music tracks — they're sold specifically for use in videos or presentations. After you pay a fixed price per song, you can usually use it however you want, as long as you stay within the boundaries specified by the music publisher. For example, some royalty-free tracks may be available for use in online videos but not in TV commercials. To understand the legal requirements around copyrighted material in detail, see Chapter 8.

To choose music for your video, follow these steps:

1. **Determine which emotion you want to convey.** For example, you may want viewers to feel happy, sad, or uplifted — or neutral.

2. **Watch a rough edit of your video several times.** Or, if you're still in the planning stage, simply review the video's storyline in your mind. Do you need fast, aggressive cuts? Are your graphics clean and simple, or more elaborate and flowery? The music you choose must match the video's storyline, aesthetic value, and editing style.

3. **Choose an appropriate genre.** You may want to use a rock-and-roll track or a country track, for example, or perhaps electronic music more closely suits your style.

4. **Set the mood.** The mood of the music you choose has to match the emotion you want to convey. To judge, determine how the music makes *you* feel when you listen to it. If it matches the emotion you chose in Step 1, you're on the right track.

5. **Control the pace of the video by controlling its musical tempo.** A song's *tempo* refers to its speed or pace. The pace of the video also has to fit the emotion you're trying to convey and the overall storyline. For example, should viewers be relaxed or breathless after watching your video? Choose a tempo between these two extremes that creates the impression you want.

6. **Search for a song.** After you choose the genre, mood, and tempo of the music in your video, search for a song. (Or, if you're truly talented, compose one yourself.) You'll likely stick with royalty-free music.

7. **Drop in the music.** After you finish creating the video, you can drop the music into your editing timeline and edit the piece to mirror the pacing of the footage.

Experiment with creating a music video that introduces your company or describes its products. A holiday-themed video often provides a good opportunity. For example, Bettina's and Andreas' company Pixability created a winter holiday video with a custom-written song to entice viewers to make creating a video their New Year's resolution. Check it out at `www.pixability.com/holiday2010`.

Picking the proper tune for your audience

As with all other elements of your video, you must choose its music with your audience in mind. Above all else, avoid alienating your audience with your choice of music. If you're unsure, we believe (and music lovers may disagree) that you should choose unobtrusive music over music that's too bold.

You should follow certain guidelines when picking a tune. The music in your video should

- ✔ **Fit the mold:** Is a certain type of music traditionally associated with your product or service? If you make skateboards, for example, you likely already realize that punk rock has long been associated with this type of product. Don't break the mold unless you purposely want to irritate your audience.

- ✔ **Be age-appropriate:** Match your video's music roughly with its targeted age group. Using the big-band sound from the 1940s to attract 20-year-olds may backfire in the same way that using autotune synthesizer pop with rap vocals is likely a poor choice if you're trying to highlight your assisted-living community.

- ✔ **Incorporate instruments:** Consider the instruments being played in the piece you're evaluating. Certain instruments are associated with particular settings or lifestyles, such as an electric guitar that works well in an urban clothing store's video or an acoustic guitar (often associated with nature) that best matches the hiking tours in a travel company's video.

✔ **Avoid vocals:** Instrumental music is almost always the best choice for background music. Vocals can be quite distracting, unless the lyrics specifically match the story of the video.

Heading in the right direction musically

Music choices can be wildly controversial because of all the emotions triggered by certain songs, so we feel somewhat shy about making recommendations. Knowing how to use the musical styles described in the following list, and being aware of musical stereotypes, can at least help get your juices flowing, however. (Feel free to snicker about our generalizations or to disagree wildly with our recommendations.)

✔ **Corporate:** This mildly upbeat, generally harmonious, and unobtrusively arranged style is used in many marketing videos. Some form of easy listening jazz or instrumental pop often works best. The sonic background of this style doesn't distract from the visual aspect of the video. But be careful not to select music that's simply bland and boring. Music should be used to *enhance* the emotional impact of your video, not to neutralize it.

✔ **Electronic:** It's modern and cutting-edge and maybe somewhat cold. Tracks with a lot of synthesizers work well in videos with a subject that's technically focused or future-oriented, such as product demonstrations of electronic gadgets.

✔ **Jazz:** Communicating sophistication and big-city glamour can work for some types of company profile videos or event videos. The jazz style can sound pretentious if it's overused.

✔ **Hip-hop:** A suggestion of boldness, street smarts, and youthfulness works well when you want to reach a younger target group. Be sure that you understand your customers, however: Not every young person enjoys hip-hop.

✔ **Classical:** The classical style adds a touch of, well, class to your videos, but may label you as conservative. Choose classical to evoke calmness, security, or reliability.

Richly arranged, Hollywood-style, orchestra music is rarely a good choice because it suggests a grandeur that your video likely doesn't deliver.

✔ **Rock:** Often adding power and boldness to a video, rock music comes in many flavors that can express vastly different moods. Floating, 1960s-style, "road movie" rock works well in travel-related videos, whereas aggressive punk rock works best in skateboard product videos.

✔ **Era:** Almost every decade has a recognizable style of music. If you want to use a style such as new wave synthesizer pop from the 1980s or flower power rock from the 1960s, ensure that the nostalgic quality of the music truly fits the topic of your video. Just because you grew up listening to a certain musical style doesn't mean that it works well in your video.

✔ **World:** Many musical styles are easily identified as originating in specific areas of the world. If your video is related to a particular country or region, the music of that area can be an appropriate choice. Clearly recognizable styles, however, such as Latin salsa and Indian sitar, should be specifically matched to suitable videos. People can be confused by musical geographical references.

You must well understand the musical tastes of your target audience. For example, avoid the assumption that all 20-year-old males enjoy heavy metal music or that every retiree in Florida enjoys golden oldies. Your clever idea for using music can backfire if your audience feels patronized or annoyed.

Knowing Where to Find Music

After you spend some quality time thinking about the music to use in your video, begin hunting for it. You can obtain the music you need for your videos in a number of ways, as described in the following sections.

Adding built-in music in video editing tools

Most of the video editing software programs we describe in Chapter 13 contain royalty-free song tracks, such as in these two examples:

✔ **Apple Final Cut Pro X:** Has 1,300 royalty-free sound effects and music tracks

✔ **Sony Vegas Movie Studio HD:** Contains 400 royalty-free music soundtracks

Some of the songs you can use from video editing software are so popular and overused (because they're free) that you risk triggering unwanted reactions from your audience. For example, a friend once complained to us that hisvideo reminded him of a late-night TV ad containing questionable content. When we watched it, we found that his video editor had used a free, built-in music track that's often chosen by these low-cost advertisers.

Incorporating stock music libraries

If you have only a small budget and you want to sound different from the standard music libraries that come with many editing programs, you can find a good selection of royalty-free stock music to download online. This list describes some options that we recommend:

- ✔ **Shockwave** (www.shockwave-sound.com)**:** Its good selection is reasonably priced. Expect to pay $30 to $50 apiece for most songs.

- ✔ **Audiojungle** (www.audiojungle.com)**:** It's less expensive than Shockwave, but its selection isn't as large. Songs cost between $10 and $20 apiece.

- ✔ **Footage Firm** (www.footagefirm.com)**:** This site sells inexpensive DVD song compilations. A disc usually has only a few good songs, but they're usually worth the price — approximately $10 per disc, including shipping.

If you want to use an iconic song such as Nirvana's "Smells Like Teen Spirit" and you have a limited budget or limited time to secure the rights, you can often find inexpensive but similar-sounding songs on stock music sites.

If you can't find a song that matches the length of your video, don't worry: Viewers don't focus on songs — songs simply enhance the pacing and mood. Therefore, a repetitive song, or looping a song to fit the length of the video, usually works well.

Finding open source music

Because of copyright laws, legally using popular music (as described in Chapter 8) is possible only if it's in the public domain or if the artists have made their music available for free (via the Creative Commons license, for example).

Websites such as Open Source Music and Opsound provide libraries of tracks that you can use for free. You can find many usable tracks on these sites, typically produced by up-and-coming musicians who want to find their audiences. Some, such as Kevin MacLeod at Incompetech, can even produce custom music for you at relatively affordable rates. (See Chapter 24.)

Classical music from the public domain can often be a good match. For example, Stanley Kubrick originally intended the stock music he chose for the movie *2001: A Space Odyssey* as a placeholder until a score was written, but he kept it.

Be careful: Classical music can be used only if you record it yourself or use a recording that's older than 70 years. Otherwise, the musicians who played the classical song have the right to royalties.

Before you use open source tracks, you must understand the exact licensing conditions under which the song is published. The Creative Commons license has several different levels, some of which prohibit commercial use. Even if a song isn't published under the traditional copyright, it's still illegal to use it outside of its license conditions.

Making your own music

If you're feeling creative and you want to make your own music, you have two key options: Use a music production software program that lets you build songs from existing clips, or record your own music from scratch.

Reusing existing material in music production software programs

Music production software programs let you easily build songs from preexisting material.

If you're looking for value, you can't beat free: Apple's GarageBand, which is preinstalled on all Apple computers, lets you easily drag and drop prerecorded music to create and customize songs from clips. These clips are usually loops, so you can have the music play as long as you want. To customize the songs, you add different instruments, one at a time.

For good but still inexpensive choices, consider these products (listed by price):

- **Mixcraft:** Approximately $75; works on PCs and is similar to GarageBand in ease of use
- **Sonar X1 LE:** Approximately $100; has more than 1GB of audio clips
- **Image Line FL Studio:** Approximately $200; for more advanced users
- **Avid Pro Tools MP:** Approximately $250; has 8GB of loops to drag and drop to quickly and easily create songs

Recording from scratch

Recording your own music is definitely the most customized way to make your video shine musically. Don't attempt it, however, if you aren't musically inclined. You need to have enough time and the proper gear to make your video sound good.

If you're using a song with lyrics, write the song along with the script so that the lyrics can reflect what's happening on the screen. For an example, check out the Pixability Video Valentine holiday video at www.pixability.com/valentine. Bettina's team worked with a local musician to create a custom song to match the script perfectly.

If you aren't using lyrics, editing the video first and then writing and recording music is the preferable order of tasks because you then know how long the song must be and which parts of the song need emphasis to match the video.

To record from scratch, you need these items:

- ✔ **A relatively fast computer with substantial CPU power:** If you're recording with a microphone, the computer must run quietly.

- ✔ **Recording software to capture the song:** You can use GarageBand, Logic, Pro Tools, Ableton, or another program. Using the cheaper (or "light") versions of these programs usually suffices unless you're recording a large number of tracks.

- ✔ **A USB or FireWire audio interface:** The interface lets you connect electric instruments (a guitar, bass, and microphone, for example) to your computer. A quality audio interface costs around $150.

- ✔ **A microphone:** The built-in microphone on your computer isn't a good sound option, so invest in a quality external microphone. An excellent choice for voice recording is the Shure SM58; its models cost $75 or $100. Note that microphones used for voice recordings aren't ideal for recording amplifiers.

- ✔ **Instruments:** Depending on the genre you're recording, you usually need at least a guitar and a bass. Drums are difficult to record, so use a software-based drum set. You can drag and drop clips to build the drum parts, or you can use a USB MIDI controller.

Putting Music in Your Video

After you have selected (or even recorded) your music, it's time to insert it in your video.

The mechanical aspect of this task is easy to complete. Follow these steps in your editing software:

1. **Gather into one folder on your computer all the music files you want to use.**

   Using one folder helps you find files easily and helps you back them up after editing. If you store your music on a CD, import the necessary tracks to your computer first by using a program such as iTunes.

2. **Import the music files into your video editing software.**

   Most editing programs can process MP3 files and most other commonly used music file formats.

3. **Add an additional audio track to your editing project.**

   Certain simpler programs, such as iMovie, have predetermined tracks for background music.

4. **Drag and drop your music piece to the new audio track. Then shift its position until it fits the timing that you want.**

5. **Watch the part of the video that now has background music in context.** Fine-tune the timing of the music, if necessary.

If you aren't sure which piece of music will work best with your video, simply import into your editing program multiple music tracks that you're considering. Drop one after the other on the audio timeline, watching the video with every piece of music, to quickly find which track you like best.

Adding emotional impact

The main purpose of your music selection is to enhance the emotional impact of your video. In the earlier section "Choosing Music for Your Videos," we describe how to find a piece of music that works best with the mood of your video.

Even the specific way in which you use music in your edit affects the video's emotional impact. Try these simple tricks to give your music more emotional impact:

- **Work with the volume level.** Music in a video shouldn't always play at the same volume level. It should be softer and drop into the background whenever it supports dialogue or a voiceover narration, and it should be fairly loud when it stands on its own and drives home an emotional point. Most editing programs let you change the volume of a particular track over time. Dramatically increasing the volume of the music track in a key video scene adds quite a powerful effect — Hollywood movies and TV shows do it all the time.

- **Determine the proper timing.** A music track doesn't have to start at its beginning when you insert it in your video. Match the music to the video's visual content. Most musical selections have *hooks* — particularly remarkable and recognizable parts. For example, the hook of Beethoven's Fifth Symphony is the famous "Ta-ta-ta-daaa." Try to match musical hooks with important moments in the video.

Cutting your video to music

When you have a piece of music that matches well the emotional purpose of your video, fine-tune your edit to maximize the effect of the music. For example, you can extend a scene slightly to fit the most dramatic moment with a remarkable hook in the music.

Most editing programs let you lock your music tracks to avoid their being affected by other changes in your video. Follow these steps:

1. **Put your musical piece on its own audio track.**

2. **Time the music so that the music begins exactly where you want.**

3. **Lock the music track.**

   Most editing programs use a tiny padlock icon to indicate locking.

4. **Watch the video and determine how to adapt the timing to best fit the music.**

   For example, shorten or stretch certain shots slightly.

5. **Make your editing changes.**

6. **Unlock the audio track.**

 Precisely matching cuts in a video with beats in the music can create quite a pleasing effect because the picture and music then seem to move in perfect harmony. Avoid overdoing it, though, because an exact match can quickly bore viewers. The best approach is to match a couple of cuts with the music and then purposely skip the next few cuts before matching again. Alternating makes the final product less predictable and maintains viewer interest.

Cutting your music to video

You may not want to alter an edit just to better fit the music. In this case, cut the music to match your video instead.

Another important reason to cut music is to omit parts that may not fit well with the visual side of your video. For example, the piece of music you selected may have a bridge section that has a slightly different mood from the rest of the track, which can be distracting in a video. Eliminate the unwanted section by cutting precisely at the end of the previous part and at the end of the bridge section.

Almost all video editing programs let you cut audio tracks also, which is good enough for completing the basic editing of your music tracks, such as cutting off unwanted intros or endings. Unfortunately, many editing programs let you cut only on the typical frame-by-frame basis of the video track (30 frames per second). This limited precision often isn't adequate for cutting music — a stray drum beat can stick out like a sore thumb.

An alternative is to cut your music tracks in advance by using an audio program such as Garage Band or Pro Tools (described later in this chapter). They let you edit audio precisely, and they provide a wealth of audio effects to help you enhance your music tracks for video use.

Recording Voiceover Narration

Many videos used for marketing employ *voiceover narration,* using offscreen narrators to tell viewers about the company's products or services. If you want to use a voiceover in your video, you have two options:

- ✔ **Record your own voice.** This option is appropriate if you have a trained, pleasant-sounding voice and a limited budget. Make a trial recording of your script, and let a trusted colleague or friend judge whether it sounds good for your video.

- ✔ **Hire voiceover talent.** You can find talented speakers, such as professional radio announcers, online or via voiceover recording studios. Visit a site such as `www.voices.com` or `www.voice123.com` to find a broad selection of voices. As with music selection, the speaker you select must match your company's products and services. Choosing a teenage voice to sell a mutual fund product — or choosing a grandmotherly voice to market the latest popular computer game — isn't likely to work. The speaker should allow you to use the recording royalty-free. Expect to pay between $100 and $1,000 for a voiceover narration, depending on the length of the script and the experience and quality level of the speaker.

Most video editing programs have a voiceover recording feature, which is useful if you're recording your own voice directly into your computer. In iMovie, you can access this feature from the Microphone icon in the middle of the screen. Figure 15-1 shows the voiceover control box; use it to set parameters such as the volume level or the degree of noise reduction (which is useful to get better sound quality). The editing program plays your video while you're recording, so you can time your narration.

If you're working with a professional voiceover artist, send that person the script with timing instructions. Professional speakers usually record scripts in their (home) recording studios according to your specifications. Sometimes, the first read delivered by a professional speaker doesn't match the style you want. Include a second read in your negotiated rate, in case you need to modify the speaking style.

Figure 15-1:
Recording a
voiceover in
iMovie.

 To record your own voiceover, invest in a mid-quality external microphone. Apart from the more advanced solutions that we discuss in the earlier section "Recording from scratch," you can buy good USB microphones well below $100 — a worthy investment because your voiceover tracks will sound much better.

 Even if you work with a professional voiceover artist, record your own voice on the video as a demonstration of the timing you want. You can send the video with your narration to the voiceover artist to specify exactly what you need. Your own recording can serve as a proxy while you're editing, and you can have a copy of the professional voiceover recording when your edit is finalized.

Adding Sound Effects

Most noises you hear in a typical Hollywood movie aren't recorded live on the set, but are added later in the process. Recording sounds on location is tricky and often creates mediocre results. That's why movie studios employ *Foley artists* (named after the inventor of this craft, Jack Foley), who specialize in generating and mixing sound effects. Even seemingly trivial sounds such as footsteps or the swishing of clothes are often created artificially. Some movie genres, such as action movies, use extremely complicated sound effect tracks that are largely responsible for the emotional impact of these movies.

Though you may not need this level of sophistication in your marketing videos, a few well-placed sound effects can add flair and credibility to them. This list describes the major kinds of sound effects you can use:

✔ **Background or ambient:** Continuous background noises that suggest where the video scene is taking place work well to establish location. For example, a busy city scene needs vehicle noises, lots of footsteps, and the occasional siren. A beach scene needs wind and water sounds. These background sounds are easy to apply.

If you can, record a few minutes of ambient sound on your video set to capture the audio character of the location.

- **Hard:** This type sound effect accompanies visible events onscreen, such as slamming doors or passing vehicles. This type is a little more difficult to apply because they must be synced precisely to the picture, though most editing programs let you do it quite easily.

- **Foley or designer:** More subtle and precisely timed effects, such as artificially created footsteps, require the expertise of a Foley artist. Certain types of subject matter, such as science fiction, need specifically designed sounds that don't exist in nature. Marketing videos rarely need this level of sophistication, but if yours do, you can find freelance audio artists on platforms such as Elance.

Most advanced video editing programs are supplied with a small library of basic sound effects that you can easily use in your edits. Just add an audio track, drag in the sound recording you want, and shift the track around until it fits the scene.

Figure 15-2 shows a timeline in iMovie with traffic background noise applied to the outdoor scenes. A second effects track features a police siren to make the scene more interesting. Note that the background music track runs through the entire scene without interruption.

Figure 15-2: Sound effects in iMovie.

You can find additional sound effects online from stock sound libraries such as Shockwave-Sound.com and Soundsnap. Most of these sounds have specific descriptions, such as "Cars passing by at 25 mph on a somewhat busy street," so you can likely find something suitable.

Mixing Your Audio Track

Much like video editing, sound mixing is an invisible art. Though most people notice only badly mixed sound, creating an appropriate sound mix is an important part of making your video work.

Sound mixing is the combination of multiple audio tracks into a coherent, great-sounding acoustic result. Advanced videos can have a dozen or more audio tracks in editing, but the final video needs a clean stereo audio track that expresses all sound elements in exactly the right way.

The mixing process consists of these general steps:

1. **Adjust sound levels.** Various sounds need to have volume levels relative to one another that enable the viewer to hear clearly. For example, don't overpower a speaking voice with background music or sound effects.

2. **Fine-tune the dynamics.** Some sounds are loud and explosive, and others are soft and continuous. A good mix adjusts these differences so that viewers don't have to continually adjust the speaker volume.

3. **Change the frequency balance.** You may be familiar with the equalizer on your stereo or MP3 player that lets you boost the bass or other elements of the sound spectrum. Similarly, certain sounds benefit from frequency enhancements. Speaking voices, for example, are easier to understand if the frequencies between 500 Hz and 2 kHz are boosted.

   Many editing programs have presets on the built-in equalizer that help you achieve a specific effect, such as boosting voices.

4. **Apply effects.** Numerous mixing effects can make an audio track sound richer or more interesting. *Reverb* adds the sound characteristics of a room, a concert hall, or even a large cathedral. An *echo generator* (or *delay*) adds a repeating pattern to a sound effect. A *pitch changer* makes a sound appear higher- or lower-pitched without changing its speed.

Figure 15-3 shows the audio inspector panel in iMovie.

This typically simple, audio control field lets the editor control the most important aspects of an audio track:

- **Volume:** This setting controls the audio track's volume level.

- **Ducking:** This automated filter turns down the volume of a background track during an event in a foreground track. For example, the background music automatically retreats slightly when somebody is speaking.

- **Fade in/fade out:** You use this setting to control whether, and how fast, an audio track softly fades in at the beginning and then fades out at the end. Using fades is often a good idea because hard audio cuts can sound rough.

- **Enhance:** Enhancing attempts to reduce background noise, such as wind or traffic. These automated filters aren't perfect, but they can make the difference between a voice track that's barely usable and one that's at least intelligible.

✔ **Equalizer:** Control the frequency balance of the track by using an equalizer. Working with the built-in presets, such as Voice Enhance, is a huge time-saver.

✔ **Normalize Clip Volume:** This button automatically enhances or reduces the volume and dynamics of the audio track to fit in with a standard mix. Try this tool first when mixing sound because sound volumes can vary wildly, depending on the source of the sound.

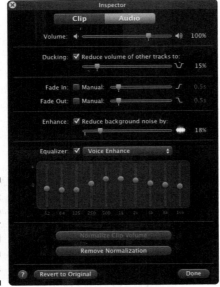

Figure 15-3:
The audio inspector control panel in iMovie.

Most video editing programs have only a limited number of audio effects and filters. If you're trying to achieve a specific effect, try premixing a sound in a sound editing program such as Garage Band or Pro Tools. These programs have a much wider range of options to create and enhance sounds.

Using tricks to make your audio sound better

What makes an audio track sound good is largely in the eye (or ear, rather) of the beholder. Some people like strong bass and loud effects, and others prefer subtle and sophisticated soundtracks.

Virtually any type of soundtrack can benefit from these tricks:

✔ **Use the equalizer to coax out the character of every sound.** For example, the sound of rolling thunder recorded on your camera's cheap, built-in microphone may sound thin and unimpressive. Boost the low frequencies to highlight the thunderous power of Thor. Or if you have an outdoor interview recording with a lot of wind noise, turn down the low frequencies to highlight the voice more clearly.

✔ **Use automated features such as the Normalize Clip Volume button in your editing program.** This button can help eliminate basic sound issues.

✔ **Use the Loudness equalizer setting on music tracks.** This setting is designed to make music sound better if it's played at a relatively low volume, which many viewers are likely to do.

✔ **Use fades.** Cutting audio isn't easy because a hard cut in the middle of a sound can appear quite rough and choppy. Use the fade-in/fade-out functionality in your editing program liberally to make the sound more fluent.

✔ **Use a compressor.** Available in many advanced editing programs, a compressor reduces the dynamic volume differences in a soundtrack and increases the volume of the average sound — typically a benefit, particularly if viewers watch your video on a laptop or mobile phone.

Ensuring audio sound quality on different types of equipment

Viewers watch videos on all kinds of different devices, including laptops and desktop computers. Some viewers use mobile phones, and others may even use big-screen TVs. All these playback devices have different levels of audio reproduction quality.

For this reason, test your video's audio mix on a number of different devices. The rich bass that sounded impressive on your home stereo may lead to annoying effects when played on a laptop speaker. And the voice track that was easy to understand when you mixed it with your headphones can sound incomprehensible on an iPhone.

Professional audio engineers store extra types of speakers and never release a track without testing it on a cheap clock radio. Follow their lead and play your video on the worst-sounding device you can get your hands on.

If you mix your video only on speakers, make a final quality check using a good pair of headphones. You may be shocked by the number of small audio flaws you missed. Headphones give you a much more precise sound image that you should use as the reference for your final mix. Many people use headphones whenever they watch videos (at the office, for example), so your mix must pass the headphone test.

Saving a botched audio track

Many things can go wrong when you record audio. As with botched video footage, some tricks at least make a bad-sounding audio track usable. This list describes the most frequent problems — and how to fix them:

- **The sound level is too low.** Many cameras record at fairly low sound levels. You can boost the level by using the Normalize Clip Volume (or similarly named) button in your editing program, boosting the track volume, or using a compressor filter.

- **The audio track has too much ambient noise.** Did the camera operator record an interview near a busy street? If so, you can use equalizer tricks to enhance the interviewee's voice. Start with the Voice Enhance equalizer setting and the Reduce Background Noise filter included in most editing programs. Then fine-tune these parameters to create the most intelligible voice track possible. Simply reducing low frequencies often works well with traffic and wind noise. If you still can't get audio you can understand, either try an advanced audio editing program such as Pro Tools or hire a freelance audio engineer to help. An experienced professional can sometimes save more sound than you would expect.

- **You can hear distracting noises in the background.** If the sound recording from the location has one or two distracting noises on it (such as a slamming door), you can often save the track by slicing out the unwanted noise and replacing it with an audio sample that has no activity. In Chapter 11, we recommend that you always record some *room tone* (silence with ambient noise) on location, and now is the time to use it.

- **The dialogue is unusable.** Sometimes you simply can't save a voice track. Maybe your talent stood too far from the microphone, or the ambient noise covers everything else. In interview situations, it's sometimes difficult to even hear the interviewer. The only way to save this kind of situation is to overdub the voice track, which involves the same person speaking exactly the same lines with exactly the same timing into a microphone in the editing studio. The result is a clean voice track. Then replace the original sound with the overdubbed track, which can be quite time-consuming. Adding ambient sound makes everything sound more natural. Overdubbing is fairly tricky and requires patience.

Chapter 16

Adding Titles and Visual Effects

In This Chapter

▶ Creating effective titles and graphics

▶ Adding magic to videos by using visual effects

▶ Making video look supersophisticated with 3-D animations and graphics

*E*verybody loves visual effects. They make Hollywood movies spectacular and so much more interesting than real life. The wizardry of the visual effects department can turn Brad Pitt into an old man in *Benjamin Button,* cars into scary robots in *Transformers,* or a handful of extras into armies of orcs in *Lord of the Rings.*

But visual effects consist of much more than these spectacular and hugely expensive Hollywood examples. Almost all videos use some kind of visual effects — often, only subtle ones.

You can use simple visual effects to make your video look better, more professional, and more interesting. Effects help you convey your message with fancy titles, easy-to-understand charts, and engaging animations. If you want to get fancy, modern technology makes even 3-D animations quite affordable.

All modern video editing programs offer some useful visual effects, from transitions and titles to color-correction features, slow-motion, and even simple animations.

Conveying Your Message with Titles

Titles don't simply get a video off to a good start. You can use them throughout the storyline to clarify topics, identify onscreen actors, or prompt viewers in what to do after they watch the video.

Inserting opening titles and closing credits

Opening titles tell viewers what the video they're watching is all about. These titles can also indicate who made the video, who appears in it, and who some of the key team members are.

Every good video can use these types of titles:

- ✔ **Opening:** An "XYZ Inc. presents" title establishes your company's brand as the first thing viewers see.

- ✔ **Main:** Make this title short, clear, and memorable. Get your audience hooked. Don't be too creative and mysterious. Clearly specify what your video is about, and make your description catchy so that it stays in viewers' minds to the end. Then they're likely to recommend your excellent video to others.

- ✔ **Secondary:** This optional title type can tell your audience more about your content. Or, if the video is part of a series, you can follow the main title with an episode title, such as *Adventures in Marketing,* Episode 4: "A New Hope."

- ✔ **Character:** If your video depicts real people, you may want to add a simple title to introduce them right away.

- ✔ **Call to action:** Make your call to action immediately before the closing credits. Viewers tend not to stick around for a video's credits, and you don't want to miss this crucial step.

- ✔ **Closing credits:** This is the moment your video team has been waiting for — to see their names on the big screen. Include everyone who contributed, even in small ways, to your video, including any outside contributors, such as the composer of your music. Credit is an easy gift to give, and people love it. Most editing programs let you create scrolling credits that can give your video a final cinematic touch.

Though most opening titles are placed at the beginning of a video, you can first draw viewers' attention with an interesting element instead. For example, you can tease viewers with one or two sentences describing the video or previewing a spectacular scene.

If you've filmed memorable bloopers or hilarious moments during your shoot (especially if your audience is familiar with key players in your video), play the bloopers as the credits roll so that audience members remain in their seats until the end. It's an entertaining, friendly way to end your presentation.

Specifying what to do next by issuing a call to action

The purpose of video marketing is to convince viewers to buy your product or service. Your video may be viewed outside the context of your website, so it *must* contain all the information viewers need to order or buy from you. A clear call to action at the end or immediately preceding the closing credits tells people how to find you, where they can find more information, or why your offer is special. Avoid using the same call to action every time — vary it depending on the content and goal of your video. If your goal, for example, is to sign up more newsletter subscribers, end your video with educational tips: "Want more tips like this? Sign up for our monthly newsletter at `www.acme. com/newsletter`."

A good call to action includes these elements:

- ✔ **The company and product name:** Use a logo, if possible.

- ✔ **The specific website address:** This address, known as the *landing page,* ties in to the offer.

- ✔ **The phone number:** An easy-to-remember 800 number works best to encourage viewers to call you.

- ✔ **A special offer that motivates people to visit the website:** Coupon codes and free items always grab people's attention, for example.

List your company's website address (or *URL*) at the bottom of the screen throughout the video. Many viewers won't watch the entire video, so the URL tells them immediately where to find you. Figure 16-1 shows how to use a website address without distracting viewers from the video's content.

A viewer's attention span is shorter than you may believe. Make your call to action clear and crisp. Avoid such uninspiring language as, "Learn more at `www.acme.com`." Give viewers a truly good reason to check you out.

Figure 16-1:
A website
address
at the bot-
tom of the
screen.

Identifying speakers in lower thirds

Most business videos feature people speaking. Perhaps you've interviewed a happy customer or your CEO welcomes viewers to your engaging new video or a well-known speaker talks about an important topic. Whatever the case may be, people want to know whom they see on the screen. One way to introduce central characters is to announce them on the voice track. But that's time-consuming and tiresome if you have more than a few characters.

A better way is to show simple titles — or *lower thirds* — at the bottom of the screen, as shown in Figure 16-2. You may recognize this element from the TV news: Whenever someone appears onscreen for the first time, the lower-third title shows the person's name and, often, title.

Figure 16-2:
A lower-
third title.

The best way to introduce someone onscreen is to insert a lower third about 2 to 5 seconds after you first show the person's face. Then let the lower third remain for about 10 seconds so that viewers have plenty of time to read it.

Apple iMovie offers a number of predefined title templates for lower thirds.

To add a lower third to your iMovie project, follow these steps:

1. **Choose the clip to which you want to add the lower third.**

   If the clip isn't in your project timeline yet, place it there.

2. Open the Title browser.

To open it, click the T icon on the gray toolbar to the right.

3. Select the title template you want to use.

The standard Lower Third template is the most flexible, but several are fancier, such as Paper, Gradient White, and Formal.

4. Drag and drop the selected title template to your clip.

For the best result, drop the template in the center of the clip to make the lower third cover the entire clip.

5. Enter the text for the lower third.

Type the text directly in the main video window.

6. Style the lower third.

Click the Show Fonts button, and select a different font or color to match the style of your video. Figure 16-3 shows some options you can use. The button labeled System Font Panel on the Font menu gives you even more options.

7. Change the timing of the lower third.

If you aren't happy with the length of the lower third, or if you want it to appear at a different spot in the clip, double-click the little blue bar above the clip. In the Inspector window that opens, you can change the duration of the lower third and change its fade-in and fade-out speeds. You can even select a different title template if you want to experiment with different styles. When you're happy with the new settings, click Done. To change the point where the lower third appears, simply drag the blue bar to the left or right.

Nothing is more embarrassing than not catching typos in someone's name, particularly when that person ends up watching your video. Proofread lower-third text carefully. If you're interviewing people you don't personally know, ask them to spell their names on camera before the interview begins.

Lower thirds can also be used to visually support the content of your video. If you're showing a long (and possibly confusing) speech, a brief phrase in the lower third can emphasize your take-away point so that the viewer can focus on the message you're trying to send.

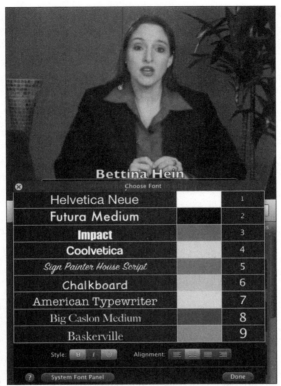

Figure 16-3:
A lower-third font selection.

Explaining by using charts and diagrams

Sometimes, live video footage isn't the best way to explain how something works or to show off a product. For example, because technical products often don't look like much from the outside, showing them in action is difficult. If you sell an abstract service, such as consulting, demonstrating it adequately on camera may be impossible.

As always, a picture is worth a thousand words. Charts and diagrams are useful ways to visualize your message. Many companies already possess visual material from brochures, websites, and PowerPoint presentations — a good starting point. You've likely put a lot of thought into these visualizations, so adapting them for your videos makes sense.

Videos need a different type of visualization:

✔ **The resolution of online videos is low.** The small video window on viewers' screens resembles a PowerPoint slide projection viewed from 60 feet away. Details are easily lost, and small fonts are difficult to read.

Make your charts simple, bold, and easy to understand.

✔ **Videos have rhythm and flow.** Nothing is more boring than viewing a static diagram for minutes at a time. Videos need movement.

Animate charts and diagrams, or zoom in on the parts you're explaining.

Insert charts into your video by using these elements:

✔ **Exported pictures:** PowerPoint, Keynote, and other presentation programs can export slides in JPEG or PNG file formats. Most video editing programs can use these files. You simply import them and then drag them to the timeline.

✔ **Screen recordings:** If you want to use an animated presentation, record it with a screen-recording program such as Camtasia or ScreenFlow.

Take your time progressing from step to step. You can always cut away the slack in your editing program.

✔ **Analog elements:** You don't always have to use fancy digital charts. Some of the most interesting videos simply show experts explaining concepts on whiteboards. To make text and diagrams easy to read, record close-up details of the drawing.

Designing titles

Most modern video editing programs offer a wide range of title templates, some of which look spectacular. In most cases, you can change fonts and colors to fit your taste and style. Take the time to experiment with these options.

The design of your titles should fit the style of your video and the branding of your company. Select colors and fonts that are compatible with the rest of your marketing material. Viewers should be able to recognize the style of your company in your videos.

A video helps you achieve your purpose, and the design of the video should help with your goal, not distract from it. Those fancy 3-D, *Star Wars*–style titles in your editing program may be fun to create, but ask yourself whether they truly fit the message of your video. Sometimes, it's better to keep things simple and ensure that viewers can focus on content.

Applying Visual Effects

Titles are necessary but also kind of boring. The fun of adding sizzle to your video starts when you begin to add visual effects, and modern video editing programs offer a wide range of effects that you can easily apply to your video.

Visual effects don't have to be flashy. Some of the most striking effects are barely visible to the untrained eye. The emotional medium of video speaks in ways that we humans don't process consciously. A few simple tricks can make a video look much more interesting and convey your message more effectively.

Moving between shots with transitions

The standard way to cut from one shot to another is to use a simple hard cut.

A *hard cut* occurs when the previous shot ends in one frame and the next shot begins in the following frame. It's the best type of cut to use 95 percent of the time.

A *transition* is a fancy way to move from one shot to the next. A transition uses a visual effect to make the cut more interesting.

You have two primary reasons to use transitions:

- ✔ Simple, soft transitions can help establish the rhythm of a video.
- ✔ The more elaborate, visible transitions signify that you're cutting to an entirely different scene.

These simple transitions are the most frequently used (and useful):

- ✔ **Cross dissolve:** One shot fades softly into the next.

  The simple cross dissolve transition is ideal for building a flowing rhythm in an edit.

- ✔ **Fade to black:** The picture fades softly into solid black, remains dark for a moment, and then fades softly to the next scene.

  Use the fade-to-black transition to separate scenes with a slightly dramatic look.

- **Dip to color:** The more exuberant cousin of the fade-to-black transition uses a color rather than black. When this effect is used with white, and is used quickly, a flash-like separator appears between scenes.

- **Wipes:** The next shot is gradually revealed, either swiping from one side to the other or moving in patterns such as circles or squares. (*Star Wars* inventor George Lucas is a big fan of the wipe.)

- **Cross blur:** The camera appears to lose focus, cuts to the next scene, and then returns to focus on the new shot.

You can find plenty more fancy transitions in most video editing programs, such as 3-D cubes, ripples that look like water waves, spinning pictures, page curls, and much, much more.

Decorative and exciting transitions are fun to see, and they work well to separate entirely different scenes. But they're the video equivalents of funky fonts in word processing: They're attractive and fresh if you use them only occasionally, but they aren't the right choices in most cases. Don't use transitions only to cut between shots in the same scene. Viewers will instinctively believe that a new scene has just begun and react with confusion if that isn't the case.

To see how to use transitions, simply pay attention to them while you watch TV. Most TV dramas and sitcoms use transitions sparingly, but you can find plenty of them in news reports, documentaries, and reality TV shows.

Correcting color and applying filters

Color is a vital tool to shape the emotional impact of a video. Movie professionals spend countless hours tweaking the color balance of their productions. The same scene can feel entirely different in warm, lively colors compared to cold bland ones.

Pay attention to the color balance the next time you watch a movie:

- Action movies use strong color contrasts, such as lots of blue and orange.

- Romantic comedies are usually subtle and warm.

- War movies generally look gritty, cold, and desaturated.

Even if you want to avoid making "artsy" color choices, correcting the colors in a mediocre shot is a good idea. Video cameras aren't as flexible as the human eye. They struggle to adapt to different lighting conditions.

Particularly when you mix natural light with light bulbs, you can show reddish faces or show windows in the background that shine in bright blue. Sometimes pictures look too dark or too bright, and in other cases, the camera exaggerates strong colors.

Fortunately, a little color correction (included in most modern video editing programs) can fix these problems. You can find the typical color correction tool, such as the iMovie video adjustments inspector (shown in Figure 16-4), in other programs, too.

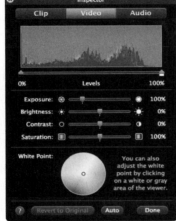

Figure 16-4:
The Video
Adjustments
Inspector
box in
iMovie 11
lets you
adapt
colors.

To optimize the look of a video in iMovie 11, follow these steps:

1. **Activate the Video Adjustments Inspector.**

   Select the clip that you want to color-correct and press V or choose Window➪Video Adjustments from the menu.

2. **Start the built-in autocorrection.**

   To start the built-in autocorrection, press the Auto button first to attempt to find a good color balance automatically. (The iMovie 11 program correctly balances the color surprisingly often.) If this strategy doesn't work well enough, try the other settings.

3. **Modify the exposure.**

   To make the picture look more vivid, the Exposure option lets you increase the intensity of the highlights (the brightest parts of the video picture) to become even brighter.

4. **Change the brightness of the picture.**

   The Brightness option lets you adapt the overall light level of the picture — helpful for brightening up elements when a shot is too dark.

   Too much brightness can result in video pictures that look quite pale.

5. **Fine-tune the contrast.**

   The Contrast option modifies the difference between the brightest and darkest parts of the picture — useful to boost shots that look flat.

6. **Optimize the color saturation.**

   The Saturation option lets you determine color strength and vividness.

   Consumer video cameras tend to exaggerate their colors anyway, so reducing saturation can sometimes make the video picture look more professional and movie-like.

7. **Change the color balance.**

   The White Point option lets you change the entire color balance to a different base color.

   • If you want a cool and corporate look, for example, select blue.

   • If you need more warmth, try orange or red.

8. **If you aren't happy with your work, go back to the original settings and start over.**

   You can reset all values at any time by clicking the Revert to Original button. Color correction involves experimenting with different settings — even the pros continually tweak the look of their videos.

9. **Click the Done button to apply your changes.**

Watch your video on at least two or three different screens. A computer monitor displays colors quite differently from a big-screen TV, which, in turn, displays colors differently from a projector connected to a laptop computer. Optimize your video's look for the type of screen that most viewers use.

Many editing programs let you choose additional video filters (or *video effects*) that you can use to give videos an interesting look. Some filters make footage look like it's from scratched old movies, other filters turn videos into science fiction flicks, and still others make videos look like *Saving Private Ryan*. Certain filters can be good starting points to tweak the look of your video. Try running your video through the different treatments to see whether it has impact on the way the video makes you feel. You may find that it creates the emotional connection your prospect was hoping for. Remember, though — less is typically more.

In certain editing programs, you can speed up or slow down footage. Apart from dramatic slow-motion effects or silly, Benny Hill–style, slapstick speed-ups, this feature can be useful to better fit a particular shot into the timing of an edit. Subtle changes in speed are barely noticeable to viewers, but can make shots look more interesting.

Cropping, rotating, and zooming footage

Professional camera operators frame their shots "just right" almost every time. But your footage likely isn't quite perfect. If too much space appears above the head of the interview subject or a distracting object appears on the edge of the shot, it's no problem — save your video project in the edit.

You can reframe video material in a number of ways:

- Most advanced editing programs let you crop footage to select the area of the video picture that you want to show. Cutting off a little of the edges lets you frame your shot perfectly, which sometimes can make all the difference between a humdrum shot and an inspiring one.

- Some programs let you rotate shots. If you tilted the camera a little when you took that epic landscape shot, don't worry — it happens. It's no big deal, thanks to the Rotation feature: Simply rotate the picture a few degrees, and the landscape then looks perfectly level.

- Many editing programs let you gradually change the framing of shots throughout a scene. You can use one part of the video picture at the beginning of the shot and use another at the end, with a fluid transition, even if the camera has never moved. One cool use of this technique is the "Ken Burns effect," named after the famous documentary filmmaker who zooms and pans around hundreds of historic photos in his films. Using the effect is a wonderful way to draw viewers' attention to a particular part of the picture, and it works with both still images and video.

To reframe a shot in iMovie, follow these steps:

1. **Go to Cropping view.**

   Select the clip that you want to modify in the timeline and press C, or choose Window➪Cropping, Ken Burns & Rotation from the menu.

2. **Select the part of the picture that you want to use.**

   You see a green frame that overlays the picture. The frame highlights the part of the picture that iMovie will show in the finalized clip. Draw the corners of the green frame until you see the portion of the picture that you want to use.

You can't change the width-to-height ratio of the frame. iMovie ensures that your new picture selection matches the aspect ratio of the entire video, which prevents your picture from appearing distorted.

3. **Add the dynamic "Ken Burns effect."**

   Click the Ken Burns button. In addition to the familiar green frame, you now see a red frame. The green frame represents the portion of the picture where the clip begins, and the red frame indicates where the clip ends. Move the corners of both frames so that you create the effect you want for the clip. For example, if you want to show the effect of "pushing in" an element, start with a bigger green frame, and end on a smaller red frame.

4. **Check to see whether your effect works as expected.**

   Verify the effect at any time by clicking the Play Clip (right arrow) button, next to the Done button, to play the clip with your new settings applied. When you're happy with the effect, click Done to apply the new settings to the clip.

To add some drama to your footage, add a slow *push-in*. This simulated, slow-zoom effect slowly enlarges the subject of the shot. The result is surprisingly powerful, literally drawing in the viewer. You can find this effect in most political and charity commercials.

Joining the Big Leagues: Motion Graphics and 3-D Animations

Subtle effects are helpful in shaping the emotional impact of a video, but sometimes you simply want to show off and dazzle your audience. In this case, bring out the big guns: motion graphics and 3-D animations.

These advanced animation techniques should be familiar to you from TV, not least because modern technology has made them quite affordable. Every small local TV station nowadays has glitzy animated introductory sequences with flying 3-D logos, and you can use the same technology (and creative talent) to spruce up your videos.

Unless you want to spend your weekends for the next year or so figuring out how to use animation software, work with a professional instead. (Yes, we're temporarily leaving do-it-yourself territory.) The software tools needed for creating animations are complex, and the skills are time-consuming to acquire. Fortunately, plenty of freelance artists and small production houses offer their services at affordable rates.

The animation standard: Pixar

Everyone knows Pixar for its movies, such as *Toy Story* and *Cars*. But Pixar was a pioneer in short, animated films. George Lucas, one of Pixar's original benefactors, asked Ed Catmull and Alvy Ray Smith to head a group to incorporate computer graphics, video editing, and digital audio into the entertainment field. In 1979, Lucasfilm Ltd. opened a division focused on computer animation, though Catmull and Smith later worried that Lucas would dissolve the department.

Lucas did not dissolve the division. Instead, he sold it to Steve Jobs, who named it Pixar, after the Pixar Image Computer, which was intended to perform complex graphics and image computations. Starting as a hardware company, Pixar grew to become the animation powerhouse we know today. Its series of short films were used as experimental films for the purpose of trying new programs and techniques on a cheaper experimental basis.

Injecting dynamism and drama with motion graphics

If you use PowerPoint, you probably have played with its built-in animations. Animation is a helpful way of letting a slide build step by step, flying in elements with different animation effects.

Professional motion graphics for videos do basically the same task, but on steroids — lots of *strong* steroids.

This list describes the most effective ways to use motion graphics:

✔ **Animated logos:** Your corporate logo (you want to display it prominently in your marketing video, right?) looks much more interesting if it's animated and builds slowly from shiny elements that fly onto the screen. Figure 16-5 shows a typical logo animation in progress. Even a traditional logo looks exciting if you add a healthy dose of visual effects.

✔ **Intro/outro wrappers:** If you're paying for motion graphics, you may as well use them wherever possible. *Wrappers* are reusable pieces of motion graphics that you can slap in front of, and at the end of, your videos. Even a simple video looks much more professional if it starts with an animated logo and ends with an animated call to action. Some video marketing software packages let you easily add these wrappers to your video without the need for actual editing.

✔ **Animated diagrams:** Explaining a product or service with charts and diagrams is always a good idea, but the additional flashiness of a professional motion graphic can make it look much more exciting.

✔ **Full animation videos:** If you want to splurge, you can even have an entire video produced with all motion graphics. This style works well for products or services that are difficult to explain using live footage. Be aware that the cost runs quite a bit higher than does a typical video.

Figure 16-5:
A logo animation in progress.

Producing 3-D animations on a budget

Remember the excitement of seeing the first 3-D computer animation movies, made by companies such as Pixar? *Toy Story* was a true breakthrough for the movie industry. This early 3-D animation still required rooms full of expensive computers.

The good news is that nowadays even a freelance artist with a powerful laptop can produce exciting 3-D graphics for you at affordable rates. (We aren't talking about the type of 3-D that requires you to wear those uncomfortable glasses — those are intended for big-time movies. You should never require this kind of additional equipment from someone viewing your marketing videos.)

Two different kinds of 3-D animations are now in use:

✔ **Pseudo-3-D animations** flip around two-dimensional objects (such as charts, photos, and text tables) in three-dimensional space. For example, a logo may "fly in" from far away, hover in the foreground, and then explode into a thousand pieces. The result can look exciting, and it's an affordable way to make existing material look flashy. Your graphics artist can probably work with programs such as Adobe After Effects or Apple Motion to create this kind of animation.

✔ **Real 3-D animations** use actual 3-D models of objects, similar to the Pixar-style animation movies. Creating these models is time consuming, but they give you full flexibility for your animation. A typical case of using real 3-D animations is architecture or design visualization. Let viewers take an in-flight tour of a planned building, or let them see your amazing new product from all angles. Graphics artists who provide this kind of animation use advanced software packages, such as Autodesk Maya, 3ds MAX, or Cinema 4D.

Locating cool animations

Producing animations isn't easy, so you may want to hire a professional artist to create them for you. Let these two suggestions help you find a good pro for your animation work:

- ✔ **Hire a video production house.** Many production companies have animation artists on staff and can advise you how to best use this type of video. An online video company, such as Bettina and Andreas' Pixability, offer them as part of their packages.

- ✔ **Find freelance artists on Internet platforms such as Elance, Mediamobz, or oDesk.** These folks can save you money if you're willing to do more work on your own. Be aware that some freelancers advertise their skills on particular programs, such as After Effects or Maya. Familiarizing yourself with the tools of the trade can help you find a good freelancer more quickly.

When you work with contractors, take the time to check their references. If they show you previous client work, ask which specific tasks they completed on every project. Before you search for a contractor, write down exactly what you want to achieve, and provide as much information as possible — for example, existing graphics that you own.

Part V
Posting and Promoting Your Video

The 5th Wave   By Rich Tennant

HELP DESK

TECHNICAL   ETHICAL

In this part . . .

After you complete a video or two, you need to get the fruits of your labor onto the web for everyone to see. The goal isn't simply to attract lots of people to watch your video — it's to attract the right people to watch. We begin this part by reviewing the hosting options for your video. We then show you how to promote it on your website, how to use social media to your advantage, and how to boost viewership by using search engine optimization (SEO). Finally, we provide you with the ways and means to measure results and improve your marketing along the way.

Chapter 17

Sharing Your Video on YouTube and Other Platforms

In This Chapter

▶ Posting your video where it can be found

▶ Transmitting video content in real time

*O*nly a few short years ago, sharing video on the Internet was a huge pain. Video makers had to deal with dozens of different file formats, users had to install special video player programs on their computers, and videos often stuttered badly.

Fortunately, a combination of new technologies and entrepreneurial ingenuity has changed this situation. Online video sharing is now so easy that virtually anyone can do it. At many different websites, Internet users can find all kinds of interesting video content, from simple, homemade clips to the latest TV shows. People are watching increasingly more video on the Internet. According to certain surveys, the average U.S. Internet user watches an incredible 17 hours of online video every month.

So the good news is that the technical hurdles to sharing and watching online video are lower than ever. But you have do some things correctly to reach your audience and to provide an optimal experience to your prospects.

In this chapter, you see how to put video on YouTube, the 800-pound gorilla of the video sharing industry. We look at alternatives that may work in certain cases, and we explore two advanced forms of online video: mobile and live streaming.

Putting Your Videos on YouTube

The most important thing to know about online video sharing is simple: You have to be on YouTube (www.youtube.com). No other video site comes even close to the importance, reach, and influence of YouTube.

How YouTube made video sharing easy

Before YouTube and its competitors came along, video sharing on the web was a complicated task. Video publishers had to support the three competing video file formats offered by Apple, Microsoft, and Real Networks. Users had to install (and frequently update) video player programs and had to know which players they had — if their computers were even compatible. If your favorite site published a video in Microsoft Windows Media format but you were on a Mac, too bad — no video for you.

This situation changed when Adobe introduced its Flash Video format (.flv). Flash software, which is now available on about 99 percent of computers, plays the colorful web animations you probably recognize from ad banners and informational graphics. After Adobe found a way to display video via Flash, users no longer had to install additional software. Problem solved.

YouTube, one of the first sites to simplify the uploading and converting of video to the Flash format, started in May 2005 and quickly won a huge following. People loved the simplicity of being able to self-publish videos that could, in minutes, play on any Internet-connected computer — a previously unthinkable task. Users also liked YouTube's social features, such as being able to comment on other people's videos or subscribe to their channels.

Only 18 months later, YouTube was acquired by Google for an eye-popping $1.65 billion. The three founders — all in their twenties — became instant multimillionaires. (It's nice work, if you can get it.)

YouTube is the website that changed the way online video works. When YouTube started in 2005, it made video sharing incredibly easy for the first time. Though YouTube had literally hundreds of competitors, it won the race for market dominance by offering a combination of simplicity and smart social features. After only 18 months, YouTube was purchased by the search engine giant Google, whose huge resources further increased the site's importance.

YouTube is now the only video sharing site that is an absolute necessity for your video distribution. Yes, YouTube is sometimes messy, crowded, and unpredictable, but it's also where most people look for videos on the topics they care about. YouTube, a cultural phenomenon, is quite simply the only video site that many Internet users visit. It's now also the second-largest search engine in the world.

Professional video makers sometimes are skeptical about YouTube because they don't like to publish their precious masterpieces on the same site where people share clips of skateboarding dogs or exploding coke bottles. But if you're in the business of marketing to people, you need to go where the people are, and in the world of online video, it's YouTube.

Creating a YouTube channel

YouTube organizes its videos into *channels,* or collections of videos that belong to a particular user. Any registered YouTube user can create her own channel and then publish her own videos, link to other people's videos, or interact with other users. And it's all free. YouTube makes money from the advertising it displays on the site.

Setting up a new YouTube channel is simple. Follow these steps:

1. **In your web browser, go to** www.youtube.com.

2. **Click the Create Account link.**

3. **Fill out the form that opens.** Among other tasks, YouTube asks for the username you want to use, your e-mail address, a password, and your birthdate, to ensure that you're old enough to use the platform.

4. **Click the Next Step button.**

5. **If you want to add a photo to your YouTube profile, add a picture of yourself by clicking the Add Profile Photo button. Then drag a photo from your computer's hard drive to the area labeled Drag a Photo Here, and click the Set As Profile Photo button.** If you have no photo handy, don't worry: You can skip this step altogether.

6. **Click the Next Step button.**

7. **Click the Back to YouTube button to complete the creation of your new YouTube account.**

8. **Click the icon in the upper-right corner that has a little downward-pointing triangle next to it. From the menu that opens, select My Channel.**

9. **Enter the YouTube channel name you want to use.** Because this name appears in many locations throughout YouTube, choose a name that reflects the topic of your channel. For example, if you're creating a channel for a company named Acme Lawnmowers, Inc., a good name is acmelawnmowers or lawnmowerexperts.

   Be specific in choosing your channel name, but don't overhype. Avoid expressions such as *buy, cheap,* and *free* because they can cause your videos to be blocked as spam.

10. **Click the Next button.**

11. **Specify the privacy settings for your channel.** If you want to use YouTube primarily for marketing, leave all options turned on. You can always change them later. Click All Done, and YouTube creates your channel.

After you set up a channel, you can personalize it and make it look more attractive. Follow these steps:

1. **Click the Edit Channel button.**

2. **If you want to change the background color of your channel, click Choose a Color and select a color you like.** Use a color that reflects your company's identity — for example, the color of your company logo. Then click Accept.

3. **Using the Background section on this page, upload a background picture to make your channel look unique.** It can be any picture that shows your product, or it can be simply an attractive background pattern. Users see only the image on both sides of the main content area in the middle of the screen.

4. **Choose Info and Settings in the top bar.**

5. **In the Title field, enter a title for your channel.** You may pick your business name, for example, or a description of the topic your channel covers.

6. **Enter a brief description text that explains what your channel is about.** This text appears on your YouTube channel page and helps users understand what you have to offer.

7. **Enter some descriptive keywords in the Tags field.** These keywords describe the topic of your channel. Use plenty of tags (at least 10 or 20) so that people can find your channel if they look for information about your topics. Separate your keywords with commas; for example: *lawn-mower, lawn care, lawn care experts.* See Chapter 20 for more tips on how to find the best tags.

8. **In the Default Tab box, choose Videos Tab.** This option ensures that your newest videos appear on your channel's front page. Figure 17-1 shows a completed form.

9. **Click Done Editing.**

Investing a bit of time in your channel's background image pays off — it not only makes your channel look distinctive but also better carries your company's brand image. As a starting point, look for *YouTube backgrounds* at your favorite search engine to find lots of freely available background images.

Sometimes, you see other YouTube channels that have highly customized layouts with large, graphical headers or even interactive elements. Unfortunately, these bells and whistles aren't available to everyone. You have to do one of the following:

- ✔ **Become a YouTube partner.** To become a partner, you need approximately 100,000 video views.

- ✔ **Be a good advertising customer on YouTube.** By *good customer,* we mean that you spend at least a high five-figure dollar amount.

Before you can reach this level of YouTube sophistication, you need to nail down some of the basics, as described in the following sections.

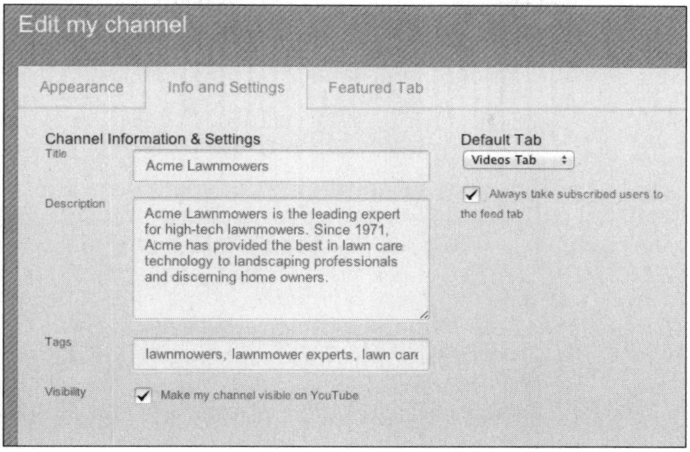

Figure 17-1:
Specifying
the title
and details
for your
YouTube
channel.

Uploading and tweaking your videos

After your YouTube channel is ready to go, it's time to upload your first video. Follow these steps:

1. **Prepare the video that you want to upload.** The video file should be ready on your computer or on an attached hard drive. YouTube accepts all widely used video file formats, such as AVI, MOV, and MP4.

2. **Go to** www.youtube.com **to ensure that you're logged in.** If you see your username in the upper-right corner, you're logged in. Otherwise, click the Sign In link and enter your username and password.

3. **Click the Upload link.** This link opens the Upload Video Files page.

4. **Click the Select Files from Your Computer button.** A file selection box appears. Select the video on your computer that you want to upload. Click Open. YouTube starts the upload and shows you a progress bar indicating how long it will take.

5. **While you wait, start adding the video information.** Immediately below the Upload Video Files section, you can enter the title, descriptive text, and tags (keywords) for your video. Choose an appropriate category.

6. **When the upload is complete and you have entered all required information, click the Save Changes button.**

7. **To watch your video, go to your channel page. Find your username in the upper-right corner, and click it. When the menu appears, choose My Channel.**

A keyword-rich title, crisp description text, and plenty of tags are important in order to be found by your intended audience. See Chapter 20 for details on how to use these elements for maximum effect. YouTube management tools, such as the Pixability video marketing software (`http://app.pixability.com`), can help you save a lot of time.

Always upload the highest-quality file format for your video. If your video is in high-definition (HD) resolution, upload it. YouTube automatically scales it down to multiple different formats that provide viewers with optimal quality.

YouTube gives you some functionality to tweak your video after you upload it. If your video is well-edited in the first place, editing probably isn't even necessary, though it can be handy if you've uploaded relatively raw videos.

To edit a video, click your username in the upper-right corner and choose Video Manager from the menu. In the list of videos that appears, click the thumbnail picture of the video you want to change. Then click the Edit Video button above the video player. Figure 17-2 shows the editor page you see.

Figure 17-2: The YouTube video editing page.

On the editing page, you can change a number of elements:

- ✔ **Trim:** Shorten your video from both sides — simply click the Trim button, and drag the gray sliders from both sides. Play the video to see whether you have achieved the effect you want. When you're happy with your choices, click the Done button.

- ✔ **Rotate:** Turn your video to one side 90 degrees, using the two rotation buttons. This feature is useful if you've recorded a video on a camera phone and the video is in portrait (upright) orientation rather than landscape (horizontal) orientation.

✔ **Stabilize:** Remove the shakiness (a common problem) from your footage. Processing longer videos takes a while, but it's typically worth your time.

✔ **Color correction:** The four buttons on the right side let you change the brightness, contrast, color saturation, and color temperature of a video. This process works much like the color correction available in most editing programs (see Chapter 16). Use color correction to fine-tune the look of your video.

Overly dark videos particularly benefit from a bit more brightness.

✔ **Effects:** Applies one of several predefined looks to your video. Simply choose the look you like, and click the Apply button.

As always, less is typically more when you're adding effects to a video.

✔ **Music:** Replace your video's audio track with music from the YouTube library. This action doesn't replace proper audio editing, but if you need a soundtrack quickly, it's helpful. The Audio tab has a style for almost every situation. Experiment with different keywords, which you can type into the Search Available Tracks box to find appropriate tracks for your video.

If you want to manipulate your videos in great deal, YouTube offers a number of sophisticated online editing tools from third-party vendors. Go to www.youtube.com/create to find several helpful tools for video creation and online editing. The editor made by WeVideo is definitely worth a try.

Managing playlists and favorites

A *playlist* is a way to group videos by common topics. It's useful when you want to

✔ **Locate video:** Playlists help your YouTube channel's visitors find the videos they're interested in.

✔ **Get found in search results on YouTube:** If you have a useful playlist about a particular topic, it will likely appear prominently whenever people look for the topic. That's good for your viewer numbers.

To manage your playlists, click your username and then select Video Manager Start by following these steps to create a new playlist:

1. **Choose the Playlist option in the leftmost sidebar.**

2. **Click the New Playlist button.**

3. **Give your playlist a title and a description. Click the Create Playlist button.**

4. **On the next page that opens, specify more details.** You can decide whether your playlist should be public or private.

5. **Click Save.**

6. **Add videos to your playlist by returning to the Video Manager list. Select the check box next to the videos you want to add.** Figure 17-3 shows an example.

7. **Click the Add To button at the top, and choose the playlist you want to use.** You can add some optional notes to your newly added video. Then click the Add Note button.

8. **Check your new playlist for correctness.** Click the Playlist link in the sidebar on the left, and then click the name of your new playlist.

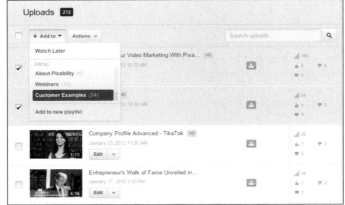

Figure 17-3:
Adding
videos to a
playlist.

A special type of playlist is the *Favorites list.* You can add videos to this list in the same way you would add them to any playlist. By default, the list of your favorite videos appears prominently on your channel, so it's a useful way to direct people to your best work.

Add your own videos to your playlists and Favorites list, and add them to other people's lists. You can add to your playlists not only your own videos but also other people's videos that you find on YouTube. If you can offer a playlist of some of the best videos on the subject (including your own, of course), viewers who are interested in a particular topic will be grateful. To add other videos, click the Add To button that you see below every YouTube video when you're logged in.

Adding annotations

In addition to the available editing functionality in YouTube, it lets you add *annotations* to your videos: These small text boxes or comic-style speech bubbles provide additional information to viewers. Annotations can link to other YouTube videos, or they can let people subscribe to your channel.

An annotation is a useful way to include an additional call-to-action element to a video.

To add an annotation, follow these steps:

1. **Go to the Video Manager page by clicking your username in the upper-right corner and choosing Video Manager from the menu that appears.**

2. **Click the thumbnail picture of the video to which you want to add the annotation.**

3. **Click the Edit Annotations link.**

4. **Click the Add Annotation button, and choose the type of annotation you want to add.** Use speech bubbles and notes for visible, colorful annotations that are ideal for calls to action, as shown in Figure 17-4.

   Titles are more discreet text elements that can convey additional information. *Spotlights* are used to point out particular parts of the picture.

5. **Position the annotation where you want it, and then add the text you want.** You can also change the font color and (for speech bubbles and notes) background color.

6. **Fine-tune the timing of your annotation.** You can choose when this element should appear and disappear. Drag it in the timeline below the video, and change its duration by dragging one corner.

Figure 17-4:
Adding annotations to a video.

7. **Choose a link.** Unfortunately, an annotation cannot link to an external site, such as your company's website. But it can link to another YouTube video, playlist, or channel. An annotation can also let people subscribe to your channel with only one click. Simply select the Link check box, and choose the type of link you want to make. Paste into the text box the web address *(URL)* of the video or playlist you want to link to.

8. **When you finish, play the video to ensure that everything appears where you want it.**

9. **Click Publish to activate your annotations.**

An annotation isn't added to a video — it's displayed *on top of it* by the YouTube video player. Viewers can turn off annotations, and viewers on most current mobile devices such as smartphones or iPads don't even see them. In other words, use annotations as additional elements, but don't rely on them for your video marketing strategy.

Understanding subscriptions

Subscribing to other channels is popular among avid YouTube users. It's an easy way to keep up with your favorite content producers. When you subscribe to another channel, you're notified about new videos that are published on the channel.

To subscribe to another channel you like, click the Subscribe button immediately above any related YouTube video.

Getting people to subscribe to your own channel has a lot of advantages. Your subscribers see all your new content, so it's a helpful way to build a loyal audience. YouTube tends to reward channels that have a lot of subscriptions with more exposure in search results and Related Videos sidebars.

In other words, having a lot of subscribers brings you more viewers, and that's always beneficial in video marketing. But how do you motivate people to subscribe to your channel? The best way is quite simply to regularly provide compelling content. In addition, at the end of your videos, use annotations that help people subscribe easily. Be generous with your own subscriptions to other people's channels. When you subscribe to their content, they often return the favor.

Interacting with other YouTube users

Though YouTube is primarily a video sharing site, it's also a social network. People can become "friends" much like they can on Facebook, they can send direct messages to each other, and they can leave comments about videos and even respond with their own videos.

To see what people are writing, click your username in the upper-right corner and then click Inbox. You see the different types of YouTube messages, such as comments, personal messages, and friend invites.

Visit your inbox regularly, and react to incoming messages. YouTube sends you e-mail notifications so that you don't miss anything.

React to personal messages, and accept all friend invites (unless they're from spammers). Having more social links on YouTube means that more people are interested in your content, which helps increase your viewer numbers.

Over time, you start to get comments and messages from viewers. Don't be shocked if the quality is sometimes low — YouTube isn't known for its high-brow online discourse. Unfortunately, the relative anonymity of YouTube encourages many users to write offensive, spammy, or just plain silly comments.

Fortunately, you can turn off the commenting function on every video, which makes sense in some cases. You can also remove offensive comments and even block users who continually violate the rules of good taste.

However, if you're truly serious about YouTube marketing, take the time to interact with your viewers. Being an active part of the community is the best way to be seen. Other people promote your content, and that's the best and most credible way to reach an audience.

Using Other Video Sharing Platforms

Though YouTube is clearly the dominant video platform, it is by no means the only game in town. YouTube's success has motivated literally hundreds of other companies to create their own video platforms. Unfortunately, none of them has even come close to YouTube's user numbers. Many competing video sites have shut down over the past few years, and others have changed their business models to focus on particular niches.

Some video sharing sites still draw a significant number of viewers, however, and can make sense as additional distribution points for marketing videos.

Vimeo

The Vimeo platform (www.vimeo.com), a favorite among aspiring filmmakers, positions itself as a higher-quality alternative to YouTube, where people who are serious about video can publish their work and watch other people's creative masterpieces.

The video quality at Vimeo tends to be significantly better than at YouTube, and the Vimeo community is much more mature and serious-minded. The site is far less cluttered and distracts viewers less with intrusive ads and pushy lists of related videos.

Unfortunately for video marketers, Vimeo prohibits videos with marketing-oriented content. Its terms and conditions explicitly prohibit content for commercial use.

However, Vimeo offers a paid plan for video marketers. For $199 per year, you can buy a Pro account to host commercial videos on Vimeo. But videos published under these accounts don't show up on the normal Vimeo community site.

Though you can find product pitches and other clearly marketing-oriented videos on Vimeo, they're technically violating the site's terms and conditions and may be removed at any time.

Because of its strict guidelines for posting commercial videos, Vimeo isn't a platform where video marketers can reach their audiences. The site's Pro plan, however, can serve as a reliable and cheap alternative to host your videos for use on your site. Check Chapter 18 for more details on this aspect.

Viddler

Another former YouTube competitor that has stopped providing free video sharing is Viddler (www.viddler.com). This site, which recently stopped offering free video upload functionality, now concentrates on video hosting for businesses, much like the Vimeo Pro plan.

Viddler prices, which start at $50 per month, are significantly higher than at Vimeo, and it offers more sophisticated features for business users, such as advanced analytics and a customizable player.

The main difference between Viddler and the countless other video hosting companies (see Chapter 18) is that it still retains social features. Users can comment on your videos directly on the site, and they can find your content based on tags. This capability may attract a few more viewers to your videos if they're hosted on Viddler. But again, Viddler isn't a direct alternative to YouTube if you want to reach a broad audience.

Dailymotion

Dailymotion is probably the closest alternative to YouTube that you can find. This French video community site is popular mainly in Europe and in certain Asian countries. Like YouTube, it's open to anybody, and it has a vibrant community of users.

For a while, Dailymotion had a tarnished reputation because it was the target of spammers and producers of questionable content. But the site has cleaned up its act and is now a viable video community that attracts many serious content producers and video marketers.

To put the market situation into perspective: Dailymotion reaches about 3 to 5 percent of the users that YouTube has; it is, at best, an addition to your YouTube strategy, not an alternative. Sharing your videos on Dailymotion can still be a good idea because it helps improve how well your videos can be found on search engines. Video search engines such as Google Video and Bing Video show results from Dailymotion next to YouTube results.

The rest

Quite a bit of confusion still exists over the many video sites that once tried to compete with YouTube, only to fall behind in the race for viewer eyeballs. Almost all these sites have completely changed their business models and no longer accept video uploads. For the sake of completeness, this list describes some of the more important sites and what they're up to now:

- ✔ **Blip.tv** (www.blip.tv) focuses on "web series" from producers of original content.

- ✔ **Hulu** (www.hulu.com) is the most popular site for long-form content such as TV shows and movies. Jointly owned by NBC Universal, News Corporation, The Walt Disney Company, and Providence Equity Partners, Hulu has opened itself to professional content producers beyond TV stations, though it isn't possible to publish your marketing videos on Hulu. Advertising options are available but costly.

- ✔ **Metacafe** (www.metacafe.com), a former YouTube competitor, is now an entertainment-focused content site and no longer lets you upload video.

- ✔ **Myspace** (www.myspace.com), the former social networking sensation, still offers a YouTube-style site where users can upload their videos. Though most other features are similar to YouTube as well, the importance of Myspace has rapidly declined. Still, it's worth a look if you're in the music or entertainment business.

- ✔ The **Yahoo! Video site** (http://screen.yahoo.com) is now an entertainment channel that shows only Yahoo!-created content.

Though technically not a full-blown video sharing site, Facebook is now an increasingly popular place to publish videos. The biggest social network lets you upload videos and share them with your Facebook friends. Chapter 19 tells you more about how to use Facebook for video marketing.

Posting Video for Viewing on Phones and Tablets

A mobile device such as a smartphone or tablet is an increasingly popular way to watch online video. Not so long ago, phones were barely powerful enough to display video in reasonable quality. But on today's sophisticated smartphones and fast wireless networks, mobile video has become a reality.

The good news is that many of the most popular video sites and video hosting services now support the most recent generation of mobile phones and tablets. There's quite a bit of bad news too: People who still use older and cheaper phones will still have a tough time watching your videos because the broadly supported mobile video standards have evolved fairly recently and are still in flux. Furthermore, mobile devices can't do everything that PCs and Macs can do with video, so it's worth your time to understand some of the limitations of mobile video.

Preparing your videos for mobile devices

Mobile devices aren't as powerful as PCs, they have smaller screens, and they typically don't have the same high-speed connection to the Internet. That's why video for mobile has to be specifically prepared with lower resolutions and for lower data speeds.

If you post your videos on YouTube, or if you use a modern video hosting service, you're in luck: These providers do the preparing for you. On YouTube in particular, you don't have to do anything to make your videos compatible with mobile devices. Most people can play them only if they go to the YouTube mobile site (http://m.youtube.com) or if they use the built-in YouTube app on an Android, iPad, or iPhone device. Figure 17-5 shows you what YouTube looks like on an iPhone.

Be sure that you understand how mobile video is different from PC-based video, as explained in the following list, because mobile video can influence some of your marketing tactics.

✓ **Most mobile devices can't use the Adobe Flash technology, which is commonly used with most PC- or Mac-based video players on the web.** The rich functionality of a YouTube video player — annotations, sharing, and subtitles, for example — isn't available on mobile devices. Most phones and tablets can only play the video itself; the other bells and whistles are missing.

✓ **The smaller screen size and lower data speed of mobile devices make your audience's viewing experience somewhat more limited than it is on a PC or Mac.** For example, small onscreen text is quite difficult to read. Keep this point in mind when you edit videos. Always consider what your videos will look like on a tiny screen.

Figure 17-5: YouTube on an iPhone.

Understanding video formats for mobile devices

Mobile video technology is still young, and it changes continually. As usual in new markets, technology companies throw around an alphabet soup of technical acronyms. You may find some of these important technical expressions when you deal with mobile video:

✔ **HTML5:** This latest version of the web's underlying layout language adds some features that make video compatible with mobile devices. Though some people refer to "HTML5 video," HTML5 isn't a video standard. It simply defines how video is integrated into web pages, including those for mobile devices. The most frequently used video standard for HTML5 is H.264.

✔ **H.264:** This standard, the most commonly used modern video file standard, is used by the iPhone and iPad and by many other mobile devices and many modern video cameras. H.264 can compress videos quite strongly without losing much picture quality.

✔ **MPEG-4:** This slightly older standard is frequently used for mobile devices as well. H.264 is the most modern flavor of MPEG-4.

✔ **3GPP (or 3gp):** This video file format was specifically developed for mobile devices and is supported by even some of the simplest and cheapest phones. Think of it as the lowest common denominator. YouTube makes most videos available in this format as well.

Streaming Live Content

Anyone can now run their own little Internet TV station on the web. Live video streaming has become widely available over the past few years, and it's now so simple that you can broadcast live video from your phone or from the built-in webcam in your laptop.

All your viewers need to do is go to a particular web page at the time of the broadcast. Live video streaming uses basically the same technology as online video players for recorded video, so your viewers don't have to install additional software. But they need a relatively fast Internet connection.

To stream live video, you need these items:

✔ **A camera:** You need a webcam or a traditional video camera that has a FireWire output. Other types of cameras, such as Flip cameras and digital photo cameras, cannot stream video and therefore cannot be used for video broadcasts.

✔ **A reasonably fast computer with a good Internet connection:** A wired connection is strongly recommended. Try to avoid wireless connections because they can be shaky. If you want to use an external video camera, you need a FireWire connection on your computer.

✔ **A streaming provider:** This type of service broadcasts your show over the Internet. You can find out more about these services in the later section "Working with streaming providers."

✔ **Video streaming software:** This normally is provided by your streaming provider.

> ✔ **A web page at which your live video player will be published and people can visit to watch the show:** Some streaming providers offer their own sites for this purpose, but you typically should have a player on a page on your own website.

Recognizing what you can and cannot do

Live streaming makes sense for video marketers in a number of scenarios, such as when you want to

> ✔ Broadcast your marketing events for customers who couldn't "attend"
>
> ✔ Conduct educational seminars *(webinars)*
>
> ✔ Announce, and demonstrate the use of, new products

A live broadcast is still an event that's special and interesting, and it's an effective way to capture people's attention. The thrill of "live TV" on the Internet often excites your audience more than any old video does.

However, just because you can stream live video from your phone or webcam doesn't mean that you should. As with normal recorded videos, people expect to see a certain level of quality. When they invest the time to show up for a live broadcast at a particular time, they want to see strong content that is well produced.

Expect your live streaming projects to be at least as much work as producing a normal recorded video. Presenting a good, live online video show requires a lot of preparation and practice.

Practice makes perfect. Complete a run-through of your show well in advance, including all necessary technical elements. This strategy is worth the effort because many minor annoyances can occur. Catch them while you can, because it's too late when you're live on the air.

Working with streaming providers

Live video streaming requires a lot of Internet bandwidth because you have to send the same video to potentially hundreds or thousands of viewers at the same time. It's a task that you can't (or at least shouldn't) do yourself. Instead, work with a video streaming provider.

These companies sell a service that lets you distribute your live video stream to many viewers. You send your show's video stream — which you produce on your computer — to the streaming provider's server, and it in turn sends your stream to all your viewers at the same time. The more sophisticated services even prepare multiple quality levels on the fly so that even people with relatively bad Internet connections can still watch your show.

Several companies provide the necessary technology to stream live video:

- ✔ **Brightcove** (www.brightcove.com)**:** The market-leading video hosting service provides live streaming as a feature for its enterprise customers. Brightcove provides the best quality we know of but at a steep price: Packages with live streaming features start in the four figures per month.

- ✔ **Justin.tv** (www.justin.tv)**:** Largely focused on consumers, this service is popular on the video game scene and certain other niches. Because Justin.tv is fully ad-financed and interrupts your show with commercials, it isn't an ideal choice for marketers.

- ✔ **Livestream** (www.livestream.com)**:** This direct competitor to Ustream offers a similar product with more sophisticated features, such as deeper analytics. The paid, ad-free plan starts at $350 per month.

- ✔ **Qik** (http://qik.com)**:** This service is optimized for streaming from mobile devices such as smartphones. Though its social media integration is strong, the site is mostly geared toward the needs of consumers, not businesses.

- ✔ **Ustream** (www.ustream.tv)**:** Using this large website — with live video channels about all kinds of topics — is free, but you have to accept the site's showing of unrelated advertising in and around your video player. It's typically a distraction for your viewers, so consider signing up for the Pro package, which removes ads and starts at $99 per month. Ustream also provides streaming software and sells additional production services.

Most streaming providers give you their own streaming software for producing a live show. Though these programs are typically quite easy to use, they're limited. If you want more sophistication, take a look at Telestream's Wirecast software (www.telestream.net): It's basically a TV studio in the form of a software program. Features such as switching between multiple cameras, adding sophisticated titles, and making 3-D transitions make your show look a lot more professional and interesting.

Attracting an audience for your live broadcast

A live video show makes sense only if you can reach a sizable audience. Don't expect people to show up like that. You have to invest some effort to motivate them to tune in.

To excite your audience, follow these suggestions:

✔ **Invite a well-known guest.** Big names attract big audiences. The guest doesn't have to be an actual celebrity — a well-known expert in your industry grabs people's attention and lends credibility to your broadcast.

✔ **If you have an e-mail list of customers and prospects, announce your show several times on it.** Clearly state the value that viewers can receive from the show. Start announcing it about two weeks before the event, and repeat the announcement one week and two days before the event.

✔ **Use your social media channels to announce your show.** Promote your broadcast multiple times on Facebook, LinkedIn, and Twitter. People often have short attention spans, and repetition helps you draw more viewers.

✔ **Produce a preview video about your show that you distribute with your announcements.** People are more likely to sign up for a live show if your preview video looks interesting.

✔ **Have a landing page where people can sign up for your broadcast with their e-mail addresses.** This strategy increases their commitment to show up and gives you additional leads. Use your preview video on this page. Send an e-mail reminder to the participants on the day of the broadcast.

✔ **Repeat the day and time of your show in all communications.** Be sure to include the time zone.

Only about half the people who sign up for a live video event typically watch it. Be sure to reach enough people to make your live show efforts worth your while.

Chapter 18

Incorporating Marketing Videos into Your Website

In This Chapter

▶ Finding a hosting service

▶ Adding video to a web page

*J*ust a few years ago, online video was still a novelty. Web video players were unreliable, and not many users had the bandwidth to watch high-quality online videos. That's why most websites using video treated the new medium as experimental, to be confined to its own special part of the site, where it could do little harm even if things went wrong.

Fortunately, this type of technical difficulty is a relic of the past. With broadband speeds available to almost everybody — even on mobile devices — and reliable technical standards well established, online video has become mainstream.

But many website owners haven't yet figured out how to use video on their websites effectively. Many are still reluctant to place videos front and center, and many struggle with the technical details. It's a pity because video is a wonderful way to catch people's attention and describe products and services.

In this chapter, you can find out where, why, and how to use video on your company's website. We explain the technical options and walk you through the process of easily adding videos to your site.

Knowing Where to Use Your Video

The first issue to address in incorporating video into your online marketing strategy is where on your company website to use video. When you use modern technology, you can embed videos limitlessly: They can live on the home page, in blog articles, on product pages, or on campaign-specific landing pages.

Use video where people can see it. Video is an attractive (and often expensive) marketing asset. If you've invested a lot of time and money into producing a fantastic video, we see no reason not to simply place it on your site's home page.

Place video in the logical place where it can best support your marketing message:

- ✔ **If a video introduces your company,** post the video on the home page.

- ✔ **If a video explains a product in detail,** add the video to the product page.

- ✔ **If a video contains a testimonial from a customer,** place it next to the product it refers to or add it to the Why You Should Choose Us section.

- ✔ **If your video is related to an event,** post the video in a blog article or news item that mentions it.

Placing video on your home page

Many people still feel that posting video on a company website's home page is a radical strategy. After all, home page real estate is extremely scarce and valuable. Even if you have plenty of elements to post there, you may simply be asking too much if you try to use all that space for a single video.

The Dropbox home page (www.dropbox.com) consists of only a Download button and a two-minute video describing the product. This simple site helped the company — one of the most successful software startup companies of the past decade — acquire more than 45 million users in only four years.

Of course, most companies have more than one product, and conflicting interests abound in assigning home page real estate. Fortunately, you can choose from the following placement strategies for using video on your home page, one of which should fit your needs. You can use video as

- ✔ **The primary eye-catching element:** This bold strategy positions your video front and center, likely filling about 50 percent of the home page area that a user can see without scrolling.

Focusing on a single home page element makes sense if your video communicates the crucial marketing message you want to convey.

- ✔ **A secondary item:** Most home page layouts have several boxes in which you can place elements such as product announcements, calls to action, or special offers. Embedding video in one or several of these boxes is a useful way to draw more attention to them. People enjoy watching videos, and a video player with a clearly visible Play button is an effective, eye-catching element.

- ✔ **Support content:** Many items on the home page have Learn More links. You can increase the effectiveness of these links by making a video the target content. Write text, such as "Watch a video about product X," to see a likely uptick in clicks on these items. The link opens a separate page where viewers can see the video and you can place calls to action and other content directly on the page.

✔ **An element in a slide show:** Many websites use as the main element of their home pages a changing information box that looks like a slide show to let viewers "flip" through a number of different messages. You can use a video as one of these messages.

Figure 18-1 shows wireframe examples of how video can be incorporated into the design of your website.

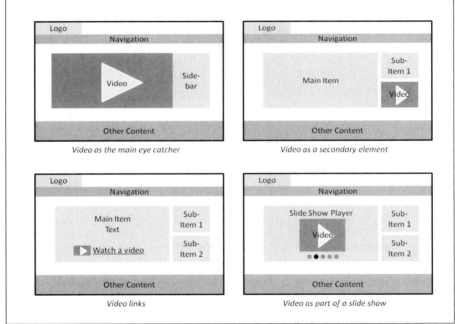

Figure 18-1: Wireframe examples showing where to place videos on your home page.

Supporting web content with video

Video can add value to almost any part of a website. Think of video as a different type of content, much like text or pictures. The right mix of these content types makes a website attractive.

This list describes some site locations where you can most effectively use video:

✔ **Product pages:** Video is arguably the best way to explain and demonstrate products.

✔ **Testimonials:** If you use customer testimonials to market products, ask a few customers to appear in a video testimonial. Filmed testimonials have much more credibility than simple text-based testimonials.

✔ **Case studies:** Attract new prospects by demonstrating how existing customers use your product.

✔ **Blogs:** Support your blog posts with expert interviews, short reports from your company events or trade shows, and in-depth educational content.

✔ **Frequently Asked Questions (FAQs):** This section of a website is important but often boring. A few short videos that answer the most important questions can help significantly.

✔ **Learning centers:** Many sites have educational sections where customers and prospects can find more information about your industry, products, and related topics. Video is one of the most effective ways to provide educational content that people appreciate and share with others.

✔ **About Us pages:** Most prospects look at this page before making buying decisions. Presenting your company in an attractive video is a perfect way to make a lasting impression.

Avoid limiting yourself to the type of video that can be categorized as "A word from our CEO." Highlighting your executives can add to your credibility, but your video strategy should advance well beyond focusing on talking heads.

✔ **Careers:** Potential employees can gain a much better perspective on your company's culture when they can watch a video about its operations.

Position videos by integrating them directly into the flow of your content. Don't hide videos behind difficult-to-find links; instead, place them directly on the page so that people can watch them with minimal effort.

Avoid the allure of pop-up video players. Though they allow visitors to immerse themselves completely in your videos, studies have shown that players decrease viewership. Use a thumbnail image that plays the video when selected.

Using video for e-commerce sites

If you sell online, anything that increases the perceived attractiveness of your products immediately affects the bottom line. That's why increasingly more e-commerce sites are using video.

Large retailers, such as the shoe seller Zappos, report an increase in sales of as much as 30 percent for products accompanied by videos. It makes sense: Customers have to make decisions about your products based only on web content. Anything that paints a fuller picture is helpful in making decisions.

Many products are hard to describe using only text and images, but they lend themselves well to video demonstrations. Even products that cannot be directly demonstrated benefit from related video content. For example, Amazon lets book authors publish videos in which they can talk about their book or let readers give testimonials.

Increasing sales and conversions

Whether you sell shoes, high-end consulting services, or submarines, using video is a means to an end: increasing business for your company. When you integrate video into your website, couple videos with elements that help you convert visitors to the next sales stage.

You must first determine, however, the action you want viewers to take after watching your video, such as

- ✔ Call you, send e-mail, chat, or fill out a contact form
- ✔ Buy your product directly from your website or from a different site
- ✔ Download more information, such as an e-book or a white paper
- ✔ Sign up for an in-person event or a webinar
- ✔ Watch another video

Your priorities for the action you want viewers to take depend on whether you're selling to businesses or consumers and on the sales process in your company. After you determine what you want viewers to do after watching, follow these steps:

1. **Include a call to action.** At the end of the video, mention the action. Before you create a video, you must consider where to use it on your website. Some video marketing software providers also let you add call-to-action *wrappers* (short clips with specific requests for action) to a video so that you can vary the call to action depending on where you're using the video.

2. **Place conversion elements close to video.** Make it easy for your website visitors to take the next action by placing conversion elements close to the video.

Examples of frequently used conversion elements are described in this list:

- ✔ **Contact information:** Place your contact information, such as e-mail address or phone number, close to the video on your site.
- ✔ **Conversion forms:** Next to the video, place a form that viewers can fill out. Marketing software companies such as HubSpot let you easily add conversion forms to any page on your website.

✔ **In-player lead capture:** Some video hosting companies, such as Wistia, let you capture your viewers' information directly in the video.

✔ **Live chat:** Let viewers ask you any questions they may have after watching the video. Place the Live Chat button next to the video player. Many qualified live chat providers such as LivePerson or Olark help you easily incorporate this element into your website.

Separating video sections

Some marketers dedicate a section exclusively to video content on their websites. We don't generally recommend this strategy, though it can make sense to achieve these two goals:

✔ **Bundle all video content so that people can easily find it.** If you have a lot of videos and you know that your users value your video content highly, having a dedicated video section can make sense.

✔ **Get optimal results for search engine marketing.** Some forms of search engine optimization (SEO) require you to use only one video per web page. To meet this requirement, create a separate video section because you may want to use multiple videos on other pages of your site. Read Chapter 20 for more details.

Integrate your videos into the other parts of your website in addition to your dedicated video section. Video is a natural part of the modern online experience, and people usually don't want to visit a dedicated video section only to watch some clips.

Working with video landing pages

Landing pages are dedicated web pages that are designed to capture leads. Most online ads link not to a company's home page, but to a landing page that provides focused information about the subject of the ad. Most landing pages also contain online forms where prospects can immediately sign up for a news-letter, download collateral and whitepapers, or request more information.

Landing pages can benefit tremendously from integrated videos. You typically have only a few seconds to capture and retain your web visitor's attention on a landing page. Useful content, well-written headlines, and an attractive design are essential, but there's no quicker and more effective way to attract attention than with a well-placed video. Some studies suggest that video landing pages can achieve a 60- to 100-percent higher conversion rate than traditional text-only pages.

Your landing page videos must be directly connected to the topic of your landing page. If you place only a generic company video on a landing page that's pitching one of your products, the video isn't effective. If you're pitching product X, feature that product (and not much else) in the video. People expect fast focused information from landing pages, and that's what entices them to convert. Make your landing page videos short, to the point, and attractive.

Hosting Your Video

If you have a website, you're paying somebody to host it. It may be a service such as Rackspace or ServInt or your internal IT department, but somebody has to provide the necessary infrastructure to run your website: server computers, data storage, powerful Internet lines, system management tools, and more.

Your website hosting covers most elements of a website, such as text, pictures, and PDF files. But video hosting is a different beast. Because video files tend to be quite large when compared to text and pictures, they need more and specialized infrastructure to be delivered properly to your audience. They also need to be combined with a video player that allows viewers to play your videos flawlessly.

Specialized video hosting services handle all these aspects and more. The following list describes the elements that a qualified video hosting service should provide — many services provide even more features, but these are the most important ones:

- ✔ **Video file management:** The hosting service provides for the easy uploading, organizing, and tagging of your video files.

- ✔ **Multiple levels of video quality:** An *encoding* service should automatically produce different versions of your video that work best for particular devices, such as PCs or smartphones.

- ✔ **Video player configuration:** The video player is configured and styled for your needs so that it fits ideally into your website.

- ✔ **High-quality delivery:** The delivery of video files to your audience at top quality requires a specialized infrastructure known as a *content delivery network.*

- ✔ **Analytics:** The hosting service should track the number of people who watch your video, how much of it they watched, and how they found your video.

- ✔ **Sharing:** If viewers want to share your video on social media or by e-mail, the hosting service should provide the necessary functionality.

Choosing between YouTube and a hosting service

The most popular video hosting service is YouTube. As described in Chapter 17, YouTube — by far the most important video sharing platform — lets you use its infrastructure to publish videos on your own website. It's easy: Click the Share button on any YouTube video, click Embed, and then copy the embed code to your website. Best of all: It's free.

Whether YouTube is a good choice for a video hosting service, and a true alternative to commercial services that cost money, depends on how you feel about its disadvantages. YouTube has a number of disadvantages that may prevent it from fitting your video hosting needs:

- ✔ **Limited control over the player:** The YouTube player has few options to customize, and many website owners feel that the familiar YouTube look doesn't quite work with their own site's design.

- ✔ **Ads:** YouTube is free, but it makes money from advertising. Even if you use your own YouTube videos on your own website, YouTube still reserves the right to show other companies' ads in these videos, either as text overlays or as TV commercials before your video begins. Unrelated ads in your videos don't make a good impression from your corporate website. Don't worry: YouTube is unlikely to show ads, not least because your video doesn't attract enough views anyway, though showing them isn't under your control.

- ✔ **Unwanted social features:** The YouTube video player shows a list of related videos after a video plays, and it lets users click through to the main YouTube site, which can distract your site's visitors.

- ✔ **Limited SEO capabilities:** Using YouTube videos on your site limits how well you can control your search engine optimization efforts — in particular, video site maps. See Chapter 20 for details about search engine optimization.

Choosing YouTube as your hosting service has another benefit: All video views on your website count toward your YouTube channel's popularity score, which in turn gives you more exposure on YouTube itself.

The bottom line: If your video marketing strategy's main goal is to draw as many views as possible for a low cost, YouTube is an excellent choice as a hosting service. If you want more control and sophistication, go with a professional hosting service.

Companies that use video successfully in their marketing campaigns use both YouTube and a professional hosting service — YouTube for capturing traffic and improving search, and professional hosting for videos that need a more sophisticated look and feel.

To turn off the list of related videos that show up at the end of your YouTube-hosted video, try this trick: Find the video URL in the embed code of your video from the YouTube site. The URL looks similar to this example:

```
www.youtube.com/embed/aD1nuwaj0P0
```

Then add the characters `?rel=0` immediately afterward to make the URL look similar to this one:

```
www.youtube.com/embed/aD1nuwaj0P0?rel=0
```

When you use this changed embed code — voilà! — the related videos disappear.

Selecting a video hosting service

If you decide to use a professional video hosting service, you first need to find one that fits your needs. Dozens of services are out there with different feature sets and price points.

Here are some of the most popular:

- **Brightcove:** Offers a broad range of packages starting at $99 per month and extending to configurations that serve some of the largest media companies in the world. Though this large provider is quite sophisticated, its main drawback is that it's comparatively difficult to use.

- **Kaltura:** Targets larger companies but also has a free, downloadable, open source edition of its product for the technically inclined. Hosting plans start at a few hundred dollars per month.

- **Ooyala:** Primarily focused on media companies and their sophisticated needs, such as ad management. Packages start at $500 per month.

- **Viddler:** Offers video hosting services starting at $50 per month. The least expensive version from this former YouTube competitor is limited, but the somewhat more expensive packages are competitive.

- **Vzaar:** Offers a bare-bones edition starting at $29 per month, though its more sophisticated versions are in the price ranges of its competitors.

- **Wistia:** Specializes in video hosting for marketers. Prices start at $29 per month, and it provides acceptable analytics and sharing functionality.

- **Vimeo:** Has recently introduced Vimeo Pro, a business video hosting service, for $199 per year. The product from this public platform (like YouTube) has a customizable player and no ads.

To find an appropriate provider, follow these important steps:

1. **Calculate your view numbers.** The most important thing to consider is the number of video views you expect. Most hosting providers have limits on the number of views that are covered by a price level, so start by estimating your volume needs. Obviously, you can't accurately predict the popularity of your videos before you start publishing them. For a rule of thumb, assume that 20 to 40 percent of your site's visitors will watch one video, and maybe 10 percent will watch several. When you review your website statistics and make this calculation, you should end up with a reasonable estimate.

2. **Decide which features are particularly important to you.** Ask yourself whether you need great flexibility in player styling or whether you're happy with a bare-bones player that stays out of the way. Determine whether you need sophisticated analytics, down to the behavior of individual users, or only a broad number of views.

3. **Sign up for free trials.** Most hosting providers provide free trial periods, and you should sign up for a few to see which one you like best.

4. **Test thoroughly a couple of your favorite services.** Spend some time with every product, and avoid making a decision based only on your first impression. Sometimes, an attractive user interface turns out to be clunky, or missing the single feature you truly need. Upload at least a couple of videos to every platform you want to test, and play through the whole process, ending with publishing a test video to your website.

Selecting a hosting provider is a somewhat technical decision, so you may want to find professional help. If you work with people in an outside web agency, they may be able to help you select a provider. If you work with a video production company, someone there may have input too. In any case, take advice from people who have worked with online video. Ask for a reference site where they have published videos using the recommended hosting provider.

Using open source players

An alternative to hosting services are standalone video players that let you "roll your own" video hosting solution. Many of these players are open source software, so you can download and use them for free. The most popular are JWPlayer and FlowPlayer.

Standalone video players solve only a small part of the overall hosting problem. You can embed their player applications into your website and customize the player's look and feel, but you still have to do the hard work of encoding your video files to the correct format and managing the deployment of your video files to your website.

Furthermore, because these free players provide no analytics and use no content distribution networks by default, some viewers will experience long buffering times or stuttering video.

Overall, a free video player is an alternative only if you're technically inclined and are willing to deal with its complexity. Otherwise, if you're on a budget, go with YouTube.

Using Video on a Web Page

After you know where to use video on your website and you have selected a hosting provider, it's time to publish your videos on your site.

Most modern websites are built using a content management system (CMS) such as Drupal, Joomla, or Typo3. Integrating video by using a CMS is reasonably easy. Some even come supplied with functionality that lets you easily include a YouTube video, or another type of video, on a page.

Still, you must complete some preparatory work and make certain decisions before you can publish your videos. This section walks you through the necessary steps.

Styling your player

Most hosting services let you change the look and feel of your video player. Consider adapting these elements to your needs:

- ✔ **Player size:** The player has to fit nicely into the layout of your web page. Generally speaking, stick with 480 x 270 pixels, or a higher resolution, because details in the video are difficult to see at lower resolutions. If you have the space available on your page, player sizes of 640 x 360 pixels or more work best.

- ✔ **Color scheme:** Ideally, your video player should fit into the color scheme of your website.

- ✔ **Buttons:** Most hosting providers let you turn off unwanted buttons and menus and other elements.

 Use as few elements as possible, and avoid turning off anything that people expect in a video player, such as the timeline (which shows the playback progress) or a full-screen button.

 Figure 18-2 shows a typical player styling tool.

- ✔ **Sharing:** Many video players come supplied with built-in social sharing functionality. Test this feature to decide whether it works for your website. Though social sharing can always put the word out, it may be distracting for visitors in certain parts of your website.

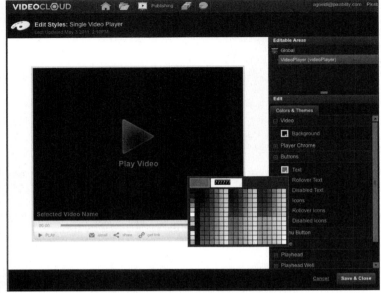

Figure 18-2:
Player
styling in the
Brightcove
VideoCloud
hosting
service.

Displaying an appropriate thumbnail picture

The first thing people see when they land on a web page featuring video is usually the video's thumbnail picture or *freeze frame*. This static picture of a video scene is typically displayed with the Play button at the top.

Selecting an effective thumbnail picture is important because it can influence strongly whether viewers click the video and watch it.

A useful thumbnail picture conveys what the video is about. The thumbnail should look immediately attractive and appealing. Show people and faces rather than static objects. You can even edit the thumbnail picture to add text to make your pitch about why people should watch this video.

Always add the Play button on top of your thumbnail picture. Internet users have learned to look for this button to identify videos, and you're likely to reduce your video play rates if you don't have one.

Determining whether to use autoplay

Most video players have the *autoplay* option, which plays the video as soon as the web page it's on has loaded. You can use your hosting service's controls to decide whether to add autoplay.

The use of autoplay is somewhat controversial. Many people consider it to be a rude way to draw attention to videos. Viewers can be embarrassed to visit a website in an office setting when they have to experience the sudden unexpected sound of a video blaring from their PCs. On the other hand, people who don't immediately pay attention to a video on Autoplay may miss out on stellar content that is truly essential to conveying the message.

Avoid using autoplay on your site's home page — it's rude. Instead, direct people to lower-level sections of your website where the appearance of videos is obvious (and therefore expected).

Inserting an embed code into a web page

All hosting services provide embed codes that let you insert videos into your web pages. An *embed code* is simply a small piece of computer code that activates the video player and displays it in the context of your web page.

An embed code can be as simple as this snippet of YouTube code:

```
<iframe width="560" height="315" src="http://www.
        youtube.com/embed/SWguMqANFZ0" frameborder="0"
        allowfullscreen></iframe>
```

Embed codes from professional video hosting services tend to be longer because they often provide more sophisticated functionality.

To insert an embed code, simply copy it to your computer's clipboard (by choosing Edit⇨Copy), go to your website's content management system, and then paste the code (by choosing Edit⇨Paste) into the correct spot in your web page.

However, inserting an embed code is often easier said than done because you have to deal with certain technical details on your website. You paste embed codes (the pieces of HTML code) into the appropriate view in your content management system to make them work. Because you have many different ways to build a website, refer to the documentation of your site's content management system to figure out exactly how to do it.

To place an embed code from a video hosting service (we use Wistia) into a page in a content management system (we use Drupal), follow these steps:

1. **In your web browser, log in to your video hosting service.**

2. **Find the video you want to embed, and click the video name.**

3. **Click the Embed link below the player.**

4. **On the next screen, select these options:**

   - *Player size:* The default size of 640 x 360 pixels may be too big for your page.

   - *Player options:* Choose whether to show the Play button and other controls.

   Figure 18-3 shows what this configuration screen looks like.

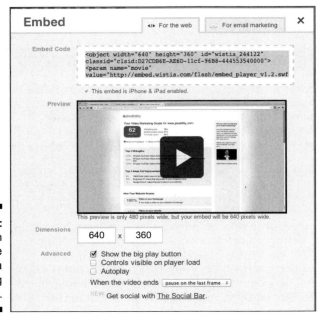

Figure 18-3: Creating an embed code in the Wistia video hosting service.

5. **Copy the embed code at the top by choosing the Edit⇨Copy command from your browser's menu.**

6. **In your web browser, visit your website and log in as a user who has editing rights.**

7. **Visit the page where you want to add the video.**

8. **Click the Edit link below the page title.**

9. **Scroll to the Body section of the page, and click the Source button (to paste HTML code).**

   This step shows you the HTML version of your page.

10. **Find the spot where you want to place your video.**

   If you're unfamiliar with HTML, simply look at the page text to locate the spot.

11. Choose Edit➪Paste to paste the embed code.

Figure 18-4 shows the result of completing this step.

12. Scroll down and click Save.

You should now see the video in your page. If the video doesn't appear immediately, reload the page.

Figure 18-4:
Pasting an embed code into your web page.

Chapter 19

Promoting Your Video with Social Media

. . . .

In This Chapter

▶ Engaging your audience with social media

▶ Using video on Facebook, LinkedIn, and Twitter

▶ Encouraging sharing in all your marketing channels

. . . .

*P*ublishing videos on your website gives you a good start in video marketing, but not all your target customers come to your website. Successful video marketers take their videos to the street — that is, they go where their audience is. Your audience increasingly uses social media sites such as Facebook and Twitter every single day. Social media can truly boost your video's exposure if you persuade others to share your video.

People love to watch online videos because it's a quicker and more entertaining way to solve the problems they're working on. People who watch a video that's truly helpful to them — or that amuses them — are more willing to share it with others. Therefore, thinking carefully about what makes your video content worth sharing *before* you create it saves time and gives you free exposure.

After you have some shareable content, you can use an arsenal of social media tools to share it. For example, Facebook, LinkedIn, Twitter, and even e-mail newsletters can be powerful drivers of video success.

Gaining Visibility with Social Media

A *viral* video is simply a video that lots of people have shared because they liked it or found it remarkable. But you can't plan viral success on the scale of millions of views. Even a larger brand, such as Nike, that can invest a million or more dollars in promoting a video doesn't always hit it out of the park. See Chapter 2 for more details about viral video.

What you *can* plan for and carefully execute is social media success with your target audience. By finding the proper venues, channels, and influencers, you can post your content where interested viewers can see it and then pass it on.

Picking your social media battles

Social media has rapidly become a wide field in which to play. You can share your videos in many different places. Here's a short list of the most important places to post videos or share links:

- Blogs
- Industry newsletters and news websites
- Online forums and communities in your sector
- Facebook
- Google+
- LinkedIn
- MySpace (still relevant if you're promoting music)
- Twitter
- YouTube

Thinking like a journalist

Journalists are trained to tell stories. When planning your sharing strategy, think like a journalist: Determine how your video can become newsworthy, or comment on current news in your industry.

Suppose that your industry has recently experienced a bad environmental scare with toxic lead paint and now everyone is talking about it — industry bloggers are buzzing, and every conference seems to host a panel discussion about the topic.

If your company has been proactive for years in eliminating toxic lead paint throughout the supply chain, a short video on how lead paint can be eliminated and what your company did to successfully make products without lead paint is instantly newsworthy:

- Bloggers may want to embed the video into their blogs.
- Your video can be showcased at your industry's next conference as a successful case study.
- Influencers may even retweet your video on Twitter.

Pick your battles. Unless you have unlimited time and resources, you can't possibly be an active community member in all these venues at the same time. Find out which channels are most important to get in front of your audience, and determine which are the most effective targets to start with.

You can leverage your social media efforts by posting content in one place and spreading it from there. Specialized social media software can help in this effort. For example, you can use the Pixability Video Marketing Software to automatically post links to your YouTube videos to Twitter, Facebook, LinkedIn, and other social media sites.

Understanding where your audience lives online

Before you start your social media efforts, step back and put your ear to the ground — or simply listen to your best customers. In Chapter 2, we discuss how to analyze your customers' needs and the problems for which they need solutions. Use this knowledge to find out more about your target customers' online habits by asking yourself these questions about them:

- ✔ **How old are my target customers?** Your social media mix is influenced by the age group you're targeting. For example, if your audience is 16-year-old skateboarders, you'll use more YouTube community features. If you're targeting 32-year-old marketing managers instead, a combination of sharing on Twitter and LinkedIn draws more attention to you.

- ✔ **Where do they live?** Depending on whether your business operates nationally or locally, your social media efforts can be targeted locally to your specific town, state, or country by following regional influencers.

- ✔ **Which events do they attend?** Your customers may congregate at important industry events, conferences, or trade shows, and all these events now have an online component, such as Twitter hashtags or coverage by industry bloggers.

- ✔ **Which websites do they visit?** Determine where your customers find their news online, which blogs they read, and where they go for advice online. You can post helpful information in these places for your target customers.

- ✔ **Which books do they read?** Finding the influential authors in your market leads you to discover where those authors publish online. You can then comment on their newest works and thoughts.

After you track down this information, you can start planning your social media strategy. Create a list of the most important places your customers visit online. You should soon discover a pattern and see that some people and places matter more than others — not all online activities and social media are created equal.

Identifying opinion leaders and influential channels

By listing all the places where your audience lives online, you have a useful starting point to identify whom your audience listens to. Every industry has opinion leaders and influential channels.

If you don't know (yet) who matters most in your industry, follow these steps on every online channel you've researched:

1. **Check the site's web traffic.** Use Compete (www.compete.com) or Alexa (www.alexa.com) to see how many website visitors a site draws per month.

2. **Verify the number of followers or "likes."** Go to the corresponding Twitter account or Facebook page of the online property you've identified and see how many followers it has relative to others in the space.

3. **Confirm connections.** See who is behind these sites by identifying the authors, editors, or top management personnel. Calculate how many connections those people have on LinkedIn.

4. **Identify who is important.** You can use online services such as Klout (klout.com) to see who is important in your space. These services measure social influence and can tell you who has interactions online with whom and whom people look up to. This step can save you a lot of time in finding the second and third tier of influencers.

5. **Find influential videos.** If your industry has well-known videos, find out who created them and where they're hosted, such as on YouTube, Vimeo, or another public platform. To find influential videos in your industry, brainstorm relevant keywords for your product or service, and use a free service such as Online Video Radar (www.onlinevideoradar.com).

After you know who matters in your space, familiarize yourself with important topics in the field. No real shortcuts are possible in this time-consuming process. Knowing your industry intimately enables you to create helpful video content and have intelligent discussions with your target audience by way of social media.

In all social media channels, you're rewarded if you create content that your audience cares about. Video is a beneficial way to differentiate yourself from all the noise in those channels, though your content must be good. Bad content usually backfires: Even if you create fancy videos, unclear or unstructured content prevents your videos from being shared. Check out Chapter 4 to find out how to send the right message.

Encouraging users to share your videos

After you've found the most relevant online properties and people in your industry, studied all the newest and juiciest industry gossip, and created remarkable videos, people should go out of their way to share your videos, right? Wrong. It's your job to bring your video to your audience's attention and make sharing easy. Follow this step-by-step approach:

1. **Set up your own social media presence.** For example, open accounts for all social media networks that matter for your audience, or start your own blog.

2. **Follow opinion leaders.** After you identify the opinion leaders, follow them on Twitter and Facebook, subscribe to their blogs, and read their columns.

3. **Post comments.** Ask opinion leaders questions, or comment on their newest content. Sign in with your real name and website URL when you comment on blogs or websites.

4. **Engage in conversations.** Monitor the places where you've commented to see whether you receive responses. Thank the responders, and engage in a conversation with them. Link to your videos if they're relevant for the conversation.

5. **Be helpful.** People often use social media as a problem-solving strategy, by posting questions on blogs or via social networks. Respond with helpful information — for example, a video or blog post that addresses the problem.

6. **Ask for feedback.** Ask for feedback on your newest videos. By following these steps, you build relationships with influencers in your target market and can likely learn more from them. If they like what they see, they're likely to share it.

Be bold enough to be controversial. Opinion leaders like to be challenged because they then have the opportunity to show off their knowledge. If your point of view is controversial but justifiable, others will respect you for *your* expertise.

To help viewers easily share your videos, ensure that your blog, your website, and your other social media channels are set up for sharing. Include the Facebook Like button, the Twitter tweet icon, and the Google+ +1 button on your site.

Establishing a Presence on Facebook

An increasing number of businesses are establishing a presence on Facebook. With more than 800 million users around the world at the time this book was written, Facebook has become a daily habit for many people. Not only are consumer brands active there, but business-to-business companies have also increasingly started using Facebook to launch their content.

Online video is among the most popular content on Facebook because users love to watch interesting content even more than they love to read it.

Boosting your business on Facebook

If your customers use Facebook to find solutions to meet their needs, your company has to have a presence on Facebook. You can create a presence in two main ways:

- ✔ Create a business Facebook Page.
- ✔ Use your personal Facebook page.

Create a business Facebook Page because you can customize it to generate customers for your company. In addition, you can support your company's efforts by liking (using the Facebook Like button) and commenting on your company's posts from your personal account.

For more information on how to create effective company Pages and market your business on Facebook, we recommend *Facebook Marketing For Dummies,* by John Haydon, Paul Dunay, and Richard Krueger (John Wiley & Sons).

Sharing video with your friends and fans

Facebook is more than a social network — it's the world's second most popular video sharing site, after YouTube.

To be successful as a business on Facebook, you have to treat your target customers as friends and let your personality shine. Engage your audience in conversations, and show the human side of your company. Video is an easy way to show off your team and let them share their expertise.

Approximately 80 percent of your videos should feature helpful hints, information about your products, and other serious content, and 20 percent should consist of videos showing what you and your team do for fun, showing off a more personal side of your business. For example, Bettina and Andreas' team at Pixability recently organized a flash mob. The Pixability community on Facebook loved the video and watched it thousands of times.

Choosing YouTube or Facebook video

You can use three methods to put video on Facebook:

- ✔ Record video with your webcam.
- ✔ Upload video directly from your drive or mobile device.
- ✔ Post videos on YouTube and publish them on Facebook.

Which variant you choose depends on what you want to do with the videos afterward.

One benefit of recording video with your webcam directly on Facebook is that you save time and money. If you want to send only a quick message to your fans, recording a quick webcam video can save time and effort.

The benefits of uploading directly to Facebook are described in this list. You can

- ✔ **Reuse your videos.** The downside of posting webcam videos on Facebook (next to their limited quality) is that you can't reuse these videos easily anywhere else. Facebook doesn't let you download them.
- ✔ **Link to videos in Facebook ads.** Facebook lets you link its ads to videos that are hosted directly on Facebook. Users can then stay within Facebook to watch your videos, which makes many of them more comfortable and can garner more views.
- ✔ **Use the videos in Sponsored Stories.** If you want your videos to show up in Sponsored Stories, you have to host them on Facebook.

(To understand how video ads and Sponsored Stories work, read the later section "Promoting video with paid campaigns.")

The benefits of using YouTube videos on Facebook are that you can

- ✔ **Accumulate more views on YouTube.** Drawing more views helps your video, search engine optimization efforts. Read more about this topic in Chapter 20.
- ✔ **See how many views your video has.** Facebook doesn't report on the number of views you've generated. YouTube counts all your embedded views, including those on Facebook.
- ✔ **Share more easily.** The Facebook video player makes it difficult to share video outside of Facebook.
- ✔ **Use annotations.** If you use the YouTube annotation function for calls to action, they also work within Facebook. Read more about annotations in Chapter 17.

Recording webcam videos on Facebook

Recording Facebook webcam videos is an easy, no-frills way to add videos to your company's Page. It works like this:

1. **Visit your company's Page.** On your Wall, you see different sharing options at the top. Click the Video icon. You see two options appear: Record a Video and Upload a Video.

2. **Click the Record a Video button.** A dialog box may appear and prompt you to allow the Adobe Player to work. If it does, choose Allow and click the Close button.

3. **Press the red button to begin recording the video.** Turn on the built-in microphone before you start. Press the button (now gray) again to stop the recording.

4. **Review your video.** You can press Play to review your video.

   If you don't like the video, press Reset to start over.

5. **Add a message.** After you're happy with the webcam recording, add to the box below it a message describing your video. You also choose with whom you want to share the video. Finally, click the Share button to publish it on your Page.

The webcam recording you've created is stored permanently in the Video section of your Page.

If you're looking for a glossy brand image, avoid using the Facebook webcam recording feature. The quality of Facebook recordings isn't good.

Just because you can quickly add videos by webcam doesn't mean that they will be compelling. Quick videos deserve the same thought, planning, and scripting as any other marketing video. Consult Chapters 3 and 4 to determine the purpose and approach for your webcam videos.

Uploading video to Facebook

To upload video to Facebook, from either your mobile device (such as a phone or a tablet) or your computer, follow these steps:

1. **Visit your company's Page.** On your Wall, you see different sharing options at the top. Click the Video icon. You see two options appear: Record a Video and Upload a Video.

2. **Click Upload a Video.** Select a video file by clicking the Choose File button. You can only upload videos that are no larger than 1024MB and no longer than 20 minutes.

   Do not upload videos that you don't have the rights to. You risk them being taken down.

3. **Add a message.** Add a message that describes your video in the box below it. You also choose whom you want to share it with. Finally, click the Share button to publish it on your Page.

Editing and tagging a Facebook video

To optimize the exposure of your Facebook videos, go to the Video section of your Page and click the uploaded video. You can now add tags to the video to tell Facebook who's in the video and where it was taken. Even more important, the Edit This Video link lets you add a title and a description and choose a thumbnail. Choose one that looks interesting and action packed. Friendly faces are also good choices.

Posting YouTube videos on Facebook

Embedding YouTube videos in your Facebook posts works like this:

1. **Upload your videos to your YouTube channel.** Follow the instructions in Chapter 17.

2. **Copy the YouTube video's URL.**

3. **Log in to Facebook, and then go to your company's Page.**

4. **Click Link at the top of the Page.** Paste the YouTube URL of your video into the box that appears. Then click the Attach button. Figure 19-1 shows what this looks like on your Page.

5. **Add a message.** Tell your Facebook fans why they should watch this video. To increase your views, mention the word *video* in your post.

Figure 19-1: How to link to YouTube videos from your company's Page.

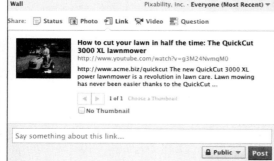

To automate the posting of YouTube videos on Facebook, use specialized video marketing software that allows you to publish your YouTube videos to your company's Facebook page. If you create video regularly and use more than one social media channel, this can a lot of save time.

To post a YouTube video on Facebook using the Pixability video marketing software, follow these steps:

1. **Log in and choose the video you want to publish.**

2. **Click the Promote button.**

3. **Click the Facebook check box. Write your post, choose to post to your company Page, and then click Send Update.**

Figure 19-2 shows how to send a Facebook update using a YouTube video with the Pixability, video marketing software.

Embedding video in your company Page

After you have video on your Facebook Page, you have to decide what to do next. Unlike your company website, which can remain relatively unchanged for a few months without harm, social media channels need to be continually updated to be effective. By actively managing your social media efforts, you stay in touch with your target audience and regularly win more fans.

Showing up in the Facebook News Feed

You don't always need to use your own videos to show up in your fans' News Feeds. You can include links to YouTube videos in your industry that your target customers will like, too.

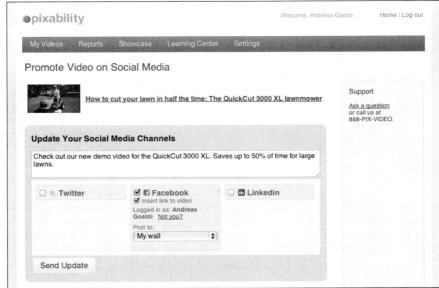

Figure 19-2: Sending a Facebook update via video marketing software.

A clever way to direct traffic back to your YouTube channel is to point your audience to other videos that show your videos in their Related Videos section.

Facebook Page welcome videos

When people who like your Facebook Page stop by for a visit, Facebook automatically brings them to your Wall. For new visitors, though, you can designate a specific tab for them to view. A cool way to increase the number of likes on your page is to let first-time visitors land on a tab that shows a welcome video.

Let viewers know what's in it for them when they visit your Facebook Page. Your welcome video should let first-time visitors know what they can expect as fans of your Page, such as whether they can find discounts, special how-to videos, or invitations to webinars.

When you're ready to start on your video landing tab, you need a special app to make it work. Follow these steps:

1. **Install the app to your Page.**

   Go to your Page and click Edit Page (in the upper-right corner). Click Apps in the navigation on the left, and then click Browse More Applications at the bottom of the page. Search for *iFrameWrapper: best FBML alternative.* Click the app, and scroll down until you find the Add to My Page link on the left. Click it, and choose your Page.

2. **Name your video landing tab.**

   Return to your Page. Your new landing tab appears in the left navigation, titled Welcome (by default). Click Edit Page and then on Apps, and then on iFrameWrapper. Then click the Edit Settings link. Enter whatever name you want in the Custom Tab Name field.

3. **Build your landing tab.**

   Click the landing tab name in the left navigation (Welcome or whatever you chose in Step 2). Then click Settings at the bottom of the tab. You can choose between HTML, CMS, and iFrames, but in order to build a simple landing page with video, stick with HTML. Finally, paste the embed code of your video. If your video is hosted on a public platform such as YouTube, look for a button labeled Share or Embed, and copy the code. Choose a width fewer than 510 pixels.

You can add more content to your landing page; it's similar to a website, so whatever you can think of to do with HTML will likely work. Text, photos, more videos — you can experiment and have fun!

Making your fans the stars can pay high dividends on Facebook. If you can persuade fans to create videos using your product, you can use the videos to draw more fans.

Promoting video with paid campaigns

The power of Facebook lies in not only using your own network of friends and fans but also promoting your content to their friends and fans. If you sign up as a Facebook advertiser, you can run Facebook ads and also Sponsored Stories. It costs money, but it may be a cost-effective way to acquire new customers.

Buying Facebook ads for your videos

After you've created videos that resonate with your target audience on Facebook, you can spread them more widely via ads. Follow these steps to get your videos seen by using ads:

1. **Create a Facebook ad at** www.facebook.com/ads/create.

2. **Select the destination you want to promote.**

   The destination of your Facebook ad can be your website, a specific landing page, or your company's Facebook Page — depending on where you've decided to place the video.

3. **Mention the word** *video* **in the title or body text of your ad.**

   This step increases your number of click-throughs.

4. **For an image, use an action-oriented thumbnail of your video with a Play button on it.**

Choose thumbnails wisely, and avoid using your logo or text in the thumbnail of the video. Facebook users like action-oriented videos, so give them a taste of what they'll see in the thumbnail.

Using Sponsored Stories for videos

A more organic way to spread the word about your videos is to use Sponsored Stories. Your fans and your fans' friends can then discover your videos via the Facebook News Feed and the Sponsored Stories column. People enjoy buying from companies that their friends trust.

Sponsored Stories are stories that are eligible to appear in your Facebook News Feed. They show up in the right column of pages on Facebook. The types of stories that can be surfaced include Page likes, Page posts, Page post likes, check-ins, app shares, domain stories, and apps used and games played. Figure 19-3 shows what a Sponsored Story looks like within your fans' Facebook pages.

To have your video discovered via Sponsored Stories, follow these steps:

1. **Create a Facebook ad at** www.facebook.com/ads/create.

2. **Select the destination you want to promote.**

   The destination should be your company's Facebook Page.

3. **Select the type of stories you want to promote.**

   Under Type, select Sponsored Stories. Under Story Type, choose Page Post Story (if you want your current fans to see the video) or Page Post Like Story (if you want your fans' friends to see the video).

4. **Select your targeting criteria and budgeting.**

   For more information about targeting, visit `www.facebook.com/adsmarketing`.

5. **Upload your videos to Facebook as described earlier in this chapter.**

6. **Create page posts including your video as described earlier in this chapter.**

   The videos show up in your fans' or their friends' News Feeds.

Videos are shown only to your fans' friends as Sponsored Stories if they liked your video in the past seven days. Keep the video content coming if you want to use this paid strategy successfully.

Figure 19-3: Sponsored Stories appear in the right column of pages on Facebook.

Tweeting videos on Twitter

An active Twitter account has become a must-have item among the social media crowd. Because updates on Twitter can be no longer than 140 characters, brevity is the key. So where does video figure into the mix?

Though you can't upload your videos directly to Twitter, you can actively promote them via links. Follow these steps:

1. **Log in to your Twitter account via** `www.twitter.com` **(or using a Twitter client or video marketing software).**

2. **Decide where to direct traffic:**

   • To your Facebook page

   • To a YouTube video

   • To a designated landing page on your website where you've embedded the video

3. **Write a pithy update.**

   Including the word *video* has been shown to significantly increase the click-through rate.

4. **For extra credit, direct the video link to some of your most influential Twitter followers by including their Twitter handles in the tweet.**

   You may be rewarded by a retweet to that follower's audience!

If you aren't shy about creating short, impromptu content to take videos on the go, use your cellphone to shoot short videos. Upload them to a service such as Twitpic, Twitvid, or Yfrog directly from your phone and send a tweet. That's instant video marketing!

YouTube is social, too

YouTube has its own social networking community, and you can find much more additional value from it for your business videos if you use its social features. (We describe YouTube in detail in Chapter 17.)

The following list describes the most important ways to engage the YouTube community:

- ✔ **Subscribe to other people's channels.** This strategy keeps you updated about content that may interest you. Best of all, because most people return the favor of subscribing, you can reach them with your videos as well.

- ✔ **Comment on other channels and videos.** Complimenting someone on her videos helps you get noticed and helps interest other people in your own content. Be authentic, though — most people can spot insincere flattery.

- ✔ **Use video responses.** This special form of a YouTube comment lets you use a video to react to somebody else's video. You can either use a video you already have or one you make specifically as a response. Again, be authentic and sincere.

   Using aggressively promotional video responses that people may see as spam can cause you to be blocked in no time.

- ✔ **Add as Facebook friends the people whose content you like.** You can "friend" people on their channel pages next to the Subscribe button. It works a lot like Facebook friendships — it's more of a social gesture of appreciation than a real friendship. You then appear on your YouTube friends' channel pages, which is another way to gain more visibility.

- ✔ **Favorite other people's videos.** Favoriting is probably the highest expression of appreciation on YouTube. It adds these videos to the Favorites list on your channel. These favorites are visible to your channel's visitors, so add only other excellent videos that fit your own goals. In a similar way, you can add other people's videos to your own playlists. Check Chapter 17 for more details.

Taking a look at other social marketing channels

Facebook, Twitter, and YouTube are the "big dogs" of social media, but depending on your business, other vehicles can attract as much attention for your videos. The key to successful video marketing is to use your videos in as many of your marketing channels as possible. Consider adding video in these locations:

- ✔ **E-mail footers:** Reference your videos in all e-mail communications. If you include a YouTube link and your recipient uses an e-mail service such as Gmail, he can even play the video directly from his e-mail.

- ✔ **LinkedIn:** Most professionals have a short résumé on LinkedIn. But LinkedIn is a social network as well. Harness the professional groups in your industry to create awareness for your videos.

- ✔ **Press releases:** Press releases that contain videos draw three times as many views as those without them. Services such as PRWeb allow you to upload videos along with your press release.

- ✔ **E-mail marketing:** When sending your company newsletter, remember to include a video thumbnail. It increases your click-throughs significantly.

Using e-mail marketing

Do you have a newsletter mailing list? Making your newsletters more fun and engaging is easy if you add a video into the mix. Research shows that you can easily double the number of clicks by substituting a boring text link with a fancy video thumbnail.

To use e-mail marketing via Constant Contact, one of the most popular e-mail marketing software providers, follow these steps:

1. **Create your e-mail newsletter as usual. Write all the text you want to use first.**

2. **Open your YouTube channel, and copy the link address of the video you want to use.**

3. **In Constant Contact, edit your newsletter, and choose Video Link from the Insert menu on the left.**

4. **Paste your YouTube link into the Video URL field, and click Create Image.**

   Constant Contact automatically creates a thumbnail picture that appears in your e-mail newsletter.

5. **Use the slide to adjust the thumbnail picture's size to fit your newsletter layout.**

6. **Click Insert to insert the video image into your newsletter.**

Your e-mail recipients see the video thumbnail as though it were a real video waiting to be played. But if they click it, they're redirected to your YouTube video.

Do not attach video to outgoing e-mail messages. The file size is usually much too large, and your e-mail messages are often rejected by corporate firewalls or spam filters. Many of your subscribers also have attachment size restrictions and immediately delete messages with large attachments — video or no video.

Linking into LinkedIn

LinkedIn is a popular channel to reach business people. Marketers who sell to other businesses should especially consider an active LinkedIn strategy.

This business network doesn't offer the option to upload video directly, but you can use your YouTube videos to great effect. Follow these steps to write a LinkedIn update with video:

1. **Log in on LinkedIn.**

2. **On your LinkedIn home page, write the text of your update in the Share and Update box.**

   Don't click the Share button yet.

3. **Go to the YouTube site, and copy the link address of the video you want to use.**

4. **Go back to LinkedIn, and click Attach a Link below your update.**

5. **In the Add URL box that appears, paste your YouTube link. Click Attach.**

   LinkedIn now gets your video's title and includes a thumbnail picture as well.

6. **Click the Share button to post your update.**

Chapter 20

Using Search Engine Optimization and Paid Ads

In This Chapter

▶ Optimizing your videos to be found on search engines

▶ Putting paid ads on YouTube

▶ Using other forms of video ads

*C*utting through the all the noise on online video sharing platforms is a challenge. The sheer amount of video content that's out there is mind-boggling, and it's growing every day. In 2010, users uploaded 48 hours of new video to YouTube every minute. That's eight years' worth of new video content loaded on the Internet every day. Even the most avid online video fans can watch only a tiny fraction of all videos that exist in the online world.

In addition to the social media tactics we present in Chapter 19, you can use two ways to attract your target audience and attract them to your videos: search engine optimization (SEO) and paid advertising.

Search engines are becoming more and more important as a source of video views. YouTube handles millions of video searches every day. The big search engines such as Google, Bing, and Yahoo! have recently begun to integrate video results directly into their main search pages. This benefit for video marketers makes doing your search engine optimization homework more important than ever.

Paid video ads are a more expensive, but effective, way to draw viewers. YouTube and certain other video platforms offer the ability to pay for views of users who have searched for a particular kind of video. The results are highly targeted views at relatively affordable prices.

Optimizing Your Video for Search Engines

Few people think of YouTube as a search engine. But the biggest video sharing site is now the second largest search engine in the world, immediately behind Google (which owns YouTube). People are using YouTube more often to find helpful how-to videos, entertainment content in a niche they particularly like, or videos about any kind of topic they care about.

What's more, the big traditional search engines such as Google, Bing, and Yahoo! have offered specialized video search functionality for a while. You can focus your search to videos if you click the Video link on Google. The big search engines cover a number of video sharing platforms and even TV sites, not just YouTube.

More recently, the traditional search engines have started to include video results directly on their main search pages, which most people use when they look for information on the Internet. So on any Google or Bing result page, you may now see a couple of videos related to the search topic.

Because not nearly as many videos exist as individual web pages, you have a much better chance of showing up as a top search result when you offer a video. Some analysts have calculated the chances to be as much as 53 times better than for a text website.

But search engines must know which videos are relevant, and not from the videos themselves. Even with today's technology, computers still cannot comprehend what a video is about. Modern speech-recognition programs can at least understand some spoken dialogue, but the precision of these automated methods isn't acceptable for search engine purposes.

It's your responsibility as the owner of a video to tell the search engine what exactly your masterpiece is about. Video sharing platforms allow you to provide a bunch of information with your video: a title, some description text, a category, and some *tags,* which are keywords that describe the content of the video.

Some video sharing platforms allow you to upload closed captions that contain every word being spoken in the video. And most platforms use grouping features such as playlists, channels, or interest groups to let you draw even more exposure with the people you want to reach.

All these elements are vital to being found by viewers — and to standing out in a long list of search results. For example, your video title is an essential factor in persuading people to watch it.

Specialized tools such as the Pixability Video Marketing Software can help you get the details right with YouTube SEO. Video SEO has many moving parts, and you can easily overlook an important step. A good tool can save you a lot of time and help you avoid errors.

Picking the right title

A good title can make a huge difference in whether people find — and ultimately watch — your video, and a good title can be essential for its success. The title you select is a key tool for standing out on search engines, and it's the most important piece of information you give to potential viewers to help them decide whether your video is worth their time.

You must understand where people will see your title and how it can influence their behavior.

Take a look at YouTube as an example:

✔ Titles show up underneath YouTube videos in full length. People have short attention spans, and many decide whether they want to spend time with your video by simply reading its title.

✔ The title also shows up next to the videos in the sidebar of your YouTube channel, where people can find related videos. YouTube limits this title to the first 50 characters, or six to ten words, so your title had better be crisp and short.

✔ In search results, people see the first ten words of your title. Again, it pays to be concise.

Because you're writing the title for both humans and search engines, writing a strong title isn't all about pure creativity. Being funny and using clever puns have their places, but a video title isn't it.

Follow these five steps to develop a strong title for your video:

1. **Focus on the key message of your video.** What particular benefit does your product or service offer? This benefit should be a part of your title.

2. **Consider which keywords your prospects will most likely search for when they look for a product such as yours.**

   Prospects aren't likely to search for your company name.

   The two or three most important keywords should be part of your title.

3. **Think about the value your video provides and about the benefit to the viewer.**

   If your video is educational in some way, you should suggest that. People (and search engines) react strongly to words or phrases such as *how-to, tricks, ideas for,* or *tutorial.*

4. **Consider whether a well-known person appears in the video.** If so, use that person's name.

5. **Create your title.**

Avoid words that can be identified as spam by search engines or e-mail systems. Terms such as *cheap, buy now,* and *free* are problems because they may catch your video in a spam filter rather than in front of your intended target.

Suppose that you sell lawn mowers and your new top model, the QuickCut 3000 XL, is absolutely the latest advancement in lawn mower technology. You make a video about it and post it on YouTube.

The worst possible title you can choose is something like this one:

The new QuickCut 3000 XL with automatic blade sharpness enhancement technology — buy now!

This title says nothing about what the product does, it provides no value statement, and it even contains a keyword *(buy now!)* that may cause it to be banned as spam.

A much better title is

How to cut your lawn in half the time: The QuickCut 3000 XL power lawn mower

The first part of the title, "How to cut your lawn in half the time," shows up in search results and in the Related Videos column on YouTube. It tells people why the video is interesting, and it communicates the value of the piece. But the full title also contains the product name (in case somebody is already in the market for it and wants to know more details) and the product category (lawn mowers).

Writing effective description text

Directly beneath the Title field, YouTube has a text field that describes the video. You have 5,000 characters (about 250 words) to explain in detail what your video is all about.

Before you invest your polished prose style into writing incredibly sublime description text, you should know this ugly secret: Few human beings are ever likely to read these words. But search engines will.

The content of the description doesn't need to be a wonderful piece of marketing copy, though it should contain as many keywords as possible. Still, the YouTube search algorithms seem to prefer real text, so avoid simply pasting long lists of keywords. Use a simple text that describes the content of your video with many synonyms. A good length for description text is around 100 words.

Just because more people are searching for *Justin Bieber* or *Angelina Jolie* than are searching for your product category doesn't mean that you should use celebrity names or other unrelated keywords in the description of your video. This *keyword-stuffing* process simply doesn't work — and can even hurt your search score. The clever YouTube algorithms ignore keywords that seem not to be related to your video's real topic.

Setting a target link

The first thing in your description text should be a link to your website. YouTube makes these links clickable, and that's a convenient way for viewers to find more information about your product.

YouTube makes a link clickable only when you use a full link, starting with `http://`. Figure 20-1 shows what a correctly set link looks like below a YouTube video.

Figure 20-1: A target link should be the first thing in YouTube description text.

The best way to capture traffic from your videos is to link to a dedicated landing page that relates to your video and contains a conversion element. An example for a conversion element is a web form to sign up to for a newsletter that allows viewers to see more videos like the ones they saw on YouTube.

Selecting effective search tags

In addition to the title and description text, YouTube lets you describe your videos in two more ways:

- **Tag:** A *tag* is a keyword that YouTube uses not only to rank its search results but also to decide which videos are related.

- **Category:** In a *category,* you describe, broadly, the genre that a video belongs to — entertainment, science, and technology, or sports, for example. Simply select the category that you feel is most closely related to the topic of your video.

After a video plays to the end, YouTube shows you a number of other videos that it thinks may be about a similar topic. In the sidebar next to every video, the Suggestions list has even more related videos. People frequently click these suggestions, so it it's effective to show up there with your videos.

Similar tags are the most important factors in the YouTube selection of these suggestions. If you assign tags such as *lawn mower* and *lawn care* to your video, it shows up as a related video next to other lawn care videos. That's free targeted traffic for you.

Try finding a lot of synonyms and related words that describe the content of your video. As always, think from the perspective of your customers. Which words can they use to search for the kind of information you offer, or which related topics might they be looking for?

Your lawn mower company should use tags such as these, starting with the tags that are most important, to reach its target market:

lawnmower	lawn mower
lawn care	lawn care tips
lawn care tricks	lawn maintenance
lawn mowing	lawn mower techniques
grass	grass care
cutting grass	backyard
backyard lawn	front lawn
yard work	mowing
mowing the lawn	lawn mower reviews
lawn mower tips	hot to mow
quickcut	quickcut 3000 xl

When you enter tags on YouTube, they're separated by commas, and tags that contain multiple words need to be enclosed by quotation marks. Here's how to enter the preceding tag list correctly in the YouTube Tag field:

lawnmower, "lawn mower," "lawn care," "lawn care tips," "lawn care tricks," "lawn maintenance," "lawn mowing," "lawn mower techniques," grass, "grass care," "cutting grass," backyard, "backyard lawn," "front lawn," "yard work," mowing, "mowing the lawn," "lawn mower reviews," "lawn mower tips" "how to mow," quickcut, "quickcut 3000 xl"

You can use as many as 500 characters for tags, which translates to about 30 tags. No tag can be longer than 30 characters. In practice, you should definitely have more than 10 tags, and coming up with more than that number is time well spent.

To find ideas for popular keywords, locate the YouTube Search box (at the top of every page on the site), and simply start typing a keyword. YouTube suggests other keyword combinations that people frequently search for. The same trick works on the main Google search engine page. Figure 20-2 shows an example.

Figure 20-2:
Using the
YouTube
search
bar to find
frequently
searched
keywords.

Choosing a thumbnail picture

Thumbnails are the little pictures representing videos that you see all over YouTube. They also show up in search results on other search engines — particularly, Google.

Choosing a good thumbnail doesn't influence your search ranking as such, though it matters a lot to entice people to watch a video when they find it. People perceive a thumbnail picture before they read the title, and the picture either draws their attention or turns them off.

When you choose a thumbnail picture, follow these guidelines:

- ✔ **Make the thumbnail clear and simple.** Thumbnails are tiny, and it's impossible to recognize any details in them.

- ✔ **Use faces whenever possible.** People click faces much more often than on anything else.

- ✔ **Choose strong colors.** You want to stand out in a sea of little thumbnail pictures.

Unfortunately, YouTube doesn't let normal users choose thumbnails freely. All it gives you is a selection of three possible thumbnails that are shot at approximately 25 percent, 50 percent, and 75 percent of your video's duration. Still, make sure to use the best one of these available thumbnails. It can influence your click rates substantially.

Other video platforms such as Vimeo let you upload your own thumbnail pictures, and that option is worth using if you publish videos on these sites.

Adding closed captioning

YouTube and certain other platforms let you upload text files that contain closed-captioning subtitles for your video. You can then reach people who have hearing impairments, and it pays off for your search engine ranking. The captions are used by YouTube search to determine the topic of your video.

You don't have to write captions yourself. Several affordable services can create these caption files for you. 3Play Media (www.3playmedia.com), for example, provides captions for only dollars per minute.

Combining Traditional SEO and Video

Your main online marketing goal is likely to attract people to your website. When users find your videos on Google, you likely want them to head directly to your website instead of to YouTube.

For this reason, combine traditional search engine optimization techniques with video. Your videos can give you more exposure in search results, and they make your website more attractive.

For SEO success, you must embed videos correctly on your website. Follow these steps:

1. **Use a dedicated video hosting service. (See Chapter 18 for details.)**

   If you place YouTube videos on your website, most search traffic goes directly to YouTube.

2. **Place only one video per web page.**

   If you have 20 videos, make 20 individual web pages. Search engines ignore multiple videos per page, and having multiple videos dilutes the effectiveness of your SEO efforts.

3. **Supply a descriptive title for your web pages, and use a keyword-rich URL.**

4. **Rather than post the video on the page, add description text that accurately describes the content of the video.**

   You can reuse some of the text that you already prepared for your YouTube channel, but avoid using it identically. Search engines don't like duplicate content.

5. **Use video site maps, as described in the next section.**

Using video site maps

It's extremely difficult for search engines to find the videos on your website. The problem is that so many different video players and video hosting companies are out there that no search engine can recognize them all automatically.

That's why Google lets you provide video site maps. A *site map* is a list of all pages on a website, and a video site map is basically the same thing, except that it lists videos. The video site map lists the videos on your website in a technical format that Google and other search engines can understand.

Creating a video site map

A video site map typically is set up by your webmaster. Site map files are written in the XML markup language, and it helps to have experience in coding traditional site map files.

Google provides a helpful tutorial about video site maps: Search for *video site maps* on Google.

Some video hosting companies such as Wistia (www.wistia.com) provide helpful tools to their customers to create these site map files automatically. All you have to do is provide the title, description, and tags, and the system does the rest for you.

Google ignores multiple video site map entries for the same web page. Be sure that you have one dedicated page per video. Otherwise, only the first video on the page shows up in the Google search results.

Though it's useful for SEO to have only one video per web page, in some cases you want to offer visitors several videos on a page to engage them more. Successful SEO is always a balance between what search engines can read and what humans like. If you need several videos on one page, the currently accepted practice is to create pages with those individual videos that are visible only to search engines.

The Microsoft Bing search engine uses a somewhat different format for video site maps: mRSS. It's less broadly supported by video hosting companies, but Google understands it as well.

Registering your site map

Let Google know that you have a video site map by registering it. The place to do this is at Google Webmaster Central, using its webmaster tools (www.google.com/webmasters).

If you have set up the webmaster tools for your website already, it's a straightforward process. Choose Site Configuration⇨Sitemaps⇨Submit a Sitemap. Enter the path to the video site map file on your website and click Submit Sitemap. Google adds your videos within hours or days.

If you haven't set up Google webmaster tools for your website yet, we recommend reading *Web Marketing For Dummies,* by Jan Zimmerman (John Wiley & Sons).

Testing your site map

To figure out whether Google has processed your video site map, perform a video search that's limited to your website. Click Video in the top Google navigation, and enter the following line in the Search bar, replacing *example. com* with your company's Internet domain:

```
site:example.com
```

This expression limits the results to your website. The results show all videos on your website that Google is aware of. If the result is empty, something is wrong with your video site map. Check it for correctness, and then resubmit it at Google Webmaster Central.

Posting Paid Ads on YouTube

If you're in a competitive industry, search engine optimization may not be enough to attract a lot of viewers to your videos. Fortunately, YouTube offers the option of using paid advertising to steer more people toward your content. YouTube calls these ads *TrueView* ads, and they're controlled through the *AdWords for video* system. Setting up YouTube ads is a relatively cost-effective way to attract more views.

YouTube ads come in four flavors:

- ✔ **In-search** ads appear on search results pages and are marked with a yellow background and the Promoted Video caption. Figure 20-3 shows a typical example. You can also set up your ads in such a way that they appear in Google's video search results and even on other websites that partner with Google.

- ✔ **In-display** ads appear on YouTube channel pages or on individual video pages, looking similar to in-search ads.

- ✔ **In-slate** ads show up on videos that are longer than ten minutes. Viewers can choose which ad, of three options offered, they want to watch.

- ✔ **In-stream** ads work exactly like TV commercials. Before viewers can see their chosen videos, they have to watch your video ad first. Viewers can skip the ad after five seconds but can also click the ad to go directly to your website.

YouTube controls which ads to show next to a particular video or search result by using keywords that you can bid on. You tell YouTube which search keywords you want your ad to appear next to, and then specify how much you're willing to pay per viewer. The right bid amount, which depends on the competitiveness of the topic, can vary anywhere from a few cents to a few dollars. YouTube then matches your bid with bids from other advertisers and shows the one or two ads that received the highest bid. Think of it as a simple auction for ad space. To find out more about how bidding for keywords works, read *Pay Per Click Search Engine Marketing For Dummies,* by Peter Kent (John Wiley & Sons).

You can benefit from this virtuous cycle: Because YouTube prioritizes videos with many views in its search results, more views generated by ads can support your SEO efforts. A higher view number also makes your video look more successful and popular.

Figure 20-3:
YouTube
Promoted
Videos
appear
on top of
search-
results
pages.

Setting up a YouTube video ad

Unfortunately, no one has yet invented a robot that sets up YouTube video ads for you. The process may sound somewhat complicated at first because the YouTube ad system is powerful, but it's fairly easy to start your first campaign. To set up a new YouTube ad, follow these steps:

1. **Log in to your YouTube channel by using the Sign In link.**

2. **Go to** `adwords.youtube.com` **and click the Get Started with AdWords for Video button.**

3. **Select your time zone and your preferred currency, and then click the Continue button.**

4. **Enter a name for your campaign in the Campaign Name field.**

5. **On the confirmation page that appears, click the Sign In to Your AdWords Account link.**

6. **Enter the username and password for your YouTube account again.** Now you're entering the AdWords for Video system, where you can set up your campaign.

7. **Enter the amount of your daily budget in the Budget field.** It's the amount you're willing to spend per day on your ads. You can increase or decrease

the budget at any time, so enter an amount that you feel comfortable to experiment with. Start with a small amount, such as $50, and increase it gradually as you start seeing the results you want.

8. **Click the Select Video button.**

9. **Enter the name of your YouTube channel.** YouTube shows you a list of your videos.

10. **Select the video that you want to use as an ad.**

Your YouTube ad may be the first thing that people see about your company, so use a video that's short, catchy, and to the point.

11. **Write your ad text.** This short bit of text appears next to the video thumbnail in your ads. You can write one headline with a maximum length of 25 characters, and you can write two lines of description text with 35 characters apiece.

Attach a catchy title, and tell people why they should watch this video.

12. **Choose the thumbnail you want to use.** YouTube gives you only four predefined options. See the section "Choosing a thumbnail picture," earlier in this chapter, for tips on how to select the best one.

13. **Enter your website address in the Display URL field.** This is the web address that viewers will see.

14. **If you want to direct viewers to a particular page other than your website's home page, enter a web address in the Destination URL field.** For example, you can use a landing page that promotes a specific product. When users click your video ad, they go to this page.

15. **Click the Save and Continue button to create your ad.** Now you need to tell YouTube where to show your ad. This target selection is a *targeting group*.

16. **Create a new targeting group by first giving the target group a name in the Name field.**

17. **Choose a maximum cost per view (CPV) amount.** This amount is the maximum you're willing to pay every time a viewer watches your video. A good amount to start with is 80 cents. You can optimize the amount later.

For in-search and in-display ads, you pay only if people click a Promoted Video ad, not for the ad simply showing up. In the case of in-stream ads, you're charged only when the viewer watches at least 30 seconds of your video ad. For in-slate ads, you pay only when someone actively chooses to view your ad. This *pay per view* method makes YouTube ads highly cost-effective.

18. **Enter three or four of the most important keywords in the Search for Targeting Suggestions field, and click the Get Targeting Suggestions button.** For example, enter *lawnmower, lawn care, landscaping* to see suggestions for ad targeting around these topics. YouTube shows you targeting options that you can use to reach your target audience.

19. **Click the Expand link next to each suggestion and click the Add button next to each keyword or placement you want to add.** You can select from four types of targets:

    • **A YouTube search keyword** lets your ad show up when users search for this particular term. Use YouTube search keywords to target users who are actively looking for specific information on a topic.

    • **Topics** are broader themes on YouTube that group similar videos. Use topics to target users who are on YouTube watching videos about subjects that interest them but who may not search actively for information. For example, select a topic such as Home and Garden to target people who may be interested in lawnmowers.

    • **Display network keywords** place your ad directly next to videos that use these keywords in their titles, tags, or descriptions. For example, choosing display network keywords such as *lawn care* places your ad directly next to videos that specifically cover lawn care.

    • **Placements** let you select specific YouTube channels and even individual videos that your target customers may be watching. This method is the most focused way to find your target audience.

20. **If you want to refine your targets further, click the Add YouTube Search Keywords and Add Targets button in the sidebar on the right to add additional keywords and placements.**

21. **Click the Save and Enable Targeting button to start your campaign.**

22. **If this is the first time you buy ads on Google or YouTube, you're asked for your billing information.** Follow the simple process on the screen to provide your credit card information.

You're billed for your AdWords account only after you start your ad campaign.

You can set up multiple targeting groups for your ads to optimize your results. For example, you can set up one target group only for search keywords, another one for topics, and a third one for specific channel placements. To add a targeting group, go to adwords.google.com, click the All Video Campaign links, select the campaign you want to change, and click the Target tab. Then click the New Targeting Group button and follow the preceding step list, starting with Step 16.

Managing YouTube campaigns is fairly similar to managing Google AdWords campaigns. You can find all the details on how to manage and optimize these types of campaigns in *Google AdWords For Dummies,* by Howie Jacobson, Joel McDonald, and Kristie McDonald (John Wiley & Sons).

Measuring your clicks

Tracking the success of your campaign regularly is essential. If you don't pay attention, you may be spending ad dollars for ineffective views, or you may miss out on interesting opportunities to reach your audience. Fortunately, the YouTube ad management tool gives you all the important numbers you need in order to manage your campaign.

Visit `adwords.google.com` and click the All Video Campaigns link to see the most important performance numbers. You also see the details for every video campaign. This list describes what the numbers mean:

- ✓ **Impressions:** How many times your ad was shown to a user (irrespective of whether they clicked on it). *Thumb* impressions refer to the little picture-and-text ads in search results and next to videos, whereas *Video* impressions count how many times your video was shown as an in-stream ad immediately before another video.

- ✓ **Views:** How many views your videos got by way of paid ads.

- ✓ **View rate:** The percentage of people who saw your ad and clicked on it and then watched the video. Don't be disappointed if this number seems low. Typical rates are well under 1 percent, but the higher the number, the more effective your ad.

- ✓ **Average cost per view (CPV):** Tells you how much you spent for one person to watch your video. This value can differ depending on the topic and the amount of competition you face, but ranges between 15 and 80 cents are typical.

- ✓ **Total cost:** The total amount you spent on all your YouTube ads.

Successful campaigns have a high view rate and a low CPV. But what the numbers should be depends strongly on your industry. Some industries, such as financial services, are highly competitive in their online marketing efforts, so expect a high CPV amount. In other industries, you may be able to draw viewers for only a few cents per pop.

The key is to watch how your campaign performs over time. When the view rate value drops and the CPV rises, it's time to optimize.

Optimizing your targeting

Because you pay for every click on your YouTube ads, you must choose highly effective keywords and placements for your campaign. When you initially create your campaign, you make certain assumptions about which targets will deliver results. Some assumptions may turn out to be wrong, and you may want to try other options over time.

Fortunately, YouTube offers a powerful way to manage targets for every video ad. Follow this step-by-step approach:

1. **Go to adwords.google.com and click All Video Campaigns.** You see a list of your video campaigns.

2. **Click the campaign you want to optimize, and then click the Segment by Targeting Group link.**

3. **Look at the campaign details.** You see the number of views you've received and the amount of money you've spent for every ad. Below these numbers, you see a list of the targeting groups that have contributed to these results.

4. **Review the list of targeting groups to determine which ones are effective.** The most important number is the *cost per view,* or *CPV* — the amount you pay for every viewer who sees your video because of that particular keyword. Low CPVs are attractive, but sometimes you may want to spend more on targeted keywords.

5. **To optimize a targeting group, click the Targets tag and then click the name of the targeting group you want to change.**

6. **Click each category link under Targeting to look at the details of how your keywords and placements perform.** You can look at detailed information for YouTube search keywords, display network keywords, topics, and placements.

7. **Remove a nonperforming keyword and placement by clicking the green button next to it and selecting Paused.** Pause keywords and placements, rather than delete them, because the performance information for paused targets is retained by the system.

8. **If you have ideas for additional keywords, click the Add Keywords button or Add Placements button to add them.**

If you aren't drawing enough views, consider increasing your bid on the targets that you particularly like. Click the Targets tab and then the Edit link next to the name of the targeting group you want to change. Increase the Maximum CPV value, and click the Save and Enable Targeting button.

Creating a call-to-action overlay

After you draw viewers to your video, you want them to then take action, by coming to your website, for example, or by signing up for your newsletter or even buying your product online.

YouTube advertisers use an attractive feature that lets you place a call-to-action message on top of your videos. This call-to-action overlay consists of a small picture, three lines of text, and a link to your website. It's an effective way to draw YouTube viewers to visit your site.

Follow these steps to create an overlay:

1. **Go to** `adwords.google.com` **and click the All Video Campaigns link.**

2. **Choose the campaign you want to change, and click the Videos tab.**

3. **Choose the video that you want to add an overlay to, and click the Add Call-to-Action Overlay link.**

4. **Add a headline and two lines of description text for your overlay.** This should be a strong call to action that entices people to click it.

   Special offers always work well.

5. **Enter the display URL and the destination URL that you want to use.** The *display URL* is the web address that people see in the overlay (`www.acme.com`, for example). The *destination URL* is the link to the page that opens when someone clicks on the overlay. It can be a product-specific page, as in this example

   ```
   www.acme.com/products/quickcut3000.
   ```

6. **Add a small image, if you want.** The image has to be a picture, in a format of 56 x 56 pixels, that's stored on your website. Add the full URL address of the picture in the Image URL field.

7. **Click the Save button.** The overlay should become active almost immediately. Play your video to verify it.

Using Other Types of Video Ads

YouTube ads are by far the most affordable and approachable type of video advertising now available. Because YouTube is dominant in the video market, it's a vital element of any video marketing campaign. But plenty of other forms of video ads are available that companies with somewhat larger budgets can use. This market is quite fragmented, and we don't have enough space in this book to describe all the details.

This list describes the most important video ad types and channels you may want to consider:

✔ **Pre-roll ad:** This ad type works similarly to traditional TV advertising — before people can watch the content, they have to sit through a short commercial. A *mid-roll* ad interrupts a video in the middle, and a post-roll ad appears at the end of a video. Pre-roll ads are most frequently used by big media companies such as CNN, ESPN, and *The New York Times*. Popular video sites such as Hulu use them as well.

If you want to buy pre-roll ads on a particular website, contact the site's ad sales team. Most sites have an Advertising link on their home pages where you can find details.

✔ **Banner ads on video sites:** Most video sites, including YouTube, allow you to place traditional online ad banners on their sites. Some of these ads use video, and others are static banners. Again, contact the ad sales staff of your favorite site to explore pricing.

✔ **Video ad networks:** These companies help you put advertising on many different video websites without the hassle of contacting every site individually. Some of the largest networks are Brightroll, Say Media, Tremor Video, and YuMe.

Chapter 21

Measuring Results and Improving Your Video

In This Chapter

▶ Knowing what to measure and why

▶ Using YouTube Analytics

▶ Working with analytics in video hosting services

You cannot manage what you don't measure. This old management maxim applies to your video strategy, too. Like all marketing channels, video marketing benefits from continual improvement. Simply posting a few videos and hoping for the best aren't sufficient — to get the most from your video strategy, you need to set your priorities.

You can improve many different aspects of your video marketing, such as investing more in content production, boosting your social media outreach efforts, focusing on video search engine optimization (SEO), or buying video ads.

To figure out what to do, critique the performance of your video marketing strategy. Fortunately, plenty of tools can provide solid data and offer insight into what works and what doesn't. As with all measurement tools, however, you have to know how to interpret the data and know which conclusions to draw from this information.

In this chapter, we explain how to gather statistics about viewings of your video and how to continually improve your video marketing strategy based on this data.

Knowing What to Measure and Why

So much data, so little time. Most people have this impression after reviewing video analytics. Like the tools for web analytics or online ad measurement that you may already use to manage your website, video analytics tools give you almost unlimited ways to track and analyze your viewership data.

The question you have to answer is which of these many data points you should pay attention to. You have to determine which measurement dimensions truly tell the story you're interested in and how the results tie in with your marketing goals.

Defining your goals

The most important step on the road to video marketing success is to fully understand which goals you're trying to achieve. Make your goals concrete, measurable, achievable, and well-defined, and ensure that they're neither too abstract nor too detailed. Goals should also have a clear deadline. Reaching 5,000 views for a video is a reasonable goal, but it makes a huge difference whether you reach it in a week or in four years.

Your main marketing goal is highly likely to improve your company's bottom line. Though this objective is an important one, it doesn't tell you what to look for in video marketing. This goal is simply too high-level and abstract to inform your video marketing activities. On the other hand, having the goal "I want to attract at least 3,000 views next week on my new YouTube video" is concrete and measurable. But you need to ask yourself how this raw number translates into business results.

 Break down abstract goals into smaller, well-defined goals that you can track. The least useful goals aren't measurable and have no clear relationship to your business outcomes. Avoid setting vanity goals that don't "move the needle" for your business. For example, the goal "We want to engage with the social media community on YouTube in order to raise our brand's profile" sounds appealing but has no distinct meaning, such as how to measure it.

Having reasonable goals depends on the nature of your business. A company that sells products on an Internet e-commerce site has goals that are quite different from the goals of a professional service business that relies on long-term relationships with clients. The e-commerce company values short-term conversions, and the professional service firm values user loyalty in its target segment.

Strive to reach these important goals in your video marketing:

✔ **Attract a large number of video views.** This goal is the most obvious one if you use online videos in your marketing effort. Drawing in lots of people to see videos in which you've invested a great deal time and money isn't an end in and of itself, but it's a first indicator that you're achieving your business goals. However, even if a million people who aren't in your target market watch your video, your business doesn't benefit. Measuring views is only the first step.

✔ **Reach many unique viewers.** Most video platforms show you the number of people you've reached, which is different from the number of views because the same person may watch multiple videos. The more people you reach, the better, if these viewers are in your target segment.

✔ **Communicate with the right target segment.** The most advanced video analytics tools break out viewer categories by age group, gender, or geographic location, and you can then decide which aspect is important to you. For example, if you sell skateboarding gear, your goal may be to target male viewers who are between 13 and 21 years old.

✔ **Inspire viewer loyalty.** If people watch multiple videos of your content and even return to see more, it's a good sign that it resonates with your audience. Being able to draw subscribers to your channel on YouTube is an important measure of viewer loyalty.

✔ **Encourage viewer engagement.** Video is a social medium on platforms such as YouTube and Facebook. Viewers can click a button to indicate that they like your video, and they can write comments about it. If your goal is to interact directly with your audience, the level of social engagement is important to track.

✔ **Increase your reach via social media sharing.** People can and do share videos that they like on social networks such as Facebook, Twitter, and LinkedIn. Encouraging loyal viewers to share is a helpful way to reach more relevant viewers because people trust recommended videos much more than ones they find by chance.

✔ **Generate click-throughs.** People who find your video appealing may also want to visit your website or, if they're already at your site, another part of it. Providing direct links to relevant content and measuring the number of clicks it attracts is important. The more click-throughs you record, the closer people come to buying — thanks to your videos.

✔ **Receive sign-up requests.** Many websites try to entice people to sign up for newsletters, information packages, or events. The number of sign-ups that result from viewing your video is a good indicator of the relevance of your content to your audience.

✔ **Produce sales.** Finally, if you sell online, you can typically measure how many people bought from you based on how they found you. If you don't sell online, get as much information as possible from your prospects about how they found you.

If your primary concern is whether a particular marketing channel, such as video marketing, increases business, you may wonder why you should even bother to measure the more granular elements, such as views, reach, and loyalty. Create goals and measurements for these more tactical aspects so that you can

✔ **Cover your entire marketing "funnel:"** People rarely buy from you when they first find out about your product or service. In many industries, the buying cycle can take months and require the completion of numerous steps. Prospects trickle down your marketing funnel step-by-step. If more people watch your videos, the opportunity to find prospects increases.

✔ **Process imperfect information:** Every marketer knows that it isn't always possible to know how a new customer found you. Data is imperfect, different marketing systems integrate less than seamlessly, and sometimes multiple channels are involved in a prospect's buying decision. Spend time studying the data carefully to determine how much business a new channel (such as video marketing) brings to you. Throwing out the baby with the bathwater is dangerous if you concentrate on pure sales goals in the short run.

At first, you may struggle to define exact values for your video marketing goals, which is normal for a new type of marketing channel. Expect your goals to shift as you eventually realize which values are realistic. You'll likely need two or three quarters of experience to grasp the normal levels of video marketing success and decide which goals you should set.

The closer your goals are to actual sales transactions, the more difficult they are to measure reliably. Measuring video views is easy, but figuring out how much you've sold because of a particular video is difficult. That's why you should use a combination of goals in every step of your marketing funnel — to paint a full picture of your video marketing success.

Focus on only three or four goals. If you have more, you likely can't focus enough to truly improve your video marketing strategy. Your goals should relate to different areas of your marketing funnel to cover early activity as well as user behavior that occurs closer to a sale.

Use the Online Video Grader (www.onlinevideograder.com) to quickly gauge how you perform in the basic dimensions of video marketing. This free tool compares you to the best video marketers in the basic categories of views, search results, and social media success.

Selecting the data you need

After you know which goals you want to pursue, calculate the specific data you need in order to measure and track your objectives.

Most video analytics tools let you track and analyze raw data in all kinds of ways, but doing so can distract you from determining how you're performing against your goals. That's why you should define the following elements for every one of your goals:

✔ **The metric you want to review:** For example, the number of views is simple to find. Other goals, such as loyalty, can be measured in many different ways, such as the number of subscribers and number of videos viewed per user. Decide which metric is truly important to your specific goal, and stick to it.

✔ **The type of granularity you need:** You may be interested in seeing data video-by-video or simply tracking it on the level of your entire YouTube channel or an entire video collection on your website. Or you may want to track particularly important videos individually while looking at the rest of the collection as a whole.

✔ **The timeframe you want to follow:** Depending on the nature of your business and your video marketing strategy, decide whether to evaluate your performance daily, weekly, or monthly.

Establishing a reporting rhythm

The point of measuring your video marketing performance against your goals is to inspire action. If you aren't fulfilling your goals, do something about it. Without action, measuring and reporting waste your time.

The best way to stay on track is to establish a fixed rhythm for reporting with clearly defined actions that you plan to take based on the results. Reviewing data too frequently or only when you feel like it can easily delay action to another day.

For the most effective approach to taking action, follow these steps:

1. **Define a reporting rhythm, and stick to it.** Many marketing departments work in a monthly rhythm, so it can make sense to tie your video marketing results to the rest of your monthly reporting. But if you're launching a large video campaign, you may want to look at your performance weekly or even daily.

2. **Clarify your agenda.** Because you may be tempted to look only at successful video campaigns and ignore weaker ones, create an agenda of all the goals and metrics you need to look at every time. Simply assembling a short PowerPoint presentation that has the same structure every time can help you easily document your progress.

3. **Involve other people.** If you work in a marketing department, you may already report your video marketing results to your boss. If you don't, involve a colleague in your reporting so that you can discuss your results and "brainstorm" a list of possible improvements.

4. **End with a list of actions.** Finally, end every reporting session by creating a list of three to five action items — tasks that should improve your video marketing performance. These actions should focus on the most important goals or on the goals that indicate where you need to make the most progress.

Keeping your reporting simple is always a good idea, particularly when you're sharing with others. For every goal, present its current value, show how much its value has changed, and indicate where you stand compared to your target. For example, you may choose the number of views you drew last month, the increase versus the previous month, and the percentage of your goal value that you achieved.

Reporting numbers is important, but including a little more color is helpful when you're sharing your results. If a viewer wrote a particularly thoughtful comment, include it. Or if a competitors made a remarkable video, show it. If you tried a new strategy that worked well, talk about it.

Taking the proper corrective action

Depending on where you stand against your goals, you should put together a plan of action because a number of different elements can influence and improve your video marketing results. This list describes a number of possible courses of action:

- ✔ **Produce better content.** If you have low viewer loyalty and you don't attract enough views per video to reach your goals, people probably don't enjoy your videos. Invest in better ones.

- ✔ **Produce more content (while maintaining quality).** If you see good results per video but the overall output of your video marketing is too limited, having more videos of similar quality can be a way to improve your results — and to help you reach more niche audiences.

- ✔ **Produce different kinds of videos.** If you see good viewer numbers for your highly produced headline videos but not many viewers turn into customers, you probably don't have the right content for each stage of the marketing funnel. Prospects expect different information depending on where they stand in the buying process. For example, a longer video explaining the details of your product for people who want to know more can be a good companion to your glossy introductory video.

- ✔ **Improve your calls-to-action.** If plenty of people watch your videos but you don't see clear business results from it (such as sign-ups or sales), your call to action may be too weak. Let people know how your products or services can help them, and tell them what you want them to do next.

- ✔ **Invest in advertising or SEO.** If you reach a small and loyal audience but you don't see much growth in your viewer numbers, try boosting the number of video views with a targeted YouTube ad campaign or search engine optimization (SEO), or both. This strategy can kick-start your results fairly quickly.

- ✔ **Improve your social media outreach.** If you don't get a sufficient number of views and action from your relevant target market, using social media to better promote your videos can help. Remember that video content is an attractive form of using social media.

Avoid the temptation to change everything at once. Make your video marketing efforts effective by concentrating on only one or two tasks at a time. Then you can complete them correctly and concentrate your efforts. And, you'll find out what really works. Having some patience and focus goes a long way toward helping you meet your goals.

Using YouTube Analytics

The sophisticated analytics tool for YouTube channel owners is named — you guessed it — YouTube Analytics. You can find it on the Video Manager menu when you log in to your YouTube account.

Figure 21-1 shows a summary report in YouTube Analytics.

YouTube Analytics is available for your channel as a whole and for individual videos.

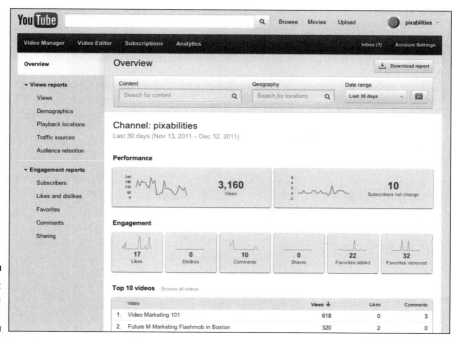

Figure 21-1: YouTube Analytics.

Tracking viewer numbers

Tracking views and viewers with YouTube Analytics is a straightforward task. You see a summary of views (for either the whole channel or per video) directly on the first page of the analytics report.

To dig deeper, choose the Views command from the Views Reports menu, as shown in Figure 21-2. You then have several interesting ways to "slice and dice" the data you see on the page:

✔ **Choose the timeframe.** YouTube Analytics shows results for the past 30 days by default, but you can select any time range you like by selecting the Date Range option.

✔ **Choose the time granularity.** You can look at daily, weekly, and monthly views, depending on your reporting period.

✔ **Look at the geographical distribution of your views.** Click the Map button to see where your viewers came from.

✔ **Look at the number of viewers.** Click the Compare Metric button and then select the Unique Viewers option to see how many people watched your video. The more videos a person watches, the more appealing your channel's content is to that person.

For in-depth number-crunching or to save results for later review, export the results of your current analytics views in Excel (.xls or .xlsx) format. Simply click the Download Report button at the top of every YouTube Analytics page.

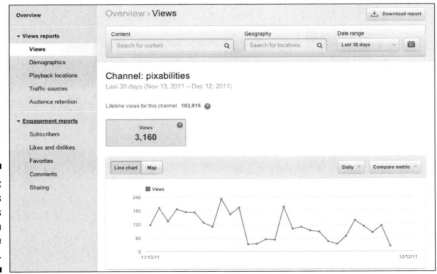

Figure 21-2: The Views Reports menu in YouTube Analytics.

Examining traffic sources

To be able to position more of your videos in high-traffic areas that are frequently visited by your target audience, you must know how they first find your videos. Find out by choosing the Traffic Sources menu option in YouTube Analytics.

The YouTube Traffic Sources report lists a wide range of sources where your videos may already have been viewed:

- **Embedded player:** Your video was viewed on another website that has embedded one of your videos. You can see a list of sites that embedded your videos.

- **YouTube-suggested video:** Views originate from an area of YouTube where the site recommends other videos to viewers — for example, in its Recommended Videos sidebar.

- **Mobile apps and direct traffic:** The source is unclear because mobile devices often don't transmit as much context information as full web browsers do.

- **External website:** A site other than YouTube has linked to one of your videos.

- **YouTube search:** Someone found your video by searching for one or more related keywords on YouTube.

- **Google search:** Someone found your video by searching at either the Google main page (www.google.com) or at its video page (www.google.com/videohp).

- **YouTube channel page:** If lots of people find your videos by looking at your channel's main page, you're doing a good job of shaping your channel.

- **YouTube features:** These views come from a variety of other YouTube features, such as playlists or your channel's Video Manager page.

- **YouTube subscription modules:** A view from a subscriber to your channel is one way to measure viewer loyalty.

- **YouTube featured video:** Occasionally, YouTube picks videos that it promotes prominently on its home page or on category pages. If you're lucky enough to have your video featured, you see its views reported in this category.

- **YouTube video annotation:** If you add these little text boxes to your video to link to other videos and someone then clicks the link, the view is reported under this category.

- **YouTube advertising:** These views are generated via paid ad campaigns on YouTube.

The ideal mix of these traffic sources depends on your content and on your target market. The important task is to track the development of your traffic mix. For example, a sudden drop in the percentage of views from search indicates that you have to do some SEO homework, as we explain in Chapter 20.

Analyzing user behavior

Ideally, your viewers are active — for example, they subscribe to your channel or write comments. YouTube Analytics gives you insight into these categories of user behavior under the Engagement Reports menu:

✔ **Subscribers:** The subscription report shows you how many people have subscribed or unsubscribed to your channel in a given timeframe.

Because subscribers are informed of all your new videos, you should have as many videos as possible.

✔ **Likes and dislikes:** Now that YouTube has replaced its five-star rating system with the simpler like-or-dislike approach, you can see how many people have reacted to your videos positively or negatively.

Encourage as many viewers as possible to click the Like button next to your videos because these votes of approval also boost your exposure in other parts of YouTube, such as search results.

✔ **Favorites:** Viewers sometimes give you the ultimate compliment by adding your video to their lists of favorites. Be aware, however, that some viewers use their Favorites lists to simply bookmark videos they want to watch later.

✔ **Comments:** Users often provide feedback by leaving their remarks on an individual video's page. (Not all comments are positive, of course.)

✔ **Sharing:** Viewers often share videos directly on their social media pages (such as Facebook, Twitter, or Google+), and sometimes they even embed them on their own blogs. Viewers can share videos outside of YouTube — for example, by adding a video's URL to a tweet — though this type of sharing isn't counted in YouTube Analytics.

✔ **Audience retention:** When you use a *video heat map* to find out how much of a video viewers have watched, you can determine which content viewers like — or, rather, at what point they stopped watching. Many people stop viewing shortly after a video begins, or near the middle, and only one-third of viewers, on average, watch the entire video. The more people who watch a video until the end, the better its content has resonated with your audience.

To compare your YouTube videos with others of similar length, click the Relative Audience Retention button.

Focus on the most important metrics when you analyze user behavior. The biggest influence on valuable viewer traffic is likely sharing via social media. Channel subscriptions are also important ways to gain loyal viewers, and audience retention tells you a lot about how much people truly value your content. Comments on YouTube are slightly less important than comments from other social media sites, so don't obsess over them.

To quickly get a handle on the level of your social media success, use the Online Video Grader, mentioned earlier in this chapter, in the section "Defining your goals." YouTube's video sharing statistics provide an incomplete view of how many people have truly shared your video because it counts only the number of times that the act of sharing a video was initiated on YouTube's own site.

Using Google Analytics to paint the full picture

To see how videos influence your business performance, tie in your video analytics with other marketing or business data that matters to you. (YouTube Analytics can take you only so far.)

One way to do this if you're using YouTube to host videos on your website is to correlate the performance of your video with the performance of your website. Though many tools are available to help you measure website performance, the most widely used tool is Google Analytics, and it's free.

To see whether your videos are helping boost your website traffic, follow these steps:

1. **Record any spikes in the number of videos viewed.**

2. **Check to see whether these spikes match the spikes in traffic to your website or to specific pages on your website.**

Unfortunately, you can't see this correlation automatically in Google Analytics or YouTube Analytics. You have to consolidate this data manually or use video marketing software that matches the data for you.

Working with Analytics in Video Hosting Services

YouTube isn't the only way to distribute video. Most video marketers use video extensively on their company websites, and you must know how to measure this part of the video analytics puzzle as well.

If you use YouTube to publish videos on your site, you're already set up with YouTube Analytics — though it doesn't give you all the information you may need and want. Hiring a video hosting service and using specialized video marketing tools can give you additional details to help you make the right marketing decisions.

Knowing what to expect from a premium service

You can use a video hosting service (we discuss them in Chapter 18) to put videos in optimal technical quality on your website and with a higher degree of control over the user experience than you would experience when using a YouTube player.

Hosting services typically provide their own analytics, and vendors have different strengths, so if you know exactly what you're looking for in your video analytics, consider this information before selecting a hosting provider.

Larger hosting services such as Brightcove and Ooyala often cater primarily to media companies. These larger content creators focus on *monetization,* or on making money from videos directly, by selling advertising on top of their videos. The analytics that these companies demand must therefore suggest how much of the ad sales pie their videos have earned (though this aspect isn't relevant to most marketers, who see video as a marketing tool, not as an end in itself).

Still, the larger hosting services provide all or most of the analytics information that you can get for videos that you host on YouTube (as described in the earlier section "Using YouTube Analytics"). Some are a bit more granular and let you access more detailed information. In some cases, you can even integrate your video analytics with your other web analytics tools, such as Google Analytics. That's very helpful if you want to see how much traffic or conversions your video content really drives.

Hosting services that are more focused on business users provide granular data at the level of the individual viewer. For example, Wistia (www.wistia. com) provides heat maps that show how much of a video a particular user watches, skips, or rewinds (see Figure 21-3). These services break down users' geographical locations and, if your video is part of your e-mail marketing campaign, for example, even tell you which people viewed the video and for how long.

Stick to the goals you've defined, and reflect primarily on the data that helps you reach these goals. You can easily become lost in all the analytics bells and whistles that certain video hosting services provide.

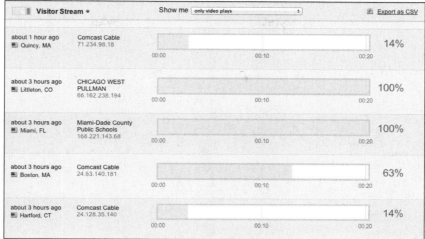

Figure 21-3:
A video-viewing heat map from the Wistia hosting service.

Using specialized video marketing tools

Because video marketing is still a complex discipline, several software providers sell tools that simplify a marketer's life by integrating multiple video marketing channels across several video platforms:

- ✔ **Caffeine** (www.pixability.com/product/caffeine)**:** Provides an all-in-one solution for video marketing and covers publishing to YouTube, Facebook, and other platforms, comprehensive analytics, video SEO, and playlist management, among others. Caffeine even matches your YouTube statistics with your Google Analytics data. This Pixability product is optimized for marketers who want to save time and realize the highest level of return on their videos.

- ✔ **OneLoad** (www.oneload.com)**:** Designed to publish videos to a large number of video platforms. OneLoad (from TubeMogul) also collects analytics from these platforms to provide a unified view of a video's success.

- ✔ **Visible Measures for Publishers** (http://corp.visiblemeasures.com/media-video-publishers)**:** Targets large brands, agencies, and video publishers with a high-end analytics solution. Its broad coverage of different video technologies and platforms provides interesting video industry statistics.

Part VI
The Part of Tens

In this part . . .

You can never have enough information, ideas, or resources for a successful video marketing campaign — and that's what the lists in The Part of Tens are designed to provide. The chapters in this part notify you in advance of video marketing pitfalls, help you get more return on your investment by listing business uses for video marketing (other than sales), and provide helpful resources to help you start marketing by video more quickly, cheaply, and effectively than you ever imagined possible.

Chapter 22

Ten Video Marketing Don'ts

In This Chapter

▶ Keeping your video message on target and interesting

▶ Making the most of online tools

There are plenty of ways to make and promote great marketing videos, but some big "don'ts" can cost you time and money. Some mistakes can even cost you customers. This short, but action-packed chapter addresses major mistakes you want to avoid like confusing your message, ignoring your audience, being unprepared, and not being objective.

Don't Let Your Message Be Vague

What good is having a killer marketing video if no one understands the message you're trying to convey? Many people feel pressure to quickly post video online or on a company website so that they don't miss the boat on video marketing. This situation often results in rushing the scripting process, resulting in a video message that's vague or pointless.

Posting a video that has a vague marketing message is worse than posting *no* video. Videos create an impression to prospects, and if your video isn't on target, you may lose prospects before they understand what you're all about.

Take the time to define your message clearly. Test the script by showing it to other people. Evaluate whether people who know you — and those who don't — respond positively. See whether test subjects can repeat back to you the main message of the video. Repeat this process after the video is shot and roughly edited. Negative feedback may prevent you from posting a video this month, or even next month, but in the end you'll know that you have a video that works for marketing your business effectively and efficiently. You can see more scripting tips in Chapter 4.

Don't Put Too Many Messages in the Video

Let's face it: Marketers have a lot to say. That's why they speak and blog and write white papers. But video is a brief medium for marketing — too many messages make your video long and complicated. Not all of your messages may be meaningful to the same target audience. Video marketing works best when you have a single brief message that you want to make memorable to a specific group of people.

Rather than complicate a video with multiple messages, split the message into parts and dedicate a single video to each part — your video then remains short and sweet. In addition to helping you target specific market segments, this strategy gives you multiple videos to post, to help with search engine optimization.

Don't Make Videos Long and Boring

Much discussion takes place in the marketing community about the proper length of marketing videos. Certain research reports have found that 2 minutes and 53 seconds is the average length of time the average viewer on the web watches a video before moving to a different activity. Many marketers believe that 2 minutes and 53 seconds is therefore the maximum attention span of most viewers. Because not every person has the same attention span (obviously), we believe that this number represents instead the average length of time that most video makers are capable of sustaining the average viewer's interest.

A marketing video has no ideal length. A video that is dull or that lacks creativity or relevance will seem long and boring at 30 seconds. Organizations such as TED (a branded series of conferences where impressive speakers are invited to give 18-minute talks), for example, regularly post compelling videos that last more than 10 minutes apiece. To create a successful marketing video, entertain your prospects and keep them interested until the last frame.

Consider your purpose and your audience when determining the length of a marketing video. In the minds of a prospect, all unwatched videos are not created equal. Though the total viewable length of a video isn't relevant to its entertainment value, it may prove to be a factor in attracting prospects to begin watching it. A short video of two to three minutes or less may entice a prospect to watch immediately. Most people can spare a few minutes to watch a video on a topic that interests them. Longer videos, of more than 5 minutes, may wait in a prospect's inbox for a day or two until the person finds time to watch. A video lasting 15 minutes or longer may wait forever to be viewed, if the topic isn't particularly compelling and relevant to the prospect.

Break long, compelling messages into smaller videos labeled Part 1, Part 2, and so on. This strategy, which puts the power back into the viewer's hand, can effectively entice someone into taking action on your marketing appeal.

Don't Forget to Prepare for the Shoot

For marketers, time is money, and nothing kills time like not being prepared when shooting a video. A video shoot involves many people and lots of moving parts. A missing prop or a forgotten battery can cause a simple three-hour shoot to turn into a painful, all-night marathon — a frustrating situation for you that may also prevent your cast and crew from working with you in the future.

While working on a location shoot with a timed deadline, Matt (sadly) left his extra camera battery at home. When the original battery drained, everyone had to wait 30 minutes for it to recharge every time Matt shot a few more minutes of video. Rather than end the shoot at 6:00 p.m., as planned, the shoot finally ended at 6:00 the next morning.

Channel your inner Boy Scout, and be prepared. Make lots of checklists and be sure to complete them. Set up a shoot a week in advance, and review the details yourself, and then again with the key players to ensure that few problems occur on the day of the shoot. To create a triple-check, set up reminders, and ask other people to remind you too. This way, everyone can sleep soundly, before and after the shoot. Check out Chapter 12 for more information about shooting preparation.

Don't Ignore the Sound Quality

What's that you say? You certainly don't want viewers to wonder what your message is when they can't hear your video. Sound is a crucial element in delivering your message, and many stumbling blocks exist to keep the message from being heard. Sound that's too soft is only one problem that can obscure your message. Background noise, out-of-sync music, and actors who mumble can all make an otherwise outstanding video useless.

In the planning and scripting stages of creating a video, choose appropriate sound bites so that you can focus on emphasizing them.

Your recording equipment should be of high quality, your shooting environments should be quiet, and your actors should speak loudly and crisply.

Edit with an ear for sound. Remove all hisses, pops, and sirens so that prospective customers feel excited, not annoyed. You can find plenty of information about creating good sound in Chapter 11.

Don't Cast without Choices

If you want your marketing videos to have an impact on their viewers, the people acting in them must convey emotion in a believable way. Recruiting someone you know, or the first person who crosses your path in your office, to appear in a video may not serve your needs when the video has to relate to prospective customers in a compelling manner.

Describing good acting or bad acting is difficult. Though some folks feel that Meryl Streep's acting is annoying, most people tout her as the finest actress of her generation. Luckily, the emoting in *your* video doesn't need to help someone win an Academy Award, but you still need to employ someone who seems authentic and who can maintain your audience's attention.

Aspire to find the best actors available under your particular circumstances. Money, timing, and location are all factors in your decision. Find two or three actors to work with for each role. Even if all the actors are mediocre, you still may observe attributes in one that are better than another, and you may be able to coach that actor to a better performance. You may even be able to swap actors in different roles for better effect.

Sometimes, however, you may not have much of a choice. If you're shooting on a low budget or in a city whose citizens have little acting talent, you may have to select from a shallow pool of talent. Even then, however, try to find at least a couple of people to choose from.

Playing in front of the camera with friends and family members can be fun, though you ultimately have a job to do when casting. You can find a ton of information in Chapter 7 on how to cast your video, which helps with your talent search.

Your video is only as strong as its weakest performance. One bad actor can distract from your message.

Don't Think That Your Video Is Good When It Isn't

Making a video is a fun and creative project. After spending large amounts of time and money on the finished product, however, you can easily become unable to view it objectively.

It's a *marketing* video, and its strategic purpose is to communicate to your prospects in a compelling manner. If your video won't help you achieve your objective, you should know that before you embarrass yourself by sending it to prospects, clients, or employees.

Set up a screening panel composed of people who will be honest with you. Choose screeners who are honest, blunt, and direct (but gentle!). Share the script with them, and show the video at various stages in the creation process. Be open-minded, and focus on critiques of the parts of the video that don't work rather than on the congratulations for the parts that do. The panel may add a little pain to the process, but it will help restrain your video making ego to your wallet, where it belongs.

Don't Omit Video from Social Media

If your company isn't a part of Facebook and Twitter, it definitely should be, because social media is an important part of every modern marketing strategy. Marketers need to be wherever their target audience is, and Internet users are spending *tons* of time on social media sites. Because everyone is overwhelmed by all the social chatter, getting people to pay attention to your company and to your message on social media isn't easy. You have to offer them a valuable and interesting product.

Video helps you stand out. Though many people nowadays blog and tweet, you should know whether your competitors have compelling video content that grabs your prospects' attention. Good video makes Facebook pages more interesting, Twitter streams benefit from links to absorbing videos, and blog articles come to life with striking video segments.

Adding video to Facebook, Twitter, and blogs not only adds tremendous value to your social media activities but also drives more viewers to your videos. People *love* to watch videos, and they love to share them. The better your videos, the more benefit you receive from social media. Don't expect your video to be the next viral video sensation, though: It doesn't have to "go viral" to be successful. Rather than aspire to attract millions of viewers, your goal should be to reach the people who comprise your target audience. A focused social media strategy that includes video is a powerful and cost-efficient way to do it.

Don't Ignore YouTube

Many marketers and video producers still have a slightly snobbish attitude about YouTube. They seem to believe that YouTube consists only of people watching silly videos of skateboarding dogs and exploding soda bottles, teenagers writing offensive comments under anonymous nicknames, and random ads popping up all over the place.

In case you wonder whether your valuable brand should be present in this chaotic environment, we can tell you: Yes, it should. The YouTube site may have lowbrow content, and it may give content owners only limited control over the presentation of their videos, but it also happens to be by far *the* dominant video platform on the Internet. After Google, the YouTube search function is the second largest search engine in the world. It's the default site for finding videos on the web, and YouTube content shows up more often than any other type of video source in Google search results. It's also the video platform that is most broadly supported by social media channels.

If you want people to find your videos, you simply must be on YouTube. You still can use a professional hosting service to post videos on your website, and you may even consider using other video sharing platforms. But YouTube is quite simply a must-have distribution channel for serious video marketing.

Unfortunately, not many people choose the correct YouTube strategy — you can't simply upload videos to YouTube and hope for the best. Spend time setting up your YouTube channel, as outlined in Chapter 17, and do your search engine optimization homework, as explained in Chapter 19. Engage in the YouTube community to drive viewer loyalty. Consider running a small ad campaign to drive viewership. All these techniques can help you draw viewers to your painstakingly produced videos.

Don't Make Only One Video

Imagine writing only one e-mail message to a prospective customer or sending only one newsletter — ever. Many people approach video this way. They seem to believe that offering a single video on their website will magically compel all their customers to buy their products.

Successful video marketers, in contrast, create videos for *several* specific target audiences. These marketers treat video as a marketing strategy that's as serious as their e-mail marketing campaigns or their search engine ads. A recent study indicates that companies successfully using video create 11 times more video than those that are unsuccessful with it.

Chapter 23

Ten Nonmarketing Uses for Business Video

In This Chapter

▶ Informing and training with video

▶ Using the video process to build better teams

▶ Improving team morale with video

*A*s video production becomes cheaper and easier with every passing day, you have increasingly more ways to incorporate the video process into your company for a variety of different purposes, including nonmarketing purposes. The ten ideas in this chapter can help improve your business — and, possibly, your life.

Internal News Show

Many companies struggle to inform their employees about company news, especially when the companies are large or growing or when their facilities are spread across a wide geographical area. To persuade employees to take the time to read corporate newsletters, consider building an internal news show.

Employees love watching their friends and colleagues "ham it up" on internal videos. A weekly news show is a perfect way to provide company information and track its delivery.

Assign a couple of employees to gather information during the week and craft a script. Don't be afraid to let them get a little silly. The more fun the show, the more likely it is to be watched every week. Use the standard news format of news anchors introducing segments of interest. Incorporate interviews and graphics. To draw viewers, limit the show to a couple of minutes, and upload and distribute a link every Monday morning. You can even track who watches the show on YouTube.

Not everyone in your company has the time or creativity to create a weekly, internal news show. Allow enough budgeted resources to make the show an important part of your culture. If members of management treat the show as a trivial pursuit, employees may treat it the same way. Try reallocating the time and money you already spend on newsletters and conference calls (and on repeating yourself), and avoid the costly mistakes that arise from the lack of good communication.

Simple Demonstrations

Showing is better than telling any day of the week. Your marketing department may have enough money in the budget to create polished videos only for customers. Wouldn't you want your staff members to see simple demonstration videos for every process and procedure you want them to perform or adhere to? If your company has an intranet or internal computer network, a library of demonstrations can be quite a useful tool.

Rather than create a suggestion box, create a suggestion *channel*. Launch a channel on YouTube where employees can upload helpful hints to benefit their colleagues. Anyone with a small camera can create a demonstration video, as we discuss in Chapter 9. The videos can provide tips and tricks related to your own product or even to tools used by employees in your company.

Training

On-the-job training is a helpful way to learn, but it usually diverts valuable work time from the experienced person who's facilitating the training. Video is a helpful way to record information from the people who create your company's policies and processes and pass it along without pulling them from their regular duties every time you need to train someone new.

Start with just a few training videos covering the most basic job responsibilities. Add a short video describing a simple task every week, and you'll soon be surprised at how quickly your efficient new training program grows. The videos don't have to be sophisticated, but at least make them fun and entertaining so that new hires want to watch and learn.

Archiving

Video is an easy and effective tool for archiving documents and other items of value. Insurance companies have accepted videos for decades as evidence of your personal property. Your business may own significant artifacts or documents that you may want to preserve electronically. Video offers a three-dimensional view that absorbs and conveys more information than photographs alone.

Record meetings and events on video for posterity. Memory is cheap, and you can store it all electronically on the web for free. You may never need to review your videos, but — who knows? — a video recording may settle a future dispute or provide valuable historical information for your next strategic planning session. Make everyone aware that you're recording the video, however, to ensure fairness and safety.

FAQ Videos

Nearly every business website has a Frequently Asked Questions (FAQ) section. Rather than write a couple of paragraphs explaining each question, use video links to serve the same purpose.

Have someone in your office who has lots of personality read letters from customers — and your company's replies. Imagine the answer girl cheerily saying, "Jane from Deerfield, Ohio, asks. . . ." and answering, "Well, Jane, so glad you asked. . . ."

Teamwork Exercise

Producing a simple video is an interactive, collaborative process that can be completed with the assistance of one person or a dozen people or more. Every part of the video process sharpens skills that are relevant to business. Scripting helps foster communication among team members, and production helps develop various management skills. By inspiring people to work together on a video, you help them create a product that has true value in an environment where they can fail safely and learn from each other and the process.

Structure helps open creative minds, so follow strict timelines and focus the exercise on the process rather than on the finished video. If your colleagues are focused and motivated, they will likely surprise you with the same creativity and quality that they demonstrate in their videos.

Company Contest

People love to compete, and making videos promotes healthy competition. You can split video teams by department or simply have participants draw straws. Give every team a camera, a topic, and a timeline, and then turn them loose. The better the prize, the better the video. After the task is complete, you can set up a red-carpet awards event to show off the videos and distribute awards.

Feel-Good Videos

Building a healthy company culture involves regularly providing employees with common cultural experiences. Whether you're touting the inspiration of your company's core values or simply praising an employee or two, honoring employees in a permanent, sharable way is better than handing out wall plaques or framed certificates that usually just collect dust.

If you make feel-good videos available in a format that's easy to upload online, colleagues can pass them on to their friends and family via Facebook, YouTube, and other social media venues.

Internal Presentations

Nothing perks up an otherwise dull slide presentation like a fun and energetic video. The process of preparing a video can help you crystallize your ideas and edit your message. The creative video process can often help inspire other entertaining moments throughout a speech. Involving others in the presentation may even boost attendance when the production crew, for example, can show off its work, too.

Music Videos for Your Company Band

Every company seems to employ someone who plays in a band. (Apparently, musicians are everywhere.) Many companies even have enough musicians to form their own bands to entertain at holiday parties. Give these bands the exposure they need, inside the company and outside of it, by helping them make music videos. Creating a video can be fun for everyone involved — including clients, if appropriate.

Chapter 24

Ten Video Marketing Resources

In This Chapter

▶ Finding the best places to buy your gear

▶ Considering industry resources

▶ Locating production services

▶ Finding the best promotional services

*T*he collaborative video marketing process has many moving parts and requires many people and many items to create an outstanding result. The industry is changing rapidly, as is its technology, and after you get started, you will see ways to improve your skills and resources. This chapter lists our favorite places to start. Oh, and yes, we list a few more than ten resources, but we thought you wouldn't mind the extra help.

Video Gear: B&H Photo Video Pro Audio

    www.bhphotovideo.com

The only thing better than a one-stop shop is one with the best prices. B&H Photo Video Pro Audio in New York City is that store. It has the largest selection of video equipment — everything from pocket video cameras to professional studio equipment. Every piece of gear you could possibly need for production, sound, lighting, and editing is available from B&H, and its prices are competitive with other stores (bricks-and-mortar or online). After looking at the B&H catalog (it's nothing short of "gearhead porn"), you'll covet video products that you've never even thought of.

If you're in Manhattan on a visit, the B&H store is worth a couple of hours of your time, just to talk with its experts and play with its amazing inventory — including a fully equipped TV studio. If you can't make the pilgrimage, all items are easily found and shipped online. Because B&H is owned and run by Hasidic Jews, its customer service department is closed from sundown Friday to sundown Saturday and on Jewish holidays.

Video Professionals: Mandy.com

```
mandy.com
```

If you lack the people, the skills, or the talent to mount a video production on your own, you can always hire a pro. Visit Mandy.com, the centralized resource for finding video production and editing freelancers all over the world. You can search by price, skill set, or geographical location to easily find a talent pool of creative video artists. You can also post your projects online so that people can contact you.

Just because someone has more video production experience than you doesn't mean that the person is qualified for your needs or can provide the artistic qualities you're looking for. Many video professionals are excellent artists who lack business knowledge. Check out their sample videos to see whether their styles are appropriate for your marketing image and approach. Above all, be clear and straightforward about your wants and needs to avoid misunderstandings that lead to lost time and money.

Content Help: ROAR! Get Heard in the Sales and Marketing Jungle

```
www.awesomeroar.com
```

Many video marketers easily become comfortable with following the production process but struggle with creating compelling content. Often, the problem lies not in the video writing process but in the lack of clear messaging in the company itself. Kevin's bestselling book *ROAR! Get Heard in the Sales and Marketing Jungle* (John Wiley & Sons) has helped thousands of companies shape their messages to say the right things to the right people in the right way.

ROAR! relates a fun (short!) parable that takes place in real-life restaurants all around New York. Inside, its exercises can help you

- ✔ Create a compelling value proposition that connects with a prospect's pain
- ✔ Truly differentiate your offering from your competition's
- ✔ Identify buyer types and craft your video message so that they respond favorably

Whether you buy the book in hard copy or download it for your e-reader (the first two chapters are free), you quickly get the tools you need to make your message work for you.

Animation: Go!Animate, Xtranormal

goanimate.com

www.xtranormal.com

If you're eager to post a video and you lack the time, money, or resources to make it happen, you can always take the route of online animation. Several tech-oriented companies are innovating in desktop animation for those who can't draw. Most of these products have full production and editing capabilities, allowing you to select and modify characters with action and voice. The two products described in this list are the easiest, cheapest, and best to use:

- **Go!Animate:** If you're a fan of Seth McFarlane-style animation, you'll love this product. You can try it for free and create great-looking, cartoon-style videos in a few easy steps. Here are some highlights:

  - Its starter version is free. More features are available at a cost.

  - Its characters are either human or animal, in 2D cartoon style.

  - You can type the lines of your dialogue to have the system create computer-generated speech, or record dialogue and use the ultra-cool lip-synching technology to match the characters' lip movements.

  - GoAnimate has more-advanced animation products to appeal to serious animators who want to customize their own creations.

- **Xtranormal:** You can use this product to create animated 3-D movies, and you can choose characters and locations by using simple drag-and-click technology. Here are some Xtranormal highlights:

  - Get basic access for free. Pay more for features or get all tools for a monthly subscription.

  - Make characters either humans or animals in 3-D computer-generated form. Advanced animation software programs are available.

  - Type the lines of your dialogue to have the system create computer-generated speech.

  - Choose different camera angles for editing to minimize the monotony of stationary characters.

Both companies let you easily download finished products to your computer or upload them to social-sharing sites such as YouTube or Facebook. If you're struggling to choose between the two, check out some amusing, informative, and racy YouTube videos by searching for *Go!Animate versus Xtranormal.* Some of them have samples of both systems (and are pretty darn funny).

Internal Video Production: H.R. Larious

www.hrlarious.com

Though employee manuals are infamously long and boring, the most significant marketing task in most companies is marketing internally to employees. A number of companies produce videos to address human resource (HR) issues, but the bulk of these videos are long, dry, boring, and forgettable — just like their published counterparts. The H.R. Larious video production company solves that problem by using humor in its videos.

The entrepreneurial women who own H.R. Larious handle common employee issues such as diversity, behavior, and safety by applying their educational backgrounds in human resources, communications, and video production to create brief, humorous videos that make the point memorably. You can customize the site's menu of already produced videos for your business or request new and unique videos specifically for your company — all at prices that are cheaper than the typical lawyer consultation.

Free Music: Incompetech

incompetech.com

Simply using the music in your iTunes folder to score marketing videos would be convenient, but that method would either violate copyright laws (as discussed in Chapter 8) or cost a ton of licensing fees. Most popular music does a good job of setting an emotional tone, but it doesn't quite work when you want to enhance the dialogue or action in a story-based movie.

Good video scoring can effectively manipulate the emotions of viewers to your advantage, which is likely one of your video objectives.

The best, and most affordable, resource for exceptional video scoring is Kevin MacLeod at Incompetech. This one-person orchestra creates and posts music segments lasting between one and three minutes on his site. This list explains why we love Incompetech (and Kevin) for scoring video:

✔ You can choose from a wide variety of music types, which you can search by several useful categories, including genre and mood.

✔ You receive a free license to use Kevin's music by simply giving him credit at the end of the video.

✔ If you can't give Kevin credit, he'll happily sell you a $5 license to use existing music.

✔ The music is easy to download and attach to your video by using any editing program.

✔ The music cuts, blends, and merges easily.

✔ The music is well produced and fun, whether it has a comedic, corporate, horror, or classical theme.

If you want custom music, Kevin can compose a custom score for your video for as little as $200 per video minute, depending on the complexity of the project. Because Kevin's approach of posting free music helps make simple scoring affordable for video makers and brings him wider exposure and more clients, he believes that more musicians should offer music royalty-free, so he also posts links to other royalty-free music sources on his blog.

Video Seminars: ROARing Video

`roaringvideo.com`

You can go a long way toward teaching yourself video marketing with the help of this book and some experimentation, but nothing replaces working side-by-side with experts. Learning directly from professional videographers can help you advance quickly and efficiently. ROARing Video has affordable, fun seminars that can help your company start making and promoting compelling and entertaining marketing videos.

Presented by two of the authors of this book (Matt and Kevin), this unique, interactive, and fun one-day workshop teaches attendees how to identify key business messages and convert them to entertaining and memorable video scripts, With guidance from a team of professional video crew members, attendees then shoot, edit, score, and post their videos online. Attendees leave with a scored and edited company video of their own creation — and with ideas for making more.

ROARing Video also presents two-day interactive workshops onsite at company locations to teach employees how to produce and integrate compelling video with effective internal and external marketing. Company employees learn to make their own videos internally, and they can work with ROARing Video to make more-advanced external videos that achieve an immediate return on investment (ROI).

Industry and Educational Information: Web Video Marketing Council, Reel SEO

```
www.webvideomarketing.org
```

```
www.reelseo.com
```

Much is going on in the world of video marketing. Dedicated video marketing professionals must keep on top of advancements in technology, production and promotion techniques, and industry changes. This list describes two prominent organizations that provide invaluable news, information, and insights about video marketing:

- ✔ **Web Video Marketing Council (WVMC):** This nonprofit agency focuses on providing its constituency with timely, relevant information and research results on a range of online video topics and technologies by way of its website, newsletter, and media partner relationships. The organization aggregates and archives directory, news, and research information on video marketing. Its weekly newsletter circulation is 30,000 strong and growing.
- ✔ **ReelSEO:** *The Online Video Marketer's Guide* is a solid resource for online video news and analysis and for tips and trends. The site features experts, columns, and videos that demonstrate best practices, resources, and creative ideas for improving your video marketing program.

Social Media Integration: FanBridge, HubSpot, Prime Concepts

```
www.fanbridge.com
```

```
www.hubspot.com
```

```
www.primeconcepts.com
```

Like video marketing, social media is a useful tool. Used by itself, social media is unlikely to make your business successful, but used effectively and integrated with other, more traditional forms of marketing, it can enhance your sales and marketing efforts with great efficiency. These three companies can boost the impact of your video marketing by way of social media channels:

✔ **FanBridge:** If you're a do-it-yourself type, you *must* manage your community and communicate with its participants regularly, via e-mail and via social networks such as Facebook and Twitter. A number of services assist in this effort, such as FanBridge, which gives you a ton of helpful tools without overwhelming you. This list describes what you can do by using the FanBridge tools:

  • Easily incorporate clickable videos into your e-mail messages

  • Add videos to your Facebook fan page

  • Convert viewers into subscribers

  • Use the Social Digest tool to automatically combine your Facebook, Twitter, and video content into a single e-mail to send to members of your community

FanBridge provides most of its tools, along with its e-mail management systems, for *free.*

✔ **HubSpot:** The main goal of online content and social media is to drive appropriate customer traffic to your door with minimal effort. *Inbound marketing* is the term for this process. The brainchild company of Brian Halligan and Dharmesh Shah, the bestselling authors of *Inbound Marketing* (John Wiley and Sons), HubSpot (www.hubspot.com) provides businesses inbound marketing software and expertise that will help your videos drive more inbound traffic to your website.

Video is ideal content for inbound marketing. When prospects arrive at your site to view your videos, HubSpot captures information about them, allowing you to more effectively and easily promote other videos and complementary content.

✔ **Prime Concepts:** Not all video marketers are ready, willing, and able to conquer the social media world on their own. With all the fast-moving changes and companies, creating an effective social media strategy can be daunting. Sometimes, farming out the whole thing is the easiest method. Prime Concepts — a national, one-stop, social media marketing resource — has people who know how to integrate marketing videos with social media.

Its founder, Ford Saeks, believes that marketing is *not* all about selling — it's about communication and building relationships. This social media guru practices what he preaches — he builds relationships by adding value first and then engages prospects with entertaining and informative video, which has led to quite a loyal following. Visit the site to download a free copy of Saeks' *Ten Tips to Leverage Your Videos Using Social Media Marketing,* at www.primeconcepts.com/smmvideos.

Promotion and Measurement: Pixability, Online Video Grader

> www.pixability.com

> www.onlinevideograder.com

After you catch the video marketing bug and start creating multiple video campaigns, you'll see that the YouTube video manager is wholly inadequate for managing a targeted campaign that provides up-to-the second analytics.

Enter Pixability — it helps companies and digital agencies create, manage, optimize, and market a portfolio of online videos. The three basic Pixability offerings are sure to create a buzz:

- **Caffeine:** Provides cutting-edge video promotion and measurement tools. This cloud-based, video marketing software platform fully integrates with YouTube and other video hosting platforms, along with social media sites such as Facebook, LinkedIn, and Twitter.

- **Espresso:** Stimulates your Caffeine software with complete video marketing services and personal guidance from the highly trained video baristas at Pixability.

- **Mocha:** Adds a shot of flavor to the Espresso and Caffeine products by incorporating full video production capabilities so that the video "mug" is always full for companies and agencies that have large budgets but don't know where to start.

Visit the site and plug in your information to instantly see how your videos measure up. The video grader shows you how to optimize your performance to ensure that your online videos are producing optimum business results.

Pixability was founded by two of the authors of this book, Bettina and Andreas, who continually use their MIT graduate degrees to create groundbreaking tools for targeting, promoting, and measuring video. It helps organizations place the right video in front of the right audience to trigger the right action.

Index

• Symbols & Numerics •

3-D effects/devices, 135,, 227, 261–264
3GPP/3gp (video file format), 282
3Play Media (closed-caption service), 326
180-degree rule, 184–185
1000 words, a picture is worth, 11
H.264 (codec), 205–206, 282
HTML5, 282
MPEG-4/MP4 files, 138, 205–206, 282

• A •

Ableton (music software), 239
accessories
 batteries, 147–148
 checklist, 171–172
 "go bag", 172
 lighting, 144–145, 155–156
 microphones, 145
 miscellaneous items, 148
 monopods and Steadicam, 146–147
 tripods, 146
action/activity, scripting, 65–67
actors. *See also* cast/casting breakdown
 about working with, 99–100
 casting calls, 106–107
 conducting auditions of, 107–109
 connecting with an audience, 100–101
 finding professionals, 364
 identifying natural talent, 109–110
 memorizing lines, 105, 111, 178
 motivation and believability, 102–104
 relationship with the director, 176–178
 talent alone is not acting, 103, 356
 tools and techniques, 101–102
 voice as a tool, 165–167
 voiceover narration, 242–243
 webinar hosting, 111–112
 using non-actors, 110–111, 119–120
 using professionals, 15–16, 104–105, 118
Adobe After Effects (software), 263

Adobe Flash Video, 205–206, 268
Adobe Premiere (software), 96, 195–197
"Aha!" moments, 60
Amazon,10, 144–145, 291
ambient sound, 158, 232, 243–244
American Federation of Television and Radio
  Artists (AFTRA), 75, 105, 119
analytics (measuring performance)
 about, 10–11, 337–338
 defining goals of the program, 338–340
 determining data needed, 340–341
 establishing a schedule, 341–342
 getting professional help, 370
 hosting services, 293, 296–297, 347–349
 planning corrective action, 342–343
 social media, 306
 using Google Analytics, 347
 using Pixability, 370
 using YouTube Analytics, 343–347
"angels"/"angel" network, 83
animation/animated videos
 about, 38–39
 adding 3-D effects, 227
 films, 262
 motion graphics, 261–264
 online software, 17, 365–366
Animoto (online video editing), 200
annotations, video, 274–276
Any Video Converter, 207
appearance waiver (release form), 120
Apple Computers. *See* editing software
Apple iPhone. *See* smartphones
Apple Motion (3-D software), 263
Apple ProRes (codec), 205–206
archetypes, 45, 53–54, 100–101
archives, video, 229, 360–361
aspect ratio, 134–136
assumption of risk, liability, 128
audience. *See* target audience/market
audio. *See also* music; sound/sound
  equipment; voiceover narration
 about the elements of, 231–232
 adding sound effects, 227, 242–244

audio *(continued)*
  improving the soundtrack, 246–247
  insuring sound quality, 247–248
  salvaging a back track, 248
  sound mixing, 244–246
Audiojungle (stock music library), 237
auditions
  callbacks, 108–109
  casting call, 106–107
  finding natural talent, 109–110
  how-to conduct, 107–108
  pros and cons of professionals, 104–105
Autodesk Maya (animation software), 263
automated online video editing, 200
autoplay, video, 298–299
AVCWare Video Converter, 207
Avid Pro Tools MP (music software), 238
Avid Studio (editing software), 197
AVS Video Converter, 207
AwesomeRoar©, 29

• *B* •

B&H Photo Video Pro Audio (store), 363
background music, 194, 198–199, 217, 223–224, 235, 245
backlighting, 152
banners/banner ads, 268, 335
batteries, 147–148, 161–162, 171–173
behavioral analytics. *See* analytics
Bing, search engine optimization, 10–11
bitly™ (URL-shortening service), 31
Blip.tv (video sharing platform), 279
blog/blogging, 12–13, 21, 139, 290
bloopers and out-takes, 250
blue screen and mattes, 95
body language, acting, 101
borrowing from others
  business locations, 90–91
  home and office locations, 89–90
  music, 124–125, 235
  respecting time and property, 91–92
  using an "angel" network, 83
  using internal resources, 33–34, 81–82
  video styles, 42
Borst, Zachary (video designer), 74
brainstorming, 23–24, 48–50, 57
Brightcove (video hosting), 284, 295, 348

Brightroll (video ad network), 335
Broadcast News, video style, 42
B-roll footage, 186–187, 224–225
budgeting. *See also* costs
  basic considerations, 14, 71
  cameras, lighting and equipment, 80–81
  casting, 74–75
  costumes, 78–79
  crew, 76–77
  estimating costs, 71–72
  fees, permits and insurance, 77–78
  in-house compared to hiring, 16
  items required, 72–73
  leveraging an "angel" network, 83
  leveraging internal resources, 81–82
  make-up, 78–79
  outsourcing, 83–84
  promotion, 33, 84
  props, 79–80
  shooting locations, 77–78
  video types, 36
  voiceover narration, 242
business videos, 21
buyer types, 52
buying decisions, 30, 57–59

• *C* •

Caffeine (software), 349, 370
call times, 170, 171
"call to action"
  adding annotations as, 274–276
  buying decisions, 291–292
  creating an overlay, 333–334
  defined, 58–59
  elements, 251
  promotion, 342
  uses in video, 44, 62, 210, 250, 262
callbacks, actor, 108–109
camcorders, 142–143
camera angles (shots)
  basic types of, 181
  breaking down the scene, 181–182
  B-roll footage, 186–187
  composition and framing, 179–180
  creating coverage, 180
  matching eyelines, 183–184
  multiple takes, 187

180-degree rule, 184–185
  scripting details, 65–67
  shooting an interview, 185–186
camera moves (pan, tilt, track), 182–183
camera operator. *See* director of
    photography
cameras. *See* digital recording devices; video
    cameras
Cars (movie), 262
cast/casting breakdown. *See also* actors;
    characters
  budgeting for, 71–72
  determining cost, 74–75
  recognizing importance of, 356
  sample budget, 73
  shooting schedule checklist, 171
  using non-professional actors, 110–111
  using union talent, 75, 105
casting calls, 106–107
Catmull, Ed (Pixar designer), 262
Celtx scripting software, 62, 64
Center for Social Media, 123
characters. *See also* actors
  animated, 17
  archetypes, 45, 53–54
  auditioning actors, 100–104
  casting breakdown, 74–75
  computer-generated, 17
  main character, 54, 167
  maintaining continuity, 179
  matching eyelines, 183–184
  side characters, 54
  storytelling, 36–37
  structural models, 54–57
  using non-professional actors, 109–111
  using professional actors, 104–109
  writing dialogue, 67
charts and diagrams, 254–255
checklists, 170–172
Chevrolet Route 66 (video contest), 74
chokepoints, communications, 22–24
chroma-key compositing (green screen)
  about the use of, 94
  basic steps, 94–95
  cost considerations, 81
  editing software, 196
  tips and techniques, 95–97
Cinema 4D (3-D animation software), 263
Cisco Systems, Inc., 140

classical music, 237–238
clip length, 211–212, 213–214, 223–224
closed-caption subtitles, 326
closing credits. *See* titles and credits
"the cloud", 198, 200, 370
Coca-Cola and Mentos viral video, 21
code of conduct, fair use, 123
codec (coder/decoder compression), 205
color balance and filters, 257–260
commercials
  about the origins of, 9
  Chevrolet Super Bowl video contest, 74
  estimating costs, 71–72
  as marketing tactic, 13
  residuals, 75
communications. *See also* internal (company)
    videos
  acting tools and techniques, 100–102
  external marketing videos, 28–31
  identifying chokepoints, 22–24
  integration strategy, 31–32
  salesmanship, 102
  training videos, 26–27
company news, 26, 359–360. *See also* internal
    (company) videos
company website, adding videos to
  creating an online strategy, 287–288
  developing a marketing plan, 31–34
  effective site locations, 289–290
  home page placement, 288–289
  landing pages, 292–293
  sales and buyer conversions, 291–292
  search engine optimization, 292
  use in e-commerce, 290–291
  video hosting, 293–296
company website, publishing videos on
  about, 297
  creating target links, 323
  developing search tags, 323–325
  displaying a thumbnail, 298
  inserting an embed code, 299–301
  player selection and styling, 297–298
  registering a site map, 327–328
  search engine optimization, 326
  selecting thumbnails, 325
  using autoplay option, 298–299
  using closed-caption subtitles, 326
  using Facebook with, 312–313
compliance, regulatory, 26

compositing, green screen, 95–97
composition and framing, 179–180
compressed file formats, 138, 204–208
consistency. *See* continuity, maintaining
container files, 205–206
content
  about, 11–12
  basics of creating, 14–15
  creating an integrated plan, 31–34
  credibility, 31, 42, 59, 243, 285, 290
  getting professional help, 364–365
  video length and, 61–62, 354–355
content management systems (CMS), 297
continuity, maintaining, 33, 115, 178–179
conversion, files, 207–208
copyright. *See also* trademarks and logos
  about, 122
  fair use principle, 123–124
  "Happy Birthday to You", 124
  ownership of scripts and videos, 120–121
  YouTube, 126
cost per view, 333
costs. *See also* budgeting
  camcorders, 142–143
  considerations before marketing, 9
  editing software, 194, 195, 197
  lighting accessories, 144–145
  music software, 238
  professional actors, 105
  session fee (minimum-scale pay), 75
  streaming live video, 284
  video hosting services, 295–296
  voiceover narration, 242
Costume Express (online orders), 78
costumes
  budgeting for, 71–73, 78–79
  maintaining continuity, 178–179
  shooting checklist, 171
  storyboarding, 63–64
crazy pain, script concept, 56
credibility, 31, 42, 59, 243, 285, 290
crew. *See* production crew
cropping, rotating, zooming, 260–261
customer assessment/needs analysis, 28, 29
CyberLink PowerDirector (software), 198

• D •

daily affirmation videos, 34
Dailymotion (video sharing), 278–279
Daum, Kevin (author)
  ROAR! Get Heard in the Sales and Marketing Jungle (Wiley), 25, 29, 52, 364–365
demographics. *See* analytics
demonstration videos, 37, 210, 360
dialogue. *See* scripts/scriptwriting
diction and dialects, 166
diffused light, 150–151
digital e-book download, 1
digital recording devices
  about, 134
  checklists, 171–172
  high-def compared to standard, 134–136
  in-camera editing, 212
  in-camera microphone, 160
  pocket cameras, 140–142
  point-and-shoot cameras, 140
  pros and cons of mini-cameras, 137–138
  shooting accessories, 144–148
  shooting location data station, 173
  single lens reflex cameras, 143–144
  smartphones, 38, 139–140, 147, 211, 247
  traditional camcorders, 142–143
  webcams, 138–139
digital storage options, 136–137
Digital Video (codec), 205–206
direct light, 150–151
direct-mail campaigns, 21, 31–32
director
  about the role and skills, 15, 113
  budgeting for, 76
  directing techniques, 177–178
  organizing the shooting location, 172–173
  pre-shoot checklists, 170–172
  relationship with actors, 176–177
director of photography, 15, 76, 114, 121
documentary films, 186, 213, 217, 220, 223, 232, 260
dramatic videos, 41–42
Drupal (content management system), 297

• *E* •

e-book download, 1
e-commerce, 290–291
editing. *See also* video editing
   about, 15
   as invisible art, 209–210
   green screen, 96
   in-house compared to hiring, 16
   unwanted sounds, 158, 248
   use of script details in, 65–67
editing software, choosing, 191–193
editing software, Mac
   Adobe Premiere, 195
   file conversion, 207–208
   Final Cut Pro, 194–195, 236
   Garage Band, 124, 194, 242, 246
   iMovie, 81, 193–194
   One To One workshops, 202
   QuickTime X, 211–212
editing software, online
   about, 198
   Animoto and other services, 200
   One True Media, 199
   Stupeflix Video Maker, 200
   WeVideo, 200
   YouTube, 198–199
editing software, Windows
   Adobe Premiere, 196–197
   Avid Studio, 197
   CyberLink PowerDirector, 198
   file conversion, 207–208
   Sony Vegas Movie Studio, 197, 236
   Windows Movie Maker, 196, 211–212
editor, 15, 76, 218
educational videos, 13, 55–56, 58–59
EepyBird (video production company), 21
Elance (Internet platform), 244, 264
electronics. *See* digital recording devices
e-mail lists, 12
e-mail marketing
   about integrating with other tools, 31–32
   adding video, 317–318
   budgeting for, 84
   getting professional help, 369
embed code, 299–301

emotions/emotional benefits
   attracting customers, 28–29
   casting actors who convey, 100–102, 179
   compelling ideas create, 47–52
   compelling script components, 52–53
   creating a feeling of, 52–62
   creating core values, 25
   events create, 32, 38
   music and, 231–235, 240–241
   shooting the scene, 180–182
   sound effects, 243
   storytelling creates, 36–37
   using archetypes, 53–54
   video editing, 223–224
   video marketing and, 10–11, 19, 35
   video styles, 40–43
   visual effects, 256
   words and pictures lack, 39
   working with non-actors, 110–111
   writing dialogue, 67
entertainment
   creating an experience, 59–60
   good scripts provide, 55–57
   videos as, 39–44
entertainment industry, 118–119
entertainment systems, 135
equipment. *See* accessories; video
      production equipment
events/event videos, 31–32, 38
Expresso (software), 370
exterior scenes. *See* shooting locations
eyelines, 183–184

• *F* •

Facebook
   advertising and paid campaigns, 314–315
   creating a presence, 307–308
   integrated marketing and, 31–32
   managing your company page, 312–313
   placement, buying, 84
   recording videos, 309–310
   tagging and editing videos, 311
   uploading videos, 310
   video sharing, 279, 308–309
   YouTube videos, posting, 311–312

fair comment, free speech, 126
fair use, legal issues, 123–124
FanBridge (social media), 368–369
FAQs, 30, 290, 361
Favorites list, 273–274
fees and permits, 77–78, 94, 121, 124, 128
file formats
    compression, 204–205
    container file types, 205–206
    conversions, 207–208, 268
    mobile devices, 281–282
    resolution, frame rate, data rate, 206–207
Final Cut Pro (software), 96, 194–195, 236
First Amendment rights, 124, 126
Flash Video (.flv), 205–206, 268
Flip cameras, 140–142
FlowPlayer (video player), 296
fluorescent light, 151
Foley sound effects, 243–244
Footage Firm (stock music library), 237
footage "on the fly", 94
frame rate (frames per second), 206–207
frame/framing, 179–180, 260–261, 298
free speech, legal issues, 124–126
freelance video support
    3-D animation, 261, 263–364
    audio, 244, 248
    budgeting, 76
    editing, 16–17, 203–204
    where to find, 364
"friending" on YouTube, 276–277, 316

• G •

gaffer/gaffer tape, 110, 115, 172
Garage Band For Dummies (LeVitus), 124
Garage Band software, 194, 238, 239, 246
Gazelles (executive coaching), 25
geographical statistics. *See* analytics
Getty Images (stock images), 225
"go bag", 172
Go Daddy (Internet hosting company), 57
Go!Animate software, 17, 38–39, 365–366
Go!Animate versus Xtranormal, 366
Goeldi, Andreas (author), 234, 264, 293, 308, 370
"gofer" (production assistant), 115

"going viral", 20–22, 75, 303, 357
Google
    acquisition of YouTube, 268
    registering a site map, 327
    search engine optimization, 10–11
    testing a site map, 328
    YouTube policies, 126
Google Analytics, 347
"gotcha" moment, script concept, 55–56
government permits. *See* permits and fees
graphics creator, described, 15
green room, 87, 173
green screen, 81, 94–97, 196
Grobe, Fritz (EepyBird founder), 21
guerrilla videos, 122

• H •

H.264 (codec), 205–206, 282
hair and make-up, 78–79, 115, 155
Halligan, Brian (author)
    Inbound Marketing (Wiley), 369
HandBrake (file conversion program), 208
"Happy Birthday to You" (song), 124
Happy Grad (Super Bowl video), 74
hard disk drive (HDD), 137
hard lighting, 150–151
Harnish, Verne (educator and coach), 25
head shots, 106–107
headphones, 158, 165, 248
Hein, Bettina (author), 203, 234, 264, 308, 370
high definition resolution (HD), 134–136
holiday-themed videos, 234, 239
Hollywood Toys & Costumes, 78
H.R. Larious (video production), 25, 366
HTML5, 282
HubSpot (media marketing), 368–369
Hulu (video sharing platform), 279
human resource videos. *See* internal (company) videos
humor/humorous videos
    about the video style, 40–41
    avoiding chokepoints, 22
    bloopers and out-takes, 250
    editing and comedic timing, 241–242
    examples, 178, 182
    getting professional help, 366

internal marketing and, 25, 26
lighting mood/tone, 150
music and sound add, 65
uses in video, 42, 43, 45, 53, 59–60

• *I* •

Image Line FL Studio (software), 238
image stabilization, 142–143, 146–147
iMovie, 81, 96, 193–194, 245–246
Inbound Marketing (Halligan and Shah), 369
Incompetech (scoring), 125, 237, 366–367
independent contractor agreement, 120
indoor lighting, 151–152
industry news and information, 26, 368
information and help. *See* resources
in-camera microphones, 160
insurance, 77–78, 94, 121, 124, 128
integrated marketing, 31–34, 84
internal (company) videos
    about, 19
    "call to action", 59
    casting talent, 81–82, 106, 109
    communications and training, 24–27
    getting professional help, 366
    "nonmarketing" uses for, 359–362
    using humor, 41
    video styles, 55
internal flash drive, 136–137
International Alliance of Theatrical Stage
        Employees (IATSE), 119
interview videos
    audio, 162
    boom mics, 165
    lighting, 155
    shooting scenes, 185–186
iPhone. *See* smartphones
iStockphoto (stock images), 225

• *J* •

jargon, video production, 5, 175–176
Jobs, Steve (computer innovator), 262
John Wiley & Sons, Inc.
    Garage Band For Dummies, 124
    Inbound Marketing, 369

*Pay Per Click Search Engine Marketing For
        Dummies*, 329
*ROAR! Get Heard in the Sales and Marketing
        Jungle*, 25, 29, 52, 364–365
Web Marketing For Dummies, 328
Joomla (content management system), 297
Justin.tv (video hosting service), 284
JW Player (video player), 296

• *K* •

Kaltura (video hosting service), 295
Ken Burns effect, 217, 260
Kent, Peter (author)
    *Pay Per Click Search Engine Marketing For
        Dummies* (Wiley), 329
keywords, 270–273, 306, 320–325, 328–333, 345
KISS (keep it short), 61–62, 354–355

• *L* •

landing page videos, 292–293
lavaliere (clip-on) microphones, 161–162
lead generation, 28–29
legal issues
    about creating videos, 14, 117
    copyrighted materials, 122–124
    defamation, 125–126
    fair use, 123
    fees, permits and insurance, 77–78
    filming in public places, 92–93, 121–122
    guerrilla videos, 122
    intellectual property, 127
    liabilities and insurance, 128
    limits of parody, 124
    litigation and lawsuits, 128–129
    music, 124–125
    ownership of scripts and videos, 120–121
    permissions (written consent), 93
    trademarks and logos, 93, 125
    using friends and colleagues, 119–120
    using union talent, 118–119
LeVitus, Bob (author)
    Garage Band For Dummies (Wiley), 124
liability insurance. *See* insurance
libel and slander, avoiding, 125–126

licensing fees. *See* fees and permits
lighting designer, 15
lighting/lighting equipment
  about, 149
  budgeting, 76
  choices and types, 150–152
  green screen, 96
  location scouting, 86–87
  optional accessories, 144–145, 155–156
  three-point lighting, 152–155
LinkedIn (business networking), 317–318
litigation and lawsuits, 128–129
Livestream (video hosting service), 284
locations. *See* shooting locations
Logic (music software), 239
logos. *See* trademarks and logos

• M •

Mac (computers). *See* editing software
MacLeod, Kevin (musician), 237, 366–367
Magisto (automated video editing), 200
make-up. *See* hair and make-up
Mandy.com (talent agency), 364
man-on-the-street, video style, 42
marketing. *See also* company website
  credibility/overcoming objections, 30–31
  as "call to action", 58–59
  communications chokepoints, 22–24
  creating a sense of urgency, 57–58
  generating leads/customers, 28–29
  integrating video into, 19, 31–34, 287
marketing performance. *See* analytics
marketing videos. *See also* internal
    (company) videos
  about creating, 14–15
  comparison to artistic videos, 37
  creating an experience, 59–60
  creating text and titles, 321–323
  critique, 228–229, 307, 353, 356–357
  defining the message, 353–354
  "going viral", 20–22
  identifying buyer types, 52
  KISS (keep it short and simple), 61–62
  live streaming, 284
  measuring effectiveness, 12–13, 15
  outsourcing, 84
  search engine optimization, 319–320

search tags, 323–325
  seeking feedback, 346
  use inside your own company, 24–27
  using closed-caption subtitles, 326
measuring performance. *See* analytics
Mediamobz (Internet platform), 264
Metacafe (video sharing platform), 279
microphones
  about the choice of, 145, 158–159
  boom microphone, 164–165
  dead microphone, 158
  in-camera microphone, 160
  lavaliere (clip-on) microphone, 161–162
  pickup patterns, 159
  recording music, 239
  shotgun mics, 93, 145, 148, 159, 162–164
  voiceover recording, 243
  wind screen, 163
mini-cameras, 137–138
miniDV tape, 137
Mixcraft (music software), 238
mobile devices, 280–282
Mocha (software), 370
models, script structure
  about the use of, 54–55
  brainstorming, 57
  crazy pain model, 56
  educational model, 55
  "gotcha" moment model, 55–56
  rational solution model, 56
  wrong way/right way model, 55
monopods, 146–147
montage videos, 44
mood, lighting choices, 150
motion graphics, 39, 227, 261–264
MPEG Streamclip (file conversion), 208
MPEG-4/MP4 files, 138, 205–206, 282
music
  about choosing, 233–234
  appropriate to the audience, 234–235
  background, 194, 198–199, 223–224, 245
  classical music, 237–238
  copyright issues, 124
  creating your own, 238–239
  emotional impact, 235–236, 240
  insertion into a video, 239–240
  matching the video to, 241–242, 366–367
  open source, 125, 237–238

reusing existing material, 238
royalty-free, 233–234, 236–237, 366–367
scripting details, 65–67
software programs, 236, 238
soundtracks, 232, 246–247, 273
stock music libraries, 237
timing of "hooks", 240
video editing and, 216–217
music videos, 362
Muvee (automated video editing), 200
Myspace (video sharing platform), 279

• N •

natural light, 151–152
news-style videos, 42–43
nudity, avoiding, 46

• O •

oDesk (Internet platform), 264
old-style newsreel footage, video style, 42
omnidirectional microphones, 159
One True Media (online editing), 199
180-degree rule, 184–185
1000 words, a picture is worth, 11
OneLoad (video marketing software), 349
one-on-one interview, video style, 42
online retailing, 10
online editing. *See* editing software
Online Video Marketer's Guide, 368
online video marketing tools, 370
Ooyala (video hosting service), 295, 348
open source music, 125, 237–238
open source video players, 296–297
optical zoom, 142
outdoor filming/lighting, 92–94, 151–152
outsourcing, video production, 84

• P •

pan, tilt, track (camera moves), 182–183
panel of experts, video style, 42
parody, legal limits of, 124
Parsons, Bob (Go Daddy CEO), 57
participant release form (waiver), 120
Party City (costume shops), 78

Pay Per Click Search Engine Marketing For Dummies (Kent), 329
pay-per-view, 12, 330, 333
PCs. *See* editing software; editing tools
performance, measuring. *See* analytics
permissions. *See also* copyrights
  fair use principle, 123–124
  guerrilla videos, 122
  location releases, 121–122
  ownership of scripts and videos, 120–121
  release form (appearance waiver), 93, 120
  use of parody, 124
  waiver of liability, 128
permits and fees, 77–78, 94, 121, 124, 128
Pixability (video editing service), 203
Pixability Online Video Grader, 214, 370
Pixability Video Marketing Software, 239, 305, 321
Pixar (movie studio), 262
pixels, 134–136
playlists, 273–274
pocket cameras, 140–142
point-and-shoot cameras, 140
PowerPoint presentation, 32, 39, 262
price. *See* budgeting; costs
Prime Concepts (marketing), 368–369
print advertising, 33
Pro Tools (music software), 239
producer, 15, 113–114
production assistant ("gofer"), 115
production crew
  basic roles and skills, 14–15, 112–115
  budgeting for, 71–73, 76
  finding professionals, 364
profanity, avoiding, 46
promotion manager, 15
promotions. *See also* video promotion
  about the basics of, 12, 15
  as "call to action", 58–59
  creating a sense of urgency, 57–58
  "going viral" on purpose, 21
props (properties)
  budgeting for, 79–80
  scripting details, 65–67
  shooting schedule checklist, 171
  using friends and colleagues, 81–82
prospecting/needs analysis, 13, 29
Pure Digital Technologies, 140

• Q •

Qik (video hosting service), 284
QR codes, 33
QuickTime (.mov video file), 205–206
QuickTime X (media player), 211–212

• R •

rational solution, script concept, 56
Real Networks, video sharing, 268
reddit (video sharing site), 12
ReelSEO (online marketing guide), 368
referrals/repeat business, 28
reflected light, 150–151
regulations. *See* permits and fees
REIT (real estate investment trust), 24
releases. *See* permissions
reputation. *See* credibility
residuals, 75
resolution, 134–136, 206–208
resources
    animation, 365–366
    books and classes, 201–202, 367
    content development, 364–365
    finding talent, 364
    internal video production, 366
    legal issues, 123
    music scoring, 366–367
    promotion and measurement, 370
    social media integration, 368–369
    stock music libraries, 124–125
    video gear, 363
    video marketing insight, 368
résumés, 106–107, 317
return on investment (ROI), 22, 72, 367
Ricky's NYC (costume shops), 78
*ROAR! Get Heard in the Sales and Marketing
    Jungle* (Daum), 25, 29, 52, 364–365
ROARing Video™ (video production), 24, 34,
    202, 367
room tone, 158, 248
rotating, cropping, zooming, 260–261
rough cuts, 218–219
royalties
    budgeting for, 71–72
    classical music, 238

open source music, 125
voiceover narration, 242
royalty-free music, 233–234, 236–237, 366–367
rule of thirds, 180

• S •

Saeks, Ford (social media marketer), 369
sales/selling
    acting is different from, 102
    buyer conversions, 291–292
    as "call to action", 58–59
    creating a sense of urgency, 57–58
    e-commerce, 290–291
    overcoming buying objections, 30
Say Media (video ad network), 335
scenes. *See* shooting scenes; video editing
Screen Actors Guild (SAG), 75, 105, 119
scripts/scriptwriting
    about the basics, 14, 64–65
    cadence (rhythm) and line reading, 178
    determining location, 86
    estimating length, 65
    in-house compared to hiring, 16
    maintaining brevity, 27
    memorizing lines, 105, 111, 178
    ownership and copyrights, 120–121
    sample page, 66–67
    shooting schedule checklist, 171
    software, 64
    storyboarding, 62–64
    use in video editing, 216
scripts, creating a compelling idea
    answering the value questions, 47–48
    brainstorming the problem, 48–50
    defining a solution, 50
    differentiating an approach, 51–52
    identifying buyer types, 52
    writing dialogue/text, 67, 322–323
scripts, creating the concept
    about the components, 52–53
    awesome experience, 59–60
    call to action, 58–59
    emotional connections, 53–54
    KISS (keep it short and simple), 61–62
    urgency to buy, 57–58
    using humor, 60
    using structural models, 54–57

SD card (storage device), 136
search engine marketing (SEM)
    about integrated marketing, 31–34
    choosing a thumbnail, 325
    closed-caption subtitles, 326
    creating a strong video title, 321–322
    describing video content, 322–323
    developing effective tags, 323–325
    optimizing videos for, 319–320
    setting the target link, 323
    social media and, 357–358
search engine optimization (SEO)
    embedded videos and, 326–328
    integrated marketing and, 31–34
    video marketing and, 10, 292, 319
Seeding™ (video marketing agency), 21
seminars, 33, 202, 367
session fee (minimum-scale pay), 75
sexuality, avoiding, 46
Shah, Dharmesh (author)
    Inbound Marketing (Wiley), 369
sharing sites. *See* video sharing
Shockwave (stock music library), 237
shooting locations
    about scouting, 15, 85
    borrowing space, 89–92
    budgeting for, 77–78
    equipment area, 173
    filming at home or office, 88–89
    filming in public places, 92–93
    filming "on the fly", 94
    green room, 87, 173
    green screen, 94–97
    guerrilla videos, 122
    in-house compared to hiring, 16
    permits and permissions, 93, 121–122
    scripting details, 65–67
    shooting area, 172
    using friends and colleagues, 81–82
    weather, lighting and sound, 86–87
    writing/following the script, 86
shooting scenes. *See also* video shoot
    basic guidelines for, 174–175
    B-roll footage, 186–187
    checklists and preparation, 355
    communicating on the set, 175–176
    director-actor relationship, 176–177
    estimating time needed, 174
    reshooting the scene, 217–218
    tips for believable performances, 178
    video interviews, 185–186
shooting scenes, techniques
    adding "handles", 176
    B-roll footage, 186–187
    camera angles and coverage, 180–182
    camera moves (pan, tilt, track), 182–183
    composition and framing, 179–180
    directing techniques, 177–178
    matching eyelines, 183–184
    multiple takes, 187
    180-degree rule, 184–185
    rule of thirds, 180
shooting schedules, 170–175, 355
shotgun microphones, 93, 159
shots. *See* camera angles
show-and-tell videos (demonstration), 37
Shutterstock (stock images), 225
Skype, 139
slides and graphics, 65–67
smartphones. *See also* mobile devices
    audio quality, 247
    video editing, 211
    video marketing, 38
    video recording, 139–140, 147
Smith, Alvy Ray (Pixar designer), 262
snail mail. *See* direct-mail campaigns
social media. *See also* Facebook; Twitter;
        YouTube
    budgeting for, 84
    choosing the channel, 304–305
    encouraging video sharing, 307
    getting marketing help, 368–369
    identifying the audience, 305–306
    integrated marketing, 12, 31–32, 303
    what's beyond the "big dogs", 317–318
soft lighting, 150–151
software
    animated videos, 17
    audio, 244
    chroma-key compositing, 96
    file compression, 205–206
    file conversion, 207–208
    music, 124, 238
    scriptwriting, 64
    storyboarding, 62
    streaming live video, 284
    video marketing, 349
Sonar X1 LE (music software), 238

sound effects, 65–67, 227, 242–244
sound mixing, 244–247
sound operator/soundperson, 15, 76, 115
sound/sound equipment. *See also*
    microphones
  basic elements, 157–158
  camcorder audio options, 143
  editing crowd sounds, 167
  filming outdoors, 92–93
  headphones, 158, 165
  location scouting, 86–87
  recognizing importance of, 355–356
  room tone, 158
  video editing and, 216–217
soundtracks
  audio tricks with, 246–247
  Garage Band software, 194
  royalty-free, 236
  value and importance, 232
  YouTube, 273
spam, 269, 277, 279, 316, 318, 322
special effects, 79–80, 95
standard definition resolution, 134–136
statistics. *See* analytics
Steadicam, 146–147
stereotypes, 45, 235–236
stock music libraries, 237
storyboarding, 14, 62–64
storyline, finding the, 218
storytelling, 16, 36–37, 200
strategy, video marketing
  budgeting for, 84
  choosing content, 11–12
  fitting the message to the audience, 358
  integrated marketing as, 31–34
  measuring effectiveness, 12–13
  promotional tools, 12
  social media, 303–306, 357–358
streaming live video
  basic elements, 282–283
  how-to best use, 283
  Internet providers, 283–284
  reaching an audience, 284–285
Stupeflix Video Maker (editing), 200
Stupid Video (video sharing site), 12
subscriptions, YouTube, 276
Super Bowl XLVI, 74

• T •

tactics, video marketing
  basic tools of, 13–14
  social media, 303–307
  using Facebook, 307–311, 312–315
  using LinkedIn, 317–318
  using Twitter, 315–316
  using YouTube, 311–312, 316
tags/tagging, 293, 311, 323–324
talent. *See* actors
talent agencies, 105
talking heads videos, 43, 210
talk-show segment, video style, 42
target audience/market
  about identifying, 14
  budgeting for, 84
  buyer types, 52
  feedback, 228–229, 307, 353, 356–357
  fitting music to, 234–235
  fitting the message to, 358
  getting professional help, 370
  ideal video length, 213–214
  live video streaming, 284–285
  sources of the traffic, 345–346
  tracking viewer numbers, 346–347
  user behavior, analyzing, 346–347
  using social media to reach, 305–306
technique, acting, 101–102
Telestream Wirecast (software), 284
television commercials, 9
*Ten Tips to Leverage Your Videos Using Social
    Media Marketing* (video), 369
testimonials, 31, 43–44, 290
3-D animation effects, 227, 263–264
3-D electronic devices, 135
3ds MAX (3-D animation software), 263
3GPP/3gp (video file format), 282
3Play Media (closed-caption service), 326
three-point lighting, 152–155
thumbnails, 32, 298, 311, 314, 317–318, 325
titles and credits, 249–255
touch points, 28
trade shows, 32–33
trademarks and logos
  avoiding legal issues, 93, 125
  as copyrighted materials, 122

graphics, 262–263
permits and permissions, 121–122
using your own, 202, 210, 251, 314
training video. *See* internal (company)
    videos; seminars
transitions, 65–67, 256–257
Tremor Video (video ad network), 335
tripods, 146
Twitter, 12, 31–32, 315–316
Typo3 (content management system), 297

• *U* •

unidirectional microphones, 159
union actors and crew, 75, 105, 118–119
Unruly Media Ltd. (marketing agency), 21
URL-shortening, 31
U.S. Constitution, 124, 126
U.S. Copyright Act of 1976, 123
U.S. Patent and Trademark Office, 125
Ustream (video hosting service), 284

• *V* •

value/value proposition
   aligning the team to the, 25
   brainstorming the problem, 48–50
   defining a solution, 50
   differentiating your approach, 51–52
   key questions of, 48
   overcoming buying objections, 30
Vegas Movie Studio HD (software), 197, 236
Viddler (video sharing platform), 278, 295
video advertising
   creating a "call to action", 333–334
   measuring effectiveness, 332
   paid ads on YouTube, 328–331
   targeting, 332–333
   types and options, 334–335
video analytics. *See* analytics
video blogging (vlogging), 139
video camera. *See* digital recording devices
video editing. *See also* editing; editing
    software
   asking for feedback, 228–229
   attempting a test project, 202
   books and classes, 201–202

data rate (compression quality), 207
exporting the final video, 229
file format compression, 204–206
file format conversions, 207–208
frame rate (frames per second), 207
picture size and resolution, 206
recording/adding music, 233–242
sound effects, 243–244
sound mixing, 244–248
using professional editing services, 203
visual and sound effects, 227
voiceover narration, 242–243
working with freelance editors, 204
video editing, beginning the process of
   deciding whether or not to edit, 210–211
   editing for length, 211–213–214, 223–224
   filling in missing material, 217–218
   in-camera, 212
   logging footage, 215–216
   reviewing the script, 216
   shooting extra footage, 212–213
video editing, making cuts
   about types of, 221–222
   beginning the rough cut, 218–219
   connecting scenes, 224
   creating rhythm, 223–224
   editing music tracks, 241–242
   finding the storyline, 218
   incorporating B-roll footage, 224–225
   moving clips and sequences, 219–220
   refining the rough cut, 225–227
   transitions, 221–222
video filters, 257–260
video hosting
   analytics, 10–11, 347–349
   choosing the provider, 295–296
   displaying a thumbnail, 298
   inserting an embed code, 299–301
   open source players in lieu of, 296–297
   player selection and styling, 297–298
   providing your own, 293
   using autoplay option, 298–299
   using social media, 357–358
   using YouTube, 294–295
video interviews, 155, 162, 165, 185–186
video length. *See also* video editing
   determining, 36, 213–214
   estimating, 65

video length *(continued)*
keep it short and simple, 61–62, 354–355
matching music to, 237
planning the schedule, 89–90, 173–174
trimming clip length, 211–212, 223–224
voiceover narration and, 242
video marketing
about the history, 9
advertising options, 334–335
benefits and consumer behavior, 10–11
creating descriptive text, 322–323
ideal video length, 213–214, 354–355
incorporating social media, 368–369
industry news and information, 368
in-house compared to hiring it, 16–17
marketing strategy, 11–13
online software, 370
ownership of scripts and videos, 120–121
production team roles, 15–16
tactics, 13–14
understanding the process, 14–15
video players. *See also* video hosting
embed code, 299
file format issues, 267, 268
open source, 296–297
selecting and styling, 297–298
streaming live video, 282–283
streaming video providers, 284
using Facebook, 309–310
using YouTube, 294–295
video production
basic steps of, 14–15, 71
believability, 35, 60, 65, 79, 178, 182
casting breakdown, 74–75
costumes, 78–79
estimating costs, 71–72
fees, permits and insurance, 77–78
finding freelancers, 364
freelance 3-D animation, 261, 263–364
freelance audio, 244, 248
freelance editing, 16–17, 203–204
in-house compared to hiring, 16–17
items required, 72–73
make-up, 78–79
outsourcing, 83–84
ownership of scripts and videos, 120–121
producing multiple versions, 229
promotion, 33–34, 84

props, 79–80
shooting locations, 77–78
team member roles, 15–16
using an "angel" network, 83
using friends and colleagues, 81–82
video production crew
assembling the, 112–113
basic roles and skills, 14–15
budgeting for, 76–77
camera operator, 114
director, 113
producer, 113–114
using added positions, 114–115
video production equipment
about, 133
boom microphones, 164–165
budgeting for, 80–81
camcorders, 142–144
choosing high-def over standard, 134–136
digital cameras, 137–142
digital storage options, 136–137
finding and buying, 363
optional accessories, 144–148
packing the "go bag", 172
recognizing importance of, 355–356
shooting schedule checklist, 171–172
shotgun mics, 93, 145, 148, 159, 162–164
3-D devices, 135
video promotion. *See also* promotions
budgeting for, 84
encouraging video sharing, 307
getting professional help, 370
target audience/market, 305–306
using Facebook, 307–315
using social media, 303–305
video scoring (music), 366–367
video sharing. *See also* marketing videos
about, 5, 267
e-mail marketing, 317–318
file formats and conversions, 268
mobile devices, 280–282
platforms other than YouTube, 277–279
social media and, 303–307
streaming live content, 282–285
using Facebook, 279, 308–309
using LinkedIn, 317–318
using Twitter, 315–316
using YouTube, 308–309

video shoot. *See* shooting scenes
video site maps, 327–328
video styles
  about, 39–40
  creating emotion, 41–42
  montage videos, 44
  news-style videos, 42–43
  stereotyping and profanity, 45–46
  talking heads, 43
  testimonials, 43–44
  using archetypes, 45, 53–54
  using humor, 40–41
video type, 35–39
Vimeo (video sharing platform), 277–278
viral videos, 20–22, 75, 303, 357
Visible Measures for Publishers (software), 349
visual effects. *See also* special effects
  about, 249, 256
  charts and diagrams, 254–255
  colors and filters, 257–260
  cropping, rotating, zooming, 260–261
  motion graphics, 261–263
  3-D animation, 263–264
  transitions, 256–257
voice, diction and dialects, 101, 165–167
voiceover narration
  about, 232
  recording, 242–243
  storyboarding and scripting, 63, 65
  uses in video, 80, 157
  video editing and, 216–217
Voltz, Stephen (EepyBird founder), 21
Vzaar (video hosting service), 295

• *W* •

waiver of liability, 128
weather, location scouting, 86
web analytics. *See* analytics
Web Marketing For Dummies (Zimmerman), 328
Web Video Marketing Council, 368
webcams, 138–139, 309–310
webinars, 14, 33, 111–112
website analytics. *See* analytics
websites. *See also* company website
  American Federation of Television and
    Radio Artists (AFTRA), 119
  Animoto (automated video editing), 200

Audiojungle (stock music library), 237
AwesomeRoar©, 29
Backstage (online casting calls), 106
bitly™ (URL-shortening service), 31–32
Blendtec video marketing campaign, 38
Blip.tv, 279
B-roll footage resources, 225
Center for Social Media, 123
costume and make-up shops, 78
craigslist, 106
Dailymotion, 278–279
EepyBird (video production company), 21
Footage Firm (stock music library), 237
Gazelles (executive coaching), 25
Go Daddy (Internet hosting company), 57
Go!Animate (software), 17, 38–39
Google Webmaster Central, 327
HandBrake, 208
Happy Grad (Super Bowl video), 74
hrlarious (human resource video), 25, 366
Hulu, 279
industry news and information, 368
International Alliance of Theatrical Stage
    Employees (IATSE), 119
Metacafe, 279
MPEG Streamclip, 208
music providers, 124–125, 366–367
Myspace, 279
open source music, 237
Pixability, 203, 214, 234, 239
ROARing Video™, 24, 202
samples of forms, 35, 119, 120–121
Screen Actors Guild (SAG), 119
scriptwriting software, 64
Seeding™ (video marketing agency), 21
Shockwave (stock music library), 237
social media marketing, 368–369
streaming live video providers, 284
3Play Media (closed-caption service), 326
Unruly Media Ltd. (agency), 21
U.S. Patent and Trademark Office, 125
Viddler, 278
video hosting services, 295
video marketing software, 349
video production resources, 363–370
video tips for believable performances,
    35, 60, 65, 79, 178, 182
Vimeo, 277–278

websites *(continued)*
  Windows Live Movie Maker, 196
  Writer's Guild of America (WGA), 119
  Xtranormal (software), 17, 38–39
  Yahoo! Video site, 279
  YouTube, 267–268
  YouTube Copyright Center, 126
  YouTube Video Editor, 199
WeVideo (online video editing), 200
Williams, John (music composer), 232
Windows Movie Maker, 196, 211–212
Windows Media (WMV), 205–206
Windows PC. *See* editing software
wireless microphones, 161–162
Wistia (hosting service), 295, 327, 348–349
Wondershare Mac Video Converter, 207
work-for-hire agreements, 120–121
workplace rules, 25
workshops. *See* seminars
writer, 15, 121
Writer's Guild of America (WGA), 119
writing. *See* scripts/scriptwriting
written consent. *See* permissions
wrong way/right way, script concept, 55

• X •

Xtranormal (software), 17, 38–39, 365–366

• Y •

Yahoo!, search engine optimization, 10–11
Yahoo! Video site (video sharing), 279
YouTube
  animated videos, 17
  buying placement, 84
  Coca-Cola and Mentos viral video, 21
compressed file formats, 138
copyrighted materials, 126
editing tools, 198–199
"friending", 276–277, 316
"going viral", 20–22, 75, 303, 357
instructional videos, 96
marketing, 10–11, 31, 357–358
posting videos on Facebook, 311–312
"rogue's gallery", 26
video sharing, 5, 9–10, 267–268
vlogging, 139
YouTube advertising
  creating ads, 329–331
  creating a "call to action", 333–334
  measuring effectiveness, 332
  optimizing targeting, 332–333
  paid ads, 328–329
  perks for good customers, 270
YouTube Analytics, 343–347
YouTube channel
  about creating your own, 269–270
  adding annotations, 274–276
  background images, 270
  editing videos, 272–273
  "friending" other users, 276–277
  linking a company website, 326–328
  playlists and favorites, 273–274
  subscriptions, 276
  uploading videos, 271–272
YouTube partners, 270
YuMe (video ad network), 335

• Z •

Zimmerman, Jan (author)
  Web Marketing For Dummies (Wiley), 328
zooming, cropping, rotating, 260–261

le & Mac

2 For Dummies,
Edition
-1-118-17679-5

one 4S For Dummies,
Edition
-1-118-03671-6

touch For Dummies,
Edition
-1-118-12960-9

OS X Lion
Dummies
-1-118-02205-4

gging & Social Media

Ville For Dummies
-1-118-08337-6

ebook For Dummies,
Edition
-1-118-09562-1

n Blogging
Dummies
-1-118-03843-7

ter For Dummies,
Edition
-0-470-76879-2

dPress For Dummies,
Edition
-1-118-07342-1

iness

h Flow For Dummies
-1-118-01850-7

sting For Dummies,
Edition
-0-470-90545-6

Job Searching with Social
Media For Dummies
978-0-470-93072-4

QuickBooks 2012
For Dummies
978-1-118-09120-3

Resumes For Dummies,
6th Edition
978-0-470-87361-8

Starting an Etsy Business
For Dummies
978-0-470-93067-0

Cooking & Entertaining

Cooking Basics
For Dummies, 4th Edition
978-0-470-91388-8

Wine For Dummies,
4th Edition
978-0-470-04579-4

Diet & Nutrition

Kettlebells For Dummies
978-0-470-59929-7

Nutrition For Dummies,
5th Edition
978-0-470-93231-5

Restaurant Calorie Counter
For Dummies,
2nd Edition
978-0-470-64405-8

Digital Photography

Digital SLR Cameras &
Photography For Dummies,
4th Edition
978-1-118-14489-3

Digital SLR Settings
& Shortcuts
For Dummies
978-0-470-91763-3

Photoshop Elements 10
For Dummies
978-1-118-10742-3

Gardening

Gardening Basics
For Dummies
978-0-470-03749-2

Vegetable Gardening
For Dummies,
2nd Edition
978-0-470-49870-5

Green/Sustainable

Raising Chickens
For Dummies
978-0-470-46544-8

Green Cleaning
For Dummies
978-0-470-39106-8

Health

Diabetes For Dummies,
3rd Edition
978-0-470-27086-8

Food Allergies
For Dummies
978-0-470-09584-3

Living Gluten-Free
For Dummies,
2nd Edition
978-0-470-58589-4

Hobbies

Beekeeping
For Dummies,
2nd Edition
978-0-470-43065-1

Chess For Dummies,
3rd Edition
978-1-118-01695-4

Drawing For Dummies,
2nd Edition
978-0-470-61842-4

eBay For Dummies,
7th Edition
978-1-118-09806-6

Knitting For Dummies,
2nd Edition
978-0-470-28747-7

Language &
Foreign Language

English Grammar
For Dummies,
2nd Edition
978-0-470-54664-2

French For Dummies,
2nd Edition
978-1-118-00464-7

German For Dummies,
2nd Edition
978-0-470-90101-4

Spanish Essentials
For Dummies
978-0-470-63751-7

Spanish For Dummies,
2nd Edition
978-0-470-87855-2

Math & Science

Algebra I For Dummies,
2nd Edition
978-0-470-55964-2

Biology For Dummies,
2nd Edition
978-0-470-59875-7

Chemistry For Dummies,
2nd Edition
978-1-1180-0730-3

Geometry For Dummies,
2nd Edition
978-0-470-08946-0

Pre-Algebra Essentials
For Dummies
978-0-470-61838-7

Microsoft Office

Excel 2010 For Dummies
978-0-470-48953-6

Office 2010 All-in-One
For Dummies
978-0-470-49748-7

Office 2011 for Mac
For Dummies
978-0-470-87869-9

Word 2010
For Dummies
978-0-470-48772-3

Music

Guitar For Dummies,
2nd Edition
978-0-7645-9904-0

Clarinet For Dummies
978-0-470-58477-4

iPod & iTunes
For Dummies,
9th Edition
978-1-118-13060-5

Pets

Cats For Dummies,
2nd Edition
978-0-7645-5275-5

Dogs All-in One
For Dummies
978-0470-52978-2

Saltwater Aquariums
For Dummies
978-0-470-06805-2

Religion & Inspiration

The Bible For Dummies
978-0-7645-5296-0

Catholicism For Dummies,
2nd Edition
978-1-118-07778-8

Spirituality For Dummies,
2nd Edition
978-0-470-19142-2

Self-Help & Relationships

Happiness For Dummies
978-0-470-28171-0

Overcoming Anxiety
For Dummies,
2nd Edition
978-0-470-57441-6

Seniors

Crosswords For Seniors
For Dummies
978-0-470-49157-7

iPad 2 For Seniors
For Dummies, 3rd Edition
978-1-118-17678-8

Laptops & Tablets
For Seniors For Dummies,
2nd Edition
978-1-118-09596-6

Smartphones & Tablets

BlackBerry For Dummies,
5th Edition
978-1-118-10035-6

Droid X2 For Dummies
978-1-118-14864-8

HTC ThunderBolt
For Dummies
978-1-118-07601-9

MOTOROLA XOOM
For Dummies
978-1-118-08835-7

Sports

Basketball For Dummies,
3rd Edition
978-1-118-07374-2

Football For Dummies,
2nd Edition
978-1-118-01261-1

Golf For Dummies,
4th Edition
978-0-470-88279-5

Test Prep

ACT For Dummies,
5th Edition
978-1-118-01259-8

ASVAB For Dummies,
3rd Edition
978-0-470-63760-9

The GRE Test For
Dummies, 7th Edition
978-0-470-00919-2

Police Officer Exam
For Dummies
978-0-470-88724-0

Series 7 Exam
For Dummies
978-0-470-09932-2

Web Development

HTML, CSS, & XHTML
For Dummies, 7th Edition
978-0-470-91659-9

Drupal For Dummies,
2nd Edition
978-1-118-08348-2

Windows 7

Windows 7
For Dummies
978-0-470-49743-2

Windows 7
For Dummies,
Book + DVD Bundle
978-0-470-52398-8

Windows 7 All-in-One
For Dummies
978-0-470-48763-1

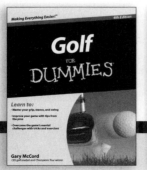

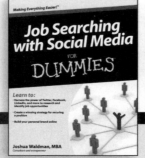

Available wherever books are sold. For more information or to order direct: U.S. customers visit www.dummies.com or call 1-877-762-2
U.K. customers visit www.wileyeurope.com or call (0) 1243 843291. Canadian customers visit www.wiley.ca or call 1-800-567-4797.

Connect with us online at www.facebook.com/fordummies or @fordummies